Other books in the series

Michael J. Lacey, editor, *Religion and Twentieth-Century American Intellectual Life*

Michael J. Lacey, editor, *The Truman Presidency*

Joseph Kruzel and Michael H. Haltzel, editors, *Between the Blocs: Problems and Prospects for Europe's Neutral and Nonaligned States*

William C. Brumfield, editor, *Reshaping Russian Architecture: Western Technology, Utopian Dreams*

Mark N. Katz, editor, *The USSR and Marxist Revolutions in the Third World*

Walter Reich, editor, *Origins of Terrorism: Psychologies, Ideologies, Theologies, States of Mind*

Mary O. Furner and Barry Supple, editors, *The State and Economic Knowledge: The American and British Experiences*

Michael J. Lacey and Knud Haakonssen, editors, *A Culture of Rights: The Bill of Rights in Philosophy, Politics, and Law—1791 and 1991*

Robert J. Donovan and Ray Scherer, *Unsilent Revolution: Television News and American Public Life, 1948–1991*

Nelson Lichtenstein and Howell John Harris, editors, *Industrial Democracy in America: The Ambiguous Promise*

William Craft Brumfield and Blair A. Ruble, editors, *Russian Housing in the Modern Age: Design and Social History*

Michael J. Lacey and Mary O. Furner, editors, *The State and Social Investigation in Britain and the United States*

Hugh Ragsdale, editor and translator, *Imperial Russian Foreign Policy*

Dermot Keogh and Michael H. Haltzel, editors, *Northern Ireland and the Politics of Reconciliation*

Joseph Klaits and Michael H. Haltzel, editors, *The Global Ramifications of the French Revolution*

René Lemarchand, *Burundi: Ethnocide as Discourse and Practice*

James R. Millar and Sharon L. Wolchik, editors, *The Social Legacy of Communism*

James M. Morris, editor, *On Mozart*

Continued on page following index

We remember Winston Churchill, above all, for his magnificent resistance to tyranny during the Second World War. But his statesmanship was more than just inspiration: He had an acute appreciation for what belongs to war and to peace.

Churchill as Peacemaker challenges the usual view that the British statesman was only a man of war. Spanning his long political career, from the turn of the century to the postwar years, this book traces his endeavors to keep the peace, or to restore it, from the little wars of Queen Victoria to the cold war. Scholars from America, Britain, and South Africa examine his choices as a statesman and his reflections as a critic to discover the fascinating, little-known story of Churchill as peacemaker.

WOODROW WILSON CENTER SERIES

Churchill as peacemaker

Winston S. Churchill in 1932. Photograph by E. F. Foley, courtesy of the
International Churchill Society (United States).

Churchill as peacemaker

Edited by
JAMES W. MULLER

September 22, 1997

To Mark Feldman
With high regard and
warm friendship

WOODROW WILSON CENTER PRESS

AND

CAMBRIDGE
UNIVERSITY PRESS

PUBLISHED BY THE PRESS SYNDICATE OF THE UNIVERSITY OF CAMBRIDGE
The Pitt Building, Trumpington Street, Cambridge CB2 1RP, United Kingdom

CAMBRIDGE UNIVERSITY PRESS
The Edinburgh Building, Cambridge CB2 2RU, United Kingdom
40 West 20th Street, New York, NY 10011-4211, USA
10 Stamford Road, Oakleigh, Melbourne 3166, Australia

First published 1997

Printed in the United States of America

Typeset in Sabon

*A catalog record for this book is available from
the British Library*

Library of Congress Cataloging-in-Publication Data
Churchill as peacemaker / edited by James W. Muller.
p. cm. – (Woodrow Wilson Center series)
Papers of the first Nation's Capital Churchill Symposium, held at
the Woodrow Wilson International Center for Scholars in Wash., D.C.,
on Oct. 28 and 29, 1994.
Includes index.
ISBN 0-521-58314-4 (hardback)
1. Churchill, Winston, 1874–1965—Contributions in peace
—Congresses. 2. Peace movements—Great Britain—History
—Congresses. I. Muller, James W., 1953– . II. Nation's Capital
Churchill Symposium (1st : 1994 : Washington, D.C.) III. Series.
DA566.9.C5C4763 1997
941.084′092—dc21   97–3851

ISBN 0–521–58314–4 hardback

To Mary Soames

Published in cooperation with the Churchill Center

The First Nation's Capital Churchill Symposium, which gave rise to this book, was organized in collaboration with the Woodrow Wilson International Center for Scholars by the Churchill Center, formally constituted in 1995 with more than six hundred founding members. The Churchill Center, whose permanent seat will be in Washington, D.C., aims to encourage the study of Sir Winston S. Churchill's life and thought; to foster research on his speeches, writings, and deeds; to advance knowledge of his example as a statesman; and, by programs of teaching and publishing, to impart that learning to men, women, and young people around the world. Aside from the ongoing series of Churchill Symposia, its programs will include an annual Churchill lecture, seminars for undergraduate and graduate students, standard and electronic libraries, bibliographic work, research and travel grants, and publishing projects and subventions. For more information about the activities of the Churchill Center, write to Richard M. Langworth, President, 181 Burrage Road, Hopkinton, New Hampshire 03229.

Contents

ix

Preface

This book offers the reader the first fruit of a collaboration between the Churchill Center and the Woodrow Wilson International Center for Scholars. The two organizations sponsored the Nation's Capital Churchill Symposium on "Churchill as Peacemaker," held at the Woodrow Wilson Center in Washington, D.C., on October 28 and 29, 1994. Jeane Kirkpatrick served as honorary chairwoman.

The symposium brought together all the authors in this book except Martin Gilbert, whose paper was read *in absentia*, and S. Burridge Spies, whose southerly academic calendar precluded his attendance. Papers were also presented by Steven J. Lambakis, a policy and strategy analyst at the National Institute for Public Policy; Frank A. Mayer, an assistant professor of history at California State University, Los Angeles; and Williamson Murray, then a professor of history at Ohio State University and now the Matthew C. Horner Professor of Military Theory at the Marine Corps University, Quantico. Warren F. Kimball, Robert Treat Professor of History at Rutgers University, participated in the symposium as a discussant, as did Patrick J. C. Powers and Paul A. Rahe, who wrote chapters after the symposium. George Seay, producer and host of *Dialogue* at the Woodrow Wilson Center, took a special interest in the proceedings.

Serving on the symposium committee with the editor were Richard M. Langworth, president of the Churchill Center; James M. Morris, director of Historical, Cultural, and Literary Studies at the Woodrow Wilson Center; and Douglas S. Russell, a director of the International Churchill Society (United States). Their aid and counsel were indispensable to the success of the symposium. George A. Lewis, treasurer of the International Churchill Society (United States), and Ronald Helgemo of the Washington Society for Churchill also made important contributions; Susan Nugent at the Woodrow Wilson Center and Adrienne Marino in the Department of Political Science at the University of Alaska, Anchorage, offered steady and resourceful staff assistance. Financial support for the project was provided by the Woodrow Wilson Center and by the Churchill Center, including a special grant from Fred Farrow.

For all who contributed to it, the pleasure of writing this book was redoubled by the conviviality of conversations with others who write on Churchill, both at the symposium and afterward. The world of academic research is humanized by congenial colleagues and friends. The editor is grateful to all of them for improving the manuscript, especially George D. Mohr and John A. Ramsden.

The idea for the symposium came from Richard Langworth, who was generous with advice at every turn. He is also the godfather of this book. More than anyone else in America, he has worked to keep Sir Winston's "memory green, and the record accurate"; and his knowledge of Churchill's life and career is matched only by his enterprise in encouraging scholarship on Churchill.

Note to the reader

The official biography is Randolph S. Churchill and Martin Gilbert, *Winston S. Churchill*, 8 vols. and 15 companion vols. to date (London: Heinemann, 1966–). The first two volumes were penned by Churchill's son and the rest by his successor. In addition to its intrinsic merit as a complete and judicious story of Winston Churchill's life, the official biography has become an indispensable source, along with Churchill's own speeches and writings, for all further research. References to the work have been made by many different methods, often prolix, incomplete, or confusing; in this book we essay a consistent, economical, and reliable method, recommending it to others in the hope that it may be generally adopted.

We cite the official biography as "*WSC*" by volume and page number, e.g., *WSC* I 358–9. The biography is complete in eight main volumes, but each main volume also has a set of two or three companion volumes to attend it. Thus far the companion volumes have carried the story part of the way through the sixth main volume; about eight more such volumes are planned. These volumes are indicated by a "C" following the number of the main volume they accompany, e.g., *WSC* II C 1989–90. Page numbers for the companion volumes run consecutively through each of the first four sets. Beginning with the fifth set, however, each companion volume is paginated separately, so these volumes are distinguished by a parenthetical number preceding the page number, e.g., *WSC* VI C (2) 240–7.

References in this book are to the British edition cited above. The official biography has also been published in the United States (Boston: Houghton Mifflin, 1966–88; New York: W. W. Norton & Company, 1993–); pagination of the American edition is the same as the British edition, except in the first two main volumes.

An unofficial appendix to the official biography is the one-volume life by the official biographer: Martin Gilbert, *Churchill: A Life* (London: Heinemann, 1991); the American edition (New York: Henry Holt, 1991) has the same pagination.

In War: Resolution
In Defeat: Defiance
In Victory: Magnanimity
In Peace: Goodwill

   —Motto of Churchill's memoirs of the Second World War

Introduction

JAMES W. MULLER

In the first chapter of his *History of the English-Speaking Peoples*, Winston Churchill quotes the observations of Britannia collected by Julius Caesar in 55 B.C. before he invaded the island. "All the Britons," he was told, "dye their bodies with woad"—a dye prepared by powdering and fermenting the leaves of the plant *Isatis tinctoria*—"which produces a blue colour, and this gives them a more terrifying appearance in battle."[1] Over the centuries, the ancient custom fell into desuetude as dyers learned to substitute indigo for woad, and Britons left off using war paint. Modern denizens of the island, who count themselves the most peaceable and civilized of peoples, might be distressed to read that their forebears painted themselves blue like savage warriors from some unsettled corner of the globe. But underneath his tasteful garb of dark suits and polka-dot bow ties, one can imagine Churchill's delight in discovering his ancestors' martial caparison. For he had a lifelong fascination with war, and to his fellow citizens he often appeared, in spirit at least, to be wearing war paint.

Churchill tells us in his autobiography that his "earliest coherent memory" was of riflemen in Dublin's Phoenix Park, and his interest in war went back to the days when he ranged his lead soldiers on the nursery floor. On the strength of this attraction, or for want of other aptitude that he could discern, Winston's father, Lord Randolph Churchill, steered him toward a career at arms. After several years in the army class at Harrow School, Winston was admitted to the military academy at Sandhurst. There for the first time he thoroughly enjoyed his studies, and he began his adult life in 1895 as a cavalry officer. Late that year he made a private visit to Cuba, where, in the company of Spanish officers trying to suppress an insurrection, he celebrated his twenty-first birthday on 30 November by coming under fire for the first time. His service in the armies of Queen Victoria was brief and eventful. Conjuring himself with great resourcefulness to one battlefield after another, in the waning years of the nineteenth

---

[1] Winston S. Churchill, *A History of the English-Speaking Peoples*, 4 vols. (New York: Dodd, Mead, 1956–8), vol. 1, 14.

century he saw action successively on India's northwest frontier, in the Sudan, and in South Africa.[2]

Although his soldiering was cut short by his election to the House of Commons in 1900 after his famous escape from a Boer prison in Pretoria, Churchill was intimately involved with Britain's twentieth-century wars. For three years before the First World War, as first lord of the Admiralty, he prepared the Royal Navy for its contest with Germany. During the war, after falling from favor in the midst of the attack on the Dardanelles, he returned to active service as a colonel on the western front; then, in the last years of the war and immediately afterward, he served first as minister of munitions and later as secretary of state for war, with responsibility for the air as well. In the 1930s, as a nettlesome independent critic of the Conservative governments of Stanley Baldwin and Neville Chamberlain, Churchill warned of the insufficiency of British preparations against the threat from Nazi Germany; in his wartime prime ministry, from 1940 to 1945, he closely supervised the campaign against Germany in his role as minister of defense. Whatever our judgment of his handling of military matters during the Second World War—and it remains a question of lively dispute among scholars—Churchill cannot be accused of neglecting them. Thus, as Robert Rhodes James remarks in Chapter 1 of this book, Churchill is often considered "principally as a man of war."

That impression is sharpened by our suspicion that Churchill's experience of war was not only extensive and unapologetic: It was also too eagerly pursued, too gamely embraced, too warmly remembered. As Churchill himself recognized in *Thoughts and Adventures*, a book of essays published during the interwar years, when war entails mass slaughter or catastrophic explosion, it is hard to find any nobility in it. By the end of the twentieth century, the spirited part of human nature has been so stigmatized as to make us condemn any such exuberance as aggression. If anything provokes us to rise up and make common cause against a dangerous heresy, it is a man who is overly fond of war.

Even the Second World War, which used to be held up as the archetypical good war against the muddled legacy of Vietnam, has now come under attack from revisionists of many stripes, working from many angles to show something more like a moral equivalency between the Axis and the Allies. In recent years, some on the right in Britain have claimed that

---

[2] Winston S. Churchill, *My Early Life* (London: Thornton Butterworth, 1930), 15, 33–4, 57–9, 97 et seq.

their country would have fared better if Churchill had been more accommodating to Hitler, while in America some on the left have claimed that their country should have been more accommodating toward Japan. What the two plaints share is their anti-Americanism. Both are far-fetched, and neither commands support from the public, who, like the French singer Edith Piaf, frankly has no regrets. Yet, although revisionism has failed to persuade Britons or Americans to stop thinking that their side was right, in a sense the two peoples have experienced a revision of spirit in the years since 1945. Only half a century later, the Second World War seems to belong to a bygone era. One example suggests the divergence of views between our statesmen and those who guided the Allies in that war: In his memoirs, Churchill takes it for granted that the requirements for military success should come before the safety of Allied civilians if the two came into conflict—that it would be ignoble to act otherwise.[3] Perhaps we should reconsider his point of view, but it is hard to imagine British or American statesmen taking that for granted today.

Although Churchill was unquestionably a man of war—as attested by the biographies and monographs that have not ceased to multiply, including this one—he was also a man of peace. He was disappointed in 1953 to receive the Nobel Prize for Literature rather than for Peace. Yet throughout his long career as a writer and statesman, beginning before the turn of the century and continuing until he retired in the mid-1950s, Churchill was as intimately involved in making peace as he was in making war.

This book was written by scholars from England, Scotland, South Africa, and the United States, trained in different disciplines and approaching their subjects with various points of view, but united by a common resolve to explore this neglected side of Churchill's life and public career: Churchill as peacemaker. Their research draws not only on published works ranging from academic monographs to political memoirs but also on interviews, personal reminiscences, and archival materials from several continents.

The first two chapters provide an overview of Churchill's peacemaking. In his unflinching first chapter, informed by his knowledge of Winston Churchill as fellow parliamentarian and biographer of Lord Randolph Churchill, Robert Rhodes James assesses Winston Churchill's reputation by presenting him as an enigma—a man both for war and for peace. In

---

[3] Winston S. Churchill, *The Second World War*, 6 vols. (London: The Reprint Society, 1950–4), vol. 6, 30, 51–2.

Chapter 2, Manfred Weidhorn, an American professor of English, surveys and interprets Churchill's career as a peacemaker, rejecting popular misconceptions to conclude that he was neither a warmonger nor a pacifist.

The next three chapters focus primarily on Churchill's reflections on peacemaking in the Victorian era but raise questions about war and peace that persisted well into the twentieth century. In Chapter 3, the American political scientist Kirk Emmert explores a question that interested Churchill from the days of Queen Victoria to the postwar era: What can imperial rule contribute to the peace and happiness of the world? Two succeeding chapters take up Churchill's reflections on peacemaking after British colonial wars. In Chapter 4, the American historian Paul A. Rahe examines Churchill's reflections on the British reconquest of the Sudan in *The River War* (1899), encompassing both his confidence in the justice of that endeavor and his doubts about the intentions of those who guided it. In Chapter 5, the South African historian S. Burridge Spies carefully unfolds Churchill's part in the dilemmas of restoring peace to Britons, Boers, and the indigenous peoples of his country after the South African War.

Chapter 6, written by the editor of this book, addresses the problems of making peace after the First World War, concentrating on Churchill's critique of Woodrow Wilson's idealistic peacemaking. The two chapters that follow describe the difficulties of reaching a settlement in two intractable disputes. In Chapter 7, the British historian Paul Addison considers the successes and failures of Churchill's attempt to bring peace to Ireland, particularly in the years leading up to the Anglo-Irish Treaty of 1922. In Chapter 8, the American attorney and writer Douglas J. Feith gauges Churchill's bona fides as a Zionist and describes his part in the Palestinian settlement after the First World War.

Two final chapters investigate Churchill's understanding of peace and war in the twentieth century, first from a theoretical and then from a practical perspective; taken together, they demonstrate that he straddled the conventional opposition between hawks and doves. Chapter 9, by the American political scientist Patrick J. C. Powers, studies Churchill's advice in the philosophical essays of *Thoughts and Adventures* on how to bring peace both to modern democracies and to the statesman's soul. Chapter 10, by Churchill's official biographer, the British historian Martin Gilbert, recounts the hardihood and tenacity of Churchill's quest for a colloquy with the Soviets in the decade after the Second World War.

With their multiplicity of subjects and approaches, it is not surprising that these authors draw different conclusions about Churchill, offering the reader divergent interpretations and sometimes outright disagreement. Yet there is also a common theme, which may serve to introduce our collective portrait of Churchill as peacemaker. Modern theorists of diplomacy, strategy, or international relations tend to fall into two camps: the warlike realists, for whom moral considerations play a distant second fiddle to the demands of *Realpolitik*, and the peace-loving moralists, who insist on cleaving to moral principles without regard for circumstances or consequences. Modern practitioners—who are usually less single-minded about their own interests than the realists, but also less oblivious of them than the moralists—fall into these camps less neatly; yet often, under the influence of theoretical counselors, they understand their own activity chiefly in terms of one or the other of these positions.

Churchill rejects them both. As these chapters attest, he is unwilling to embrace the unbending formulas or the idealistic confidence of the moralists, judging them too simplistic for actual political situations; nor does he inhabit the bleak world of the realists, whose indifference to ethics strikes him as practically inhuman. Neither peace nor war is always the right choice. Self-respect might prove a better guide in politics than a doctrinaire self-absorption or self-denial; it might draw our attention to the human things, prized by Churchill but neglected by realists and moralists alike, that matter so much in politics: friendship, conversation, and honor. After all, neither realism nor moralism teaches us to enjoy the company of other men—but Churchill did, both in war and in peace.

1

The enigma

ROBERT RHODES JAMES

The quandary of Winston Churchill may be simply expressed: There were so many Winston Churchills. This baffled his contemporaries and often inspired their mistrust; it has caused historians and his biographers comparable problems.

Let us survey this phenomenon. Politician, sportsman, artist, orator, historian, parliamentarian, journalist, essayist, gambler, soldier, war correspondent, adventurer, patriot, internationalist, dreamer, pragmatist, strategist, Zionist, imperialist, monarchist, democrat, egocentric, hedonist, romantic—the list seems endless. Churchill was also impulsive, hard, inspirational, infuriating. Did anyone, apart from his wife, ever really know him? What kept him going at such an amazing pace for so long? What was his mainspring? Why did he have so few real friends? Why was he so solitary a figure?

We are confronted with a daunting series of questions, and few satisfactory answers, but the quest for them remains one of the most intriguing ones in modern historiography. Most great men tend to diminish in stature as time passes and new perspectives lead to new evaluations; in Churchill's case the sheer complexity of his personality, and the fact that he touched almost every known aspect of life, makes him look increasingly formidable and mysterious.

This is not, of course, the universal view. One conspicuous feature of the current wave of denigratory portraits in Britain is that they are all written by young men of somewhat limited horizons with no personal political experience; also, none of them has even seen Churchill in person, let alone met him. Of course, this is not essential for a biographer, but in my view it helps. And for those of us who were alive in 1940—and what a year it was to be alive in England—there is an imperishable emotion of gratitude and affection that inevitably colors our view of him. This has never made me uncritical of him, but my criticism is tinged with awe at the magnitude of his scale and achievements—at that ferocious energy and zest for life. He is just too big for us to comprehend.

My former boss at the foreign office, Lord Carrington, as usual expressed the feelings of the 1940 vintage perfectly:

I remember in the summer of 1940, guarding three and a half miles of beach between Hythe and Folkestone, with 48 Guardsmen, 46 rifles, two Bren Guns and my pistol and reflecting with great sympathy on the appalling fate of any German division which landed on my beach. We were, of course, very naïve and no doubt stupid, but morale and leadership plays an enormous part in our attitudes, and nobody who was alive at the time can ever forget the effect of Winston Churchill—his presence, his manner, his speeches, his determination and his courage, and what a decisive effect it had on all of us.[1]

Here, I should emphasize that there is nothing wrong with serious historical revisionism; perspectives change, new evidence emerges, and hindsight has its virtues as well as its perils. It was only relatively recently, for example, that we became aware of the crucial role played in the Second World War by the cryptologists at Bletchley in their unraveling of the secrets of the German codes. Indeed, the enormous and still growing literature on that war still produces surprises—some quite small, it is true, but constantly changing our perceptions. The brutality of the Wehrmacht has astonished researchers given access to the records captured by the Russians and only recently made available to Western scholars. Also, Churchill's own war memoirs have been critically reassessed, and the necessary correctives applied.[2]

Inevitably, assessments of individuals will alter, and not usually to the advantage of their reputations. But there is a considerable difference between this and character assassination.

It is true that what Sir Michael Howard has described as "Churchill-mania"—especially in the United States—went too far, and it may be that I unwittingly started a more realistic approach in my study of his career up to 1939 that was published in 1970; I subtitled it "A Study in Failure," which gave some people, who had only read the title, the idea that this

---

[1] Lecture, Royal United Service Institution, April 1995.
[2] See inter alia, Robin Edmonds, *The Big Three: Churchill, Roosevelt, and Stalin* (London: Hamish Hamilton, 1991) and Robert Blake and Roger Louis, eds., *Churchill* (Oxford: Oxford University Press, 1993; rpt. 1994).

was the first denigratory biography of the great man.[3] Of course, it was
not, as Lady Churchill and other members of the family quickly realized
and appreciated. It was an attempt to regard him as an historical rather
than a contemporary figure—which was why it ended in 1939—and as
a fallible human being of great gifts and qualities but also of erratic judgment and weakness. But we have gone from Churchillmania to something
like Churchillphobia, of whose exponents David Irving is the most sinister and Clive Ponting the most ludicrous.

In my case, also, I am biased in that Churchill was immensely kind to
me as a very young man. As an Oxford undergraduate I had formulated
the daring plan of writing the biography of his father, Lord Randolph;
Churchill, the first—and indeed only—biographer of his father, was not
at all encouraging. When it was published,[4] when I was twenty-six, there
was general astonishment at the sheer cheek of it all, but when Churchill
read it he made it widely known that he thought very well of it, and wrote
me a letter of glowing congratulations. Beaverbrook invited me to Cherkley,
and Lord Rosebery to Mentmore, with the request that I write a biography
of Rosebery's father. Churchill himself arranged for family papers to be
brought from Chartwell to his London house for me to study under
congenial circumstances in Hyde Park Gate. When in 1962 the Turkish
authorities refused me permission to visit the Gallipoli battlefields, then
a closely guarded military zone, I obtained a letter from his private secretary, Anthony Montague Browne, seeking the ruling to be reversed. Naturally, it was, and quickly. I was to be one of the ushers at his funeral, but
the imminent birth of our youngest daughter prevented this.

I would not claim that I knew him, but from my earliest political memories he was the dominant personality in my life—my prime minister, my
party leader, my hero. My father took me to Blenheim in 1946 to a great
Conservative rally, where I beheld Churchill in the distance on a platform, orating to a vast audience. That was my first sight of him, at the
age of thirteen. I saw him at rather closer range in action in the House
of Commons in his glorious Indian summer between 1951 and 1955, and
then frequently during his nine years as a silent, and eventually stricken,
backbencher, when I was a clerk of the House of Commons. Indeed, on
the day he left the chamber for the last time it was I who opened the great

---

[3] Robert Rhodes James, *Churchill: A Study in Failure, 1900–1939* (London: Weidenfeld &
Nicolson, 1970; rpt. 1994).
[4] Robert Rhodes James, *Lord Randolph Churchill* (London: Weidenfeld & Nicolson, 1959;
rpt. 1995).

doors for him and helped him into his wheelchair. By then the great frame
had shrunk, and the eyes looked lifeless, but this was no husk of a man.

Even in his last years as a member of Parliament, Churchill's mere
arrival in the chamber caused excitement. Visitors in the public galleries
would be galvanized, and a buzz could almost be felt in the House itself.
Labour members who had booed and jeered him, and on occasion actually shouted him down, rushed to welcome him; when he rose to leave
there was almost a sigh of disappointment. "He may not utter a word,"
as Woodrow Wyatt wrote in April 1954,

> yet as long as he sits on the bench, the great head moving round, the face animated
> or so lifeless that it has the quality of a bust worn by time, the charged temper of
> the atmosphere is sustained. Every gesture, every move of hand to ear, is signifi-
> cant. When he gets up to go, something of the vitality of the House goes with him.
> It settles down to a quieter jog, like a reception after the champagne is finished.[5]

Here was grandeur, and what would now be called "charisma." Here was
a political star, even in extreme old age. It was magical. Perhaps there is
some harm for a biographer to have fallen under "the wand of the magi-
cian," but not much, because I have always seen him as a fascinating, but
very imperfect, human being, and not a wholly attractive one.

Few ultimately successful political careers were for so long so bitterly controversial. Many considered that he had no principles at all, and
was an adventurer and a charlatan, the man who had broken his parole
with the Boers and then made himself a national hero by escaping; the
Conservative who had ratted on his party when it was disintegrating and
suddenly declared himself a Liberal—only to return to the Conservatives
twenty years later when the Liberals themselves disintegrated; imperious,
reckless with other men's lives, it was claimed, he was held responsible
for the loss of much of the Royal Naval Division ("Winston's private
army") at Antwerp in 1914, for the tragedy of Gallipoli in 1915, and the
hapless British intervention in the Russian civil war from 1919 to 1921.
Indeed, there were few British misfortunes in the first two decades of
the twentieth century that were not in part blamed on him. There was,
of course, much injustice and malice in this, but politics can be a harsh
and unforgiving calling. The remarkable thing was that he kept bouncing
back after reverses that would have destroyed most men both in their
reputations and in their personal self-confidence.

---

[5] Woodrow Wyatt, "Churchill as Parliamentarian," *Encounter* 2, no. 4 (April 1954), 5–
13.

As Desmond Morton, who for a time knew him particularly well, has written, Churchill had few real friends, and had an unattractive habit of discarding people when they ceased to be useful to him or had become an embarrassment.[6] Morton was one of them, but so were many others.

Perhaps there is validity in the comment of his onetime ally and supporter, Bob Boothby, another discard: "Winston was a sh—, but we needed a sh— to defeat Hitler."[7] Alan Brooke was not the only colleague who found him insufferable, arrogant, selfish, impulsive, often outrageously rude, and intolerant; others close to him, like Jock Colville, although often infuriated by his whims and orders, adored him and would have died for him. As Colville, at first a vehement critic and later an almost—but not entirely—total admirer, later wrote: "Few public figures in all history have assumed so many mantles, displayed such an unlikely mixture of talents, experienced over so wide a span of years such a variety of triumphs and disasters, and been successively so suspected and so trusted, so disliked and so admired by his fellow countrymen."[8] But, as Colville also remarked, and rightly, "He was as strange a mixture of radical and traditionalist as could anywhere be found. He was certainly not conservative by temperament, nor indeed by conviction a supporter of the Conservative Party. On the other hand . . . he disliked the abolition of anything which had colour and tradition behind it."[9] And it is to Colville that we owe the priceless story of how, when he announced that he was going to join the Royal Air Force, Churchill's main concern was that he could take "your man" with him, the idea of going to war without one's personal valet being an unthinkable sacrifice.[10] Of course, his detractors quote this to demonstrate how appallingly out of touch Churchill was, but it was part of that style which Isaiah Berlin has immortalized in his superb *Mr. Churchill in 1940*, as "riding in triumph through Persepolis."[11]

To the end he remained a highly controversial personality, much hated as well as much revered. I vividly recall a newsreel of his eightieth birthday celebration in Westminster Hall being booed in an Oxford cinema in 1954, and a startlingly large number who were quite unmoved by his

---

[6] Quoted in Rhodes James, *Churchill: A Study in Failure, 1900–1939*, 287.
[7] Private discussion with Lord Boothby, also reflected in his *Reflections of a Rebel* (London: Hutchinson, 1978).
[8] John Colville, *The Fringes of Power* (London: Hodder & Stoughton, 1985), 124.
[9] Ibid., 128.
[10] J. Wheeler-Bennett, ed., *Action This Day* (London: Macmillan, 1968), 60.
[11] Isaiah Berlin, *Mr. Churchill in 1940* (London: John Murray, 1964), 17.

death and magnificent funeral, putting down the emotion to nostalgia and sentimental memories of our imperial past.

CHURCHILL'S ROMANTIC VIEW

There was something in the last criticism. Churchill's romantic view of the British and their history now gets short shrift from most professional historians, but how many of them could have written, or conceivably have written, anything like his account of the Battle of Blenheim in his biography of Marlborough? And what politician of our times could have called a defeated nation to arms and exhilaration by reminding them of the triumphs of their ancestors? Oddly enough, only Hitler and Mussolini and the Japanese leaders. Thus Wellington's soldiers and Nelson's sailors fought against Moltke's Uhlans and the Roman legions. This is one aspect of the Second World War that has always fascinated me. When the *Bismarck* was sunk, the victorious British admiral cabled the Admiralty: "She fought to the end in the great traditions of the German Imperial Navy." And Churchill himself greatly admired and respected the German soldier, with his own traditions. I have always thought it significant that he found it difficult to accept the cold-blooded bestiality of the German killing machine, in which the Wehrmacht was more deeply involved than we realized, until the evidence was overwhelming. Even then, he differentiated between "the Narzees" and the ordinary German, not comprehending, or wanting to comprehend, the extent of the war guilt.

Similarly, remembering the gallant *poilus* of the First World War, and recalling the valor of Napoleon's armies, he was wholly unprepared for the collapse of the French armies and their commanders in 1940. "Thank God for the French Army!" had been his prewar cry. He had also convinced himself that the days of the tank—very much his own brainchild—and the submarine were over, and that modern warships had nothing to fear from aircraft. As with his romantic opinion of the heroic French army, these opinions had to be swiftly revised, but not before near catastrophe.

A MAN OF WAR AND PEACE

It is inevitable that Churchill is thought of principally as a man of war. Indeed, much of his life had been devoted both to the study of war and to involvement in it, from a subaltern on the northwest frontier of India to leadership of his country in the greatest war in history. From the Malakand Field Force to Korea, with two world wars thrown in, from a cavalry charge at Omdurman to thermonuclear weapons—this is quite a span. From this fascination with war to being called a "warmonger" was a very short step, and many crossed it—particularly in the awful 1930s, when the British were petrified by the mere thought of another European war, and wanted to listen to those who told them that it was impossible, and did not want to hear someone telling them that unless they rearmed on a massive scale it was inevitable. Even an admirer and friend, Alan Herbert, wrote of Munich, "I did think that he [Churchill] rather enjoyed a war; and, after three years in the infantry, in Gallipoli and France, I did not. I wanted Mr. Chamberlain to be right, and keep the peace success-fully. I voted sadly for Munich: and the whole thing made me ill."[12]

But Churchill, as Paul Addison has reminded us,[13] was also a peace-time minister and politician. Indeed, he was considerably longer in office in peacetime than in war, and held all the major domestic ministries, a simple fact that tends to be overlooked. In his first period in politics he could almost be described as a pacifist, so strong were his denuncia-tions of military expenditure. His closest political ally after he had joined the Liberals in 1904 was Lloyd George, who had courageously opposed the South African War, and who was then in his fiercest Radical period. Churchill was against spending money on dreadnoughts and for spending it on social reform. As Addison has written, "He was the principal driving force behind the Liberal welfare reforms of 1908–11, both at the Board of Trade and as Home Secretary," yet there were many who were skep-tical about the depth of his commitment, even Violet Bonham Carter expressing doubts about his sincerity;[14] but, although it is always danger-ous to try to affix political labels to this exceptional man, he was not the son of the populist Tory Democrat Lord Randolph for nothing, and his speeches in this period have a fire and sincerity. Deeply influenced by what he had seen in Germany, Churchill appointed the young William Beveridge to examine the possibility of labor exchanges, which he then introduced. He was also one of the pioneers of national insurance, and, had he been reelected in 1945, would have introduced the national health

---

[12] A. P. Herbert, *Independent Member* (London: Methuen, 1950), 109.
[13] Paul Addison, "Churchill and Social Reform," in *Churchill*, ed. Blake and Louis, 57–78.
[14] Violet Bonham Carter, *Winston Churchill as I Knew Him* (London: Eyre & Spottiswoode and Collins, 1965), 161.

service. As Addison has nicely put it, "He saw it as the duty of his class, and hence of the state, to protect the weak and the poor."

THE ARISTOCRAT AND SOCIAL REFORM

David Cannadine and other critics have placed excessive emphasis on the fact that Churchill was an aristocrat.[15] The fact was that he was a very poor one, who throughout his life had to earn his own living by his own endeavors and abilities; if he demanded a high standard of living, he worked for it, and admired others who did the same.

This is an important, and often underestimated, point.

British politics have always been, and in many respects still remain, a rich man's occupation. When one looks at the British prime ministers of this century it is striking how many were independently rich, or certainly were comfortably well-off. Churchill was envious of Balfour's lack of concern for mundane matters of family finance, but the same could be said of every other major Conservative politician—and many Labour and Liberal—Anthony Eden being an outstanding exception, another point of common interest between them.

Churchill's sympathy for, and action on behalf of, the unfortunate and poor is now unhappily derided in my country by some Conservatives as "paternalism," "wetness," and "gutless Keynesianism." The new god is something called "market forces," when in reality it is a return to Victorian laissez-faire liberalism. The world in which Churchill grew up may have been one of the British Empire at its apogee, but it was also one in which the child mortality statistics for Belfast were worse than those for Calcutta, and where both in town and country there was desperate poverty. The young Churchill read, with horror, the reports of Seebohm Rowntree and others about urban squalor and destitution, which in the English countryside, after the terrible agricultural slump of the 1870s and 1880s, he could see for himself. He also saw the tragedy of old people like his beloved nurse, Everest, ill-rewarded in their lives and left to die in total poverty. The institution, by Lloyd George and Churchill, of the basics of a state pension fund was an achievement he always looked back upon with pride—and rightly so.

But there was also unquestionably a strong element of political calculation in his approach, as there had been in his father's. He knew that

---

[15] David Cannadine, "The Pitfalls of Family Piety," in *Churchill*, ed. Blake and Louis, 9–20.

if people were not given work, decent living conditions, and opportunities they would seize them for themselves. The French Revolution had been a nasty shock for British Conservatives; the revolutions of 1848 that had swept Europe and deposed many monarchies had been perhaps even nastier for the established order. With considerable skill Disraeli had transformed the Conservative Party into the party of constitutional and social reform; Lord Randolph took it even further, as did his son.

Charles Masterman wrote of Churchill during this period that "He desired in England a state of things where a benign upper class dispensed benefits to an industrious, *bien pensant*, and grateful working class";[16] there was some truth in this barbed comment, but although Churchill accepted the need for social reform to preserve established institutions, there was more to it than that. It is true that, as Violet Bonham Carter has written, "Though he had supported himself by his own tireless industry he was not acquainted with poverty," and that as a radical social reformer "He was—quite unconsciously—wearing fancy-dress, that he was not himself";[17] yet the actual record is more in Churchill's favor. There is also a certain charming naïveté in him. He enjoyed the good things in life, and wanted others to do so as well, provided that they did not fight him for them. He had much better relations with trade unionists than is often realized, but once he got into a battle he was determined to win it—until his last government, when something close to domestic appeasement became government policy.

As Isaiah Berlin and others—notably Leo Amery—have remarked, Churchill's views on most matters changed very little in his long lifetime,[18] and this is particularly ironic in view of the frequent charges of inconsistency and opportunism flung at him throughout his political career. In his social reform phase, which ended abruptly when he went to the Admiralty in 1911, he was very careful to distance himself from socialism and socialist measures, most vehemently in his election address at the 1908 Dundee by-election. "The cause of the Liberal Party is the cause of the left-out millions" was a call for a more humane system of society, not its transformation into a centralized state.[19] (Lloyd George was equally emphatic, comparing socialism with sand that gets everywhere and clogs

---

[16] Rhodes James, *Churchill: A Study in Failure, 1900–1939*, 35.
[17] Bonham Carter, *Winston Churchill as I Knew Him*, 164.
[18] Leo Amery, *My Political Life*, 2 vols. (London: Hutchinson, 1955), vol. 2, 510.
[19] Robert Rhodes James, ed., *The Complete Speeches of Sir Winston Churchill*, 8 vols. (New York: Chelsea House/Bowker, 1974), vol. 1, 1025–35.

everything up.) Churchill saw himself as the inheritor of the vision of his father's Tory democracy, now abandoned by the Tories. He was also, unashamedly, a populist, and the violence of his language, which delighted huge Liberal audiences, appalled his former Conservative colleagues.

The trouble was, as he frankly admitted in a letter to his mother, "I v[er]y often yield to the temptation of adapting my facts to my phrases,"[20] which was true, and was one of the sources of the mistrust in which he was widely held. But Masterman was wrong in dismissing him simply as "a Rhetorician," because there was always much thought behind Churchill's rhetoric, however full-blooded. As the compiler of all his speeches, in eight volumes of a thousand pages each, I am in a better position than most to testify to this. There were bad speeches; there were often very calculated political ones; he believed, rightly, in the power of oratory and rhetoric, but also in that of argument—and it is this that separates him emphatically from the mob-style orators of our century. Nonetheless, he did occasionally—and until his prime in the mid-1930s—yield to the temptation of adapting the facts to his phrases.

His Conservative opponents went further; they accused him of having committed the ultimate betrayal of his background and class by embracing socialism, when in fact he never remotely did. His memorable intervention in a Commons debate on domestic matters in 1939—"There is no more far-seeing investment for a nation than to put milk, food, and education into young children"—was in fact put into effect by his wartime government by Woolton at the Ministry of Food and R. A. Butler at the Ministry of Education, and he became convinced of the need for a national health service.

None of this makes him a great social reformer along the lines of a Shaftesbury, a Lloyd George, or a Beveridge, but he admired Roosevelt's remarkable domestic achievements, and his solicitude for British civilians during the war was profound. "People in high places," he remarked to Boothby, "do not realise how perfectly bloody life is for most people."[21] When Boothby proposed free milk for children Churchill agreed with alacrity; free orange juice and cod liver oil followed. For all the horrors of the Battle of the Atlantic, which was one of the decisive turning points of the war, and one too often neglected, the British people as a whole were better fed and clothed during the war than most had ever been. I

---

[20] *WSC* II C 933. For intelligence of this citation, see "Note to the reader," on p. xiii of this book.
[21] Boothby recollections.

remember vividly as a child before the war seeing the thin white faces and shabby clothes of the malnourished poor children of London; by a remarkable irony, the war was the best thing that could have happened to them.

It could be claimed that all this was to boost civilian morale; it certainly did, but the causation was more profound and personal, as his ministers knew. What he failed to appreciate was that this highly organized central direction of food, goods, and supplies was becoming so popular and appreciated that people wanted it to continue after the war and had no desire to return to the miseries of the 1920s and 1930s, for which they held the Conservatives to blame. The shrewder Conservative canvassers in the 1945 general election recognized that the huge enthusiasm for Churchill personally was not going to be translated into Conservative votes.

But Churchill himself was not really a Conservative at all, except in the sense that he believed deeply in established, proven institutions, particularly the monarchy, Parliament (by which he meant the House of Commons, having no time whatever for the Lords), and the majesty of the British judicial system. These he certainly wanted to conserve, as he wanted to conserve the British Empire. But the Conservative Party of the interwar period was a miserable thing. As Duff Cooper once commented, it was much easier for a poor man to enter heaven than for a poor Conservative to enter the House of Commons.[22] Safe seats were almost blatantly bought by the highest bidder, with results that might have been foreseen. It is significant that the first serious reforms of this outrageous custom began during the war under Churchill's leadership and were confirmed in the late 1940s when he was leader of the party, thereby opening for the first time the opportunity of men and women of moderate means to enter Parliament as Conservatives. The first, and spectacular, signs of this were the 1950 and 1951 intakes, which began to make the party, for the first time in its remarkable history, more representative of the electorate.

Churchill's democratic instincts, which were strong and lifelong, did not extend to women. He had opposed their getting the vote before 1918, and ten years later he was the only cabinet member who opposed extending it to all women. He was invariably courteous to women—apart from a few exceptions, such as Lady Astor, whom he cordially detested—but he considered them politically immature and too emotional to be trusted

[22] Duff Cooper, *Old Men Forget* (London: Rupert Hart-Davis, 1953), 128. See also Stuart Ball, *Parliament and Politics in the Age of Baldwin and MacDonald* (New Haven: Yale University Press, 1992).

with serious matters of state. He was outraged when the Commons in 1944 voted for equal pay for women and men teachers, and at once slammed down a motion of confidence to have the vote rescinded. This did him no good at all in 1945.

This was remarkable because of his love and reverence for his wife, who held very strong political views, usually considerably to the left of his, and he later adored the queen, to the barely concealed mirth of his private office. He had to be persuaded very hard to have a woman in the 1951 cabinet, and did not look notably downhearted when she turned out to be a total failure. It is not difficult to guess at how he would have reacted to Margaret Thatcher, who was told by Lady Churchill that "this was one of Winston's blind spots."[23] His attitude to women in politics was the same as that toward scientists, "on tap but not on top." But he had been one of the pioneers of widows' pensions and other reforms of real and enduring benefit to women and children, so this "blind spot" should not be held too seriously against him.

Nor should his flirtation in the 1930s with electoral reform. Until 1918 the vote for men had a property qualification, as it did for women until 1929, and Churchill regretted the new era of one person one vote, regardless of the individual's contribution to the nation. He proposed that certain categories of deserving people should receive two votes: "They would all be persons who had to face the real problems of life in a manner quite different from the lodgers of all kinds of both sexes, dependent or otherwise."[24] His nostalgia for a lost golden age when "we had a real political democracy led by hierarchy of statesmen, and not a fluid mass distracted by newspapers"[25] was symptomatic of his mood. On another occasion, in his essay on John Morley, he lamented that "The tidal wave of democracy and the volcanic explosion of the West have swept the shores bare," so that "All we have is vague mass-driftings interrupted from time to time by spasmodic mob votes."[26]

This was, of course, considered to be extremely reactionary, and people took as little notice of his views on this topic as they did on everything else he was then writing and speaking about. But his opinion that only those who had a real stake in the nation should be permitted to vote is not so Victorian and undemocratic as it first appears, and the context is

[23] Private information.
[24] Winston S. Churchill, article in *Evening Standard*, January 17, 1934.
[25] Winston S. Churchill, *My Early Life* (London: Odhams Press, 1947), 354.
[26] Winston S. Churchill, *Great Contemporaries* (London: Fontana, 1957), 84–5.

important. The Nazis had proved masters of mob organization, and the French democracy had virtually broken down; Italy was a dictatorship, which Churchill openly admired; initially he supported Franco in the Spanish civil war, which was unsurprising considering his loathing of communism. After a visit to Spain by his son-in-law, Duncan Sandys, he completely changed his attitude, but by then another European nation was in the grip of a fascist dictatorship.

Churchill was not alone in being fearful that this ugly tide could, in one form or another, cross the channel to Britain. If we now regard Mosley's British Fascist Party with derision and incomprehension, the violent clashes between its followers and avowed communists in the streets of London seemed very frightening then. Most of Europe was in constitutional and political turmoil, with the twin gods of communism and fascism fighting for men's souls (and lives). What guarantee could there be that Britain would be inviolate, and that in a wave of hysteria and panic the electorate might not vote into power something like an elective dictatorship? If all this now seems very alarmist, there was much to be alarmed about in Europe between 1933 and 1939.

Churchill's apparently quixotic attempt to keep King Edward VIII on the throne during the 1936 abdication crisis was part of this fear. There were personal factors: he felt a deep sympathy for, and loyalty to, the lonely king; he was a fervent monarchist—"Monarchial Number One," as his wife teased him;[27] and the possibility of this hallowed institution being jeopardized by what seemed to him a triviality genuinely horrified him. He was bitterly criticized at the time for his actions, and virtually howled down in the Commons, and he himself quickly realized that King George VI and Queen Elizabeth were a vast improvement on the former king. But again, in the context of the time, it was not so foolish nor irrational a stand as it seemed to be then, and afterward. It cost him dearly; as he later wrote, "I was myself so smitten in public opinion that it was the almost universal view that my political life was at last ended,"[28] and for a while that was his own opinion also. Harold Macmillan wrote of "the catastrophic fall in Churchill's prestige."[29] The new king and queen eyed him with considerable doubt, and were not enthusiastic about his accession to the premiership in May 1940; nor were many others in the political establishment, nor in the Labour Party.

[27] Philip Ziegler, "Churchill and the Monarchy," in *Churchill*, ed. Blake and Louis, 187.
[28] Winston S. Churchill, *The Gathering Storm* (London: Cassell, 1947), 171.
[29] Harold Macmillan, *Winds of Change* (London: Macmillan, 1966), 480.

CHURCHILL DISTRUSTED AND DETESTED

The official biography of Churchill by Randolph Churchill and Martin Gilbert rightly exonerates him from the trade union myth—which has proved remarkably enduring—that as home secretary he sent troops to shoot striking miners in Wales in 1911. In fact he was very cautious and sensible over this episode, but Randolph Churchill passed very hurriedly over his father's reactions to a rail strike in the same year, in which Churchill mobilized 50,000 troops to deal with the emergency and gave officers full responsibility to act as they thought fit without reference to the home office—"as though Armageddon was upon us," in the caustic words of A. G. Gardiner. It was an episode that earned him a particular niche in the demonology of organized labor, and merited Lloyd George's comparison of him with "a chauffeur who apparently is perfectly sane and drives with great skill for months, then suddenly takes you over a precipice."

Churchill's role in British intervention in the Russian civil war in 1919— again, not nearly so irresponsible and lamentable in retrospect as it seemed at the time, and for a long time afterward—and in the 1926 general strike further increased the animosity against him, not only in the Labour Party and movement but in the Baldwinite ranks who craved for "peace in our time, O Lord." They did not realize that, once the strike was called off, Churchill was almost the only senior minister who wanted to give the defeated miners a reasonable settlement, following his principle of "in victory, magnanimity." But the Conservatives were determined to exact their full tribute from their defeated enemy, with a resultant bitterness against them that lasted for a generation, and of which Churchill was an undeserving recipient. His determination as prime minister to remedy this false impression may have gone too far—particularly in the years between 1951 and 1955—but was understandable. Nonetheless, the labels of war-monger and "enemy of the working man" proved difficult to eradicate; they were descriptions about which he, and his official biographers, were especially sensitive and which they were anxious to refute. But politics, however unfairly and unreasonably, is about perceptions of men, and no amount of subsequent explanation and careful arraignment of the facts can hope to obliterate contemporary assessments, however wrong they may be.

There is rather more to be said for Churchill's period as chancellor of the Exchequer between 1924 and 1929 than has been generally admitted, although Keynes's *The Economic Consequences of Mr. Churchill* contained some fairly incontrovertible censures. But although Churchill did not convince his colleagues of the virtues of a national minimum wage, nor of imposing taxes on wealth gained directly as a result of war profiteering, he was a strong supporter of Neville Chamberlain's proposals for reducing the age provision for pensions to widows from seventy to sixty-five years of age, and provided the necessary funds. But he was not at ease with himself at the Treasury, and the sureness of touch that he had so often demonstrated in other offices—although not invariably—was far less evident. It was not a period in his life on which he looked back with much pleasure or satisfaction.

EXPECTATIONS FOR THE POSTWAR WORLD

It was often claimed, then and later, that in the Second World War Churchill was uninterested in postwar plans, being obsessed with military victory. His speeches and remarks gave strength to that impression— "everything for the war, whether controversial or not, and nothing controversial that is not *bona fide* needed for the war," he declared in October 1943—but, as so often with him, it was not so simple as that. It was true that he could become irritated with grandiose utopian proposals for a New Britain while the old one was still engaged in a desperate war against very formidable enemies; it was also true that he came to realize that the eventual victory might be in many respects Pyrrhic, with Britain relatively impoverished and inferior to the United States and the Soviet Union; but he recognized that the British people expected, and were entitled to, a much better life than the one they had had before 1939. But he did not make this clear. Fisher's old cry of approbation, "He was a *war* man!" now came to haunt him politically.

At no point in the war did the British expect to be defeated, but after the great succession of victories between 1942 and 1944 they were nonplussed that the war was going on so long. When I returned to Britain at the beginning of 1945, I was not only struck by the scale of the bomb damage in Liverpool, London, and the southern coastal towns, which was far greater than we had been led to believe, but by the general air of exhaustion. The V-1 and V-2 attacks were very unpleasant experiences; the German Ardennes offensive in the winter of 1944–5 caused something approaching panic in some quarters, and a sick feeling in the stomach to most of us. The advance of the Allies seemed interminably slow on all fronts after the wild excitements of the post-Normandy stampede by the British and Americans to the German borders and the huge Russian gains to the east. The Allies were overwhelmingly more powerful than the Germans and Japanese, but the folly of "unconditional surrender" was now manifest. It was not Churchill's fault that the war was not over by the autumn of 1944, but the last nine months of the war made the British war-weariness a serious matter. Morale never cracked, but it came perilously close to doing so.

One factor, which Churchill underestimated, was the belief that the postwar world should be a better one. Indeed, it was the theme of Labour, the trade unions, and the Army Education Corps that it would be, but not under the Conservatives. When Churchill told General Slim, commander of the Fourteenth Army, that he was optimistic about the forthcoming general election in 1945, Slim told him bluntly, "My Army won't be voting for you."[30] Admiration for the heroism of the Russian army and people was carried to excessive lengths in the British press, Mrs. Churchill unwittingly helping the process with her enthusiastic leadership of the Red Cross to Russia fund. Almost wholly ignorant of the true nature of the evils of the Soviet regime, the British began to applaud socialism as such, and attempts by his ministers to interest Churchill more in the home front were not successful. Concentrating upon the problems and dangers of war—and they continued virtually up to the German surrender in May 1945—he was unaware that the tides of political feeling were turning ominously against his party and government.

POSTWAR AMBITIONS

His defeat in 1945 astounded and wounded him. He was urged by his family and colleagues not to take it personally, but he did. Like most political leaders, he relished the appurtenances of office, and was desolate when they were abruptly withdrawn. The British treat ex–prime ministers ungenerously, in contrast with the American treatment of former presidents. But far more important to Churchill was the removal of power. As the Conservatives rebuilt themselves into a modern progressive party between 1945 and 1950, Churchill's only interest lay in the capacity of these new plans and Charters to win votes, and he was deeply suspicious

---

[30] Ronald Lewin, *Slim* (London: Leo Cooper, 1976), 246.

of policy commitments that might prove embarrassing in office; in this his instincts were right, but to the thrusting young Conservatives and their leaders in Parliament—Eden, Butler, and Macmillan in particular —this was inadequate, and at one point the chief whip, James Stuart, was deputed to suggest to him that he should step down as leader of the opposition. Churchill was incensed, and the matter was dropped, but it was significant.

Nonetheless, Churchill was exceptionally aware, throughout his life, of other people's perceptions of him. The dominant one after the war was that, although he had been a great war leader, he was too old, too uninterested in social reform, too dangerously bellicose in the increasingly grim international situation of the late 1940s. Very few people knew that the Attlee government, in great secrecy, had embarked upon the manufacture of a British atomic bomb; indeed, the fiction that Attlee had personally persuaded Truman not to use atomic weapons in Korea seemed to point up the essential difference between the two men. Churchill accordingly tolerated the activities of his colleagues and young Conservatives in entirely changing the image of the party at home, while he became increasingly oppressed by the nuclear menace.

When he did return to power in 1951 this became almost an obsession, and seriously imperiled his relations with Eden, who had never shared Churchill's enthusiasm for summits—particularly after Yalta—and did not have his pro-American enthusiasms. And he could see no signs whatever, and with good cause, that the Soviet leaders were open to any kind of negotiation. On Stalin's death in 1953 Churchill at once seized what he thought was a priceless opportunity of doing serious business with the new regime, only to be balked by Eisenhower and Eden. On this subject he made perhaps the worst single speech of his career, which plunged the Commons into bitter tumult and reduced his colleagues to embarrassed silence. The idea that nuclear war was inevitable—and there were many who believed just that—repelled him. The development of the hydrogen bomb, with its appalling implications, spurred him on further. He was certainly never a unilateral disarmer, or any kind of disarmer, but he could not accept that reasonable men could not come to a *modus vivendi*, nor that the wartime alliance could not somehow be re-created.

There were those who considered that these were perilous, quasi-senile dreams of an old man still wanting to hold center stage in world affairs, and hopelessly unrealistic. They do not seem so now. Indeed, his concerns have a nobility and vision about them that are admirable.

"THE LARGEST HUMAN BEING OF OUR TIME"

One of the principal quandaries in Churchill's character lay in its contradictions. He could be romantic and sentimental, but also hard and fierce; he was capable of kindnesses and acts of generosity, but also of total lack of consideration, and even cruelty; he could be ebullient and zestfully optimistic, then subject to dark moods of depression; he could be the best of company or the worst; he could be elaborately courteous and then, usually unthinkingly, snubbingly offensive; no one, not even his wife, could easily anticipate his moods. He had remarkably few real friends, and many of his favorite pastimes were essentially solitary. He could be excessively impressed by mavericks and adventurers, and dismissive of less enthralling personalities, yet even here he could see through charlatans, although it sometimes took rather a long time. He certainly overvalued Alexander and underestimated Slim—whom he had never met until he had established his unique reputation—but his assessments of Wavell and Auchinleck, which so enraged their admirers, now look eminently shrewd. He played Roosevelt as an expert angler with a brave and slippery salmon, and it is an open question as to which won this elaborate and fascinating contest of wills and personalities. He certainly saw Stalin rather more clearly, although perhaps not clearly enough until 1945. Arrogance was never a vice of which he could be accused, but neither was modesty. He saw himself and his life in heroic terms, but even his egocentricity had its charms and value—because he was, as Berlin has rightly and simply written, "the largest human being of our time."

2

A contrarian's approach to peace

MANFRED WEIDHORN

When a private secretary suggested to Winston Churchill that the shocking electoral defeat of 1945 would at least enable him to get some rest, he answered despondently, "No, I wanted to do the Peace too."[1] The great war leader and alleged warmonger as peacemaker? That Churchill frequently in his career was called The Man of War, or The Old Warhorse, and was branded a "warmonger" needs no certification. We all know about his early love of toy soldiers, his attendance at a military academy in lieu of college, his youthful eagerness to rush off to frontier wars on three continents, his exemplary work at the Admiralty, his service at the front lines in the First World War, his eagerness to meet force with force, his belief that war is sometimes necessary and even healthy, his warnings about the rise of the Nazi military machine and then of the Soviet one, and, above all, his unique wartime leadership as both Fabius and Scipio, first on the defensive in 1940 and then in helping forge an alliance to destroy the Nazi monster. We know, as well, about his personal courage in the face of hostile fire, his intellectual brilliance in mastering the minutiae of army, navy, and air force strategic deliberations, his abiding interest in military technology and his consequent role in helping develop the tank, the warplane, and the artificial harbor, and, perhaps most impressive of all, his amazing memo of 1911 that accurately predicted the course of the first forty days of combat in the imminent First World War, a memo that ultimately won glowing praise from generals, politicians, and historians.

Less well known, however, are his achievements in peacemaking. One reason for this ignorance is the tendency of persons of action to specialize,

---

[1] Martin Gilbert, *Churchill: A Life* (New York: Henry Holt, 1991), 857.

24

and of observers to oversimplify. As Churchill himself put it, "We are all right-handed or left-handed. . . . Those who can win a war well can rarely make a good peace, and those who could make a good peace would never have won the war."[2] The assumption, therefore, is that if Churchill excelled at warmaking, he could not have been good at making peace.

A second reason for this skewed vision is that violence always sells better than tranquillity. "War," Thomas Hardy saucily said, "makes rattling good history,"[3] but peace is poor reading. We all proclaim our love of peace, yet the best-selling books and movies are invariably about war, whether in outer space (*Star Wars*) or on the domestic scene (*The Godfather*).

But the most compelling reason for Churchill's anemic reputation as a peacemaker is that his approach has been readily misunderstood. He does not quite belong to either of two schools of thought that have arisen in response to the question of how to deal with the bloody-mindedness of human nature. One school, founded by Jesus, holds that violence should be met with nonviolence only. This is clearly not Churchill's way. In any case, the pacifism in the words and deeds of Jesus has rarely been taken seriously by most Christians. The principle of the just war evolved by St. Augustine provided the necessary loopholes. Yet, though pacifism is a philosophy for the very few, in diluted form it is widespread in the modern world and subject to much lip service. Usually discarded as a usable idea, its simulacrum is idolized.

The other school of thought rests on the principle of fighting fire with fire. This is a far more popular line of thought, given the natural proclivity for revenge and retaliation. Churchill, it needs hardly to be said, is closer to the latter group, and his strong articulation of its viewpoint has contributed to his reputation for bellicosity. Particularly disquieting to some was his attack on what he took to be the former's sentimentality, the rhetorical pacifism that allows many people to substitute noble words for direct grappling with grim reality. At issue is the sentimentality of all those who, as Churchill put it in the early 1930s in criticizing disarmament conferences, think that stating a desire for peace helps in any way to obtain it. Just as objectionable is the sentimentality of the general public, which is seduced by protestations of the love of peace. This verbal,

---

[2] Winston S. Churchill, *A Roving Commission* (New York: Scribner's, 1930; rpt. 1941), 331. In my *A Harmony of Interests* (Madison, New Jersey: Fairleigh Dickinson University Press, 1992), ch. 3, I study the complexity of Churchill's attitude to war.

[3] Thomas Hardy, *The Dynasts* (London: Macmillan, 1923), 54.

ersatz pacifism, which villains either proclaim or exploit, plagues the modern world. As Churchill observed, "Any declaration or public speech against armaments, although it consisted only of platitudes, . . . has always been applauded, and any speech . . . which set forth the blunt truths has been incontinently relegated to the category of 'warmongering.'" Or, as he said again soon after the Second World War: "Peace will not be preserved by pious sentiments expressed in terms of platitudes or by official grimaces."[4]

Churchill's presentation of the issues, however, differentiates him from the unthinking proponents of the hard line. He stands out not only because of his willingness to attack the popular, noble-sounding pacifist rhetoric, but also because of his eloquent enunciation of his position in six decades of public affairs, his being often borne out by events, and, chiefly, his unorthodox approach. For, despite his occasional advocacy of force and his notoriety as a warmonger, the story of his career finds him repeatedly among the compromisers. Once war was inevitable, he indeed turned into a vengeful sword of the nation, but that was not the course he pursued so long as alternatives to war existed. This ability to make important distinctions sets him off from both the hawks, who bring to all questions the same idealism or blood lust, and the doves, who bring to all questions the same reasonableness or squeamishness.

THE FIRST THREE DECADES

For one who was putatively a war-lover, Churchill has a long record of criticizing the making of war. In his first book, *The Story of the Malakand Field Force*, he remarked on the futility of that campaign. All the barbarity, losses, and expenditure, he feared, would not achieve a "permanent settlement."[5] He thought that a superior policy in Asia and Africa was to conquer and govern with silver rather than steel, that is, with money rather than bullets. A few years later, when criticizing in the same fashion the conduct of the Boer War, he obtained a chance, the first on what was to be a long list, to apply his beliefs and to affect the course of events. Making it clear that he was for compromise, he described himself in 1902 as "tolerant [and] moderate," as someone hating "extremists whether

---

[4] Gilbert, *Churchill: A Life*, 506, 868.
[5] Ibid., 79; Winston S. Churchill, *The Story of the Malakand Field Force* (London: Longmans, Green, 1899), 270, 311–12.

they be Jingoes or pro-Boers." That attitude catapulted him into a major role in the peacemaking that ended the Boer War.

Generosity was the centerpiece of his approach to the enemy. At the colonial office, he helped draft a constitution for the Transvaal as part of the policy he advocated of granting self-government to the defeated South Africans. His motive was, frankly, national selfishness, but enlightened selfishness. As he put it, far better is it for Britain to show "courage and distinction" by granting autonomy in its hour of triumph than to have it "jerked and twisted" away, with "humiliation" rather than grace, at a later time of possible British weakness. To that end he worked for equality between the defeated Boer and the victorious Briton. Prime Minister Campbell-Bannerman lavished high praise on Churchill for his major role in "this courageous and righteous policy . . . the finest and noblest work" of modern Britain.[6]

Nor was this nobility confined to foreign affairs. Fifteen years later, he brought the same openness to the festering Irish problem at home, with equally glittering prizes to show for his effort. Though his father had opposed home rule, Churchill modified his position in 1904 and was, by 1912, advocating home rule strenuously. The First World War suspended serious discussions on this provincial matter, but, as soon as the war ended, the Irish crisis became central again. With violence escalating, Churchill appealed for negotiations to replace the killing. To be sure, he played a prominent role in the British resort to counterterrorism, but at least he was one of the first to see the futility of that strategy. A half-year later, declaring the failure of force to resolve the struggle between the government and the Irish revolutionaries, he again urged negotiations without preconditions.

This time he was listened to, and, as in the case of South Africa, his eloquent words dispatched him into the maelstrom of events. He became once again a chief negotiator. He prevailed on the cabinet to waive, as a sign of British good faith, the death penalty for all Sinn Feiners convicted of murder. The ensuing discussions rendered the two sides, in his words, "allies in a common cause." It next fell to him to guide the resulting Irish Treaty through Parliament and then to head a cabinet committee charged with implementing it. When Irish extremists rejected the treaty and resumed violence, Churchill established, together with the Sinn Fein negotiator

---

[6] Gilbert, *Churchill: A Life*, 149, 151, 176, 182; *WSC* I 504–5, II 144–53, 158–61; William Manchester, *The Last Lion*, 2 vols. to date (Boston: Little Brown, 1983–), vol. 1, 390.

Michael Collins, a boundary commission to work out, farm by farm, the exact borders between the North and the South. After introducing the Irish Free State bill in Parliament, he worked with Arthur Griffith, founder of Sinn Fein, on a constitution.

He thus not only played a major role in the emancipation of Ireland but was lavishly commended by many observers. His "skill and patience," they said, as well as his "exercise of judgment," even marked him out for a possible leadership role in the future. Among Michael Collins's last words before being assassinated was a sentence which could be the rubric for Churchill's entire career, at least among those who see him as a candidate for the honor of "man of the century": "Tell Winston we could never have done anything without him."[7]

With the wisdom of hindsight, of course, we can see that liberality toward the Boers resulted in forty years of oppression of black people and that freedom for the twenty-six counties resulted in civil war, as well as, later, a quarter century of violence in the remaining six counties. Further, his arranging, at the Cairo Conference of 1921, the map of the Arab world left orphaned by the death of the Ottoman Empire did nothing to prevent seven decades of conflict between Arab and Jew or between Iraq and Kuwait. These adverse developments might *prima facie* tarnish Churchill's image.

Such an interpretation of events is, however, unfair. It confounds the short run with the long run. In the short run, Churchill's work held up nicely, as it extricated Britain from vexatious quagmires. In the long run, it did not hold up, but in the long run nothing does, for everything is in flux. If Churchill were to be blamed for remote unintended consequences, George Washington would have to be held responsible for perpetuating slavery and preparing the way for civil war, and Jesus, for crusades and inquisitions. The test is rather what was the best that the politician was able to accomplish in his time and place. As Churchill himself defined the issue in his eulogy on Neville Chamberlain, "In one phase men seem to have been right, in another they seem to have been wrong. Then again, a few years later, when the perspective of time has lengthened, all stands in a different setting. . . . The only guide to a man is his conscience . . . the rectitude and sincerity of his actions."[8] Though it is easy to find defects,

[7] Gilbert, *Churchill: A Life*, 164, 250, 258, 427, 440–9; Manchester, *The Last Lion*, vol. 1, 720–35; Robert Rhodes James, *Churchill: A Study in Failure* (New York: World, 1970), 144–5, 150.

[8] Winston S. Churchill, *The Second World War*, 6 vols. (Boston: Houghton Mifflin, 1948–53), vol. 2, 550.

from one vantage or another, in the settlements Churchill arranged, one must always remember that politics is the art of the possible. By that standard, Churchill's peacemaking in these cases looks very good indeed.

A different sort of moderation and pragmatism presented itself in the years before the First World War when Churchill in 1912 urged a naval holiday, i.e., an agreement by the two major sea powers, Britain and Germany, to a moratorium on the construction of warships. The offer was ignored, and war became imminent. Yet, far from thirsting for the blood of Germans, Churchill in these ominous times joined in the attempt to prevent the cataclysm. In July 1914, he urged Grey to defuse the European crisis. Wanting to do his "best for peace," he favored British neutrality, "so long as no treaty obligation or true British interest is involved. . . . Balkan quarrels are no concern of ours." He was for a while not willing to go to war with Germany even if Belgium were invaded.[9]

A consequence of the First World War was, of course, the Bolshevik Revolution. One of the things best known about Churchill is that he was the first and most strident postrevolutionary anti-communist and that he moved heaven and earth, in his own famous words, to "strangle Bolshevism in the cradle." Hardly known at all is that this same man was willing to make peace with the new Russia, even willing to guarantee in person the survival of the Bolshevik government, if only it would resume the war against the Germans. That offer, seeking peace on a lesser front for the sake of war on the major front, might of course be dismissed as no evidence of Churchill's pacific nature. Yet, with the First World War over, late in 1918, he was still ready to deal with the Bolsheviks—though he doubted that they would respond until they realized that "we had the power and the will to enforce our views." And when the subsequent Allied attempt to overthrow the new regime failed, Churchill was once more prepared to negotiate with its leaders, however wicked they might be, because, he said, they were "a force of order." In other words, his anti-communist idealism had given way to a dose of realism. Indeed, as hostilities next erupted between Russia and Poland, he wanted Britain to mediate a peace between them rather than to side with Poland and thereby try again to undo the revolution. His position now was that, if certain terms were met, Britain should recognize Bolshevik Russia. His policy on this matter is, like that on the Tonypandy affair and on the general strike, an example

---

[9] Gilbert, *Churchill: A Life*, 243–4, 258, 263, 268–9, 271; Manchester, *The Last Lion*, vol. 1, 449, 468.

of the injustice perpetrated by common wisdom, by what is called reputation. People remember the idealistic (or fanatical) attempt to stifle Bolshevism and forget the pragmatic aftermath.[10]

A second conclusion to be drawn from Churchill's early record as a peacemaker is that he was often a pragmatic compromiser to begin with, or, when not so, a leader who replaced obsessive hostility with practical accommodation for the sake of peace. This mellowing can be seen even in situations in which his behavior was dubious or erratic—as on Turkey in 1922 and on India in the early 1930s. In the case of the former, after having made some hawkish noises that alarmed many people, he came around to urging Lloyd George to fashion a peace with Turkey and to evacuate British forces from Chanak rather than to suffer a military defeat. And in the case of India, where his noisy stand is generally regarded, not entirely fairly, as one of the black marks on his record, it should be recalled that after the Second World War he finally did quietly yield on the question of granting independence.[11]

The imbroglio over Bolshevik Russia remains, however, more complex than these last two cases. His change of attitude toward the fledgling communist state was due not only to realism, or perhaps fickleness, but also to a considered, if somewhat wrongheaded, idea. So far was he from being, despite his occasional ambiguities and others' suspicions, a lover of war, that he could in fact be accused on certain occasions of excessive optimism about human nature. He had an almost naïve (and somewhat conservative) faith in the power of money and time to restrain the bellicose, sadistic impulses in individuals and nations. His theme at various junctures was that, while a nation might make warlike pronouncements, the passage of time would bring prosperity and that such social change is a great solvent of truculence. Thus he said of Germany, after the Agadir crisis in 1911, that war was not inevitable because "It may be that in a few years' time the democratic forces in Germany will again have greater control of their own Government, and that the landlord ascendancy which now exists will be replaced by more pacific . . . elements."[12]

A decade later he was saying something similar of the new regime in Russia: peace and reorganization "may well prepare the way for the unity of Russia through a political evolution. . . . A cessation of arms and a promotion of material prosperity are inevitable, and we must trust . . . to

---

[10] Gilbert, *Churchill: A Life*, 389–90, 405, 420–2; but see Rhodes James, *Churchill: A Study in Failure*, 137.
[11] Gilbert, *Churchill: A Life*, 450–2, 876, 884.   [12] Ibid., 242.

peaceful influences to bring about the disappearance of this awful tyranny and peril."[13] He occasionally articulated similar sentiments during the cold war. In 1957 he wrote, "Russia is becoming a great commercial country. Her people experience every day in growing vigour those complications and palliatives of human life that will render the schemes of Karl Marx more out of date."[14]

Churchill's naïveté here is embarrassing. He was completely wrong about Germany, which needed the catalyst of two disastrous defeats to turn it inward in the manner he had predicted or hoped for. The eventual implosion of the Soviet empire might seem to vindicate the second prophecy, were it not necessary to overlook a lot of painful history that he did not adequately foresee.

Perhaps a better example of prescience on the matter of seeking peace can be found in Churchill's *obiter dicta* on a pair of subjects of relatively lesser importance on the world stage. Both had to do with the Middle East. In the 1921 Cairo Conference devoted to the new shape of the Arab world, Churchill proposed autonomy for the Kurds in northern Iraq, lest a future Iraqi ruler were to oppress the Kurdish minority. And nearly a quarter of a century later, as his thoughts turned again to that region, he urged King Ibn Saud to help arrange a lasting peace between Jew and Arab by establishing a Jewish Palestine within a larger Middle Eastern Arab federation.[15] Both suggestions are as relevant today as when they were made—and ignored—long ago.

UNDERSTANDING THE ADVERSARY

This, then, was the core of Churchill's work as a peacemaker in the first half of his career. Few politicians can match it. Encompassing the opening three decades of the century, this record was, with a few notable exceptions, relatively noncontroversial. Far different was the case with the second half, spanning the 1930s and 1940s, when the epithet of "warmonger" was often hurled at him in connection with his Cato-like warnings about Hitler and Stalin. The challenges offered by South Africa and Ireland, impressive and important though they seemed at the time, proved

---

[13] Ibid., 420.
[14] Winston S. Churchill, *Memoirs of the Second World War*, abridged by Denis Kelly (Boston: Houghton Mifflin, 1959), 1015.
[15] Gilbert, *Churchill: A Life*, 434, 825.

to be minor compared to the global threats perceived to be emanating later from Germany and Russia.

To understand his notoriety in the second half of his career, we must confront a philosophical principle. Before doing so, however, we should pause to ask at this stage of the inquiry what lay behind the long and rich peacemaking record so far. What principles governed his behavior? What mind-set did he have that enabled him to find doorways that other politicians and diplomats missed? How did his thinking deviate from the unimaginative norm?

Surely one important element was his taking the proper measure of war. If Churchill was somewhat naïve on the question of the strength of the acquisitive drive relative to the aggressive drive, he was not naïve about war itself. Confronting him here was not the pacifist's sentimentality, but the war-lover's romanticization of combat. The idea that war is beautiful or at least noble is widespread among those who confine their acquaintance with it to books and movies, as well as those who have porous memories. Churchill himself early in life had a weakness for this adorned view, and it resulted in an occasional purple passage by him, as well as much rhetoric by others, then and later, about his putative love of war. Yet despite his juvenile celebrations of its beauties, he was from the beginning aware of its downside. He shared in the ambivalence to which General Robert E. Lee famously confessed and which Churchill quoted in his *History of the English-Speaking Peoples*: "It is well that war is so terrible—[otherwise] we should grow too fond of it!"[16]

No war-hater could be so well tutored as Churchill in the horrors of war. For one thing, his presence at no fewer than four wars by the age of twenty-six is more frontline experience than nearly all politicians and most generals gather in a lifetime. And from these experiences he brought back the bad news. In the campaign in northwest India, he reported, native savagery was met with British savagery, including the use of the "appalling" new dumdum bullet, the effects of which he dared not allude to in print. In *The River War* he realistically described the sufferings of the unattended injured and the panorama of death.[17]

He soon put his experience and insight to practical use. At the start of his parliamentary career, in 1901, he painted a grim picture of what the

---

[16] Winston S. Churchill, *A History of the English-Speaking Peoples*, 4 vols. (New York: Bantam Books, 1963), vol. 4, 132.

[17] Winston S. Churchill, *The River War*, 2 vols. (London: Longmans, Green, 1899), vol. 1, 104, 440, 445; vol. 2, 195–7, 378.

wars of the future would be like, a picture fully borne out by events. On the eve of the First World War, he repeated such warnings, saying that a war involving two "highly scientific nations" would be devastating. In the 1920s he painted even grimmer pictures of future wars, which would involve weapons somewhat like the nuclear bombs and missiles that in fact were developed. After the Second World War, he feared that another war might occasion the end of civilization and even "possibly disintegrate the globe itself." And late in life he was harping anew on the "unspeakable and unimaginable horrors" of a Third World War.[18] This is hardly the rhetoric of a war-lover.

But neither is it the rhetoric of a pacifist. For, war horrors or not, patriotism and duty were the first priority. If war was a "curse," tyranny was a "darker curse."[19] When a potentially aggressive tyrant was on the world stage—as in the years between 1911 and 1914, the 1930s, and the late 1940s—Churchill was a zealot for the cause of arming to the teeth. This prompted those innocents who saw no impending aggression to label him a warmonger. But a true warmonger would favor expansionist aggression by one's own nation. Churchill never did so, and, in fact, in periods with no threat looming, he was avid for retrenchment in military spending. That was the case in 1901 and 1903, when he attacked St. John Brodrick's proposal to enlarge the standing British army at a time of widespread peace.[20] Later, whether as a radical Liberal in 1908 or as the new Conservative chancellor of the Exchequer in 1925, he wanted to make reductions in naval spending in order to pay for the social welfare legislation which he proposed.

Declaring one's hatred of war is to most modern people easy and obvious. More challenging is the attitude taken once war is inevitable. According to an old saw, when war begins, the first casualty is truth. One form of mis- and disinformation that quickly gains currency has to do with the enemy. The people of a country at war learn to regard their counterparts as less than human. Any residual good sense or decency is destroyed by the propaganda machinery of the government. Having got the nation into a war, the politicians, if only to justify themselves, must whip up public sentiment against the enemy, lest the war be fought halfheartedly. The vocabulary of hate—"kraut," "Jap," "gook," "slope," "dink"—is meant to dehumanize the enemy in order to make it easier to

---

[18] Gilbert, *Churchill: A Life*, 79, 143, 245, 872, 923, 930, 935; Winston S. Churchill, "Shall We Commit Suicide?" *Nash's Pall Mall Magazine* (September 24, 1924), 1994 rpt., 8.
[19] Weidhorn, *Harmony of Interests*, 61.   [20] Gilbert, *Churchill: A Life*, 143, 153.

kill him without incurring a guilty conscience. Politicians, when not sharing in that orgy of hate, exploit it.

Not Churchill. He had a unique way of regarding the adversary. He
knew the wisdom of Talleyrand's maxim *"n'ayez pas de zèle"* ("not too
much zeal"). No matter how much his policy may whip up public sentiment against the enemy, the wise leader knows better. After all, he may
have to negotiate peace some day with that same enemy. This possibility
is not theoretical. Just consider the massive changes of recent years: an
Israeli government, after swearing up and down through decades that
it would never negotiate with terrorists, at last secretly, and then openly,
held talks with the Palestine Liberation Organization. A British government that made the same avowal about the Irish Republican Army made
the same turnabout. A South African government that looked upon the
African National Congress as its mortal foe ended up handing power over
gracefully. Clearly in each case the vow of abstinence was partly a bargaining chip and partly a posture for public consumption, and the talks
that canceled the vow represented politicians coming to terms with reality. Politicians often ignore their own rhetoric, for what gets you elected
is not what enables you to govern.

Despite a consequent vulnerability to the charge of being a liar, a politician is thus an informal devotee of the golden rule: love your enemy
as you would love yourself. Even the politician who lacks such wisdom
will not, for prudential reasons, bring hatred and fanaticism into cabinet
room deliberations. Churchill credits Bismarck with the observation that,
in order to fight the enemy, one must first understand him.[21] That is, one
must put oneself into the enemy's shoes, comprehend where the enemy is
coming from, and be able to say that, were one in the enemy's place, one
would hardly act differently. This gesture of empathy is often beyond the
reach of the common man who, concerned with his livelihood, is largely
ignorant of history, untrained in analytical thinking, imprisoned in un-
examined assumptions, a creature of his culture and his herd, and, therefore, susceptible to the political passions of the moment. For proof, just
listen to the statements of most callers on radio talk shows, as well as
many of the hosts.

So here we have another key to the understanding of Churchill's
unique approach to the prosecution of war: One makes war intelligently so
that one can make a peace that lasts. While the populace emotes blindly,

---

[21] Churchill, *Second World War*, vol. 3, 581.

the politician reasons and looks ahead. That is why, throughout the many wars in which Churchill participated, his attitude to the enemy was unconventional.

One can see this principle at work very early, in the Cuban Revolution of 1895, which Churchill observed at close hand at the tender age of twenty-one. His instincts favored the Spaniards, partly because they, like the British a century earlier, were fighting to maintain an empire and partly because they were his hosts and treated him kindly. In his dispatches, therefore, he tended, without strong partisan feelings, to present the war from the perspective of what would now be called the colonial oppressors. Yet Churchill's nonconformity and intelligence enabled him to bypass his predispositions and to see the merits of the cause of the Cuban guerrillas. In his private letters, he revealed that the scope of the Spanish corruption and exploitation appalled him so much as to force from him the concession that "a national and justifiable revolt is the only possible result of such a system." Later he even reproached himself, again in private, "for having perhaps done injustice to the insurgents" in his somewhat "uncandid" newspaper articles.[22]

When he participated two years later in the British frontier wars as a soldier and correspondent rather than as an observer, he took the difficult and rare step of bringing to bear on his own country *in print* the dispassionate attitude that it had been easy to take in private toward a foreign power like Spain. He actually extolled the virtues of the Pathans, dervishes, et al.—"valiant warriors," whose state was "tolerable" to them.[23] Such sentiments may not seem like much but, when placed alongside the usual view, held by frontline soldiers and by homebound civilians, that the Pathans and dervishes—like, later, the Boers, the Germans, the Russians, the Arabs, and the Argentinians—are "savages" and "barbarians," it *is* significant.

In the third of the frontier wars, Churchill likewise showed respect toward the Afrikaner enemy of Britain. He carried this disinterestedness to a climax when, in his maiden parliamentary speech, he paraphrased Chatham on the American colonists: "If I were a Boer I hope I should be fighting in the field." This famous utterance brings out as well as anything can the need for an approach at the top that is inspired by a detached analysis of the facts rather than by the roiling waves of popular emotions.

[22] Gilbert, *Churchill: A Life*, 60.
[23] Manfred Weidhorn, *Sword and Pen* (Albuquerque, New Mexico: University of New Mexico Press, 1974), 35.

As is well known, that little gem of a sentence caused an unfavorable reaction in the House and at large. It demanded more understanding than most people, even most politicians, could muster.[24]

Churchill was in fact continually on the lookout for actions that, though cheered on by the bulk of the populace and officialdom in the name of chauvinism, actually degraded Britain in the eyes of either an adversary or a fair-minded observer. In 1901, he protested publicly against the execution of a Boer commandant and tried to prevent the execution of another. When British troops slaughtered six hundred peasants in Tibet in 1904, Churchill was understandably outraged, and by adopting the point of view of the victims, he could also see the counterproductiveness of the action: "Are there any people in the world so mean spirited as not to resist under the circumstances to which these poor Tibetans have been subjected?" In 1906 he criticized British pacification measures in Nigeria: "The chronic bloodshed which stains the West African seasons is odious and disquieting." The British crushing of a Zulu revolt in Natal was referred to by him as "the disgusting butchery of the natives." The shooting by British troops of three hundred unarmed Indians in Amritsar in 1920 he called "monstrous . . . we cannot admit this doctrine [of frightfulness] in any form."[25]

If these reactions sound unexceptional, the product of common decency, we are fooling ourselves. In the American operation in Panama a few years ago, which was mounted to apprehend a single individual, hundreds of Panamanian civilians were killed and buried in a mass grave. Was there any voice of conscience in the halls of power, at the pulpit, in the media, or in the American population at large nagging us the way Churchill thought fit to nag the officials of his own government and country? A man who talked the way he did is bestirred not by the war-lover's venom but by the peacemaker's sensitivity and common sense.

The same largeness of mind operated in the domestic sphere. In the strikes of 1910, he reached out to the workers by having them talk to the industrial arbitrator. His calling the owners "very unreasonable" shows that he understood what the workers faced. Indeed, in turbulent dislocations a year later, he insisted that the strikers, being "very poor [and] miserably paid," had "a real grievance" and were "an unduly strained class of workers." He withheld troops while seeking conciliation; strikers should be confronted with unarmed auxiliary police who could do the job, not

[24] Gilbert, *Churchill: A Life*, 139, 149.   [25] Ibid., 145, 163, 183, 422.

with soldiers. During another strike, in 1921, he complained that the miners' needs were not appreciated.[26]

Even in the general strike of 1926, in which he came to be seen as a rabid right-winger, he was in fact a moderate. He struck a conciliatory note; he praised both the union negotiators and the Labour M.P.s for their moderation; he insisted that the miners' grievances should be attended to; he again urged keeping the military out of sight. Chosen chief government negotiator because of his conciliatory role, he fought for the workers whenever they had what he considered to be a real grievance; he accepted, for instance, the miners' demand for a minimum wage. Seeing the owners as "recalcitrant" and "unreasonable," he wanted to press them, but the cabinet would not back him.[27]

He brought this enlightened, conciliatory approach with him to other domestic issues. His administration of the prison system was marked by his hunting out cases of unwarranted severity. And, in early 1919, when he came to the war office just as there was deep unrest among soldiers demanding immediate demobilization, he promptly improvised a scheme that was seen as fair by all sides. In the face of a new mutiny, General Haig wanted the ringleaders shot, but Churchill overruled him on the grounds that no blood had been spilled by the mutineers.[28]

Such an attitude prevailed in the great wars. Two minor incidents that showed Churchill rising above patriotic cant and rant involved his using ceremonial language in his declaration of war on Japan and in his praise of General Rommel. Both gestures aroused criticism, on which he commented, "This churlishness is a well-known streak in human nature but contrary to the spirit in which a war is won or a lasting peace established."[29]

Churchill's capacity to give the devil his due is truly remarkable. He could see something positive even about the dictators who arose in the interwar period. Impressed at first by Mussolini, he said in 1926, echoing his pro-Boer statement of 1901, "Had I been an Italian, I am sure I would have been wholeheartedly with you from start to finish." Even Hitler he judged dispassionately as late as 1937, and again with echoes of the pro-Boer statement: "If our country were defeated I hope we should find a

[26] Ibid., 220–1, 231–2, 478; Paul Addison, *Churchill on the Home Front, 1900–1955* (London: Pimlico, 1993), 143–4, 162–3.
[27] Gilbert, *Churchill: A Life*, 475–9; Rhodes James, *Churchill: A Study in Failure*, 193; Addison, *Churchill on the Home Front, 1900–1955*, 259–68.
[28] Gilbert, *Churchill: A Life*, 225, 406–7.   [29] Churchill, *Second World War*, vol. 4, 67.

champion as indomitable to restore our courage." To be sure, like all decent people, Churchill decried the evils of the fascist regimes, but that was, on the part of many anti-fascists, cheaply bought self-righteousness. He alone took the statesman's extra step of trying to see what was valid about the obnoxious rulers, why they had arisen in the first place, and how they managed to remain in power. As he said of the German re-occupation of the Rhineland in 1936, if one were a German and disliked the regime, one would still take pride in Hitler's daring feat.[30] Without such an understanding of one's adversaries, one could not hope to contend with them.

When the dictators' behavior forfeited the benefit of the doubt they had been given, he switched his sympathy from them to their subjects. He tried in various wartime speeches to separate the leaders (and their backers), with their monstrous guilt, from average Italians and Germans. To the British man in the street, the Italians and Germans might be just so many "wops" or "krauts," but Churchill would not, as Burke would not, "indict a whole nation."[31] Indeed, as late as the early 1930s, Churchill had spoken sympathetically of the "just grievances of the vanquished" (i.e., the Germans) needing to be attended to.[32]

The relevance of this wise objectivity to our own concerns cannot be overestimated. When the Ayatollah Khomeini came to power, he was derided by people and politicians in the West as a lunatic. Yet the man was motivated by—or at least loved for—his piety and his patriotism, two values much appreciated in the West as well. Using the politician's golden rule the way Churchill did, we would realize that, had Khomeini adhered to our religion and our country or had we been Muslims and Iranians, most of us would have loved him too. This is not to exculpate Khomeini but to inculpate us for misreading the facts and resorting to a shallow, dismissive word like "lunatic" to cover up our self-centeredness.

MAGNANIMITY

When the defeated adversary finally comes to the negotiating table, the inclination of most people is to rake in the spoils of victory and to sate themselves on revenge and riches. That was not Churchill's way. For reasons of fairness as well as of enlightenment and prudence, he took

---

[30] Gilbert, *Churchill: A Life*, 480, 580; Winston S. Churchill, *While England Slept* (New York: Putnam, 1938), 252; Rhodes James, *Churchill: A Study in Failure*, 285.
[31] Gilbert, *Churchill: A Life*, 793.   [32] Ibid., 511.

the larger view. The famous motto of his Second World War memoirs
—"In war, Resolution; In defeat, Defiance; In victory, Magnanimity; In
peace, Goodwill"—was adapted from the Romans as early as in his 1930
autobiography.[33]

A *pacifying* if not a pacifist principle, it is more easily recited than
enacted. Churchill had nothing to be ashamed of in this regard. He consistently practiced what he preached, even at the beginning of his career.
In *The River War*, he lamented the fact that the British allowed barbarous
elation to overcome magnanimity in victory. And he drew up an indictment: the victory at Omdurman was "disgraced by the inhuman [British]
slaughter of the wounded [Sudanese]." Kitchener allowed "acts of barbarity." The tomb of the Mahdi was destroyed and the corpse of the
Mahdi desecrated in a gesture that was at best "vandalism and folly" and
at worst "wicked." Official statements about these matters were filled
with "mendacity" to the point of ridiculousness.[34] In this case, Churchill
was so respectful of the Sudanese opponent (as well as of the rules of war
and British self-regard) and so outspoken about it as to incur the anger
of General Kitchener and imperil his nascent career. Some would call this
"courage."

We saw his important role in the peacemaking that followed the Boer
War. Now we can see the magnanimity that made it possible. Churchill
believed that while using tough military measures, "We must also make
it easy for the enemy to accept defeat. We must tempt as well as compel."
The victors were to forswear the luxury of revenge lest it drive the losers
to desperation and to a guerrilla war, with "years of bloody partisan
warfare." Once the Boers finally desisted from their guerrilla war, Churchill, unlike the Conservatives, sought their reunification with the British.
Only an "honorable agreement" with a "brave enemy" would result in
a lasting peace. Predictably, he was severely criticized for his "peaceful
telegrams."[35]

Likewise, right after the First World War, Churchill advocated magnanimity in peacemaking. A major instance of the clash of untutored
passion and discriminating intelligence occurred at this time. Throughout
the Western world, hatred and vindictiveness toward the loser ran rampant.
People wanted to make Germany pay until it squeaked like a pip. That

[33] Churchill, *Roving Commission*, 331.
[34] Gilbert, *Churchill: A Life*, 98–100; Weidhorn, *Sword and Pen*, 35; Churchill, *River War*,
vol. 2, 212, 225.
[35] Gilbert, *Churchill: A Life*, 125–6, 149.

the burden of reparations would fall on the common man and not on the aristocrats, plutocrats, and generals who started the war was irrelevant to them. Some politicians knew that this was poor peacemaking, but, in order to remain in power, they went along; not Churchill. He demurred when Lloyd George suggested that the kaiser should be shot and when most politicians and the press favored harsh peace terms for Germany. Anything severe, he believed, would reduce German workers to "a condition of sweated labor and servitude." Churchill was of course right because, while assuaging the British and French voters, the onerous Treaty of Versailles eventually spawned Hitler and the Second World War. It was a case of penny wise, pound foolish.[36]

And when that avoidable war came, Churchill once more wanted to go easy on the German people. As early as September 1944, in the heat of battle, he deprecated proposals to deindustrialize Germany because "There are bonds between the working classes of all countries, and the English people will not stand for the policy." At Yalta, arguing again against exploiting a defeated Germany, he reminded Roosevelt and Stalin that the heavy reparations demanded of it after the last war had been a disaster.[37]

Churchill's farsightedness was especially noteworthy with regard to Germany. Hatred of the Germans has long festered in the peoples bruised by them over the course of the bloody twentieth century. But for Churchill, as soon as either war was over, future hostilities could be prevented only if rancor and vindictiveness yielded to prudence and vision. In 1921 he said that unless France and Germany were reconciled, the struggle between them would soon be renewed. He therefore opposed Britain's making a treaty with France in 1925, which would have alienated Germany; far better was something like the Locarno Treaty, which brought all the major European powers together.[38]

After the Second World War he resurrected this old theme. At the risk of shocking public opinion and irritating the French, as he put it, he urged the reconciliation of France and Germany. Germany should be invited to join in the military defense of Western Europe—even if the French needed some convincing about this and even if Britain and France needed to remain united in order to keep Germany honest. Finally, in June 1954, talks between President Eisenhower and Prime Minister Churchill resulted in West Germany's becoming an equal partner in the West European

[36] Ibid., 402–4; Rhodes James, *Churchill: A Study in Failure*, 245.
[37] Gilbert, *Churchill: A Life*, 793, 818.   [38] Ibid., 439, 471.

community, this being the fruition of an idea Churchill had advanced eight years earlier, and indeed a full generation earlier.[39]

REALISM

These, then, are some lessons to be drawn from Churchill's peacemaking: one must be flexible, that is, one must have an inclination, like a chess player's, continually to reevaluate the overall situation (as Churchill did with Russia, but not with the Empire); one must understand that war is a painful and dubious last resort; one must realize that the enemy may be a mirror image of oneself. Consequently, one must practice magnanimity and enlightened selfishness rather than pettiness or avarice. With such a far-seeing approach, how did Churchill ever obtain the reputation of a warmonger? Why did his controversial behavior in the Russian and Turkish crises of 1919 and 1922 eclipse all his other deeds?

The answer has to do with the second half of his career and is to be found in one word, "realism." What separates the inept, sentimental, naïve peace *lover* from the successful peace *maker* is that elusive concept. Like much else in life, realism is in the eye of the beholder. For Churchill, realism meant accepting as a given that at certain junctures men are war-like and rapacious and that only force can stop force. Such an attitude enmeshes one in power politics. It prompted Churchill, who had been throughout the decade of the 1900s on the side of military retrenchment and moratoria on warship building, to change course in 1911. He became a war hawk, to the consternation of the many optimists, meliorists, and liberals whom he left behind clinging to the old dovish faith in a better, war-free world. He had seen a rising, ambitious, threatening Germany, something which they would or could not see. Remember also that he had discovered in the frontier wars a killer instinct in himself and in others. That sense of original sin or innate aggressiveness caused him to ignore the widespread, quasi-pacifist feeling that, in the twentieth century, Europe had finally learned to put war behind it.

This realism accompanied him throughout his career but became most important and controversial in the phase that saw the sway of Hitler and Stalin. The need to arm for the sake of peace, an idea whose time had come in 1911, repeated itself in the 1930s, with that same Germany

---

[39] Ibid., 872–3, 890–2, 921, 928, 932.

playing the villainous role, albeit in Nazi rather than imperial trappings. And then, after the Second World War, realism informed Churchill that a dormant giant, Russia, had been awakened by the bitter blows of the Hitlerian invasion and was now, whether out of a determination never to be invaded again or out of a messianic zeal to spread the new gospel, looking as if it had entered an expansionist phase.

That same realism, on the other hand, prevented Churchill from becoming an idealist or fanatic who would not desist from hostilities until the earth was purged of the communist evil. It instructed him that a major power, which could not be wished away by daydreaming, need not be wiped out by force. Although to most conservatives Stalin was worse than Hitler, Churchill made a distinction between domestic horrors and external aggressiveness. Hitler's Germany had been expansive in a way that Stalin's Russia was not. The latter only grabbed what fell his way but did not go about shaking the tree the way Hitler did. Russia therefore could be lived with. Here was a *via media*, which, at the risk of offending purists, involved carving out with the Great Bear spheres of influence for the sake of the greater good of establishing peace.[40] Americans claimed to be shocked by such cynical traditional diplomacy. Yet if Roosevelt spoke of ushering in a new world without wicked old ideas like the balance of power and the spheres of influence, Churchill knew that human nature had not changed as a result of the victory of the Allies.

Making an accommodation with Russia would, of course, be hard on the peoples of Eastern Europe, who would be consigned to living under an oppressive Russian hegemony and a communist social system, not to speak of dooming the Russian people to a perpetuation of their brutal regime. Yet not for Churchill any John Foster Dullesian crusade to roll back the Iron Curtain. The question is, was not this compromise of his, which was based on realism rather than visionary aspirations, better than the alternative of stumbling into a Third World War for the purpose of liberating oppressed peoples and achieving only mass destruction? Churchill had, after all, earned his realism about Russia in the crucible of experience; he had paid his dues to idealism when he had tried to strangle Bolshevism in the cradle.

The situation became ticklish in Greece, which was plagued by a violent communist movement. Greece had been left out of Russia's sphere of influence, as part of an arrangement which Stalin honored. Churchill

---

[40] Ibid., 796, 798, 815.

therefore felt free to use force; Poland and other Eastern European countries had to be written off because of the presence of Russian troops, but making war on the Greek communists did not run the risk of Russian intervention. Here was a case of peacemaking requiring the bloodshed of a "just war." And Churchill even flew in person to Athens to complement the use of force with an attempt to make a peace or at least a truce.[41]

Realism in diplomacy requires not only the acceptance of traditional concepts like spheres of influence but also a capacity to live with paradox. Churchill's attitude to peace and war can easily be misunderstood, because his approach was based on the idea that you have to zig in order to zag. That is, we live in a paradoxical world where the straight line is not the shortest distance between two points and where the obvious is specious. For many modern people, swayed by diluted pacifism, if you want peace, you must act peaceably. On occasion, such a procedure may work, but for Churchill, the case is sometimes, or often, that if you want peace you must arm for war. You must, in short, negotiate from strength. That was his position in March 1914. A powerful British navy was, for him, "the one great balancing force which we can contribute to our own safety and the peace of the world." The theme recurred right after the war, when confronting Russian Bolshevism instead of German imperialism. The Bolsheviks would not negotiate until they realized that "We had the power and the will to enforce our views."[42]

So, too, in dealing with Arab violence in Palestine in 1921, Churchill stressed the importance of using force on behalf of law and order. And when in 1926 some Chinese warlords attacked British subjects, Churchill approved strong measures. "There is no evil worse than submitting to wrong and violence for fear of war. Once you take the position of not being able in any circumstances to defend your rights against the aggression of some particular set of people, there is no end to the demands that will be made or to the humiliations that must be accepted." In other words, no appeasement from weakness. In 1932 a British foreign secretary urged, with widespread approval, disarmament as the way to keep the peace in Europe. Churchill's response was that as long as France and Germany were equally armed, war would follow. Better "a one-sided peace than a war between equally well-matched powers."[43]

Such a stance could easily be misinterpreted—especially, at various

[41] Ibid., 813–14.   [42] Ibid., 256, 405.
[43] Ibid., 437, 480, 506, 511.

times, by the Germans, Russians, Arabs, and Chinese affected—as war-mongering and sanctimoniousness. That charge is of course an over-simplification of a complex situation; it ignores the fact that a show of force went hand in hand with another Churchillian imperative—that concessions were to be made "on their merits and not under duress." And Churchill, we saw, often looked for the merits of the other side. But the other side was not to claim merit by resort to compulsion. In the miners' strike of 1926, when the miners showed signs of wanting to talk, Churchill demanded that there be "a clear interval" between the strike and the negotiations, "nothing simultaneous." The government's position was to be, "Tonight [you] surrender. Tomorrow [we show] magnanimity." So, too, in the case of the Germans, his policy was: "The removal of the just grievances of the vanquished ought to precede the disarmament of the victors."[44]

The difficulty in all these examples is, of course, the question of who gets to determine which grievances are "just." Churchill's policy of coming to the negotiating table with a superior force tends to foreclose any protracted discussion of that issue. Other nations may therefore be tempted to arm themselves in order to achieve parity at the table, and an arms race is under way.

Despite this solecism, Churchill's unfashionable approach sometimes risked belaboring the obvious for an audience that would neither see nor hear any evil, as when the gap between the realistic and the merely well-intentioned ways of looking at the world became painful to him in the 1930s. In 1933, as Hitler was surging to power, the flower of English youth, as represented by the students of the Oxford Union, voted by almost two to one not "in any circumstances to fight for King and Country." This sentiment meant embracing nonviolence, if not downright pacifism. In the abstract, the Oxford youths, having read about the horror and futility of the First World War, were correct; the war against Imperial Germany may well have been morally ambiguous and practically futile. But given what was happening in Germany in 1933, they picked the very worst time to arrive at their wisdom. Wilhelmine Germany, whether culpable or not, could hardly match Nazi Germany for evil. This was no occasion for practicing moral equivalence between Britain and Germany. Churchill was chagrined to see how such wrongheadedness contrasted markedly with the fervor and militancy of German youth, who

[44] Ibid., 437, 477, 511.

were being trained in the martial arts and were all too eager to die for their fatherland.[45]

The English students were merely reflecting their society. For some years the push for unilateral disarmament remained strong in labor and leftist circles, at the very time that Germany was rearming. Nor was the British government any better; its policy of urging France to disarm and of ignoring German grievances while Germany was still weak was, to Churchill, a sure way to war. Even with the Nazis in power and practicing terror, disarmament remained the "shrill cry of the hour," and Churchill's warning about imminent peril only brought him opprobrium. When Hitler later militarized the Rhineland, the European powers understandably felt too unprepared militarily and psychologically to challenge the Germans, and Churchill found it ironical that "I have been mocked and censured as a scaremonger and even as a warmonger, by those whose complacency and inertia have brought us all nearer to war." That he favored war, he had to repeat, early and late, was a "foul charge." Peace was still possible, but only if Germany faced a "military preponderance. . . . There is safety in numbers." An alliance of all nations sharing borders with Germany would constitute "an overwhelming deterrent against aggression."[46]

His quarrel with the political establishment evolved inevitably into a question of semantics. In 1939, he proclaimed his goals to be a strongly armed Britain and "peace with honor." The slogan was the same as Chamberlain's, but the way to achieve it was different. Peace and honor are not interchangeable: "What men call honor does not correspond always to Christian ethics." That is, contrary to popular sentimentality, force is a factor in the equation; sometimes honor requires war. Moreover, just as "peace with honor" can be interpreted rightly or wrongly, so can "appeasement": "The word 'appeasement' is not popular, but appeasement has its place in all policy. Make sure you put it in the right place. Appease the weak, defy the strong."[47] In other words, appeasement from weakness is evil, just as peace at the price of honor is neither peace nor honor.

As the Second World War drew to a close, Churchill again looked to negotiations from a position of strength. He first contemplated in September 1943 the new problem created by a resurgent Russia. The war having knocked out the two military titans, Germany and Japan, Russia would become the greatest land power. Only the might of the English-speaking

---

[45] Ibid., 513; Rhodes James, *Churchill: A Study in Failure*, 249–53.
[46] Gilbert, *Churchill: A Life*, 514, 533, 552, 559, 506, 556.
[47] Ibid., 610, 890; Churchill, *Second World War*, vol. 1, 321.

people would keep the peace. He therefore urged the armies of the Western Allies to capture Berlin and to penetrate as far east as possible to prevent Russian encroachments. These lands were to be held until a peace settlement was reached. A settlement was possible, but a show of strength was needed beforehand. He saw no contradiction between building up defenses and concurrently settling with Russia. "Peace is our aim, and strength is the only way of getting it. We need not be deterred by the taunt that we are trying to have it both ways at once. Indeed it is only by having it both ways at once that we shall have a chance of getting anything of it at all."[48]

This ambidextrous or paradoxical approach was naturally greeted in many quarters as self-contradictory and "alarmist," just as the speeches of the years between 1932 and 1938 had been. The reason is obvious: in 1946, the American and British people were tired of war, and they had been for four years conditioned to look on Russia as a brave ally. Anyone who abruptly presented that nation as a new enemy was bound to be dismissed as a warmonger, especially by that sizeable number still smitten with the idea that "Uncle Joe" Stalin's Russia was the site of the "great experiment" and of a future that worked. That the statesman's elasticity in grappling with changing circumstances is not shared by the populace makes him the messenger who must be silenced.

And Churchill's critics did have a trenchant observation. Churchill overlooked the possibility that, if one side builds up its military power, even for the noblest of reasons, the adversary is not brought to acknowledging the goodness of that side but merely escalates its own military effort. The historian's objectivity forces one, furthermore, to note that Churchill's reputation for prescience on the cold war rests on the mainstream assumption that the Soviet Union replaced Nazi Germany as the source of evil. There is, of course, a revisionist school that pins the blame rather on the West for initiating the cold war out of insensitivity to Russian vulnerability and fear of the spread of communism. As a skeptic by philosophical conviction, I find neither explanation definitive. Instead of an ideologically driven theory, I prefer—without in any way diminishing the internal horrors of the Stalinist regime—the psychological explanation that both sides, victims of mutual paranoia, blundered into what might be called the symbiosis of self-fulfilling prophecies. That interpretation of events leaves Churchill's reputation in connection with the early, Iron Curtain phase of the cold war rather uncertain.

---

[48] Gilbert, *Churchill: A Life*, 753, 816, 834, 838–9, 866–8, 923.

Yet that ambiguity in no way reduces the value of his contribution to peacemaking in the later, post–Iron Curtain phase of the cold war. Churchill always insisted on keeping the door open. He was willing to make "friendly gestures" to Russia, such as letting it have three votes in the United Nations and letting it send its fleet to the Pacific as well as through the Dardanelles. He refused to join a United States of Europe movement because of its undue hostility toward Russia. He said that Russia should be seen as a potential partner. The way to peace was to "bring matters to a head with the Soviet government and, by formal diplomatic processes, with all their privacy and gravity, to arrive at a lasting settlement."[49]

Indeed, in his closing years in public affairs, his one great theme was to urge negotiations with the Russians for a final settlement, but only when they realized the allied power and consequently showed an interest in talks. Were a peace conference held prematurely, he cautioned, its breakdown could lead to warlike rumblings. In the early 1950s, a series of developments sharpened his desire to embark on a mission to bring the United States and the Soviet Union together. At first, the election of Eisenhower made him more fearful of war. Then the death of Stalin, a half year later, gave Churchill hope for a fresh start. As the Americans did not agree, he was perfectly willing to go to Russia without them. That the Americans were against even that solitary trip was, along with the lack of a Soviet response, very disappointing to him. Settling with Russia meant recognizing the existence of the evil of communism, accepting the spheres of influence, and all the rest. To true-blue conservatives this was heresy, and the American possession by a Manichaean vision prevented their responding to what they considered to be his softheaded approach to peace.

Still he persisted; he was sure he could convince the Americans of the legitimacy of détente since he had the credentials of having been the one who had originally helped put together "the world front against communist aggression." He told leading American congressmen that communism is indeed a tyrant, but "meeting jaw to jaw is better than war." In July 1954, he again suggested talks between himself and the Soviet leaders as a prelude to a general summit meeting and settlement.[50] So eager was he to round out his career by ending the cold war that he remained in power despite failing health and growing restiveness in his party and

---

[49] Ibid., 819, 822, 872–3, 879. [50] Ibid., 881, 889, 903, 908–11, 921, 926–8.

government. It was all in vain, and what would have been the greatest feat of peacemaking of his—or anyone's—career eluded him. Just as in 1936 and 1938 he had had to defer to the British prime minister, so now he had to defer to the leader of the free world, the American president.

THE RHINELAND AND MUNICH CRISES

The result is that, while the first half of his career as peacemaker is marked by his accomplishments in connection with South Africa and Ireland as a political insider, the second half is marked by his failures in connection with Hitler's Germany and Stalin's Russia because he was an outsider. The Second World War took place, and the cold war dragged on for decades. But should he not get credit for playing a role he had always celebrated, that of being a "great fighter for a lost cause"?

That the lost cause was the cause of peace was ignored by many people because he proposed to obtain it through a policy of strength. This policy represents the one way in which Churchill deviates most from popular misconceptions about him. The reliance on strength implies a commitment to use it when called for. But should force ever be used? The answer hinges on that grand philosophical divide referred to at the beginning of this chapter, that between the hawks who say that force is necessary and the quasi-pacifists who believe that alternatives exist.

The tendency of many liberals, of certain pious Christians, of people with good intentions and generous spirits, is to deprecate violence. They fear that a military buildup must lead to hostilities. Civilized people, they assert, can do better. Dialogue, reasoning, negotiations, compromises—these can replace childish displays of military might. To which one must say, more power to such souls! However much they may be subject to derision, without them mankind would still be in the caves. What motivates them, as Churchill himself acknowledged, is not mere squeamishness but the precepts of the Gospel or the imperatives of being civilized.

Nor is this quasi-pacifism confined to liberals. Moderates and even conservatives are sudden converts to nonviolence when the violence comes from radical segments of society. Let some group of terrorists set off a bomb in the name of a leftist cause, and behold conservatives sermonizing that "violence is never right." They mean, of course, violence against the current status quo, not antique violence like the Glorious Revolution of 1688 or the American Revolution that established a new status quo and that leaves the conservatives comfortably in power.

Churchill did not indulge in absolute statements about violence, pro or con. Without theorizing much about the matter, he came down in a series of crises on the side of action, that is, threatened or manifest violence. His central idea is either borrowed from or parallels a central insight of Machiavelli's, another man who did not blench at the thought of violence. Machiavelli's basic contention is that, as a result of human depravity, turning the other cheek may guarantee one a place near the throne of God but is certain to result in defeat in this world. Whether out of cowardice or decency or principle or indecisiveness, men shrink from violence. By avoiding it, they hope to eradicate it. And it *is* true that some difficulties, whether in international, domestic, or even family politics, when postponed, disappear. But many do not.

The problem, as Machiavelli sees it, is that the attempt to avoid violence in the short run, when it is limited, results not in removing violence but paradoxically in ensuring it on a far larger scale later. Machiavelli cites the contrasting examples of the tolerant Florentine government and the ruthless Cesare Borgia. The latter brought unity, order, and peace to the Romagna, while "The Florentine people, . . . to avoid the name of cruelty, allowed Pistoia to be destroyed." He who exercises cruelty for the sake of unity "will be more merciful than those who, from excess of tenderness, allow disorders to arise, from whence spring bloodshed and rapine. . . . It is much safer to be feared than loved." Even more to the point was Machiavelli's dictum on the Romans, who "never allowed [disorders] to increase in order to avoid a war; for they knew that war is not to be avoided, and can be deferred only to the advantage of the other side. . . . One ought never to allow a disorder to take place in order to avoid a war, for war is not thereby avoided, but only deferred to your disadvantage."[51]

These words mirror Churchill's own on the Rhineland crisis of 1936. When Hitler broke the Treaty of Versailles and marched the German army into the Rhineland, Britain and France should have acted. With the Allies still militarily stronger and the German army not yet built up, a show of willpower would have forced the Germans back. Unfortunately, lack of preparedness and fear of violence, understandable after the carnage of the recent Great War, paralyzed the Allies. As a result, Hitler concluded that the Allies were led by "vermin" and that bluster, bluff, and force would

---

[51] Niccolò Machiavelli, *The Prince and the Discourses*, trans. Luigi Ricci (New York: Random House, 1940), 11, 14, 60–1.

carry all before him. This conclusion took him a long way before it finally brought him down.

Churchill was, of course, right. Neither the light German forces occupying the Rhineland nor the light divisions backing them were in any condition to resist a forceful police action by the superior French forces nearby. Such a humiliating development might have meant the end of Hitler. Perceived as a reckless, unbalanced gambler, he might have been overthrown by German generals acting in the name of patriotism and sanity to prevent a disastrous German misstep. No blood would have been shed, but even if a little blood had been shed, the result would have been the same—the probable avoidance of the Second World War. The world paid dearly for this monumental mistake. That is why, looking back after the war, Churchill came up with one of his memorable utterances, dubbing it "The Unnecessary War."

Study of the Rhineland crisis shows that each side overestimated the other side's forces and resolve. That would have led to mutual paralysis had it not been for the man of destiny and consummate diplomatic poker player, Hitler, who stepped into the vacuum and bluffed the French. The other man of destiny, Churchill, would have called Hitler's bluff, but he was in no position to do so. All he could do was virtually to shriek in the press, concerning the "hideous drift" to war, "Stop it! Stop it!! Stop it now!!! NOW is the appointed time." That sentence may well have been the most prescient of his long career, but no one listened to him.[52]

---

[52] Gilbert, *Churchill: A Life*, 861; *WSC* V 713–14, 718; Winston S. Churchill, *Step by Step* (New York: Putnam, 1939), 3–4, 8. While not immediately urging action to repel Hitler's illegal move, Churchill did make clear within a few days the need to assemble forces to support the French and to stop the drift to war. That the German government was ready to retreat at the least sign of French resolve is crystal clear. More speculative is the corollary that Hitler would have been overthrown as a result of such a setback. See Hajo Holborn, *A History of Modern Germany* (New York: Knopf, 1969), 768–9; A. J. P. Taylor, *English History, 1914–1945* (New York: Oxford University Press, 1965), 386; A. J. P. Taylor, *The Origins of the Second World War*, 2d ed. (New York: Fawcett, 1961), 97; William Shirer, *The Collapse of the Third Republic* (New York: Simon and Schuster, 1969), 260–2, 267–8, 280–1; William Shirer, *The Rise and Fall of the Third Reich* (New York: Fawcett, 1960), 400–3; Joachim C. Fest, *Hitler*, trans. R. and C. Winston (New York: Harcourt, Brace, Jovanovich, 1973), 497; Alan Bullock, *Hitler*, rev. ed. (New York: Harper & Row, 1962), 343; Robert J. O'Neill, *The German Army and the Nazi Party, 1933–1939* (New York: Heinemann, 1966), 128–9. The problem was that in France and Britain, the people, the press, the government, and the military lacked both the prescience and the nerve to match those of Hitler and to undertake the small police action necessary to avert a large war later. (See Holborn, *A History of Modern Germany*, 769–70; Shirer, *The Collapse of the Third Republic*, 251, 254–7, 260–5, 268–9, 272–3, 276, 278, 280–3; Taylor, *English History*, 368, 387–8; Taylor, *The Origins of the Second World War*, 97–8, 100–1; Paul-Marie de la Gorce, *The French Army*,

And why did the world make such a mistake? Here we come upon the crucial thesis of both Machiavelli and Churchill, the heart of the misconception about Churchill as a warmonger. Realism means acceptance of violence as a form of policy. People considering this matter are in the grips of a common but fatal error. The choice is not, as liberals, pacifists, and earnest Christians would have it, between violence and nonviolence; it is rather between a little violence and a lot of violence, between early, educative, abbreviated violence and late, debilitating, protracted violence, between the violence that prevents and the viꞏ'ꞏnce that feeds on itself. What people will not concede is that sometimes noꞁ.ꞏiolence is simply not an option.

Churchill took an approach contrary to commonly held views of peacemaking because he subscribed to this Machiavellian premise rather than to the sentimental one that violence can be avoided and that violence only begets more violence. He signed on to the unpopular idea, articulated by Nietzsche no less than Machiavelli, that violence is a necessary ingredient in civilization itself, that without violence there is no progress. As he said in his instructions to the British general in charge of suppressing the Greek communists in 1944: "It would be a great thing for you to succeed in this without bloodshed if possible, but also with bloodshed if necessary." To be sure, Cesare Borgia's way, if constantly followed, leads to Hitlerism and Stalinism, but Churchill (like Machiavelli) means only that democracy must *occasionally* sully itself with the use of force and cannot always be the pure polar opposite of tyranny. Circumstances may "make it right and imperative in the last resort . . . that the use of force should not be excluded."[53]

Articulating this grim truth is no way to win a popularity contest. But that is because of another widespread confusion. The difference is not between the war-hating good people and the war-loving Churchill but

---

trans. Kenneth Douglas [New York: George Braziller, 1963], 261–3.) There was "no realistic chance of . . . threatening a preventive war," concludes Rhodes James, and Churchill was among the very few who "saw the full probable implications for Britain and Europe" (289–90). While the mainstream view, following the lead of Churchill in his speech of November 1945, is that here was one of the great turning points of history (Gilbert, *Churchill: A Life*, 861; Holborn, *A History of Modern Germany*, 768–9; Shirer, *The Collapse of the Third Republic*, 263, 280–1; Shirer, *The Rise and Fall of the Third Reich*, 403, 405), some have dissented (Taylor, *Origins of the Second World War*, 100–1; Taylor, *English History*, 386–7; Rhodes James, *Churchill: A Study in Failure*, 288–9) and others remain agnostic.

[53] Gilbert, *Churchill: A Life*, 807; Churchill, *Second World War*, vol. 1, 320. For a historical exploration of this theme, see my "Violence and Progress," *Centennial Review* (Summer 1970), 241–66.

between two different ways of trying to avert war—the optimistic, pacific, sentimental one and the pessimistic, realistic, Machiavellian one. As Churchill once said in an essay, "In all great controversies much depends on where the tale begins."[54] The aphorism means in this connection that all those people making the pacifist assumption that nonviolence is a viable course of action will naturally see Churchill as a bloodthirsty warmonger. He for his part saw these quasi-pacifists as deluded in regarding preventive action to be "unreasonable, rash, below the level of modern intellectual thought and morality."[55]

The Machiavellian moment came again in September 1938. Churchill several times urged Britain, either alone or, preferably, in conjunction with France and Russia, to present Hitler with an ultimatum over Czechoslovakia. This medicine was too strong for Chamberlain. Churchill concluded that, because of military unpreparedness, "We seem to be very near the bleak choice between War and Shame. My feeling is that we shall choose Shame and then have War thrown in a little later, on even more adverse terms than at present." When he soon found out, during a visit to France, that Germany had had few soldiers on the French border at the time of the Munich crisis, he was all the more certain that firmness would have prevented war. Yet even if fighting had broken out, "We should have been far better off than we may be at some future date." Sure enough, the ultimatum not given over Czechoslovakia had to be given a year later over Poland, when Germany was finally prepared for war. Or, as he put it after the war, in words echoing Machiavelli on Florence and Pistoia, "There is no merit in putting off a war for a year if, when it comes, it is a far worse war or one much harder to win." Moreover, as in 1936, the non-violence practiced by the Allies probably saved Hitler from being deposed by German generals.[56] Once again the choice between little and big violence was misinterpreted as one between no violence and violence.

---

[54] Winston S. Churchill, *Great Contemporaries* (New York: Putnam, 1937), 122.
[55] Churchill, *Second World War*, vol. 1, 347.
[56] Gilbert, *Churchill: A Life*, 595, 608; Churchill, *Second World War*, vol. 1, 320; Manchester, *The Last Lion*, vol. 2, 352–6; Rhodes James, *Churchill: A Study in Failure*, 372–5. That there was some sort of generals' plot at this time is clear, but its prospects for success have been much debated. For the optimistic view, see Holborn, *A History of Modern Germany*, 787; Shirer, *The Collapse of the Third Republic*, 354, 391–4; Shirer, *The Rise and Fall of the Third Reich*, 516–17, 548, 550, 554–7, 575; O'Neill, *The German Army and the Nazi Party*, 162–3; Fest, *Hitler*, 562–3. Doubts over its prospects have been expressed by Shirer, *The Rise and Fall of the Third Reich*, 555, 558; O'Neill, *The German Army and the Nazi Party*, 165; Bullock, *Hitler*, 470; Williamson Murray, *The Change in the European Balance of Power, 1938–39* (Princeton: Princeton University Press, 1984), 205–6.

Nor is Churchill's argument vitiated by the contention advanced by almost all historians that, given the state of public opinion and military unpreparedness in 1938 and especially in 1936, there was no chance— even if Churchill had been prime minister—of a strong Allied reaction to Hitler's first expansionist steps. In light of the fact that German public opinion and military preparedness were likewise not ready for war, that observation merely shows Churchill's insight to have been rare and precious. It places him in the tragic predicament of other prophets, that of having the intelligence and the will, but not the means of action. It leaves his analysis of the widespread error intact. What most people saw only with hindsight he had foreseen.[57]

Most politicians, of course, do realize, like Churchill, that peace requires strength and that force is sometimes a necessity. But they are unable or unwilling to break the logjam caused by the electorate's sentimental, half-baked pacifism. Churchill, by contrast, knew that what distinguishes the statesman from the mere politician is a willingness to educate the voters and a determination, on critical issues, to lead them instead of being led by them. Churchill was, therefore, a contrarian not only in the views which he held but also in his eagerness to translate these views into action.

Now we can agree that, in regretting the electoral defeat of 1945 with the poignant lament, "I wanted to do the Peace too," Churchill was not being delusional or paradoxical. His record shows him to have earned the right to make that claim. When he said in his 1930 autobiography that good warmakers are poor at peacemaking and good peacemakers are poor at warmaking, he concluded, "It would perhaps be pressing the argument too far to suggest that I could do both."[58] This was written less with irony than with seriousness, less with humility than with accuracy, less with hindsight at the relatively small though well-appreciated triumphs in South Africa and Ireland than with mystical foresight into his much-maligned and misunderstood Herculean efforts to cope with the challenges presented by the two bloodiest tyrants in history.

[57] Had Churchill been heeded in 1936 or 1938 and had war then broken out, Germany would in all likelihood have been defeated and Hitler disgraced, but Churchill would have emerged with a revitalized reputation as a warmonger. That is because the world would not have known the horrors that it had been spared. Churchill was in a no-win situation. Either his warnings were ignored or, if heeded, his reputation would be besmirched. See my "Misunderstanding History," *Proceedings of the International Churchill Societies, 1992–1993*, ed. Richard M. Langworth (1995), 123–36.

[58] Churchill, *Roving Commission*, 331.

3

The peaceful purposes of empire

KIRK EMMERT

Winston Churchill's reputation for leadership is borne to us on the tides of war. Above all, he is honored for saving Great Britain in its darkest hour from defeat, or from being fatally compromised, and for inspiring the subsequent Allied victory over Hitler. His political life thus reminds us of the sense in which circumstances make the leader. If he had been denied this opportunity for war leadership, if, for instance, his prominent opposition to home rule for India had fatally undermined his effective political career in the early 1930s, what would we think of him today? We would probably not view him as a failure,[1] but also surely not as one of the preeminent leaders of our century. The circumstance of being wartime leader of Britain did not guarantee Churchill's preeminence, but it made possible the Churchill we know. It was the indispensable opportunity, the stage, which allowed him fully to develop his hitherto unrealized capacity for political leadership.

Churchill would be comfortable with this association of his reputation with war leadership. He was aware of the darker side of war. Years before the atom bomb, he warned of the potentially devastating power of modern military technology.[2] Experience and study taught him that war is generally cruel and destructive, particularly for ordinary citizens. But his spirited nature, along with his understanding of war's political and

---

[1] The title of Robert Rhodes James's book *Churchill: A Study in Failure, 1900–1939* (London, 1970) calls our attention to the dependence of Churchill's reputation on his leadership in the Second World War. Through 1939 Churchill was a failure in the sense that he had not obtained the greatest prize, the office of prime minister, and had a decidedly mixed political reputation. At the same time, of course, he had many successes in his political career, to say nothing of his accomplishments as an author.

[2] See "Shall We All Commit Suicide?" and "Fifty Years Hence," in Winston S. Churchill, *Amid These Storms: Thoughts and Adventures* (New York: Charles Scribner's Sons, 1932), 245–52, 269–80.

moral impact, also led him to see its other side—the light that cannot exist without the shadows. Churchill found that the danger, finality, and high stakes of war intensified life, raising it to a higher level of existence. From his youthful exuberance at being shot at on the Indian frontier, through his more measured exhilaration in 1914 upon his successful deployment of the British fleet to Scapa Flow, to his admiration for the spectacle of the D-Day armada, Churchill drew energy from the drama and peril of war. He knew that the way of life and very existence of whole nations might be at stake in the clash of great armies on the battlefield. "Battles are the principal milestones in secular history," he observed. "Great battles, won or lost, change the entire course of events, create new standards of value, new moods, new atmosphere, in armies and nations, to which all must conform."[3]

In addition to its political and historical importance, Churchill thought that war can call forth admirable human qualities in a nation's citizens and leaders. As a war prime minister, he admired and was deeply moved by the courage and fortitude displayed by ordinary citizens and soldiers as they conducted their private lives and met their public duties. And at the highest level of affairs he knew from experience that only those with great strength of soul and extraordinary capacities could meet the stern demands of war. Herbert Asquith was "probably one of the greatest peacetime Prime Ministers we have ever had," Churchill observed. "His intellect, his sagacity, his broad outlook and civic courage maintained him at the highest eminence in public life. . . . In or out of power, disinterested patriotism and inflexible integrity were his only guides." Ultimately, however, Churchill concluded that Asquith did not rise to the level of events in the Great War: "In war he had not those qualities of resource and energy, of prevision and assiduous management, which ought to reside in the executive." Thus the nation was well served, in Churchill's view, when Asquith gave way in 1916 to Lloyd George, who, although he lacked some of Asquith's virtues, could ride and tame the whirlwind of war.[4]

In his capacity for wartime leadership Churchill was closer to Lloyd George than he was to Asquith, but this is not the deeper reason why he ultimately ranked wartime above peacetime leadership. For Churchill the

---

[3] Winston S. Churchill, *Marlborough: His Life and Times*, 2 vols. (London: George G. Harrap, 1947), vol. 1, 843; vol. 2, 381.

[4] Winston S. Churchill, *Great Contemporaries* (New York: G. P. Putnam's Sons, 1937), 126.

supreme political accomplishment is to have "held with honor the fore-most stations in the greatest storms,"[5] for to acquit oneself well in such positions requires the most admirable political and moral virtues on the grandest scale. The attainment of such virtue, along with the resulting fame, is not sufficient reason for statesmen to seek out war. But when war must come, it provides scope for the rare political capacities of a leader like Churchill, capacities which are, or seem to be, unneeded and, as Churchill's life testifies, often unwelcome in less perilous times.

This perhaps unsettling association of the highest kind of leadership and war—this admiration for the warrior-statesman—is not, however, Churchill's last word. The distinction between war and peace illuminates the nature of political leadership, but Churchill suggests that it is also prob-lematic. The inherent ambiguity and indistinctness of politics is in tension with any effort to understand it by making "crisp and sharp" distinc-tions.[6] The distinction between war and peace partakes of this ambiguity. In foreign relations, formal peace often obscures the underlying reality of a continuing war. Thus at the beginning of *The Gathering Storm*, Churchill observes that the two world wars should be understood, rather, as one war, "another Thirty Years' War."[7] This does not mean that politics is simply coterminous with war: Peace is not a chimera. But politics is often more warlike than it first appears, and measures which might seem war-like—rearmament, forming alliances, sending an ultimatum, using limited force—may actually promote peace. Since war and peace are often, perhaps usually, intertwined, and wartime leadership is seen as most demanding (and thus most prized), a very high level of statesmanship might be attain-able even when a nation is formally at peace, as was Britain during the 1930s. Moreover, there may be, as we shall see, a form of more peaceful rule—imperial rule—which approaches in its scope the demands of war-time rule but exists in peacetime, or near peacetime, and actually pro-motes peace in some ways.

Beyond its ambiguity, focusing on the distinction of war and peace (e.g., wartime versus peacetime leadership) stresses the conditions of politics to the neglect of its purposes. Healthy political communities and their leaders do not consider war as an end in itself. Even those who

---

[5] Ibid., 263.

[6] Churchill, *Amid These Storms*, 53. In preferring the British to the American Constitution, Churchill observed that "in our affairs as in those of Nature there are always frayed edges, borderlands, compromises, anomalies."

[7] Winston S. Churchill, *The Second World War*, 6 vols. (Boston: Houghton Mifflin, 1948–54), vol. 1, iii.

purport to be dedicated to war actually prize war because of the opportunities it offers to display the military virtues and the glory that they think follows from victory. More commonly, the purpose of war is thought to be victory issuing in peace: By preparing the way for peace, the warrior-statesman is the true peacemaker. But while peace may be desirable in itself, it is usually seen not as the sole or highest purpose of politics but as the precondition for pursuing those purposes. Radical pacificists aside, peace is usually not thought to be desirable at any cost. Perhaps Churchill could have bought a precarious, tutelary peace with Hitler in 1940, but that kind of ultimate subordination to the will and barbaric purposes of a ruthless leader was unacceptable to Churchill and, under his leadership, to a decent, freedom-loving British people.

Although Churchill's life and writings seem to be mostly about questions of war and peace, their broader, more significant theme is the purposes served by war and peace. Churchill the peacemaker sought peace because of the purposes that could be served by peaceful rule. For Churchill, these purposes were embodied in the remnants of the aristocratic imperial regime he experienced in his youth and in the emerging, and later fully grown, liberal democratic order of his later years. Churchill's inclination to view the external relations of Britain in light of these broader aristocratic and democratic purposes can be seen perhaps most clearly in his understanding of the British Empire and of its relation to modern democracy. Focusing on these purposes also brings to light the deeper reasons why Churchill sought to moderate Britain's understanding and conduct of its imperial and foreign relations. In defending the Empire Churchill promoted a view of its purposes that was intended to moderate its expansion, benefit its imperial subjects, and elevate British public life and character.

EMPIRE: SECURITY AND THE POWER TO PREVAIL

From his earliest writings, and the first stirrings of his political career, Churchill was a moderate, "middle thinker"[8] regarding the Empire. He rejected the extreme views of those who supported "Little Englandism"[9] (an inward-looking nation with minimal foreign responsibilities) and the views of "our unbridled Imperialists, who have no thought but to pile up armaments, taxation, and territory."[10] Prior to the rise of mass democracy

---

[8] *WSC* II C 105.   [9] Churchill, *Great Contemporaries*, 5.
[10] Quoted in *WSC* II 32.

in the 1920s, Churchill thought that the major threats to moderate empire originated with two different kinds of expansionists: the power politicians and the moralizers. Under their tutelage, legitimate national concerns with security and morality were radicalized to the point of losing sight of the proper purposes of empire.

The connection between the quest for security and imperial expansion is a major theme of Churchill's early writings on the Empire. He recognized that commercial and security concerns were intertwined in the development of the Empire but concluded that the quest for security was a more fundamental and problematic cause of national expansion than the quest for wealth and markets.[11] In his *History of the English-Speaking Peoples*, Churchill argues that the growth of English naval power was a precondition for the expansion of British commerce and the establishment of the Empire. Repeatedly, pursuit of commercial advantage required control of foreign territory; securing these new possessions necessitated further, often reluctant, expansion.[12] In India, or later in the Second Empire, initial control and expansion of territory usually was undertaken, despite official indifference and occasional opposition, by private British citizens and groups seeking greater wealth and security. The larger these foreign domains became, the more military security seemed to dictate absorption of further territory, including key points on the route back to England.[13] This security impetus to imperial expansion is the major theme of Churchill's first book, *The Story of the Malakand Field Force*, in which he argues that an essentially satisfied, defensive empire was led to fight and expand just to protect its existing possessions.

On the Indian frontier, Churchill learned that extensive empires are seldom wholly at peace throughout their widespread domains. In his account of the Malakand Field Force he initially contends that this, and by implication other frontier wars, were provoked by the warlike dispositions and fierce independence of frontier tribesmen. He goes on to acknowledge, however, that these mountain tribesmen's initial attacks were provoked by the British "Forward Policy," which was aimed at thwarting

[11] Regarding expensive efforts to maintain imperial prestige on the Indian frontier, Churchill observed, "Imperialism and economics clash as often as honesty and self-interest": Winston L. Spencer Churchill, *The Story of the Malakand Field Force*, new imprint (London: Longmans, Green, 1901), 220. Commenting on America's interest in Cuba, he noted that "people do not fight to death for economic principle or to keep up the price of sugar. It is one cause of many." (*WSC* I C 854: letter dated January 5, 1898.)
[12] Winston S. Churchill, *A History of the English-Speaking Peoples*, 4 vols. (New York: Dodd, Mead, 1956–8), vol. 3, 223; vol. 4, 99–100.
[13] Ibid., vol. 2, chs. 7–10; vol. 3, ch. 15; vol. 4, chs. 16, 19.

Russian designs on Afghanistan.[14] British expansion was compelled by the need for security against a rival power; it was, he concludes, more the cause than the effect of the tribal uprising. "I am inclined to think," Churchill observed in a letter to his mother, "that the rulers of India, ten years ago or a hundred years ago, were as much the sport of circumstances as their successors are to-day. . . . The force of circumstances on the Indian frontier is beyond human control."[15] In a subsequent article on frontier policy, Churchill predicted that military necessity would soon impel, and thereby justify, British absorption of Afghanistan:

We can neither retire nor for ever stand still. . . . It is too late to turn back. The weary march of civilization and empire lies onward. We must follow it till the Afghan border is reached and thence beyond, until ultimately India is divided from Russia only by a line of painted sign-posts, and by the fact that to transgress that line is war.[16]

In India, and subsequently in Egypt,[17] military necessity led the imperial government, contrary to its own inclinations, into deeper involvement in local affairs and absorption of new territory. Churchill supported these expansions and criticized those who tried to ignore military necessities, but he preferred a more pacific, inward-looking imperial policy. Prior to the "Forward Policy," the Indian Empire had "turned its tireless energy to internal progress and development," convinced that British rule had reached its "natural frontier" at the foot of the Himalayas. Churchill wrote of the "wisdom of Anglo-Indian statesmen" who worked to maintain this "purely defensive," internally oriented imperial policy "which contained so many elements of finality and so many guarantees of peace."[18] But he also knew that, in time, external forces will overwhelm any imperial quest for peace and permanence: empires do not have "natural" boundaries. Britain, like Rome in its golden age, "would have been content to rule alone in moderation,"[19] but other nations demurred. "We

---

[14] Churchill, *The Malakand Field Force*, 305.

[15] Ibid., 310; *WSC* I C 807.

[16] Winston S. Churchill, "The Ethics of Frontier Policy," *United Service Magazine* XVII (August 1898), 508. In one of his dispatches to the *Daily Telegraph*, Lieutenant Churchill observed that "the frontier policy makes itself, and is dictated by circumstances rather than by men" (A Young Officer, "The War in the Indian Highlands," *Daily Telegraph*, November 6, 1897, 7).

[17] Winston Spencer Churchill, *Lord Randolph Churchill*, 2 vols. (London: The Macmillan Co., 1906), vol. 1, 225–6.

[18] Churchill, *The Malakand Field Force*, 305, 310.

[19] Churchill, *The English-Speaking Peoples*, vol. 4, 386 (concerning the Roman Empire, see vol. 1, 35–6, 44–7).

have won for ourselves, when other powerful nations were paralyzed by barbarism or internal war," Churchill told the House of Commons in March 1914,

an exceptional share of the wealth and traffic of the world. We have got all we want in territory, but our claim to be left in undisputed enjoyment of vast and splendid possessions, largely acquired by war and largely maintained by force, is one which seems less reasonable to others than to us.[20]

What was for the British a source of pride and satisfaction was for others a possession to envy and an accomplishment to emulate. Churchill surmised that the Germans, in particular, might ask:

Are we to be limited to Europe? Is the old grey sea-wolf England to enjoy the dominance of the world and of the oceans? . . . Are we to be denied "our place in the sun?" . . . We are late, but we are going to have our share. Lay a place at the table for the German Empire . . . or if not we will thrust you from your seats and carve the joint ourselves![21]

Empires cannot rest and enjoy their plenitude. Envy of the powerful, fear of their strength, a desire to have one's rightful share of the spoils lead other major powers to challenge the supremacy of a dominant empire. These threats to imperial security, along with the inevitable hostility of border peoples and restless subjects, compel every empire, Churchill suggests, to adopt its version of a "Forward Policy." In practice, a satisfied, defensive, moderate empire is compelled to unending, and in this sense unlimited, expansion. Unwillingly, its behavior approaches that of a deliberately expansive, aggressive empire.

Granted, external necessity renders precarious any inward-looking, narrowly defensive empire. But do most empires, even the British Empire, arise largely out of necessity rather than out of deliberate, expansive design? In *The River War*, Churchill's second book about the Empire, he amends his earlier teaching that the Empire grew almost entirely as a response to military necessity fueled by commercial expansion. After describing Britain as a "vigorous nation," Churchill observes that "All vigorous nations of the earth have sought and are seeking to conquer." The primordial desires which drove the frontier tribesmen to attack the Empire are present in all nations. Civilization restrains and channels these desires into more pacific activities, but it cannot eliminate or fully control them. At crucial junctures they can influence decisively the external politics of

[20] Quoted in *WSC* II 683.   [21] Churchill, *Great Contemporaries*, 22–3.

civilized nations, which may then disguise their striving for predominance by donning the mask of military necessity. Modern European civilization is "more powerful . . . , but not less aggressive" than were those of Rome or Islam; the "impulse of conquest hurried the French and the British to Canada and the Indies." Churchill did not exempt the British Empire from his observation that "the spirit of empire" is the desire for power, "the desire to prevail, [a] great fact which practical men must reckon with."[22]

How, then, in his quest for moderate empire did Churchill reckon with military necessity and with the desire to prevail? To begin, he distinguished between arguments of security and arguments of power. He thought that imperial expansion could be politically sound and morally legitimate if grounded in military necessity but not if it rested on a claim of superior power or ability to prevail. The difficulty with the security impetus to empire, however, is to distinguish true from spurious claims of necessity and then to find some way to restrain spurious claims. Churchill's solution was to call for stricter assessments of what constituted a threat to security and, in barren areas such as the Indian frontier, to stress the economic cost of expansion. Thus he opposed an expansion that would not pay for itself, a position he described as "pay as you go."[23]

While hoping for some restraint from these approaches, Churchill also understood that they were insufficient. He was aware that economic restraints are often ineffective or absent; expansion often pays its own way and, even if it does not, prosperous areas of a large empire can finance expansion in more barren areas. Moreover, the effort to limit empire by taking a stricter view of military dangers runs counter to an imperial need to take a more expansive view of dangers to imperial security than would be reasonable for a smaller, non-imperial nation. Unlike lesser nations, empires must respond decisively to seemingly minor challenges to their rule because their authority rests on their reputation for being militarily invincible. Any sign of weakness could undermine imperial prestige, thereby encouraging further challenges to imperial authority.[24] Given these difficulties, a stricter view of dangers might retard imperial expansion,

---

[22] Winston Spencer Churchill, *The River War: An Historical Account of the Reconquest of the Soudan*, 2 vols. (London: Longmans, Green, 1899), vol. 1, 19, 17, 19–20.

[23] Churchill, *The Malakand Field Force*, 270, 309, and "Ethics of Frontier Policy," 506–8.

[24] "The great drama of frontier war is played before a vast, silent but attentive audience, who fill a theatre that reaches from Peshawar to Colombo, and from Kurachee to Rangoon" (Churchill, *The Malakand Field Force*, 223; see also 222, 298).

but Churchill saw no responsible way to sever the link between imperial security and imperial expansion.

But why not avoid expansion and seek security by being small and insignificant, an inward-looking island nation protected by a modest fleet? At the end of the nineteenth century this was clearly not an option for Britain. But it was not, in any case, a desirable course in Churchill's view, for such nations survive only by exercising a diplomacy of shifts and maneuvers from "which pride and virtue alike recoil."[25] More significantly, and to anticipate my subsequent argument, to renounce empire would be to deny a vigorous people the opportunity to attain a high level of human excellence by undertaking the demanding political tasks occasioned by imperial rule.

The desire for power or to prevail poses both a practical and a theoretical challenge to Churchill's advocacy of moderate empire. Clearly, a power-seeking empire makes other empires and nations less secure, thereby raising incentives for their expansion through alliances or by forging their own empires. But Churchill's deeper problem with the power defense of empire is that it promotes unlimited expansion and says nothing about the quality or other purposes of this expansive rule. If the desire and power to prevail is sufficient justification for rule, if any higher claim to rule than superior strength is denied, tyranny can no longer be distinguished from just rule. From his earliest writings and travels abroad, such a posture was unacceptable to Churchill. Thus, following his first trip to America, he condemned Spanish rule of Cuba as "intolerable." Later, in *The River War*, he denounced Egyptian rule of the Sudan between 1819 and 1883 as "a hateful sham," the "iniquitous . . . oppression" of a "tyrannical government" whose "aim was to exploit, not to improve the local population."[26] And in 1897, before he began his political career, Churchill criticized Lord Salisbury and the "cruel" and "shameless" policy of his "Machiavellian government," which would not support Greeks and Cretans who were being "oppressed" by the Turkish Empire.[27] In all these instances Churchill argued explicitly or implicitly that political power should be guided by a higher standard of right—what as a war correspondent he called the "eternal standard of right and wrong independent of and superior to climate, custom and caprice."[28]

[25] Churchill, *Marlborough*, vol. 1, 72.
[26] *WSC* I C 616; see also Churchill, *The River War*, vol. 1, 20–3.
[27] *WSC* I C 734, 740, 750–1.
[28] Winston S. Churchill, "The Soudan Campaign," *The Morning Post*, September 28, 1898, 5.

The power to prevail is not an adequate claim to rule, at home or abroad. While meeting its legitimate security needs, an empire should be guided by a higher principle of right. But as with security, this appropriate moral concern can be taken so far that it undermines moderate empire. Churchill considered this second major threat to limited empire in *The River War*, where he argued that the proper kind of higher standard largely eluded the British in their reconquest of the Sudan. The problematic aspects of the River War stemmed not from unwarranted expansion generated by power-seeking Machiavellianism, but from moral excesses associated with religious and philanthropic sentiments. Religious sentiments aroused by the death of the martyred Christian hero General Charles Gordon fostered in many Britons a near-fanatical desire for revenge. In addition to prompting reprehensible actions such as the desecration of the Mahdi's tomb, this "avenging of Gordon," was not, Churchill observed, "a dignified emotion for a great people to display."[29]

Equally unacceptable was the moral indignation that arose from humanitarian sentiments activated by the "misery of the Dervish dominion." Keenly aware of the great distance between themselves and the lowly natives, sanguine concerning the possibilities for their improvement, humanitarians became impatient with the intractability of the Dervishes' behavior and condition and their seeming indifference to the selfless ministrations of would-be benefactors. The philanthropists' mounting impatience turned into indignation directed at the very people they sought to benefit. Those who were at first pitied in their misery came to be seen as "vile" savages who were somehow culpable for their own and others' degradation. Some of the cruelties committed by the Empire in the River War could be traced, Churchill argued, to attitudes fostered by humanitarians who could not "contemplate military operations for clear political objects unless they can cajole themselves into the belief that their enemy are utterly and hopelessly vile."[30]

Even before he entered public life Churchill distrusted "all booms of sentiment"—religious, humanitarian, patriotic—because they "carry men too far and lead to reactions."[31] To avoid being captured by these booms

---

[29] Churchill, *The River War*, vol. 2, 388, 393. "The idea of revenge, ever attractive to the human heart, appeared to receive the consecration of religion. . . . The spirit of the Crusades stirred beneath the surface of scientific civilization; and as the years passed by, there continued in England a strong undercurrent of public opinion which ran in the direction of 'a holy war' " (ibid., vol. 1, 169).

[30] Ibid., vol. 2, 394.

[31] *WSC* I C 938.

of sentiment, and by the moralistic or the narrowly aggrandizing policies associated with them, Churchill suggested that the Empire should be guided by the standard of honor, of not doing anything unworthy of a great people. He returned to this formulation throughout his life, but in *The River War* he also indicated the need for a more specific political standard that encompassed the full range of the Empire's proper purposes. This notion of a broadly conceived Empire was grounded in, but not exhausted by, the need to sustain security and economic prosperity. It culminated in the Empire's role as a "great civilizing power."[32] Churchill saw in civilizing empire the cure to the diseases of unlimited and tyrannical empire.

CIVILIZING EMPIRE

Churchill's view of civilizing empire is based on the view that human beings have an obligation to improve themselves that takes precedence over any rights they might claim to self-government or liberty. He confessed ignorance of the ultimate grounds of this obligation, but he was convinced that to deny it was to renounce man's purpose for living, to deny man's humanity. If, he wrote, the reader of *The River War* should inquire

> to what end the negroes should labour that they may improve; why they should not remain contented, if degraded; and wherefore they should be made to toil to better things up so painful a road, I confess I cannot answer him. If, however, he proves that there is no such obligation he will have made out a very good case for universal suicide.[33]

Nor is it sufficient to do "well" or "good enough to justify the means" expended. "Perfection must remain the human ideal,"[34] for only if human beings strive to attain their full human potential can they achieve true dignity and self-respect. We owe it to ourselves and to civilization—to our participation in the accumulated fruits of man's efforts to attain excellence—to make this effort.

Churchill's various studies of his "great contemporaries" illustrate that nature provides human beings with varying, unequal capacities for excellence, which they must develop through their own efforts: no person or institution can simply bestow excellence on someone. But neither

---

[32] United Kingdom, *Parliamentary Debates*, 4th ser., vol. 171 (March 13–27, 1907), col. 534.
[33] Churchill, *The River War*, vol. 2, 398–9.   [34] Ibid., vol. 2, 189.

can human beings improve without the external assistance of families, laws, and other economic and political institutions, including occasions to employ their developing capacities. At its best, in Churchill's view, empire is an institution or form of rule which provides this assistance and thereby narrows the gap between a person's or a nation's potential and its present condition. Empire is a human contrivance whose highest purpose is to compensate for the stinginess of God or nature in providing for our attainment of our full humanity. More specifically, empire is the political relationship that exists when a civilized nation rules an uncivilized nation without its consent for the sake of the mutual improvement of both rulers and ruled. The civilized are elevated by ruling, the uncivilized by being ruled.

Since their improvement serves their own interests and requires their own efforts, why should the uncivilized not be left to develop themselves? Churchill did not think that either deliberate intention or natural inclination was sufficiently strong in most human beings to lead them toward collective improvement. On the frontier and in the Sudan he found the natives to be "ignorant of their barbarism," and thus of their need to improve, and "tenacious of liberty" to continue living as they wished.[35] He acknowledged that in time, and under favorable circumstances, some peoples could develop through a natural course of competitive striving for resources and survival.[36] But in light of man's overriding obligation to improve, the precariousness and long duration of this natural course of development led him to conclude that it had to give way, whether or not the ruled agreed, to the more rapid and assured civilizing agency of imperial rule.

Imperial rule proper—rule of the civilized over the uncivilized—is despotic. Its justice depends not on the voluntary consent of its subjects but on whether it is true to its purpose, the improvement or civilizing of rulers and ruled. To accomplish this, the imperial rulers must be substantially superior in strength and merit to the ruled.[37] This superiority and the distinctness of the rulers promote acceptance of imperial rule. A just empire seeks the highest form of consent to its rule of which its subjects are capable. Thus on the Indian frontier, where the natives respected only superior force, they were treated, properly in Churchill's view, in accordance with their limited outlook. But in Uganda, where the more

---

[35] Ibid., vol. 1, 18–19, 190; see also Churchill, *The Malakand Field Force*, 6–7.
[36] Churchill, *The Malakand Field Force*, 113.   [37] WSC I 423.

advanced natives could acknowledge the superior political and administrative skill of their British rulers, consent to imperial rule was sought by providing efficient, fair administration.[38]

Churchill thought that imperial rule promotes civilization by providing circumstances that assist the natural course of human development. In order to become civilized or to "improve," human beings must "labour" up a "painful . . . road," a journey which demands the strenuous employment of their physical, moral, and mental faculties. Since they lack a strong natural propensity to become fully civilized and are averse to painful toil, the uncivilized require a strong, immediate "incentive to work" so that they may improve. Their basic needs for food, shelter, security, and minimal comfort provide this incentive for self-exertion. Willingness to labor is a function of the scale and intensity of human needs and the immediate availability of resources to meet these needs. Nature promotes civilization by giving man basic needs but providing him, in most instances, with meager resources. This scarcity induces a competitive struggle against inhospitable aspects of nature, against internal impediments such as the desire for ease, and against other human beings. The "pressure of competition" is nature's means for gradually promoting civilization.[39]

Empire assists this "action of nature" in three important ways: by expanding human desires, increasing the resources to meet these desires, and providing circumstances more conducive to their satisfaction. The most crucial circumstance empire provides is an "organized government" which establishes peaceful "law and order"[40] and respect for private property and the "fruits of work, enterprise, or thrift."[41] Empire then broadens and augments the desires of the uncivilized by bringing them into contact with "busy, practical, matter-of-fact, modern" civilization[42] and, more directly, by promoting trade and commerce.[43] Finally, it provides greater means for meeting these desires by financing large capital improvements, particularly in irrigation and railways.[44] This whole imperial enterprise rests, Churchill stresses, on the power of modern science,

[38] Winston S. Churchill, *My African Journey*, rpt. from 1908 edition (London: The Holland Press, Neville Spearman, Ltd., 1962), 84.

[39] Churchill, *The River War*, vol. 2, 397–8.   [40] Ibid., vol. 2, 405, 411.

[41] Winston Churchill, "Mr. Wells and Bolshevism: A Reply," *Sunday Express*, December 5, 1920, 1.

[42] Churchill, *The Malakand Field Force*, 122.

[43] Churchill, *The River War*, vol. 2, 27, 403–5; see also Churchill, *The Malakand Field Force*, 37.

[44] Churchill, *The River War*, vol. 2, 405–12; see also Churchill, *My African Journey*, 150, and final chapter.

whose technological fruits make possible these capital improvements and give the empire decisive superiority in war.[45] Thus modern civilizing empire assumes an ambiguous posture toward nature, employing scientific technology to overpower nature[46] but at the same time using and assisting natural forces to foster civilization. Nature is both the antagonist and the friend of civilization.

Churchill thought that even in its direct dependencies the imperial government should be relatively remote and noninterventionist, restricting itself to providing fair, efficient administration, enforcement of law, freedom of commerce, and capital to assist economic development. With India as his model, he favored minimal intervention in native religion or education. Promoting economic growth took precedence,[47] for it was the best means, in his view, for taming religious fanaticism.[48] Economic growth also directly improved physical well-being, a precondition for addressing moral and mental improvement.[49]

The limited scope of imperial government reflects the limited aspirations of civilizing empire for its subjects. Once they are minimally civilized, once they acquire a minimal capacity to govern themselves, imperial rule proper gives way to an imperial rule limited by obligation to seek the uncoerced consent of the ruled. Under this modified, more consensual form of imperial rule Churchill favored expanding somewhat the scope of imperial governance.[50] But at this point he had moved beyond imperial rule proper.

Churchill thought that the uncivilized need the external assistance of empire in order to fulfill their obligation to improve. Far from allowing the powerful simply to do as they wish, he also argued that empire was not just if it did not help to elevate its uncivilized ruled. But he did not hold that the moral foundation of such a just empire lay in the obligation of the civilized to succor the needy or less advanced, nor in their right

---

[45] Churchill, *The River War*, vol. 1, 276–7, 308; vol. 2, 164.

[46] Churchill, *My African Journey*, 89, 111.

[47] Churchill, *The Malakand Field Force*, 314; Churchill, *The River War*, vol. 2, 215, 402–3; Churchill, *The English-Speaking Peoples*, vol. 4, 80–1, 88–90.

[48] Churchill observed that "credulity and fanaticism" are "now passing away from the earth under the combined influence of Rationalism and machine guns" (*The Malakand Field Force*, 230).

[49] Churchill, "The City of Omdurman," *The Morning Post*, October 8, 1898, 5. In arguing against the establishment of Khartoum College, Churchill noted that "there must be some wealth before there is any wisdom . . . ; we must irrigate before we educate" (ibid.). See also *WSC* I C 767.

[50] Churchill, *My African Journey*, chs. 5 and 6, 59–85.

to such assistance. Rather, he situated the higher grounds for empire in an imperial people's obligation and desire to improve themselves, to pursue their own good, broadly and nobly conceived. Empire is not a burden to be endured but a welcome opportunity for individual and national self-improvement.

This defense of empire highlights the aristocratic, non-Christian thrust of Churchill's moral outlook.[51] He saw noble pride or noble self-regard as the moral posture of fully civilized human beings and nations. They want, and because of their character and capacities they deserve, the best things for themselves. And they consider human excellence and the honor accorded to it—rather than, for example, bodily pleasure, wealth, or power—to be the things most worth having. Nobly proud individuals view great responsibilities as their due, just as proud, honor-seeking nations tend to be outward-looking and expansive.[52] Thus in 1945 Churchill

hoped that power would be accorded to me to try to make the settlement in Europe. . . . I had the world position as a whole in my mind, and I deemed myself to possess knowledge, influence, and even authority, which might be of service. I therefore saw it as my duty to try, and at the same time as my right. I could not believe this would be denied me.[53]

The beneficiaries of the noble self-regard of men like Churchill or his illustrious ancestor the Duke of Marlborough have, strictly speaking, no claim on the assistance they receive. These benefactors are not obliged to the less advanced or to aid undifferentiated humanity. Rather, they consider themselves obligated to be true to themselves, to the high standard of civilized excellence they have made their own, and they see themselves as honor-bound to promote civilized behavior. Thus Churchill explained that unconditional surrender meant that "the victors have a free hand," that the Germans "have no rights to any particular form of treatment." This did not mean, however, that the Allies were "entitled to behave in a barbarous manner." The "victorious nations owe it to themselves to observe the obligations of humanity and civilization." If we are bound, Churchill argued, "we are bound by our own consciences to civilization."[54]

The self-seeking activity of the noble harmonized the individual and the common good. Churchill observed that the Duke of Marlborough

---

[51] Churchill observed: "It is baffling to reflect that what men call honour does not correspond always to Christian ethics. Honour is often influenced by that element of pride which plays so large a part in its inspiration" (*The Second World War*, vol. 1, 321).

[52] Churchill, *The English-Speaking Peoples*, vol. 1, 476; vol. 4, 298, 331.

[53] Churchill, *The Second World War*, vol. 6, 590.   [54] Ibid., vol. 4, 689–90.

"was a builder for England, for posterity, and for himself. No one of these purposes could be removed without impairing the others, and part of his genius lay in their almost constant harmony."[55] These often conflicting individual and common goods are harmonious because the individual good is understood as culminating in the pursuit of human excellence and, equally important, excellence is understood as possession of the moral character and political skills to govern well. These are the moral and political virtues—justice, courage or strength of soul, prudence, perseverance, imagination, self-restraint—possessed and displayed by great political leaders and illustrated in Churchill's life of Marlborough, in his histories of the two world wars, and in his essays on his "great contemporaries."

From the time he was an ambitious young officer, Churchill understood that these virtues could be fully developed—and human excellence thereby attained—only by holding high public office. Human excellence is tied to demanding political activity because the virtues of the fully civilized person are brought forth and perfected by doing deeds that require those virtues for their accomplishment. Human beings develop their intelligence by reasoning, their judgment by making decisions, their rhetorical powers by speaking, and their moral virtues by performing just, courageous, generous, or moderate acts. These political and moral virtues can be nurtured, then, only in situations that call for them or give them scope: human beings need "a stage" on which our "gifts" can be developed and displayed.[56] Without the need to give some group or individual their due there can be no substantial realization of a capacity for justice; without substantial peril, no courage; without political responsibilities, no true prudence. Churchill suggests that man is political not just in the sense that he needs to live together with others for security and prosperity, but that he needs to engage in politics to realize his potential for moral and political excellence. In quest of adequate scope for his own abilities Churchill went from sport—polo and hunting—to war to politics, activities that he ranked according to the comprehensiveness of the demands they made upon him and, secondarily, the benefits others derived from his activity. In reflecting on his own life he indicated that ruling a civilizing empire was the culmination of his effort to find scope for, and thereby to develop, his powers.

Churchill considered British eagerness and facility for governing to be

---

[55] Churchill, *Marlborough*, vol. 1, 620.
[56] Churchill, *The English-Speaking Peoples*, vol. 3, 149.

evidence of a highly civilized people. Their Empire provided them with
sufficient opportunities to develop these capacities. Within the broader
British Empire, he observed, "The peculiar gifts for administration and
high civic virtues of our race may find a healthy and honourable scope."[57]
Following his trip through eastern Africa, Under Secretary Churchill
observed that the "African protectorates . . . afford rare scope for the
abilities of earnest and intelligent youth. A man of twenty-five may easily
find himself ruling a large tract of country and a numerous population."[58]
In Egypt and India Churchill was impressed with the "educating force"
of imperial military responsibilities; the young imperial officers were "more
resourceful and more intelligent, better fitted to lead men in war, than
their comrades in the British army."[59] At the peak of affairs in the major
imperial possessions was the equivalent of Lord Cromer who, by 1899,
had

> reigned in Egypt for nearly sixteen years. . . . His status was indefinite; he might
> be nothing; he was in fact everything. His word was law. Working through a
> handful of brilliant Lieutenants . . . Cromer controlled with minute and patient
> care every department of the Egyptian administration and every aspect of its
> policy. . . . He had maintained a tight hold upon the purse strings and a deft
> control of the whole movement of Egyptian politics.[60]

From the district or squadron officer to Lord Cromer, the virtual mon-
arch of millions, the empire provided scope for, and thereby helped to
actualize, the British capacity for military and civic virtue.

In addition to providing these positions abroad, empire augments the
scope of major offices in the home imperial government. This was impor-

---

[57] Churchill, *My African Journey*, 143.
[58] Ibid., 23–5. When he visited a district commissioner's office in the East African Protectorate, Churchill found two officers—a soldier and a civilian—presiding "far from the telegraph, over the peace and order of an area as large as an English county, and regulat[ing]
the conduct and fortunes of some seventy-five thousand natives, who have never previously known or acknowledged any law but violence or terror. . . . The District Commissioner must judge for himself, and be judged by his actions. Very often . . . the officer is
not a District Commissioner at all, but a junior acting in his stead, . . . sometimes for a
year or more. To him there come day by day the natives of the district with all their
troubles, disputes, and intrigues. . . . Disease and accident have to be combated without
professional skill. Courts of justice and forms of legality must be maintained without
lawyers. Taxes have to be collected by personal influence. Peace has to be kept with only
a shadow force. All these great opportunities of high service, and many others, are often
and daily placed within the reach of men in their twenties—on the whole with admirable
results" (ibid.).
[59] Winston Spencer Churchill, "The British Officer," *Pall Mall Magazine*, January 1901, 71.
[60] Winston S. Churchill, *A Roving Commission: My Early Life* (New York: Charles Scribner's
Sons, 1942), 216.

tant to Churchill because he considered virtue most praiseworthy when it exists on the grandest scale, the magnitude of virtue being a function of the magnitude of the events which it seeks to direct. Many peacetime actions of imperial leaders have worldwide ramifications, which affect the lives of tens or even hundreds of millions. Usually, the demands of peacetime imperial rule provide greater scope for political excellence than the wartime leadership of lesser nations. In this sense, empire is the most effective, peaceful means of promoting human excellence. Still, when Churchill suggests that the highest possibilities for statesmanship came to those who "held with honor the foremost stations in the greatest storms,"[61] he implies that the grandest scope for virtue comes to those who lead great imperial nations in perilous wars. He considered 1940 to be the "most splendid, as it was the most deadly, year in our long English and British story," for in that year Britain "proved itself capable of bearing the whole impact and weight of world destiny."[62]

The Empire did more, however, than provide scope to develop the political capacities of the British; it helped to make a capacity for civic virtues, and an eagerness to cultivate them, a kind of second nature of the British nation. By requiring certain military and political tasks, empire calls forth certain virtues and thus a specific type of human being, who then comes to be honored for his contribution to the nation's well-being. In this way an empire molds the character of its governing nation. In the peroration of a speech given in October 1898, Churchill called for

young men who do not mind danger [and] older and perhaps wiser men who do not fear responsibility. The difficulties and emergencies with which the Empire is confronted will give us these men in plentiful abundance—and they in their turn will help to preserve the very Empire that calls them forth.[63]

The Empire benefited those relatively few who went abroad to govern and defend and those who held high office in the imperial government, but what about the common citizens who remained at home? Churchill argued that they too were better off in an imperial Britain because the Empire made them more secure and prosperous, as well as increasing their

---

[61] Churchill, *Great Contemporaries*, 263.
[62] Churchill, *The Second World War*, vol. 2, 628.
[63] Quoted in *WSC* I 422–3. Churchill observed that Sir Bindon Blood "is one of that type of soldiers and administrators, which the responsibilities and dangers of an Empire produce, a type, which has not been, perhaps, possessed by any nation except the British, since the days when the Senate and the Roman people sent their pro-consuls to all parts of the world" (*The Malakand Field Force*, 80).

economic and social opportunities through possible emigration to a colony.[64] Their awareness of being part of a nation that ruled "in majesty and tranquility by merit as well as by strength over the fairest and happiest regions of the world"[65] fortified citizen patriotism and imparted a larger, more political dimension to their lives. The unavoidable stress on foreign and imperial affairs, and the "indispensable discipline and privations" required to sustain the nation's imperial position, also pushed its citizens to discipline their own desires in the name of the broader good. And since the maintenance of this position required considerably more moral and political virtue from the nation's leaders, the Empire helped to sustain a fuller view of human excellence and a "bolder spirit of life" than would have otherwise survived in an increasingly democratic and commercial nation.[66]

Churchill's views on empire show that promoting human excellence was a major goal or purpose of his political thought and action. His defense of civilizing empire is grounded in the principle that the highest purpose of human life is to cultivate moral and political virtue. Empire is the ultimate means to this end, for only imperial nations can provide adequate means to develop this virtue in its finest form. At the same time, this focus on the highest purpose of empire points toward the other dominant purpose of Churchill's political life—promoting democratic liberty. And ultimately it points away from politics altogether to an awareness of the limits of all political endeavors.

DEMOCRATIC EMPIRE

Empire cannot stand alone, for in its focus on ruling others it does not directly address how a people should rule themselves. But do not the principles of empire suggest that these people should rule themselves aristocratically, for then there would be a general harmony in their governing principles at home and abroad? This was not Churchill's view, for he advocated a civilizing and democratic empire. As an advocate of democratic empire, he sought to combine two quite different views of the purposes and means of governance—one democratic, the other decidedly

---

[64] Winston Spencer Churchill, *London to Ladysmith via Pretoria* (London: Longmans, Green, 1900), 40–1.

[65] Quoted in *WSC* I 422–3.

[66] Winston Churchill, "The Country Calls for Virility, Realism, Action," *Daily Mail*, November 16, 1931, 12.

aristocratic. The democratic view is grounded in human equality derived from a commonly shared humanity, the imperial view in human inequality as manifested in the superiority of the fully civilized to everyone else; the democrat insists on the primacy of rights, the imperialist on the primacy of obligations, and thus on what is honorable; the democratic elevation of freedom and individualism contrasts with the imperial stress on virtue and man's more political nature; and while democratic government promotes the private pursuit of happiness and seeks legitimacy in popular consent, the purpose of imperial government is to promote civilization, and "intrinsic merit" is its title to rule. If democratic empire is to be a viable form of governance, these fundamentally different principles, and the practices which spring from them, must be made to coexist within one nation and government.

Why did Churchill seek to promote this tension-ridden, hybrid form of rule rather than advocating a more aristocratic Britain or abandoning his seemingly undemocratic notion of civilizing empire? Necessity certainly played its part, for Churchill knew that the forces promoting the democratization of Britain would prevail in the first decades of this century. More significant, he supported popular government in principle, as being a superior form of rule. Opposed to mass democracy as an extreme and degraded version of popular rule,[67] Churchill favored an institutionally restrained, open, and somewhat deferential and hierarchical form of democracy. He was a democrat in the sense that he was prepared, following Tory democracy, to "Trust the People" to make sound judgments and to serve their country provided they were properly informed and led. He thought that democratic leaders should be subject periodically to popular control and evaluation. But for him the first question was not, Is the regime sufficiently democratic? but, rather, Does it make provision for, and support, vigorous, prudent leadership? His "democratic ideal" was "the association of us all through the leadership of the best."[68]

Finally, Churchill advocated democratic empire because he thought this union could benefit both partners, moderating empire and elevating modern democracy. Aware that democratic liberty and equality might undermine domestic support for empire, he sought during his first ten years in Parliament to increase popular support for the Empire—particularly

[67] See, for instance, Churchill, "Mass Effects in Modern Life," *Amid These Storms*, 255–66.
[68] Churchill, *The English-Speaking Peoples*, vol. 1, 66; see also Winston S. Churchill, "This Age of Government by Dictators," *News of the World*, October 10, 1937, 12.

among the expanded electorate—through his numerous writings about the Empire.[69] During these years Churchill tended to view democracy more as an ally than a foe of the restrained empire he advocated. The democratic stress on improving the material and moral well-being of the majority and of the less fortunate would, he hoped, moderate the tendency of the Empire to draw too much of the nation's attention and resources toward imperial affairs and expansion. Thus the other side of Churchill's advocacy of moderate empire was his support for a more nearly equal, democratic pursuit of justice at home; he also saw this increased attention to domestic affairs as a means to moderate concern with foreign, imperial affairs. This outlook was reflected in the prominent part he took in promoting the Liberal Party's domestic reforms in the years prior to the First World War, as well as in his close association with Lloyd George.

If democracies rightly and necessarily give prominence to domestic affairs, democratic empires prudently do the same; for support for the Empire rests, Churchill suggests, on the physical and social condition, character, and patriotism of the democratic electorate. "To keep our Empire," he observed in one of his earliest political addresses, "we must have a free people, an educated and a well-fed people. That is why we are in favor of social reform."[70] More than a decade later, in defense of proposed Liberal reforms, he observed that

the security and the predominance of our country depends upon the maintenance of the vigour and health of our population. . . . If Great Britain is to remain great and famous in the world we cannot allow the present social and industrial disorders with their profound physical and moral reaction, to continue unabated and unchecked.[71]

Churchill argued, in sum, that the democratization of the British regime could benefit the Empire by encouraging a more restrained imperial policy and by fostering a broader, healthier, more virtuous foundation for the Empire—a regenerated British people.

Conversely, Churchill thought that the emerging democratic regime in Britain could be elevated by supporting and going out to govern the Empire it inherited. Extensive foreign responsibilities help to broaden the

---

[69] See, for instance, Winston S. Churchill, *For Free Trade* (London: Arthur L. Humphreys, 1906), viii–ix; A Young Officer (Churchill), "The War in the Indian Highlands," *Daily Telegraph*, December 6, 1897, 10; Churchill, *The Malakand Field Force*, 14.

[70] *WSC* I 422. (From a speech at Southsea, October 31, 1898.)

[71] United Kingdom, *Parliamentary Debates*, 5th ser., vol. 4 (October 19—December 3, 1909), col. 854.

scope and politicize the content of democratic politics. The demands of empire call for restraint of the largely private, narrowly self-seeking desires and weak-spiritedness which often predominate in a liberal, democratic society during the "comfortable monotonies" of peacetime.[72] Repeatedly, Churchill argued that the British Empire could be sustained only if the nation were brave, persevering, restrained, honorable, and farsighted, concerns that were particularly important to him in his lonely, and seemingly imprudent, battle against the India Bill in 1931.[73] By calling for these qualities, empire strengthens a modern democratic people's regard for, and ability to serve, the common good and fosters those virtues without which no individual or community can become truly self-governing.

Did the union of modern democracy and empire promise, as Churchill argued, an enriching marriage of opposites, or a strife-ridden, debilitating struggle of incompatibles? Initially, Churchill thought that it would be possible to rule according to the "old principles" of empire abroad while following modern, democratic principles at home.[74] He suggested that this might be accomplished by forging a somewhat unequal union. Thus within a fundamentally democratic regime, one geographically segregated, subordinate institution—empire—would be informed by a nondemocratic view of justice and the human good. The clear and ultimate supremacy of the democratic principles would minimize the possibility of unsettling tensions caused by a struggle between different governing principles. And the geographic separation would keep empire from being overwhelmed by the dominant democratic principles of the regime.

Churchill hoped that democratic empire would provide the basis for the kind of intermediate course in political affairs that he consistently favored throughout his life. At its best, democratic empire promised many of the benefits of a rightly constituted mixed regime but accomplished this through a regime, which remained largely, and fundamentally, democratic. By providing freedom and equal civil and political rights for all Britons, improving the well-being of the lower classes, and granting all citizens the franchise, the democratic regime would acknowledge

---

[72] Churchill, *The Malakand Field Force*, 253.
[73] Churchill, *The River War*, vol. 1, 22, 77; vol. 2, 237; Churchill, *Marlborough*, vol. 2, 996; Churchill, *For Free Trade*, 43; Winston S. Churchill, "Mesopotamia and the New Government," *The Empire Review*, July 1923, 694; *WSC* I C 67, III C 1453; Winston S. Churchill, *India: Speeches and an Introduction* (London: Thornton Butterworth, 1931), 97; Winston S. Churchill, "Life—the Greatest Secret of All," *Answers*, March 18, 1933, 4; Winston S. Churchill, "Will the British Empire Last?" *Answers*, October 26, 1929, 5.
[74] Quoted in *WSC* I 318.

mankind's fundamental equality and do justice to the claims of the many. By encouraging the pursuit of political and moral excellence, the Empire would acknowledge man's obligation to improve and do justice to the capacities of the more excellent few. Given these complex purposes, an imperial democracy would come closer than any other viable political order to reconciling the good of each individual with the good of the community. Imperial democracy was the institutional representation and practical resolution of the two major strands or dominant purposes of Churchill's political orientation—aristocratic virtue and democratic equality and freedom.

Aware from the start that the union of empire and democracy was problematic, Churchill became increasingly apprehensive after the end of the First World War that the British experiment in democratic empire might fail. With the coming of what he viewed as an increasingly degraded form of mass democracy in the 1920s and 1930s,[75] he saw a regime increasingly in need of, but increasingly incapable of assuming, the bracing and elevating responsibilities of empire. Under such circumstances, the additional needs of empire might well further undermine, rather than regenerate, British democracy. Moreover, while democratic needs might moderate empire, the Empire still tended to attract resources and attention away from pressing domestic needs, for imperial problems often seemed more urgent, interesting, and important than domestic needs.[76] But if empire, the junior partner in this union, contributed to its downfall, the dominant partner—democracy—was the primary source of its incompatibility.

Churchill found that the democratic principles of the British regime undermined the authority of the Empire abroad, while at home mass democracy provided an inadequate political, institutional, and moral foundation for sustaining empire. He did not think mass democratic elections usually selected the potentially most able political leaders. Even if capable leaders did on occasion win office, the electorate was not inclined to support their initiatives.[77] Nor did mass democracy provide a solid institutional base to support the Empire. Unable to rise to the level of a nonpartisan,

---

[75] The shortcomings of this mass democracy are stressed in Churchill's essays on the Earl of Rosebery and on John Morley in *Great Contemporaries*, 3–18, 77–88, and in his essays "Election Memories," "Mass Effects in Modern Life," and "Fifty Years Hence," in *Amid These Storms*, 201–15, 255–66, 269–80.

[76] *WSC* II C 111, 182.

[77] See United Kingdom, *Parliamentary Debates*, 4th ser., vol. 178 (July 11–24, 1907), col. 411; Churchill, *Lord Randolph Churchill*, vol. 1, 61; Churchill, *Amid These Storms*, 203; and Churchill, *Great Contemporaries*, 6–7.

traditional institution, the Empire necessarily became subject to partisan controversy with the advent of fully democratic, party government. In addition, mass democracy, grounded in a volatile mix of narrow self-interest and moralistic sentiments, did not provide the solid moral foundation either in noble self-regard or in long-range self-interest that Churchill viewed as essential to empire.

Finally, even before the First World War, Churchill reluctantly recognized that the Empire could not be isolated from the ruling principles of the mother country.[78] The "old principles" of imperial rule were fatally undermined as subjected peoples adopted the new, democratic principles of their home country, asserting their right and ability to govern themselves.[79] Moreover, the rulers and defenders of the Empire, themselves committed democrats, adopted a more equalitarian understanding of the "old principles," thereby undermining the legitimacy of imperial rule and the national and individual self-assurance required to rule others. Thus Churchill's advocacy of democratic empire exposes, but does not in the longer run resolve, the tension between his political aspirations to promote human excellence or virtue and to promote equalitarian freedom—to further the ultimate purposes of aristocracy and of modern democracy.

THE LIMITS OF POLITICS

Just as Churchill doubted, despite his hopes and advocacy, that democracy could be wedded to empire, he feared that civilizing empire might be unlimited in extent. If it remained true to its purpose, a civilizing empire would act justly to the ruled and behave in a civilized way. The standard of civilization does not, however, limit in principle the extent of imperial expansion. The imperial view of what it means to be civilized—possessing political virtue on a grand scale—encourages imperial expansion to the ends of the earth; the larger the empire, the greater the number and scope of imperial offices at home and abroad. In practice empire might be restrained by rival powers, limited resources, or domestic needs, particularly in a democracy. But given its view of human excellence—of humanity's highest purpose—what limits imperial expansion in principle?

Beginning with his earliest writings on empire, Churchill suggests two kinds of answers to this problem of unlimited expansion: awareness of

[78] WSC II C 1376.
[79] See, for example, Narayan G. Jog, *Churchill's Blind Spot: India* (Bombay: New Book Co., 1944).

the imperfect, short-lived nature of all political endeavors, and dethrone-
ment of political and moral virtue as the highest purpose of human life,
and thus of the political community. Awareness of the imperfect character of political solutions lay behind Churchill's stance as a moderate
reformer who sought to deflate utopian political expectations while avoiding cynicism, fatalism, and apathy. Thus Churchill holds up for our admiration the grand political accomplishments of the Duke of Marlborough
but at the same time teaches that Marlborough's "success[es] bred failure" and that England's momentary "prosperity prepared collapse, by
which again new, larger, and more painful efforts were extorted": brief
success obtained, only to be followed again by decline. Political affairs, he
concludes, are governed by a "mysterious law which perhaps in larger
interests limits human achievement, and bars or saves the world from clear-
cut solutions."[80] In war "high comradeship and glorious daring" give way
to "disillusion and prostration"; the greatest victories lead almost inevitably to "weakness, discontent, faction, and disappointment."[81] In this
imperfect world, "We often see that capable rulers by their very virtues
sow the seeds of future evil and weak or degenerate princes open the
pathway of progress."[82]

At the beginning of *The River War*, Churchill clearly suggests that the
British Empire was not exempt from the sobering disproportion between
intention and accomplishment that plagues humankind's worldly efforts.[83]
Later in the book he observes that

All great movements, every vigorous impulse that a community may feel, become
perverted and distorted as time passes, and the atmosphere of the earth seems
fatal to the noble aspirations of its peoples. . . . There appears no exception to this
mournful rule, and the best efforts of men, however glorious their early results,
have dismal endings.[84]

And toward the end of *The River War* he notes that he fears for the future
of the British Empire precisely because of its accomplishments: all great
empires have been destroyed by success and none has "enjoyed so full a
measure of that fatal glory as the British."[85]

Churchill further depreciates political accomplishments in *The River*

---

[80] Churchill, *Marlborough*, vol. 2, 191–2.
[81] Winston S. Churchill, *The World Crisis*, 4 vols. (London: Thornton Butterworth, 1923–
       9), vol. 2, 18; vol. 4, 10.
[82] Churchill, *The English-Speaking Peoples*, vol. 1, 315.
[83] Churchill, *The River War*, vol. 1, 18–19.   [84] Ibid., vol. 1, 57–8.
[85] Ibid., vol. 2, 237.

War by contrasting the mutability and ephemeral nature of human affairs with the constancy and eternity of the unchanging Nile, which is indifferent to the passing moral, political, and religious distinctions which divide men.[86] He cautions against the false sense of human omnipotence that technological power gives to a scientific civilization: "The terrible machinery of scientific war had done its work. The Dervish host was scattered and destroyed. Their end, however, only anticipates that of the victors; for Time, which laughs at science, as science laughs at valour, will in due course contemptuously brush both combatants away."[87] The insignificance of human beings in the presence of the power and beauty of the unchanging Nile prompted Churchill to reject the view that man can attain a kind of immortality through glorious political accomplishments:

The past in relation to the present is but a fleeting moment. . . . Each generation exults in the immediate possession of life, and regards with indifference, scarcely tinged by pride or pity, the records and monuments of those who are no more. The greatest events of history are insignificant beside the bill of fare. . . . The past is insulted as much by what is remembered as by what is altogether forgotten.[88]

Through his depreciation of the possibilities for eternal glory and his comparison of unchanging nature with the transitory and imperfect nature of all political institutions and accomplishments, Churchill sought to moderate the aspiration for political greatness, which is the ultimate cause of empire.

But the question remains: If not politics, then what highest purpose and way of life should be sought by those who seek full human excellence? However flawed they may be, if political accomplishments are the highest human achievements, the best human beings and nations ought to, and will, commit themselves wholeheartedly to the grandest political project—an expansive empire. Moderate empire can be reconciled with the commitment to human excellence only if political and moral virtue are not seen as the peak of human attainment, only if there is a human purpose and way of life equal or superior to political excellence. In his early (and only) novel, *Savrola*, and later in his essay "Painting as a Pastime," Churchill explicitly calls into question the superiority of political accomplishments and suggests, thereby, the highest grounds of limited empire.

Churchill presents Savrola as a political leader driven by his ambition to found a republican government by overthrowing the dictator of

---

[86] Ibid., vol. 1, 8–11.   [87] Ibid., vol. 2, 226.
[88] Ibid., vol. 1, 11.

Laurania. Savrola becomes disillusioned with politics when he sees that the moderate revolution he favors has been captured by radicals who will shun him once they attain power. More significant, he is drawn away from politics by his attraction to stoical contemplation and by his love for the beautiful Lucile. Savrola did not fix his "thoughts on the struggles and hopes of this world."[89] He "loved to watch the stars for the sake of their mysteries" and longed "to live in dreamy quiet and philosophic calm in some beautiful garden, far from the noise of men and with every diversion that art and intellect could suggest."[90] Savrola's love also had an earthly object, the beautiful Lucile with whom he flees from Laurania, the locus of his political activity. Savrola tells Lucile that "honour" has "no true foundation, no ultra-human sanction. Its codes are constantly changing with times and places." True beauty, in contrast, is "eternal": it conforms to "an eternal standard of fitness." Churchill concludes *Savrola* with Gibbon's observation that history is "little more than the register of the crimes, follies, and misfortunes of mankind."[91] *Savrola*, in sum, depreciates political activity in the name of philosophic contemplation and love of the beautiful.

In his essay on painting, first published in 1921, Churchill amends the harsh view of politics in *Savrola* by suggesting that there are a number of ways of life that, if not superior, are equal to that devoted to politics. "Painting a picture," Churchill argues,

must require an intellect on the grand scale. There must be that all-embracing view which presents the beginning and the end, the whole and each part, as one instantaneous impression retentively and untiringly held in the mind. When we look at the larger Turners . . . , we must feel in presence of an intellectual manifestation, the equal in quality and intensity of the finest achievements of warlike action, of forensic argument, or of scientific or philosophic adjudication.

The art of the painter reflects the harmonies that form the common core of the greatest human accomplishments in war, politics, art, and science. The "same mind's eye that can justly survey and appraise and prescribe beforehand the values of a truly great picture in one . . . homogenous comprehension, would also with a certain acquaintance with the special technique be able to pronounce with sureness upon any other high activity of intellect."[92] Pursuit of political excellence is then only one of a number of

[89] Winston S. Churchill, *Savrola*, new ed. (New York: Random House, 1956), 30–2.
[90] Ibid., 31–4, 86.   [91] Ibid., 233–4, 78, 81, 241.
[92] Churchill, *Amid These Storms*, 312, see also 309–10.

equally worthy, or perhaps more worthy, human purposes, none of which requires a political position. The limits to political striving are established by the existence of other equally elevated human activities. The civilized impetus to imperial expansion is restrained by the recognition that it is possible to become fully civilized in a non-imperial nation.

The peaceful purpose of empire is to promote political and moral excellence. But empire cannot stand alone: in the modern world it must be tied to a democratic regime, which moderates and gradually undermines it. Empire is also qualified by the fact that political excellence is only one of a number of worthy human purposes. The practical implications of this view of the relation of empire to other political and nonpolitical purposes would seem to be that existing empires should pursue a moderate imperial policy and that those nations that are not imperial should pursue a moderate, honorable foreign policy that does not aspire to empire and, as long as circumstances permit, remain non-imperial.

4

The *River War*: Nature's provision, man's desire
to prevail, and the prospects for peace

PAUL A. RAHE

Before Winston Churchill became a peacemaker, before he became a statesman, before he entered politics in the first place, he had ample occasion
to reflect on war and on the forging of peace. In his capacity as a soldier,
journalist, and contemporary historian, he witnessed conflict and attempts
at pacification in Cuba, in India's northwest territories, in the Sudan, and
in South Africa, and in the last three cases, he wrote extensively about the
struggle itself and about its aftermath. Two of these early works—*The
Story of the Malakand Field Force* and *The Boer War*—have been recently reprinted.[1] But the third—*The River War: An Historical Account
of the Reconquest of the Soudan*—is today virtually unknown. It was first
published in a two-volume edition in 1899; it was twice reprinted that
year and twice again the next; and then it then was allowed to go out of
print.[2] When the book reappeared in 1902, it did so in a much abridged,
one-volume edition supplemented by a chapter on the aftermath of the
war.[3] This was then reprinted with a new preface in 1933.[4] The original
has been unavailable for nearly a century, and there is reason to suspect
that Churchill was himself responsible for its neglect. In its original form,
The River War was written "without fear or favour" (I x),[5] and in it

---

[1] See Winston S. Churchill, *The Story of the Malakand Field Force: An Episode of Frontier War* (New York: W. W. Norton, 1989), and *The Boer War* (New York: Dorset Press, 1991).

[2] Winston S. Churchill, *The River War: An Historical Account of the Reconquest of the Soudan*, 2 vols. (London: Longmans, Green, 1899).

[3] See Winston S. Churchill, *The River War: An Account of the Reconquest of the Soudan* (London: Longmans, Green, 1902).

[4] See Winston Churchill, *The River War: An Account of the Reconquest of the Sudan* (London: Eyre & Spottiswoode, 1933).

[5] All citations within the text refer to the original two-volume edition of the book. I follow the original spelling throughout.

Churchill may have been too frank for his own good. The abridged edition was published after its author had entered Parliament. There are limits to what a young politician, newly embarked on his career and intent upon ingratiating himself with his colleagues and a wide range of associates, can prudently say. In *The River War*, Churchill speaks his mind with a candor that later he could rarely afford.[6]

That *The River War* has suffered neglect is a misfortune, for it is the longest and most interesting of Churchill's early works, it is arguably one of his most enlightening books, and it deals with a subject that is of greater interest to us today than it has been at any time since the outbreak of the First World War. Ten years ago, if one were asked to recommend a book dealing with the larger questions of war and peace, the obvious place to begin would have been Thucydides' account of the Peloponnesian War. Nowhere can one find a subtler depiction of the moral and practical dilemmas faced by the statesman in a world torn by conflict. Moreover, Thucydides' environment was bipolar—as was ours in the great epoch of struggles on the European continent that stretched from 1914 to 1989— and Thucydides' war pitted a maritime power, such as the United States was, against a power, such as Germany or the Soviet Union, threatening dominance on land. But the two great world wars are now long gone, the cold war has come to an end, and we no longer find ourselves hovering on the verge of conflict with a single foe. Our situation more closely resembles the plight of the late Victorians than that of Pericles, Archidamus, Alcibiades, and Lysander. And while we still have much to learn from Thucydides, there is something to be said for suggesting that contemporary students of international politics read Winston Churchill's lively accounts of the dirty little wars that his countrymen had to fight late in the last century in defense of their empire and their way of life.

The River War is by far the best of these. No one who reads the original two-volume account will have any difficulty in understanding why Churchill was eventually awarded the Nobel Prize for Literature. Like Thucydides' history, Churchill's great neglected work is a prose epic. His themes—the Nile and its peoples; the conflict between Islam and modernity; the origins, character, and course of the Mahdist revolt against Egyptian rule within the Sudan; the resistance mounted by General Gordon at Khartoum; the fecklessness of Gladstone's Liberal administration; and

---

[6] For a comparison of the two editions, see James W. Muller, "War on the Nile: Winston Churchill and the Reconquest of the Sudan," *Political Science Reviewer* 20 (1991): 223–63. This seminal essay is the starting point for all serious discussions of Churchill's book.

the campaign of reconquest ultimately mounted on behalf of Egypt and Britain by Sir Herbert Kitchener—offered him the same sort of canvas available to Thucydides, and he took the endeavor as an occasion for reflection on the moral responsibilities attendant upon great power and as an opportunity to explore the relationship between civilization and decadence, that between barbarism and courage, and that between modern science and the changing character of war. In an age when we are likely to be called on to respond to ugly little conflicts marked by social, sectarian, and tribal rivalries in odd corners of the world—the Arabian peninsula, the Caucasus, the Horn of Africa, the Balkans, central Africa, the Maghreb, and the Caribbean, to mention the most recent examples—I can think of no historical work that better deserves our attention.

THE NATURAL SETTING

In Chapter 1, after a brief initial paragraph announcing the work's themes and inviting its readers to "admire the perseverance" of his own countrymen, "who pursue their policies in spite of delay and disaster to victorious ends" (I 1–2), Churchill turns to the geography of what he calls "the military Soudan," describing in detail the countryside that stretches from Omdurman to the border of Egypt. In doing so, he provides a setting for the subsequent narrative. But his focus is not merely or even primarily geopolitical, for his chapter is as much a reflection on the general setting for human endeavor as it is an account of a particular place.

Churchill's description of the Sudan resembles Herodotus' account of Egypt: each historian treats his subject as a gift of the Nile. The "great river" is for the Sudanese "their only means of growth, their only channel of progress." The Sudan is linked with Egypt "by the Nile, as a diver is connected with the surface by his air-pipe. Without it there is only suffocation." Khartoum owes its importance to the fact that it lies by "the confluence of the Blue and White Niles": it is the focal point through which all trade from "the real Soudan . . . moist, undulating, and exuberant," makes its way to the North (I 2–3).

Churchill's attention, however, is focused not on the real Sudan, but on that other Sudan with its "deserts of surpassing desolation" through which the great river flows northward from Khartoum to Aswan for some 1,200 miles. "This," he exclaims, "is the Soudan of the soldier."

Destitute of wealth or future, it is rich in history. The names of its squalid villages are familiar to distant and enlightened peoples. The barrenness of its scenery has been drawn by skilful pen and pencil. Its ample deserts have tasted the blood of brave men. Its hot, black rocks have witnessed famous tragedies. It is the scene of the war.

"This great tract," Churchill observes, "stretches with apparent indefiniteness over the face of the continent." It is marked by "level plains of smooth sand—a little rosier than buff, a little paler than salmon," and these are "interrupted only by occasional peaks of rock—black, stark, and shapeless." Its "fine sand," when driven by the wind, he compares with "a fiery snow, such as might fall in hell." In this environment, "the earth burns with the quenchless thirst of ages, and in the steel-blue sky scarcely a cloud obstructs the unrelenting triumph of the sun" (I 3–4).

Churchill's bleak depiction of the northern Sudan is broken only by his mention of the Nile, which flows through the desert, except in time of flood, as "a thread of blue silk drawn across an enormous brown drugget." Though "vital" to all who live along it, the great river "is never so precious as here." A man on a journey will "cling to the strong river as to an old friend, staunch in the hour of need. All the world blazes, but here is shade. The deserts are hot, but the Nile is cool. The land is parched, but here is abundant water. The picture painted in burnt sienna is relieved by a grateful flash of green" (I 4).

Even here, however, Churchill evidences misgivings—for the Nile is attractive only in comparison with the desert. Its reeds are "unnourishing"; its grasses "grow rank and coarse from the water's edge." The soil becomes "dark" and "rotten" after the flood recedes. The local vegetation is "inhospitable," and the thornbushes bristle "like hedgehogs" and thrive "arrogantly." The soldier may find these bushes useful for building temporary fortifications and the artist may judge them beautiful, but the ordinary traveler will be more impressed by his own torn clothes. One may, of course, admire the caustic plant: "Its long stalks are garnished with pale green leaves, and from the jointed branches large, luscious-looking fruits depend." But upon close examination the fruits turn out to be "bladders puffed with air and filled with a poisonous white milk, which produces blindness if by chance it is squirted in the eye." To Churchill's way of thinking, these are "malignant growths." Only the palm trees can be judged "kindly" with their clusters of dates; only they serve to remind the visitor that "nature is not always mischievous and cruel." One is left with an impression of terrible desolation (I 4–5). But Churchill takes care to qualify this dismal account. Though the Nile displays "an abundance of barrenness" and evidences "monotony" except when compared with the desert, "there is one hour when all is changed." Shortly before the setting of the sun, "a delicious flush brightens and enlivens the landscape." And even when the sun disappears and the colors fade, "the stars light up and remind us that there is always something beyond" (I 5–6).

Churchill's depiction of the northern Sudan with its "pitiless sky," its "oppressive distance," and with "the mockery of the mirage" does more than set the tone for the tale that he relates. It raises questions as well concerning the prospects for peace given "the insignificance of man" in the scheme of the universe. "A philosopher might draw comfort," he writes, "from the reflection that strife is rightly relegated to unprofitable regions, and may acidly observe that those who seek to destroy each other have no right to rail at Nature." But it is not clear that Churchill is such a philosopher. He knows that strife is not always or even generally relegated to unprofitable regions. In any case, this war has its origins not in the desert but in the Nile. The great river is not only "the life of the lands through which it flows." It is also "the cause of the war. It is the means by which we fight; the end at which we aim. . . . Without the river none would have started. Without it none might have continued. Without it none could ever have returned" (I 6–9).

Were the earth truly desolate, were there no Providence natural or divine, there would be no wars: men fight over that to which they "pay their tribute of respect and gratitude." They fight over "the great river," which "has befriended all races and every age," which "has borne with an impartial smile the stately barges of the Pharaohs and the unpretentious stern-wheel steamers of Cook."

It has seen war with the wide *balista* and the short Roman sword, and has witnessed the military employment of quick-firing guns and Lyddite shells. Kingdoms and dominations have risen and fallen by its banks. Religious sects have sprung into life, gained strength in adversity, triumphed over opposition, and relapsed into the obscurity of non-existence. The knowledge of men has grown, withered, and revived. The very shape and structure of the human form may have altered, but the Nile remains unchanged.

It is only by reflecting on that which remains unchanged, it is only by contemplating the "mission" of the Nile "to relieve and vivify" through "the annual miracle of its flood," it is only by considering its capacity to become "thick and red, laden with the magic mud that can raise cities from the desert sand and make the wilderness a garden," it is only by pondering the fact that it inspires "a feeling of mystic reverence" that one can understand the causes of war and the prospects for peace (I 8–10).

Churchill begins his narrative with an extended reflection on nature because he wants his readers to contemplate the events that he will relate *sub specie aeternitatis.* He acknowledges that his war will in the near future "seem almost insignificant." If judged in relation to the present, he acknowledges, "the past . . . is but a fleeting moment," for

each generation exults in the immediate possession of life, and regards with indifference, scarcely tinged by pride or pity, the records and monuments of those that are no more. The greatest events of history are insignificant beside the bill of fare. The greatest men that ever lived serve to pass an idle hour. The tremendous crash of the Roman Empire is scarcely heard outside the schools and colleges. The past is insulted as much by what is remembered as by what is altogether forgotten.

All of this notwithstanding, Churchill thinks his task a worthy one. It is characteristic of human beings that "the desire to live extends beyond the span of life" and that they "long for a refuge in memory, when the world shall have slipped from beneath their feet like a trapdoor." Someday, he adds, in the distant future some chronicler may try to "write for his present a history of our past"; and, while "rummaging among old books," he may come across *The River War* with its tale of "the untimely destruction of three hundred thousand human lives" (I 11).

It is on this note that Churchill ends his initial chapter. Nowhere does he echo Thucydides' bold claim that his work is not a tragedy, a comedy, or a satyr play designed for the dramatic competition at a religious festival and that it "was composed as a possession for all times rather than as contest piece *(agonisma)* meant to be heard straightaway."[7] But we need not doubt that, behind a semblance of modesty better suited to our egalitarian age, the aristocratic Englishman harbored ambitions as grand as those of his ancient predecessor. He, too, ends the first section of his history with a reflection on memory, the passage of time, and the question of immortality.

THE HUMAN SETTING

After describing the natural endowment of the Sudan, Churchill turns to its human endowment. At the beginning of his second chapter, he briefly surveys the resources of the southern Sudan, which is an example of "prolific Nature," well-watered, replete with lush vegetation, a great variety of animals, and "countless millions of birds, butterflies, and beetles."

[7] Thucydides 1.22.4. All translations from the Greek are my own.

Then, he considers "the human inhabitants of the Soudan," who would be numerous but "for their vices and misfortunes." As it happens, "War, slavery, and oppression have ... afflicted them until the total population of the whole country does not exceed at the most liberal estimate three million souls" (I 12–14).

Churchill approaches the Sudan's human endowment in a manner likely to offend delicate sensibilities today. He speaks of race, which puts one on one's guard, but a racist he is not. In using that English word, since grown so precise and evocative, he is less concerned with biological than with cultural differences. His approach is that of Aristotle or perhaps that of the baron de Montesquieu. He has in mind the distinctions that characterize what we would term not races, but peoples and nations. "The huge area" of the Sudan "contains many differences of climate and situation, and these have produced peculiar and diverse breeds of men." This is his claim. And he does not hesitate to describe "the two main races" of the Sudan—"the aboriginal natives, and the Arab settlers"—in language that would today be considered not only judgmental but insensitive, impolite, and perhaps even profoundly immoral (I 14). One can hardly imagine a university press accepting for publication a work containing such an account.[8] In other words, Churchill speaks blunt truths that nearly everyone now privately or at least tacitly concedes but that one can no longer safely utter in the public arena. He speaks of civilization and barbarism, and he has no compunction regarding moral judgment of the habits and customs of nations and peoples, including his own. His account has a distinctly Herodotean flavor.

"The indigenous inhabitants of the country," he begins, "were negroes as black as coal." They were "strong, virile, and simple-minded savages," and they "lived, as we may imagine prehistoric men—hunting, fighting, marrying, and dying, with no ideas beyond the gratification of their physical desires, and no fears save those engendered by ghosts, witchcraft, the worship of ancestors, and other forms of superstition common among peoples of low developement." If Churchill's assessment is largely negative, it is not wholly so. The aboriginal Sudanese "displayed the virtues of barbarism," and these are not mean virtues: "they were brave and honest." In any case, "the smallness of their intelligence excused the degradation of their habits. Their ignorance secured their innocence." But

---

[8] For the standards now applied, see Marilyn Schwartz and the Task Force on Bias-Free Language of the Association of American University Presses, *Guidelines for Bias-Free Writing* (Bloomington: Indiana University Press, 1995).

Churchill's "eulogy" of the indigenous population is and "must be short, for though their customs, language, and appearance vary with the districts they inhabit and the subdivisions to which they belong, the history of all is a confused legend of strife and misery, their natures are uniformly cruel and thriftless, and their condition is one of equal squalor and want." Churchill may respect, but he is not inclined to romanticize the primitive (I 14–15).

Though the black peoples of the Sudan outnumber "the Arabs," he soon adds, the latter "exceed" the former "in power"—for "the bravery" of the former "is outweighed by the intelligence of the invaders and their superior force of character." The initial Arab conquest, which followed close upon the death of Muhammad, and the subsequent waves of Arab immigration introduced a new "element" into the Sudan, which spread throughout the country "as water soaks into a dry sponge. The aboriginals absorbed the invaders they could not repel. The stronger race imposed its customs and language on the negroes. The vigour of their blood sensibly altered the facial appearance of the Soudanese." And then, "for more than a thousand years, the influence of Mohammedanism" permeated the Sudan. In the North, by Churchill's time, the process was complete, "and the Arabs of the Soudan are a race formed by the interbreeding of negro and Arab, and yet distinct from either." In the South, especially in the most remote and inaccessible districts, the process had then barely begun, "and between these extremes every degree of mixture is to be found" (I 15–16).

Churchill did not admire the result. He found the Arabs of the Sudan "a debased and cruel breed, more shocking because they are more intelligent than the primitive savages." The problem was simple: "The stronger race soon began to prey upon the simple aboriginals; some of the Arab tribes were camel-breeders; some were goat-herds; some were Baggaras or cow-herds. But all, without exception, were hunters of men." And so they dispatched over a period of centuries "a continual stream of negro captives" to the great slave markets of the Arabian peninsula. As the invaders spread their "blood, religion, customs, and language" among the black Sudanese, they "harried and enslaved them." And for centuries, the Sudan was synonymous with chaos and war (I 16–17).

Then, something happened in "the outer world." While events in the Sudan went unheeded, "another civilisation reared itself above the ruins of Roman triumph and Mohammedan aspiration—a civilisation much more powerful, more glorious, but no less aggressive." And the spirit of conquest—which caused the English and the French to move on Canada and the Indies, the Dutch to seize the Cape, and the Spaniards to capture Peru—induced Egypt's Muhammad Ali to conquer the Sudan (I 17–18).

After recounting this event, Churchill pauses to consider the question of empire. His discussion of imperialism is no less unsparing than his account of primitive barbarism and Arab oppression in the Sudan. He begins, in the manner of Virgil, with the presumption of the conquerors.[9] "What enterprise," he asks, "that an enlightened community may attempt is more noble and more profitable than the reclamation from barbarism of fertile regions and large populations?"

> To give peace to warring tribes, to administer justice where all was violence, to strike the chains off the slave, to draw the richness from the soil, to plant the earliest seeds of commerce and learning, to increase in whole peoples their capacities for pleasure and diminish their chances of pain—what more beautiful idea or more valuable reward can inspire human effort? The act is virtuous, the exercise invigorating, and the result often extremely profitable.

But, even in the best of circumstances, there are problems. "As the mind turns from the wonderful cloudland of aspiration to the ugly scaffolding of attempt and achievement, a succession of opposite ideas arise." To begin with, empire rarely pays for itself: "Industrious races are displayed stinted and starved for the sake of an expensive Imperialism which they can only enjoy, if they are well fed." And, at least at its inception, it is unappreciated by its beneficiaries: "Wild peoples, ignorant of their barbarism, callous of suffering, careless of life but tenacious of liberty, are seen to resist with fury the philanthropic invaders, and to perish in thousands before they are convinced of their mistake" (I 18–19).

Moreover, the invaders are no less human than their less civilized adversaries, and the power that they wield does nothing to liberate them from their own vices. As Churchill puts it, "The inevitable gap between conquest and dominion becomes filled with the figures of the greedy trader, the inopportune missionary, the ambitious soldier, and the lying speculator, who disquiet the minds of the conquered and excite the sordid appetites of the conquerors." Although he believes that there is more to be said on behalf of empire than our contemporaries are inclined— at least in public—to admit, Churchill finds himself forced to confess that, "as the eye of thought rests on these sinister features, it hardly seems

---

[9] Cf. Virgil, *Aeneid*, 6.847–53.

possible for us to believe that any fair prospect is approached by so foul a path" (I 19).

He is not, however, content to let it rest at that. Where others in a later generation might be inclined to wash their hands of the whole matter and to measure their moral accomplishment by their avoidance of contact with endeavors in which one inevitably becomes soiled, he retains something of the instinctive moderation and sober understanding that inspired Thucydides. His premise is simple: "The desire to prevail is not . . . a matter of reason but of constitution. It is only one form of the spirit of competition, the condition of our continued existence. All the vigorous nations of the earth have sought and are seeking to conquer." He does not claim that this "instinct" is "wise." But he does suggest that it may be "healthy: for, as in the Roman State, when there are no more worlds to conquer and no rivals to destroy, nations exchange the desire for power for the love of art, and so by a gradual, yet continual, enervation and decline turn from the vigorous beauties of the nude to the more subtle allurements of the draped, and then sink to actual eroticism and ultimate decay." Churchill refrains from following the logic of this "argument even to the depths which average men can plumb." He stops short of examining "whether a conspiracy for the arrest of developement is justified by the unexpected powers which the science of man has snatched from Nature." Already, at the end of the last century, he was aware that man may be unable to cope with and wisely make use of the opportunities that modern technology affords. Here, however, he refrains from further exploring this theme, and he merely suggests that the historian must "recognise the desire to prevail—the spirit of empire—as a great fact, which practical men must reckon with" (I 19–20). Those who study war and peace must begin with the presumption that spiritedness cannot be wished away: the desire to rule is as much a part of the human endowment of the Sudan as is the desire not to be ruled by those of an alien nation or race.

CORRUPTION, REFORM, AND REVOLUTION

Churchill ends his brief discussion of imperialism with a pithy observation: "that, if even noble races soil themselves by pursuing the path of conquest, it would be well if mean breeds avoided it altogether." This remark serves as an introduction to his account of Egyptian dominion in the Sudan. The conquest took place in 1819; the Egyptians were ejected in 1883. Their rule in the interim was "not kindly, wise, nor profitable."

Its aim was to exploit, not to improve the local population. The miseries of the people were aggravated rather than lessened: but they were concealed. For the rough justice of the sword there were substituted the intricate laws of corruption and bribery. Violence and plunder were more hideous, since they were cloaked with legality and armed with authority. . . . The Egyptians had only pressed upon the tortured face of the Soudan the bland mask of an organised Government.

That government had one other defect: it was not just "iniquitous" (I 20–1); it was weak. It combined "public incapacity and private misbehaviour." Its army was "badly trained, rarely paid, and very cowardly." "Never was there," Churchill insists, "such a house of cards as the Egyptian dominion in the Soudan. The marvel is that it stood so long, not that it fell so soon" (I 24–5).

Responsible for "the actual outburst" were two seemingly quite different men. "One was an English general, the other an Arab priest." But despite their striking difference in "conditions," they were similar in the crucial regards.

Both were earnest and enthusiastic men of keen sympathies and passionate emotions. Both were powerfully swayed by religious fervour. Both exerted great personal influence on all who came in contact with them. Both were reformers. The Arab was an African reproduction of the Englishman; the Englishman a superior and civilised developement of the Arab. In the end they fought to the death, but for an important part of their lives their influence on the fortunes of the Soudan was exerted in the same direction.

In Charles Gordon, who twice governed the Sudan, and in Mohammed Ahmed, who was called the Mahdi, nature had its way, for they were cut from the same cloth. Prior to their appearance on the stage, the Arab tribes of the Sudan "were destitute of two moral forces essential to all rebellions." They lacked "the knowledge that better things existed," and they were without "a spirit of combination." If Gordon afforded them the former, the Mahdi provided the latter (I 25–6).

Chinese Gordon was the first to influence events. Churchill found him a truly "extraordinary" man—"a type without comparison in modern times and with few likenesses in history." "Rare and precious," he writes, "is the truly disinterested man." But his disinterest was matched with an absence of "mental ballast. Mercury uncontrolled by the force of gravity was not on several occasions more unstable than Charles Gordon. His moods were capricious and uncertain, his passions violent, his impulses sudden and inconsistent" (I 26–8). He enters the picture because Egypt was under pressure from the powers of Europe to suppress the slave trade. His appointment as governor of the Equatorial Province was meant to be taken as a sign that the Egyptians were serious about tackling the problem. But, in Gordon's hands, what may have been intended as "a pretence" became "very real." He traversed the country, he put an end to the trade, and "he scattered justice and freedom among the astonished natives. He fed the infirm, protected the weak, executed the wicked. To some he gave actual help, to many freedom, to all new hopes and aspirations." His impact on the country was profound, but he was, as he knew only too well, "the herald of the storm." In putting an end to the slave trade, he destroyed "the greatest institution in the land" and thereby "undermined the whole social system." Moreover, in the process, Gordon taught the Sudanese that conditions did not have to be what they had so long been: "Oppressed yet ferocious races had learned that they had rights. The misery of the Soudanese was lessened, but their knowledge had increased." What Gordon had begun could not easily be stopped (I 28–32).

But Gordon's reforms were not a sufficient explanation for the revolt of the Sudan. This took the Mahdi as well. The latter's influence could not, however, be comprehended unless one reflected on another dimension of our human endowment that many of the more enlightened of Churchill's contemporaries were and even more of our own are inclined to scant. "Few facts," Churchill observes,

are so encouraging to the student of human developement as the desire, which most men and all communities manifest at all times, to associate with their actions at least the appearance of moral right. However distorted may be their conceptions of virtue, however feeble their efforts to attain even to their own ideals, it is a pleasing feature and a hopeful augury that they should *wish* to be justified. No community embarks on a great enterprise without fortifying itself with the belief that from some points of view its motives are lofty and disinterested. It is an involuntary tribute, the humble tribute of imperfect beings, to the eternal temples of Truth and Beauty.

One consequence of this encouraging fact is that suffering and oppression are insufficient to cause a revolution. Before a people or a class "will take up arms and risk their lives some unselfish and impersonal spirit must animate them." In highly civilized countries, men may evidence "pride" in the country's "glorious traditions" or "a keen sympathy with surrounding misery" or "a philosophical recognition of the dignity of the species," and this may be sufficient. Savage nations are, however, denied these motives by ignorance. But they have by way of compensation "the mighty stimulus of fanaticism."

The French Communists might plead that they upheld the rights of man. The desert tribes proclaimed that they fought for the glory of God. But although the force of fanatical passion is far greater than that exerted by any philosophical belief, its unction is just the same. It gives men something which they think is sublime to fight for, and this serves them as an excuse for wars which it is desirable to begin for totally different reasons.

Churchill denies that "fanaticism" is or can ever be a genuine "cause of war." It is, he says, "the means which helps savage peoples to fight. . . . What the horn is to the rhinoceros, what the sting is to the wasp, the Mohammedan faith was to the Arabs of the Soudan—a faculty of offence or defence" (I 32–3).

Churchill is aware of the tendency, so evident in discussions of today's worldwide Islamic revival, especially on the part of "those whose practice it is to regard their own nation as possessing a monopoly of virtue and common-sense, . . . to ascribe every military enterprise of savage peoples to fanaticism." And he valiantly resists this inclination. In his judgment, those who suggest that "the revolt in the Soudan was entirely religious" have fallen prey to folly. He himself is willing to assert that "the revolt of a great population has never been caused solely or even mainly by religious enthusiasm." That which is necessary is not always sufficient, and it is scarcely "less absurd to contend that the revolt in the Soudan was caused by fanaticism, than to assert that the French Revolution was brought about by the great admiration which the French people had for the philosophy of the 'Contrat Social' " (I 34–5).

The Sudanese had ample reason to revolt. "Their country was being ruined; their property was plundered; their women were ravished; their liberties were curtailed; even their lives were threatened. Aliens ruled the inhabitants; the few oppressed the many; brave men were harried by cowards; the weak compelled the strong" (I 35). In short, justice was in all respects being denied. And if Charles Gordon, during his brief tenure as governor, taught Egypt's Sudanese subjects "that better things existed," Mohammed Ahmed provided them with the requisite "spirit of combination" (I 26).

Mohammed Ahmed was able to do so because the Muslims of the Sudan adhered to the Shukri belief that "some day, in a time of shame and trouble, a second great Prophet will arise—a *Mahdi* who shall lead the faithful nearer God and sustain the religion" (I 42). In 1881, shame and trouble were in more than sufficient supply, and in that same year, the Expected One appeared. "A large proportion of the religious teachers of heathen and other countries are devoid of enthusiasm," Churchill observes, "and [they] turn their attention to the next world because doing so affords them an easy living in this" (I 37–8). But there are exceptions, and Mohammed Ahmed was such a one. He was so fervently devout that he proved unable to tolerate a measure of dissipation on the part of the sheikh to whom he had attached himself. When the young man broke with his teacher, his protest against "the decay of religious fervor and the torpor of the times" caused a stir, and it was soon rumored that he was the Mahdi—"the expected Guide" (I 42, 45). At Mohammed Ahmed's side, fanning the flames, stood the cunning Abdullahi—"a man of determination and capacity" who was resolved "to free the Soudan of foreigners, and to rule it himself" (I 43–4). Initially under the aegis of Mohammed Ahmed and then on his own, Abdullahi achieved his aim.

When summoned to Khartoum to justify himself before the Egyptian governor, Mohammed Ahmed "proclaimed a holy war against the foreigners, alike the enemies of God and the scourge of men," and he revealed himself as "God's holy prophet 'the expected Mahdi'" (I 47). The revolt might have been nipped in the bud—but the two rival companies sent to fetch the rebel leader fired on one another, and Mohammed Ahmed's followers eliminated most of the survivors. When they similarly made short shrift of a second expedition sent in pursuit, the Sudan erupted in general revolt (I 47–50).

Churchill is perfectly prepared to blame Mohammed Ahmed in part for all the blood that was spilt, but he suggests that "the unjust rulers who oppressed the land" and "the incapable commanders who muddled away the lives of their men" as well as "the vacillating Ministers who aggravated the misfortunes" shared in responsibility for what happened. He was even willing to come to the Mahdi's defense. "It should not be forgotten," he contends,

that he put life and soul into the hearts of his countrymen, and freed his native land of foreigners. The poor miserable natives, eating only a handful of grain, toiling half-naked and without hope, found a new, if terrible magnificence added to life. Within their humble breasts the spirit of the Mahdi roused the fires of patriotism and religion. Life became filled with thrilling, exhilarating terrors. They existed in a new and wonderful world of imagination. While they lived there were great things to be done; and when they died, whether it were slaying the Egyptians or charging the British squares, a Paradise which they could understand awaited them. The materialist may deplore the loss of life, the interruption of trade, and the destruction of property; but the true philosopher, who realises that men's souls as well as their stomachs are capable of developement, will view the tumult with impassive eye. (I 55–6)

Churchill took note of the fact that many a Christian who evidenced respect for Islam treated the Mahdi as an impostor. "In a certain sense," he comments, "this may be true. But I know not how a genuine may be distinguished from a spurious Prophet, except by the measure of his success." In his lifetime, he then adds, the Mahdi's accomplishments exceeded those of "the founder of the Mohammedan faith." If the Mahdi's cause eventually went down to defeat, it was only because it "came in contact with a mighty civilisation and the machinery of science." Churchill could imagine a day when "prosperity should come to the peoples of the Upper Nile, and learning and happiness follow in its train," and he had little doubt that then "the first Arab historian who shall investigate the early annals of that new nation, will not forget, foremost among the heroes of his race, to write the name of Mohammed Ahmed" (I 56).

QUICKSAND

None of this would have much mattered to the government of Great Britain had it not been for William Gladstone's intervention in Egypt at about the same time—for when Britain rescued the khedive from a revolt mounted by his Egyptian subjects, it assumed responsibility for the country's welfare, and no one in Cairo was prepared to relinquish Egypt's claim to the Sudan (I 50–5). In consequence, gradually and inadvertently, the British were drawn in, and every step they took for the purpose of extracting themselves had the effect of placing their prestige on the line.

The process began innocently enough. The khedive's British advisers simply acquiesced in a concerted attempt on Egypt's part to suppress the revolt. When the khedive's army, led by a retired officer of the Indian staff corps, was slaughtered by the increasingly professional forces of the Mahdi, Gladstone's government advised the abandonment of the Sudan, and having offered advice that the Egyptians could not refuse, the occupying power found itself unable to refuse the Egyptians the aid that they needed in order to put into practice the policy advised. Abandonment required evacuation—for, at Khartoum in particular, the Egyptians maintained a substantial establishment. No one trusted the Egyptians to undertake the task on their own, and the obvious candidate for leadership was judged repugnant (I 57–64).

His name was Zubair, and, though Sudanese, he had been cooling his heels in Cairo for some years while under house arrest. Before Charles Gordon had ever set foot in the Sudan, this Zubair had been a force in that land—for he was the most notorious slave trader in its long history. Only he had the knowledge and the local standing to "stem the tide of Mahdism" and "restore the falling dominion of Egypt," or "at least save the garrisons of the Soudan." The Egyptians suggested Zubair, but Gladstone and his cabinet demurred. "Their aim" when they intervened in Egypt "was philanthropic and disinterested" and, high-minded as they were, they "would countenance no dealings with such a man" (I 62–4).

The only alternative was Charles Gordon. For obvious reasons, the Egyptian government was averse to sending a Christian to effect an evacuation in the face of a rebellion launched in the name of Islam. Sir Evelyn Baring, Britain's man on the spot, quite rightly feared that Gordon's appointment would only further inflame the Sudanese. All were forced to yield. Fortified "by that belief in personality which too often misleads great men and beautiful women," Gordon threw himself into the endeavor. The general was no admirer of the Egyptian administration; like Gladstone, he viewed the Sudanese as "a people rightly struggling to be free" (I 63–8). To his great credit, upon arrival in Egypt, Gordon quickly recognized that he would need the aid of the very scoundrel whose suzerainty he had brought to an end. He reiterated his request upon reaching Khartoum. "Never was so good a case made out for the appointment of so bad a man," Churchill remarks. "The Envoy Extraordinary asked for him; Colonel Stewart, his colleague, concurred; the British Agent strongly urged the request; the Egyptian Government were unanimous; and behind all these were ranged every single person who had the slightest acquaintance with the Soudan" (I 68–70). But all of this was to no avail.

Her Majesty's Government refused absolutely to have anything to do with Zubair. They declined to allow the Egyptian Government to employ him. They would not entertain the proposal. They scarcely consented to discuss it. Parliament and the nation approved their decision, and it has never since been impugned. It was in no degree a party matter. The position which all men assumed was, that great States cannot stoop to employ such agents.

Churchill leaves it to "the historians of the future" to occupy "their leisure and exercise their wits in deciding whether the Ministers and the people were right or wrong; whether they had a right to indulge their sensitiveness at so terrible a cost; whether they were not more nice than wise; whether their dignity was more offended by what was incurred or by what was avoided." He intimates that the question is largely academic and turns on "whether the end justifies the means, whether it is right to commit a smaller sin to avoid a greater wrong" (I 71).

But while he appears to acknowledge the existence of a moral quandary, Churchill also points to the considerations by which it can be resolved. After all, he observes, the consequences of Britain's refusal were obvious. "Either the British Government were concerned with the Soudan, or they were not. If they were not, then they had no reason or right to prohibit the appointment of Zubair. If they were, they were bound to see that the garrisons were rescued." Churchill regarded it as "an open question" whether his countrymen were "originally" responsible for safeguarding the garrisons. Gordon thought that they were, "and he backed his belief with his life." "Others," he adds, no doubt thinking of himself, "may hold that governments have no right to lay, or at any rate, must be very judicious in the laying of, burdens on the backs of their own countrymen in order that they may indulge a refined sense of chivalry towards foreigners." England was not responsible for Egyptian misgovernment in the Sudan— but "the moment Zubair was prohibited, the situation was changed. The refusal to permit his employment was tantamount to an admission that affairs in the Soudan involved the honour of England as well as the honour of Egypt." In substituting its judgment for that of the Egyptians, Britain assumed responsibility for what eventually transpired (I 72–3).

This passage should give the reader pause, for in it Churchill displays the fine sense of judgment that would later distinguish him from the appeasers of the 1930s. When faced with the threat posed by Hitler, they dithered in part because they found it morally repugnant to seek an alliance with Stalin. When they might have encouraged a military coup against the Nazi leader, they recoiled before the prospect of soiling their hands by involving themselves in a plot to overthrow an elected civilian government. They indulged their sensitiveness at a terrible cost; they were more nice than wise. In refusing to commit the smaller sin, they incurred a far greater wrong.

Some might be tempted to contrast Churchill with Gladstone and with the appeasers of the 1930s by describing the former as an exponent of *Realpolitik*, but they would be in error. The author of *The River War* was, like Thucydides, exceedingly hardheaded. In judging questions of policy, he was concerned first and foremost with results, and he did not pussyfoot around. But if he was neither sensitive nor nice, if he seemed at times insensitive and blunt to the point of being unfit for polite company, it was not because he was inattentive to the demands of morality. It was, rather, because, again like Thucydides, he adhered to the practical wisdom inherent in an older, more manly moral code.[10] Churchill was saved from a specious and irresponsible moralism by the inheritance that saved him also from *Realpolitik*. His old-fashioned—one might even say pagan—sense of honor caused him to adopt a morality of consequences in place of the morality of intentions that guided men like Gordon and Gladstone. He wasted no time examining the purity of his own intentions; he concerned himself not one whit with the problem of dirty hands. He assessed where the English government's obligations lay, and he considered the likely results of the various policies under consideration. Small sins were nothing when compared with great wrongs.

In contrast with Gordon, Churchill doubted that his country should assume responsibility for the consequences of Egypt's misgovernment of the Sudan: England's honor was in no way at stake; it had undertaken no obligations in this regard; and its first duty was to look after the welfare of its own. In contrast with Gladstone, he recognized that England could not forbid Egypt the means to carry out a policy forced on Egypt by England without thereby assuming responsibility for what transpired. And, of course, in the end, as Churchill's narrative makes clear, Great Britain was drawn into the morass by the very tactics that were meant to extricate itself therefrom—for, in practice, no nation can indefinitely ignore the dictates of honor. They are too closely bound up with the nation's long-term self-interest for that to be the case. In reading Churchill, one comes to realize that honesty in the original sense of the word is generally the best policy and that sensitivity and niceness are all too often euphemisms for a self-defeating form of self-congratulatory self-indulgence. *The River War* is a book that the policymakers in Europe and the United States who stood about wringing their hands about the horrors being perpetrated in the former Yugoslavia should have been made repeatedly to read. With Churchill they could then have asked, "Is this always to be our method of war and conquest—blunders, follies, bloodshed, an ill-timed or ill-conceived expedition, useless heroism and withdrawal, and then years afterwards a great army striking an overwhelming blow?" (II 48).

---

[10] In this connection, see Paul A. Rahe, "Thucydides' Critique of *Realpolitik*," *Security Studies* 5, no. 2 (Winter 1995–6): 105–41.

THE VERY MODEL OF A MODERN CHRISTIAN GENTLEMAN

Churchill cannot help but admire Charles Gordon. Single-handedly, the envoy brought home to his countrymen the requirements of honor. Once he reached Khartoum, he recognized that he lacked the wherewithal to effect an evacuation. He had, however, the means with which to make his own withdrawal. This he resolutely refused to do.

Gordon considered that he was personally pledged to effect the evacuation of Khartoum by the garrison and civil servants. He had appointed some of the inhabitants to positions of trust, thus compromising them with the Mahdi. Others had undoubtedly been encouraged to delay their departure by his arrival. He therefore considered that his honour was involved in their safety. Henceforward he was inflexible. Neither rewards nor threats could move him. Nothing that men could offer would induce him to leave Khartoum till its inhabitants were rescued. The Government on their side were equally stubborn, but since their firmness was unattended by personal danger it has seemed less admirable to the nation. Nothing, however sacred, should induce them to send troops to Khartoum, or in any way involve themselves in the middle of Africa. (I 73–4)

As Churchill observes, "the deadlock was complete." Had the British sent someone else, he might have withdrawn. "But the man they had sent was the one man of all others who was beyond their control, who cared nothing for what they could give or take away." And by means of his journals, Gordon made sure that the ministry bore what he called "the indelible disgrace of abandoning the garrisons" (I 74–5).

In this situation, the Mahdi saw his opportunity. Gordon's arrival had been disconcerting: it suggested that reinforcements might follow. But Gordon's announcement that he had come solely to effect an evacuation was reassuring. It invited the blockade of Khartoum that the Mahdi soon launched (I 76–81). Churchill found it a marvel that the city managed to withstand the siege for nearly a year. "That one man," Churchill remarks, "a European among Africans, a Christian among Mohammedans, should by his genius have inspired the efforts of 7,000 soldiers of inferior race, and by his courage have sustained the hearts of 30,000 inhabitants of notorious timidity, and with such materials and encumbrances have offered a vigorous resistance to the increasing attacks of an enemy who, though cruel, would yet accept surrender, during a period of 317 days is an event without parallel in history." In contemplating Gordon's conduct during the siege of Khartoum, he adds, "even the philosopher" will be "perplexed by the unforeseen magnificence of a human soul"; in consequence, he "will find his mournful reasonings disturbed by a bright gleam of doubt" (I 81–2).

No less remarkable was Gordon's impact on politics in Britain, for he won the struggle with Gladstone—albeit at a terrible cost. Churchill's father raised in Parliament the question of Gordon's safety. There was in due course a motion of censure (I 92–3), and though Gladstone "did not feel justified in involving the nation in operations in the heart of the Soudan for the purpose, not of saving the life of the envoy—for Gordon had but to embark on his steamers and come home—but simply in order to vindicate the personal honour of a man," he ended up being forced to do just that. As Churchill put it, "The Government which had long ignored the call of honour abroad, was driven to the Soudan by the cries of shame at home" (I 94). That the relief expedition arrived too late to save Gordon only reinforced his political victory (I 95–107). Gladstone's administration was returned to office in the election of 1885, but the outcome was public "despondency," and Britain lost in prestige. "The European opinion about Great Britain was not dissimilar from that lately held about Italy after the Abyssinian defeats, or about Spain since the Cuban War. It was not denied that the soldiers were brave. That was also admitted in the cases of Italy and Spain. They had failed, and Continental observers did not hesitate to declare that this failure was only the beginning of the end." Equally important was the fact that "in a hopeless way the belief was widely shared in England" as well (I 109).

Churchill's admiration for Gordon is qualified in one particular. The man's sense of honor was rooted in a species of religious sentiment that verged on fanaticism. If "his honour as a man" had the effect of putting "all courses which he did not think right, once and for all out of the question," and if it thereby "allayed many doubts and prevented many vain regrets," it was "his faith as a Christian" that served as "the real source of his strength. He was sure that beyond this hazardous existence, with all its wrongs and inequalities, another life awaited him—a life which, if he had been faithful and true here upon earth, would afford him greater faculties for good, and wider opportunities for their use" (I 89–90).

To convey all that Gordon's faith involved, Churchill turned to his journals and to their revelations concerning the general's treatment of the Austrian officer Rudolph Slatin. The latter had governed Darfur for the Egyptians, and for four years he had battled the Mahdi's rebellion. He had "the reputation of a brave and capable soldier," and those who knew him well "unhesitatingly confirmed" the impression left by his memoirs that he was "a man of feeling and of honour." But Slatin had "committed an act which deprived him of Gordon's sympathy and respect." When his soldiers at Darfur became discouraged in the face of defeat "and attributed their evil fortune to the fact that their commander was an infidel under the curse of the Almighty," he declared himself "a follower of the Prophet, and outwardly at least adopted the faith of Islam" (I 83–4).

Eventually, Slatin was forced to surrender—and "the religion he had assumed to secure victory, he observed to escape death." From the Mahdi's camp on the outskirts of Khartoum, he wrote secretly to Gordon to explain his surrender, to excuse his apostasy, and to ask that he be allowed to escape to Khartoum. Gordon was, however, "inflexible." His journals betray his contempt; and when Slatin's missives arrived, he insisted on treating him as a man who had been allowed his freedom on condition of a promise not to escape—which was not the case. As Churchill makes clear, Slatin's position differed not one whit from that of the black captives from the Egyptian army who had been made to serve the Mahdi, who deserted to Khartoum in considerable numbers, and who were welcomed there. Even when Slatin's correspondence with Gordon was discovered and he was put in chains and fed on a diet otherwise reserved for horses and mules, Gordon displayed no compassion. To make matters worse, Gordon desperately needed Slatin. "He was alone. He had no one in whose military capacity he could put the slightest confidence." It would have been preposterous for a man "who would have employed Zubair and bowed to expediency" to have rejected the Austrian officer's aid. But Gordon did so nonetheless. Slatin he could not countenance because of his apostasy. The old slavemonger Zubair may have been vicious and evil, but he "had never 'denied his Lord'" (I 84–7).

THE RULE OF AN ARMY

Churchill has little to say concerning the rule of the Mahdi, for Mohammed Ahmed outlived the sack of Khartoum by barely five months. He shifted the capital to the western bank of the White Nile at Omdurman, and he had a mosque, an arsenal, and a house built there for his own use. Then the typhus struck him down, and he was buried beneath the room in which he had expired (I 113–16). Churchill leaves it to his readers to imagine what would have taken place had the new prophet lived past the age of thirty-seven.

In the event, power fell to the Mahdi's caliph the crafty Abdullahi. The man had "achieved his not inconsiderable desires."

His country was at his feet. He had obtained the supreme authority in the Soudan. It remained, however, to preserve it. Like Macbeth he reflected, "To be thus is nothing; but to be safely thus——" And all the actions of his reign were directed to the strengthening of his own position. He ruled a turbulent people who had learnt their power, tigers who had tasted blood. The nice methods of constitutional Government were scarcely suited to such a task. Sterner and bloodier measures were necessary. Nor was Abdullahi the man to shrink from the harshest or the most treacherous expedients. His cruelty indeed may escape notice in a land where all men hold life cheap and regard suffering with callous indifference; but his low and unscrupulous cunning must excite the disgust and indignation even of the most tolerant chronicler. He was a crafty, vain, and savage man, faithless in all respects save one. His unswerving loyalty to the Mahdi must be credited to him as a single virtue (I 117).

Having thus condemned the man, Churchill goes on to concede that Abdullahi's "talents" were "indisputable." The man "understood affairs of peace and war; had studied the characters of his countrymen; and knew exactly how he might avail himself of their fanaticism. He could take advantage of their weaknesses and utilise their strength. With punctilious care he fostered their religious prejudices." In public, he "always preserved that dignified gravity which has distinguished the noblest of their race," and he observed "the forms of legality," bowing "before the judgment of the courts which were his instruments" and paying "an exaggerated respect to judges whom he effectively controlled by fear and bribery" (I 117–18).

After thus assessing the character of the Mahdi's caliph, Churchill qualifies his conclusion, for he recognizes that "the Khalifa is not rightly judged by the standards of European civilisation." To locate the man's "peers," he suggests, one must look to "barbaric potentates," such as Persia's shah or Afghanistan's amir.[11] In any case, "no execution" that Abdullahi "ordered at Omdurman was more terrible than those which, with the approval of the British Government, accompanied the suppression of the Indian Mutiny. His chastisement of rebellious tribes was less brutal than the massacres of Armenians, and far more rational than the anti-Semitism from which even the most polite nations have not purged themselves." What the caliph accomplished was straightforward: he managed to hold and retain the sovereignty by the instrument by which it had been won—the sword (I 118–19).

This was not easy. The Mahdi's "garrisons mutinied" against his successor; "Emirs plotted; prophets preached"—and beyond the borders of the Sudan stood the Abyssinians, the Egyptians, and outposts manned by

[11] Note, in this connection, Churchill, *The River War*, vol. 2, 216–19.

the English and the Italians. For thirteen years, Abdullahi managed. "Self-preservation was the guiding principle of his policy, his first object and his only excuse" (I 119–21). He eliminated rivals; he instituted a standing army; and he established his own tribe as a privileged body in Omdurman, enriched by the caliph, hated by the dispossessed, and therefore fiercely loyal to their benefactor and protector (I 121–5). Abdullahi's own tribe the

Taiasha Baggara controlled the black Jehadia, once the irregular troops of the Egyptians, now become the regulars of the Khalifa. The black Jehadia overawed the Arab army in the capital. The army in the capital dominated the forces in the provinces. The forces in the provinces subdued the inhabitants. The centralisation of power was assured by the concentration of military material.

To supplement these arrangements, the caliph struggled to keep the various tribes and clans in balance. "Such," Churchill admiringly concludes, "was the statecraft of a savage from Kordofan" (I 125–6).

In the thirteen years that passed before Britain's reconquest of the Sudan, Abdullahi managed to retain control within Khartoum, to inflict a terrible defeat on the Christian kingdom of Abyssinia, and to put down a religious revolt in the West (I 140–2). His authority survived all of this and famine and pestilence as well (I 142–4). But although the caliph's accomplishments were impressive, Churchill withholds his endorsement. He concedes that it might seem "at first a great advantage that the peoples of the Soudan, instead of being a multitude of wild, discordant tribes, should unite of their own accord into one strong community, actuated by a common spirit, living under fixed laws, and ruled by a single sovereign." But he weighs against these advantages the cost.

"There is," Churchill observes, "one form of centralised Government which is almost entirely unprogressive and beyond all other forms costly and tyrannical—the rule of an army."

Such a combination depends, not on the good faith and good will of its constituents, but on their discipline and almost mechanical obedience. Mutual fear, not mutual trust, promotes the cooperation of its individual members. History records many such dominations, ancient and modern, civilised or barbaric; and though education and culture may modify, they cannot change their predominant characteristics—a continual subordination of justice to expediency, an indifference to suffering, a disdain of ethical principles, a laxity of morals, and a complete ignorance of economics. The evil qualities of military hierarchies are uniform. The results of their rule are universally unfortunate. The degree may vary with time and place, but the political supremacy of an army always leads to the formation of a great centralised capital, to the consequent impoverishment of the provinces, to the degradation of the peaceful inhabitants through oppression and want, to the ruin of commerce, the decay of learning, and the ultimate demoralisation even of the military order through overbearing pride and sensual indulgence.

In the case of the Sudan, this was aggravated by the fact that "the Dervish Empire developed no virtue except courage, a quality more admirable than rare. The poverty of the land prevented magnificence. The ignorance of its inhabitants excluded refinement." It lacked the "high sense of personal honour" and the "ennobling patriotism" that elsewhere compensated for "a low standard of public justice" and for "economic follies." "Of the military dominations which history records," Churchill remarks, "the Dervish Empire was probably the worst" (I 112–13).

To the dervish cause, Churchill did make one concession. "In the passage of years," he wrote, "the Arabs might . . . have worked out their own salvation, as have the nations of Europe." In time, the army might have become "effete," and having withered and disappeared, it might have left behind "only the consciousness of nationality." Then, "a wise ruler" might have arisen to "establish a more equitable and progressive polity." In Churchill's judgment, "the natural course of developement is long, but true." In the end, however, "the Dervish dominion," which "was born of war" and "existed by war," was doomed to fall in the same fashion: "by war."

It began on the night of the sack of Khartoum. It ended abruptly thirteen years later in the battle of Omdurman. Like a subsidiary volcano it was flung up by one convulsion, blazed during the period of disturbance, and was destroyed by the still more violent shock that ended the eruption.

In the process, the natural course of the Sudan's development was interrupted, and "the British people" chose "a shorter though more terrible road for the tribes to follow" (I 113). Whether that interruption was favorable to the prospects for peace deserves consideration.

SCIENTIFIC CIVILIZATION

In the aftermath of the relief expedition, Churchill tells us, "when all the troops had retreated to Wady Halfa and all the Soudan garrisons had been massacred, the British people averted their eyes in shame and vexation from the valley of the Nile" (I 147). In time, however, the efforts of Sir Evelyn Baring and his chief aides bore fruit.

The Khedive and his Ministers lay quiet and docile in the firm grasp of the Consul-General. The bankrupt State was spending surpluses upon internal improvement. The disturbed Irrigation Department was vivifying the land. The derided army held the frontier against all comers. Astonishment gave place to satisfaction, and satisfaction grew into delight. The haunting nightmare of Egyptian politics ended.

Gradually, imperceptibly, "another dream began—a bright if vague vision of Imperial power, of transcontinental railways, of African Viceroys, of conquest and commerce" (I 148–9). When Sir Alfred Milner's celebratory *England in Egypt* was published in 1893, its "words rang like the trumpet-call which rallies the soldiers after the parapets are stormed, and summons them to complete the victory" (I 150). Men ceased to avert their gaze from Khartoum.

As it happened, the Egyptian army was ready to play its part. The old army had been disbanded at the end of 1882; and a new force was formed to take its place under the leadership of Sir Evelyn Wood, the first British sirdar of Egypt's army (I 150–2). "It was hardly possible," Churchill observes, "that the fertile soil and enervating climate of the Delta would have evolved a warrior race." Neither oppression nor poverty served to inspire the requisite patriotism. The *fellahin* of Egypt possessed courage —"a courage which bears pain and hardship in patience, which confronts ill-fortune with indifference, and which looks on death with apathetic composure"—but they lacked the necessary "desire to kill." They might be "cruel," but they were "never fierce." Theirs was "the courage of down-trodden peoples." They were "obedient, honest, sober, well-behaved, quick to learn, and above all physically strong" (I 152–3). From this material, the English officers managed to forge an army capable of defending Egyptian frontiers against the dervish empire to the south.

In 1884, the sirdar added to this nascent force the first of a series of battalions of Sudanese blacks. Where "the Egyptian was strong, patient, healthy, and docile," Churchill observes, these new troops possessed "delicate lungs, slim legs, and [a] loosely knit figure." They were "always excitable and often insubordinate"; they were "at once slovenly and uxorious." But the Sudanese soldier "displayed two tremendous military virtues" his Egyptian counterpart lacked. "To the faithful loyalty of a dog he added the heart of a lion. He loved his officer, and feared nothing in the world." It was, Churchill emphasizes, "the introduction of this element" that made of Egypt's army "a formidable military machine" (I 156). In 1885 and again in 1889, this machine repulsed the dervish attack.

When the British began once again to contemplate Khartoum, they thought of Charles Gordon as well.

The personal character of "the Christian hero" had produced a profound impression upon the people of Great Britain. His death at the hands of infidel savages transformed him into something like a martyr. There was an earnest desire on the part of a pious nation to dissociate his name from failure. The idea of revenge, ever attractive to the human heart, appeared to receive the consecration of religion. What community is altogether free from fanaticism? The spirit of the Crusaders stirred beneath the surface of scientific civilisation; and as the years passed by, there continued in England a strong undercurrent of public opinion which ran in the direction of "a holy war." (I 169)

This was exacerbated by the publication of books by escapees from the dervish dominion—prominent among them a tome penned by the long-suffering Austrian, Rudolph Slatin.

The misery of the Dervish dominions appealed to that great volume of generous humanitarian feeling which sways our civilised State. Extremes of thought met. Jingoism found—not for the first time—support at Exeter Hall. The name of Gordon fused the military, the fanatical, and the philanthropic spirits into one strong and moving influence; to this were added the impulse of the national pride in the regeneration of Egypt and the momentum of modern Imperialism; and these three forces—the sentimental, the intellectual, and the political—gradually overcame the fear and hatred of Soudan warfare which a long series of profitless campaigns had created in the mind of the average taxpayer. (I 169)

In the meantime, the Tories came to power; the Italians were defeated by the Abyssinians at Adowa; and it was feared that the dervish empire would attack the Italians at Kassala. With encouragement from Germany and Austria-Hungary, the new English government decided to make a demonstration on the Wady Halfa frontier. Though caught off guard, the Egyptians seized the opportunity. An attempt by France to prevent Egypt from securing the necessary funds was thwarted, and the sirdar was given instructions authorizing him to prepare an expedition into the Dongola province of the Sudan (I 170–81). When that expedition succeeded, the cabinet elected to reconquer Egypt's lost province in its entirety.

The man selected for the task was Horatio Herbert Kitchener, an English officer knowledgeable in Arabic who had hurried to Egypt at the time of the British occupation and who had made himself indispensable. By the time of the expedition, he had become sirdar of the Egyptian army (I 159–66). Churchill manages to convey a mixture of admiration and distaste. The man was "little known to and less liked by his brother officers."

His promotion on the recommendation of Sir Evelyn Baring produced "astonishment" and even "disgust" in the Egyptian army. But Kitchener had revealed "strange powers of organisation" while serving as adjutant general in the war office in Cairo, and his subsequent performance more than justified the British agent's confidence in him (I 164–6).[12]

The details of the fighting need not detain us. It suffices to say that the British soldiers and officers and the Egyptian and Sudanese battalions commanded by the latter distinguished themselves, and that the dervish forces displayed ingenuity and great courage. Churchill tells the story in detail, but he intimates at the outset that Kitchener's "strange powers of rapid and comprehensive arrangement" were decisive (I 187). The real campaign was fought not against the caliph Abdullahi and his minions but against nature, and it displayed man's desire to prevail as that desire articulated itself within scientific civilization. Kitchener personified this force. He was responsible for the "machine-like preparations" for the "destruction" of the dervish dominion (I 218).

Some were inclined to attribute victory to "the 'Sirdar's luck.'" Churchill is perfectly prepared to concede "the influence of Fortune." As he puts it, "countless and inestimable are the chances of war." But he denies that accident determined the outcome. "Much depended on forethought: much on machinery; little was left to chance" (I 235–6). Moreover, early on, as Churchill makes clear, Kitchener and his army were beset by every species of misfortune: weather, disease, and mechanical failure stood in their way (I 236–74). If the army persevered, it was because the sirdar's "organising talents" were equal to the unforeseen crises that they confronted. The man's "grasp of detail and power of arrangement were never better displayed" than in an emergency. "He knew the exact position of every soldier, coolie, camel, or donkey at his disposal" (I 253).

The element crucial to victory was the railroad. "In a tale of war," Churchill observes, "the reader's mind is filled with the fighting." Mindful of his audience, in his narrative, the author of *The River War* does not stint in this regard. He tells us of "the battle—with its vivid scenes, its moving incidents, its plain and tremendous results," for he knows that it "excites imagination and commands attention," and he recognizes that "the eye is fixed on the fighting brigades as they move amid the smoke; on the swarming figures of the enemy; on the General, serene and determined, mounted in the middle of his Staff." But, at the same time, Churchill

---

[12] See also ibid., 151, 154.

insists on discussing at length "the long trailing line of communications," which all too often passes "unnoticed." He concedes that "victory" may be a "beautiful, bright-coloured flower," but he contends that "transport is the stem without which it could never have blossomed" (I 275–6).

Churchill's tale concerns the conquest of nature by scientific civilization. The lessons that he teaches should not be lost on a generation that witnessed the defeat of Iraq in the Gulf War.

It cannot be denied that a battle, the climax to which all military operations tend, is an event which is not controlled by strategy or organisation. The scheme may be well planned, the troops well fed, the ammunition plentiful, and the enemy entangled, famished, or numerically inferior. The glorious uncertainties of the field can yet reverse everything. The human element—in defiance of experience, probability, and logic—may produce a wholly irrational result, and a starving, outmanoeuvred army win food, safety, and honour by their bravery.

Having acknowledged all of this, Churchill then adds that "such considerations apply with greater force to wars where both sides are equal in equipment and discipline." It was his conviction that "in savage warfare in a flat country the power of modern machinery is such that flesh and blood can scarcely prevail, and the chances of battle are reduced to a minimum." He concludes, then, that "fighting the Dervish was primarily a matter of transport. The Khalifa was conquered on the railway" (I 276–7).

It would therefore be tempting to think the war on the Nile a mundane event. Churchill insists that it was not: the conquest of nature has its heroes as does the conquest of men. Kitchener was one such. He managed to advance the project despite the obstacles it faced, and in a tight spot he was perfectly prepared to gamble. The railway was necessary because of the cataracts that made the Nile at various points unnavigable. For the most part, the army could build its railroad along the river—but that was not possible in the long stretch from Merawi to Abu Hamed. The crucial question was whether, under conditions of war, it would be possible to extend the line across the Nubian desert. The sirdar

appealed to expert opinion. Eminent railway engineers in England were consulted. They replied with unanimity that, having due regard to the circumstances, and remembering the conditions of war under which the work must be executed, it was impossible to construct such a line. Distinguished soldiers were approached on the subject. They replied that the scheme was not only impossible, but absurd. Many other persons who were not consulted volunteered the opinion that the whole idea was that of a lunatic, and predicted ruin and disaster to the expedition.

In this situation, Kitchener listened to the advice and "reflected on it duly." Then, he ordered that the railway "be constructed without more delay" (I 283–6). He oversaw the work himself. "Usually ungracious, rarely impatient, never unreasonable, he moved among the workshops and about the line, satisfying himself that all was proceeding with economy and dispatch." In the process, he won "the affection of the subalterns. Nowhere in the Soudan was he better known than on the railroad. Nowhere was he so ardently believed in. That he deserved the confidence is beyond dispute. That he reciprocated the affection is more doubtful" (I 297).

Kitchener's gamble paid off (I 286–309). "On the day that the first troop train steamed into the fortified camp at the confluence of the Nile and the Atbara rivers," Churchill remarks, "the doom of the Dervishes was sealed."

It had now become possible, with convenience and speed, to send into the heart of the Soudan great armies independent of the season of the year and of the resources of the country; to supply them not only with abundant food and ammunition, but with all the variegated paraphernalia of scientific war; and to support their action on land by a powerful flotilla of gunboats, which could dominate the river and command the banks, and could at any moment make their way past Khartoum even to Sennar, Fashoda, or Sobat.

In Churchill's judgment, "though the battle was not yet fought, the victory was won. The Khalifa, his capital, and his army were now within the Sirdar's reach. It remained only to pluck the fruit in the most convenient hour, with the least trouble and at the smallest cost" (I 308–9).

IN DUBIOUS BATTLE

In reading Churchill's narrative, one cannot help but detect a triumphant tone. His first volume, which takes the form of a history, tells the story of the reconquest up through the battle of Atbara on 8 April 1898 (I 310–462); the second, which takes the form of a memoir, begins with a firsthand account of Churchill's own involvement in the final campaign and the battle of Omdurman on 2 September 1898 (II 1–227). Although he has prefaced this account by arguing that the result of the struggle was a foregone conclusion, he takes care at every point to assess the strategy and tactics employed by each side. After discussing the decisive battle's immediate aftermath (II 228–300) and the Fashoda incident (II 301–21), in the same spirit, he reviews the conduct of the war as a whole (II 322–79). To the dervish empire Churchill gives its due, but his pride in his own countrymen, in their technical skills, and in what they have made of the human resources of Egypt and the Sudan is evident on many a page.

It would be comparatively easy to depict Churchill as a naïve adherent to the doctrine of progress. He certainly has no compunction in speaking of his colleagues as "the educated soldiers of a civilising Empire" and in describing the battle of Omdurman as "the most signal triumph ever gained by the arms of science over barbarians." His satisfaction in the victory effected by "the soldiers of scientific war" is apparent in his choice of words. "Within the space of five hours the strongest and best-armed savage army yet arrayed against a modern European Power had been destroyed and dispersed, with hardly any difficulty, comparatively small risk, and insignificant loss to the victors" (II 100, 144, 164). Elsewhere as well, Churchill celebrates the accomplishments of modernity.

While en route up the Nile, he stopped first at the Temple of Luxor and then at the Temple of Philae. Of the former, he wrote:

Something in the strange shapes of the great pillars appeals to the human love of the mystical. It requires no effort of imagination to roof the temple and fill its great hall with the awe-struck worshippers, or to occupy the odd, nameless chambers at the far end with the powerful priests who crushed the body and soul out of ancient Egypt. Now that the roof is off and the sun shines into all the nooks and corners, we may admire the beauty of the work without fearing its evil purposes. (II 7–8)

In this passage, as in those critical of the religious passions guiding Charles Gordon and Mohammed Ahmed, Churchill reveals himself as a child of the Enlightenment. In his account of the Temple of Philae, he presents himself also as a proponent of economic development; its "celebrated ruins" provoked in him a keen "hostility." He found himself "offended" by its broken pillars and walls. "The past," he writes, "looked down on the present, and, offended by its exuberant vitality, seemed grimly to repeat the last taunt that age can fling at youth: 'You will be as I am one of these days'" (II 9).

The real object of Churchill's annoyance was not the temple itself but the antiquarians. He favored the project of building a great dam at Aswan for the purpose of improving Egyptian irrigation to the south. Preeminent among the opponents of the scheme were the defenders of the temple, which would be left submerged by the rising waters (II 7–19). Churchill refrains from assailing "the small but beautiful ruin"; he is prepared to "believe that the god to whom it was raised was once worthy of human reverence"—but only if that god "would willingly accept as a nobler memorial the life-giving lake beneath which his temple would be buried." Otherwise, "it would be time for a rational and utilitarian generation to tear the monument of such a monster to pieces," for the sacrifice of 1,485 million cubic meters of water would be "the most cruel, most wicked, and most senseless sacrifice ever offered on the altar of a false religion." But his real opponent is neither the temple nor its god.

Behind it stand the archæologists. Because a few persons whose functions are far removed from those which may benefit mankind—profitless chippers of stone, rummagers in the dustheaps of the past—have raised an outcry, nominally on account of the tourists, the sacrifice of water—the lifeblood of Egypt—is being offered up. The State must struggle and the people starve, in order that professors may exult and tourists find some space on which to scratch their names. (II 18–19)

When forced to choose between the living and the dead, between progress and nostalgia, between modernity and antiquity, the young Churchill was not inclined to hesitate.

This fact helps explain his willingness to contemplate the loss of life that the reconquest of the Sudan required. When he considered "the melancholy end" of the "brave men" who fell in the war, Churchill suggested that "theirs is no worse than the common fate of man." He was persuaded that

when we are ourselves overtaken by death, the surroundings of home and friends will not make much appreciable difference. To struggle and choke in the hushed and darkened room of a London house, while, without, the great metropolis is planning and contriving—while the special editions report the progress of the latest European crisis, and all the world is full of the business of the morrow—will not seem less unsatisfactory than, when thrilled with fierce yet generous emotions, to die in the sunshine and be spaded under before the night (I 441–2).

In any case, he had little doubt that something good had been accomplished. "The destruction of a state of society which had long become an anachronism—an insult as well as a danger to civilisation; the liberation of the great waterway; perhaps the foundation of an African India; certainly the settlement of a long dispute"—Churchill regarded these as "cenotaphs which will scarcely be unregarded during the present generation" (II 204).

Churchill was no friend to Islamic rule. "How dreadful," he wrote, "are the curses which Mohammedanism lays on its votaries!" Among these are "fanatical frenzy" and a "fearful fatalistic apathy" that give rise to "improvident habits, slovenly systems of agriculture, sluggish methods

of commerce, and insecurity of property." He deplored its "degraded sen-
sualism" and argued that "the fact that in Mohammedan law every woman
must *belong* to some man as his absolute property—either as a child, a
wife, or a concubine—must delay the final extinction of slavery until the
faith of Islam has ceased to be a great power among men." He conceded
the bravery and loyalty of individual Muslims, but he insisted that the
influence of Islam "paralyses the social developement of those who follow it." In his opinion, there is "no stronger retrograde force . . . in the
world." He was so impressed by its power as "a militant and proselytising
faith" that he was led to remark, "Were it not that Christianity is sheltered
in the strong arms of science—the science against which it had vainly
struggled—the civilisation of modern Europe might fall, as fell the civilisation of ancient Rome" (II 248–50).

Churchill did not doubt that the reconquest was a just war. To indicate
why, he drew attention to the Egyptian claim and reminded his readers
that the dervish dominion was "an annoyance to civilised nations" (II
392–6). He also pointed to the map. "To unite territories that could not
indefinitely have continued divided; to combine peoples whose future
welfare is inseparably intermingled; to collect energies which, concentrated, may promote a common interest; to join together what could not
improve apart—these are the objects which, history will pronounce, have
justified the enterprise" (II 389–90). In this spirit, Churchill devoted the
last eighteen pages of his work to a discussion of the future development
of Egypt and the Sudan and to the institutions and spirit of administration
most likely to contribute to that end (II 396–414).[13]

At no time, however, does Churchill allow his enthusiasm for modern,
European scientific civilization to get the better of his judgment. He takes
note early on of the British propensity "to regard the re-conquest of the
Soudan as a work of deliverance." But he has little use for the "pathetic
pictures of the unspeakable joy of the Arab, freed from the accursed yoke
of the Khalifa," that "have been drawn with [such] skill and elaboration"
(I 456–7). He does not blame the sirdar for choosing in his dispatch to
regard the "natural manifestation of joy on the part of the townsfolk" of
Khartoum "at hearing they were not to be put to the sword as their
satisfaction at their deliverance from the rule of the Khalifa," but he
cannot countenance the claim (II 173–4). He is impressed by the fact that,
in the aftermath of the great battle, the caliph Abdullahi "found safety

---

[13] See also ibid., 226–7.

and welcome among his flying soldiers" and that "the surviving Emirs hurried to his side" (II 180–2). And critical though he is of the man, he feels compelled to confess that it is preposterous to suppose that "his rule was odious to his subjects" and that "the British and Egyptian armies entered Omdurman to free the people from his yoke." "Never," reports this eyewitness, "were rescuers more unwelcome" (II 394–5).

Moreover, Churchill refuses to attribute the "valour" of the dervish soldiers to "mad fanaticism." Such a claim he considers "a cruel injustice." "Why," he asks, "should we regard as madness in the savage what would be sublime in civilised men?" In the process he displays flashes of the resoluteness that would become visible again in 1940 and 1941. "I hope," he writes, "that if evil days should come upon our own country, and the last army which a collapsing Empire could interpose between London and the invader were dissolving in rout and ruin, that there would be some—even in these modern days—who would not care to accustom themselves to a new order of things and tamely survive the disaster" (I 162).

In the same spirit, despite his pronounced distaste for Islam, Churchill comes to the defense of the Mahdi. He visited the man's tomb shortly after the great battle, and he pondered the fact that

this place had been for more than ten years the most sacred and holy thing that the people of the Soudan knew. Their miserable lives had perhaps been brightened, perhaps in some way ennobled by the contemplation of something which they did not quite understand, but which they believed exerted a protecting influence. It had gratified that instinctive desire for the mystic which all human creatures possess, and which is perhaps the strongest reason for believing in a progressive destiny and a future state.

Churchill then fiercely deplores the sirdar's decision to profane the tomb, raze it to the ground, exhume the corpse of the Mahdi, separate his head from his limbs and trunk, and ship it to Cairo. "Whatever misfortunes the life of Mohammed Ahmed may have caused," he remarks, "he was a man of considerable nobility of character, a priest, a soldier, and a patriot. He won great battles; he stimulated and revived religion. He founded an empire. To some extent he reformed the public morals. Indirectly, by making slaves into soldiers, he diminished slavery." Churchill denies that it is possible for "an impartial person" to read the testimony of figures such as Rudolph Slatin "without feeling that the only gentle influence, the only humane element in the hard Mohammedan State, emanated from this famous rebel." He looked after his prisoners; he protected the Christian priests from the mob (II 211–13). In his concern for the well-being of those in distress, he displayed the very qualities of character that the leading representative of scientific civilization seemed to lack. It is no accident that Churchill's reflections on the Mahdi are soon followed by his grisly account of Kitchener's failure to make provision for the dying and the wounded survivors of the dervish host (II 219–26).[14]

When he reexamines the arguments of those who defended Kitchener's decision to profane the Mahdi's body and tomb, Churchill notices a certain "confusion of thought" suggestive of "insincerity." Some dismissed the matter as something of "little consequence" on the grounds that the Mahdi was "a fallen idol" who no longer commanded the loyalty of the Sudanese Arabs. Others contended that the prophet's influence was so "great" and his memory "so powerful" that his tomb would otherwise have become "a place of pilgrimage" inspiring "an element of fanaticism" likely to disturb the victors' rule. Apart from the obvious contradiction, Churchill finds both arguments "absurd." If the Sudanese no longer cared for the Mahdi, "it was an act of Vandalism and folly to destroy the only fine building which might attract the traveller and interest the historian." He finds it "a gloomy augury for the future of the Soudan that the first action of its civilised conquerors and present ruler should have been to level the one pinnacle which rose above the mud houses." If, as was quite obvious, the Sudanese still revered their prophet, then, Churchill declares, "to destroy what was sacred and holy to them was a wicked act, of which the true Christian, no less than the philosopher, must express his abhorrence" (II 213–14).

There was a point to Churchill's objection that went beyond moral indignation. He was concerned also with the maintenance of public peace. As he points out, what Kitchener had done would have been "condemned" as well "by the wise public servants who administer the Indian Empire." It was, he notes, an offense against the penal code of India for anyone to insult the religion of anyone, whether true or false. "It is," he explains, "because respect is always shown to all shades of religious feeling in India by the dominant race, that our rule is accepted by the mass of the people." But pacification is not Churchill's first concern. "If the Soudan," he concludes, "is to be administered on principles the reverse of those which have been successful in India, and if such conduct is to be characteristic

---

[14] See also ibid., vol. 1, 439–40; vol. 2, 93–4, 195–7.

of its Government, then it would be better if Gordon had never given his life nor Kitchener won his victories" (II 214–15).

As this last observation should remind us, Churchill was a peacemaker who was never prepared to purchase peace at just any price. From the outset, he cared more for nobility than for peace, and he was never simply a partisan for his own country and its way of life. That he admired much in Kitchener one need not doubt. But there was much as well in that representative of scientific civilization that gave him pause. He ends his discussion of the aftermath of the great battle of Omdurman with a reflection that returns his readers to the perspective that he offered at the beginning of his book: "The terrible machinery of scientific war had done its work. The Dervish host was scattered and destroyed. Their end, however, only anticipates that of the victors; for Time, which laughs at science, as science laughs at valour, will in due course contemptuously brush both combatants away." He can imagine that in time, when "a mighty system of irrigation" has made "a fertile garden" of the "desolate plain of Omdurman," a farmer may turn up "a skull amid the luxuriant crop" and remark on the fact that on that ground a battle had once taken place (II 226). But Churchill is by no means certain that the Sudan will ever see so mighty a system of irrigation.

In the funeral oration recorded in Thucydides' histories, Pericles suggests that through Athens and the greatness of its imperial achievement his compatriots will secure in fame and glory a species of eternal life: "We inspire wonder now, and we shall in the future. We have need neither for the panegyrics of a Homer nor for the praises of anyone to whose conjecture of events the truth will do harm. For we have forced every sea and every land to give access to our daring (tolma); and we have in all places established everlasting memorials of evils [inflicted on enemies] and of good [done to friends]."[15] In his last recorded speech, the Athenian statesman asks his compatriots to look forward to the day when Athens will no longer exist.

Remember that this city has the greatest name among all mankind because she has never yielded to adversity, but has spent more lives in war and has endured severer hardships than any other city. She has held the greatest power known to men up to our time, and the memory of her power will be laid up forever for those who come after. Even if we now have to yield (since all things that grow also decay), the memory shall remain that, of all the Greeks, we held sway over the greatest

---

[15] Thucydides 2.41.4.

number of Hellenes; that we stood against our foes, both when they were united and when each was alone, in the greatest wars; and that we inhabited a city wealthier and greater than all.

Pericles concedes that imperial Athens is envied and loathed, but argues that such hatred is short-lived—since "the splendor (*lamprotes*) of the present is the glory of the future laid up as a memory for all time."[16]

Churchill makes no such claims on England's behalf; he is aware that Athens might not be remembered had Thucydides not acted in Homer's stead. And if he takes pride in his country's conquests, he does so at least in part with an eye to the civilizing effects of Britannia's rule. He does, however, demand of his readers what Pericles reportedly asked from his listeners. Early in the first volume, when he has occasion to comment on the progress of the religious and political revival inspired by Mohammed Ahmed, Churchill prefaces his discussion with a series of melancholy observations. "All great movements," he writes,

every vigorous impulse that a community may feel, become perverted and distorted as time passes, and the atmosphere of the earth seems fatal to the noble aspiration of its peoples. A wide humanitarian sympathy in a nation easily degenerates into hysteria. A military spirit tends towards brutality. Liberty leads to licence, restraint to tyranny. The pride of race is distended to blustering arrogance. The fear of God produces bigotry and superstition. There appears no exception to the mournful rule, and the best efforts of men, however glorious their early results, have dismal endings; like plants which shoot and bud forth beautiful flowers, and then grow rank and coarse and are withered by the winter. (I 57–8)

He can face this sad fact, and, far more easily than Pericles, he can recognize and cope with time's judgment on the relative insignificance of human endeavors, for he shares in "that instinctive desire for the mystic" which the Mahdi inspired in the Sudanese, because for him it is "the strongest reason for believing in a progressive destiny" (II 212). To be precise, Churchill proves able to "reflect that decay gives birth to fresh life, and that new enthusiasms spring up to take the places of those that die, even as the acorn is nourished by the dead leaves of the oak or the phoenix rose from the ashes of the pyre, that the hope strengthens, that the rise and fall of men and their movements are only the changing foliage of the ever-growing tree of life, while underneath a greater evolution goes on continually" (I 58).

It is by no means certain that the author of *The River War* was a

[16] Ibid., 2.64.

believing Christian. As he evidences in his discussion of the manner in which "the human love of the mystical" was exploited at the Temple of Luxor for the purpose of subjugating mankind (II 8), in his youth, Churchill displayed a fierce dislike of the phenomenon that his fellow Englishman James Harrington was the first to dub "priestcraft."[17] It is clear, however, that he had a profound respect for the notion of providence and that he deemed a belief in nature's provision, or in that of nature's God, essential to the spiritedness that gives rise in man to the noble and healthy desire to prevail.

As we already have had occasion to note, Churchill finds something to celebrate even in the desolation that stretches out from the Nile. There, he writes, just before sunset, "a delicious flush brightens and enlivens the landscape. It is as though some Titanic artist in the hour of inspiration was retouching the picture, painting in dark purple shadows among the rocks, strengthening the lights on the sand, gilding and beautifying everything, and making the whole scene live." Eventually, of course, the colors dissolve as the sunlight wanes, and everything becomes dark and "grey, like a man's cheek when he is bleeding to death." Then, travelers such as Churchill "are left sad and sorrowful in the dark," but eventually "the stars light up and remind us that there is always something beyond"(I 5–6).[18] One cannot reread this passage after having perused the entire book without being reminded of what Churchill has to say concerning the journals that Charles Gordon penned during the siege of Khartoum. "Reading their pages," he writes, "the soldier may draw instruction from the military events; the Christian will rejoice in the grandeur of his faith; the patriot may exult in the pride of nationality; and even the philosopher, perplexed by the unforeseen magnificence of a human soul, will find his mournful reasonings disturbed by a bright gleam of doubt" (I 81–2).[19] This understanding of the universe and of man's place in it, this awareness of nature's beauty and of the transcendent realm to which it points, and this disposition of wonder and awe in the face of a man of great soul

---

[17] In this connection, see Mark Goldie, "The Civil Religion of James Harrington," in *The Languages of Political Theory in Early-Modern Europe*, ed. Anthony Pagden (Cambridge: Cambridge University Press, 1987), 197–222.

[18] See also Churchill, *The River War*, vol. 1, 438; vol. 2, 188, 245.

[19] Cf. Immanuel Kant, *Kritik der Praktischen Vernunft*, II Beschluss, in Kant, *Werke in Zehn Bänden*, ed. Wilhelm Weischedel (Darmstadt: Wissenschaftliche Buchgesellschaft, 1968), vol. 6, 300, which should be read in light of Ronald Beiner, "Kant, the Sublime, and Nature," in *Kant and Political Philosophy: The Contemporary Legacy*, ed. Ronald Beiner and William James Booth (New Haven: Yale University Press, 1993), 276–88.

provided Winston Churchill with the equanimity that he needed to function effectively as a prudent statesman and enabled him to accept, and
even embrace, the limits of politics—as it provides us with the context
within which to interpret his endeavors in the pursuit of peace and enables
us to understand why, in certain circumstances, he preferred war.[20]

[20] One may wish to compare Kirk Emmert's discussion, on pp. 79–81 of this book, of
Churchill's novel *Savrola* and of his later essay "Painting as a Pastime."

5

Peace and two wars:
South Africa, 1896–1914

S. BURRIDGE SPIES

In June 1891, when he was forty-two years old, Lord Randolph Churchill wrote to his seventeen-year-old son, Winston, from South Africa: "I expect when you are my age you will see S[outh] Africa to be the most populous and wealthy of all our colonies."[1] Not all South Africa was, in fact, under British colonial rule in 1891. There had been a duality of white political power in South Africa between British-imperial and Boer-republican control for nearly forty years—by 1891 independent black authority south of the Limpopo River had been eliminated. That situation was the result of the Great Trek (the mass exodus of Dutch-speaking farmers from the Cape Colony) to the interior in the 1830s and subsequent British official policy. After an initial attempt to annex the territory in Natal occupied by these white farmers (who have come to be known as Voortrekkers), Britain granted independence to the white inhabitants north of the Vaal River (1852) and in the territory between that river and the Orange River (1854). Thus, independent Boer republics, the South African Republic and the Orange Free State, were created.[2] Chaotic conditions in the former republic enabled Britain to annex the Transvaal in 1877 in the hope of implementing the scheme of the British colonial secretary, Lord Carnarvon, to form a federation of British states in South Africa. A successful Boer rebellion against British rule and the defeat of the British army at Majuba in 1881 led to a new British government's restoring a somewhat limited form of Boer independence in the Transvaal.[3]

---

[1] Quoted in *WSC* I 152.
[2] T. R. H. Davenport, *South Africa: A Modern History*, 4th ed. (London: Macmillan, 1991), 44–8, 170–1; H. J. van Aswegen, *History of South Africa to 1854* (Pretoria: J. L. Van Schaik, 1991), 254–96.
[3] Davenport, *South Africa*, 177–9.

There is no doubt that the factors Lord Randolph believed would lead to large-scale immigration to, and prosperity in, South Africa were the conditions he observed in the Transvaal or South African Republic under President Paul Kruger. The discovery of gold on the Witwatersrand, the highveld heart of the Transvaal, in 1886 had led to the founding of Johannesburg, the influx of vast numbers of Uitlanders (that is, Outlanders or foreigners, who were mostly British subjects) to the republic, and the enrichment and transformation of Kruger's state. Nineteen years earlier, diamonds had been discovered in the disputed territory of Griqualand West, but the claims of the other Boer republic, the Orange Free State, had been overruled and the diamond lands had been annexed by the British government.[4]

Lord Randolph Churchill in June 1891 had fewer than four years to live. According to one of his biographers, he had gone to southern Africa in search of sport, gold, and health.[5] He had stayed with the premier of the Cape Colony, the capitalist and imperialist Cecil John Rhodes, in Cape Town and dined in Salisbury (now Harare) with Rhodes's associate Dr. Leander Starr Jameson and other officials of the British South Africa (or Chartered) Company—which aimed to develop the territory north of the Limpopo. Lord Randolph also invested in gold mines being opened on the Witwatersrand by deep-level mining techniques.[6]

THE JAMESON RAID

In December 1895, Rhodes, Jameson, Chartered Company officials, deep-level mining interests, and the colonial secretary, Joseph Chamberlain, became embroiled in what has become known as the Jameson Raid. In essence, Rhodes, Chamberlain, and certain mine owners aimed to overthrow Kruger's state by force. They foresaw an uprising in the Transvaal against Kruger's government by certain mine owners, who had political grievances (particularly Kruger's raising of the residential qualifications for Uitlanders to obtain the franchise) and economic complaints, and planned an invasion of the Transvaal by a Chartered Company force led by Jameson. A strip of territory in the Bechuanaland Protectorate had

[4] Ibid., 174–5; J. S. Marais, *The Fall of Kruger's Republic* (Oxford: Clarendon Press, 1961), 1.
[5] Robert Rhodes James, *Lord Randolph Churchill* (London: Weidenfeld & Nicolson, 1959), 349.
[6] Ibid., 351; R. F. Foster, *Lord Randolph Churchill: A Political Life* (Oxford: Clarendon Press, 1981), 373–4.

been acquired by the Chartered Company especially for this purpose as a "jumping-off ground" from the colonial office. After the overthrow of the republican government, British sovereignty would be proclaimed over the Transvaal. Some historians have stressed the economic motives of the main role-players, but Rhodes's political ambitions, aided and abetted by Chamberlain and some mine owners, were the prime factors.

The Jameson Raid was a fiasco—but it had extremely serious consequences. Jameson and a force of about 600 men invaded the Transvaal on 30 December 1895, even though the revolt in Johannesburg never came about. Rhodes, in Cape Town, did not act to stop Jameson. A Boer force confronted Jameson's force near Krugersdorp, west of Johannesburg, and after suffering some casualties the raiders surrendered and were sent to jail.[7]

The Jameson Raid is important in the context of this chapter both for the attitude of the youthful, politically conscious Winston Churchill at the time—probably the earliest statement of his views on peace and war in South Africa—as well as for his interpretation of the event in later years.

Winston Churchill had received a commission in the cavalry regiment, the Fourth Hussars, in February 1895.[8] By January 1896 the twenty-one-year-old subaltern had returned home from the United States and the seat of operations in Cuba (where he had spent some of his leave to "observe" the war between Spanish troops and rebel forces). Back in Britain, in the exalted company of Arthur Balfour, the Unionist First Lord of the Treasury and leader of the House of Commons, the prominent Liberal H. H. Asquith, and the wealthy Lord Rothschild, Churchill commented to his mother on the Jameson Raid. His attitude was somewhat ambivalent. No doubt influenced by the views of his fellow guests, he mused:

I expect that Dr. Jameson and his officers will be dealt with as severely as the government know how. I have not heard a word of excuse or sympathy from anyone. Mr Balfour—particularly—seemed to think that they deserved exemplary punishment. . . . I suppose they are right and that these men who never considered us—or English interests—should in their turn receive no consideration from us.[9]

---

[7] On the Jameson Raid, see Marais, *Fall of Kruger's Republic*, 64–95; Jean van der Poel, *The Jameson Raid* (Cape Town: Oxford University Press, 1951); Elizabeth Longford, *Jameson's Raid: The Prelude to the Boer War* (Johannesburg: Jonathan Ball Publishers, 1962); Jeffrey Butler, *The Liberal Party and the Jameson Raid* (Oxford: Clarendon Press, 1968). On the debate on the economic causes of the raid, see particularly G. Blainey, "Lost Causes of the Jameson Raid," *Economic History Review* 18 (1965): 350–66, and R. Mendelsohn, "Blainey and the Jameson Raid: The Debate Renewed," *Journal of Southern African Studies* 6, no. 2 (1980): 157–70.

[8] WSC I 243–4.   [9] WSC I 265–80.

Nevertheless Churchill could not hide his sympathy for the raiders. As he continued his letter, he stated, "But all the same I venture to doubt the advisability of severity. South African opinion and South African interests ought not to be altogether disregarded and the whole of the Cape would vigorously protest against—and bitterly resent—the infliction of such a punishment."[10] A truer reflection of Churchill's views in 1896 on the Jameson Raid may well be summarized in the words he wrote more than thirty years later:

> I need scarcely say that at 21 I was all for Dr. Jameson and his men. I understood fairly well the causes of the dispute on both sides. I longed for the day on which we should "avenge Majuba." I was shocked to see our Conservative Government act so timidly in the crisis. I was ashamed to see them truckling to a misguided Liberal Opposition and even punishing those brave raiders.[11]

After the surrender of Jameson and his men, Kruger handed them over to the British government. Five of the fifteen officers with Jameson were tried in London for violating the Foreign Enlistment Act. They were found guilty—Jameson and one other officer received prison sentences of fifteen months (Jameson was released after four months because of illness), the others five to seven months.[12] Cecil Rhodes was forced to resign as prime minister of the Cape Colony[13] (a modern historian has described him as "a burnt-out case" after the raid).[14] A British parliamentary committee of inquiry (nine of the fifteen members—including Chamberlain, who also sat on the committee—were supporters of the government) condemned Rhodes's conduct, but exonerated Chamberlain and the colonial office of being implicated in the raid.[15]

The raid had other important repercussions: Kaiser Wilhelm II's telegram of congratulations to Kruger at defeating the raiders increased Anglo-German antagonism, Kruger's government gained a legitimate pretext for building up Boer armaments, Boer-British relations in South Africa suffered an enormous setback, and the possibility of war in that country increased immensely.[16]

---

[10] *WSC* I 280.
[11] Winston S. Churchill, *My Early Life: A Roving Commission* (London: Fontana, 1965), 106.
[12] Van der Poel, *Jameson Raid*, 179–81.   [13] Ibid., 155.
[14] Iain R. Smith, "The Origins of the South African War (1899–1902): A Reappraisal," *South African Historical Journal* 22 (1990): 32.
[15] Van der Poel, *Jameson Raid*, 199, 227–8.
[16] Ibid., passim; Longford, *Prelude to the Boer War*, passim; Davenport, *South Africa*, 188–9.

After the First World War Churchill (who as a member of the Liberal Party had helped institute conciliatory measures in South Africa after 1902) expressed views on the Jameson Raid far removed from his remarks and attitude in 1896. He maintained: "I date the beginning of these violent times in our country from the Jameson raid in 1896."[17] A few years later, in his autobiographical work on his early years, he averred: "In December 1895 there had occurred in South Africa an event which seems to me as I look back over my map of life to be a fountain of ill."[18] The Cape politician J. X. Merriman expressed remarkably similar sentiments in 1917: "Our troubles date from Jameson's ill-considered enterprise."[19]

But the overriding sentiment of Churchill at the time, or shortly after the Jameson Raid, was one of intense patriotism, and an ardent desire for a showdown with the Transvaal Boers. Toward the end of 1896 or the beginning of 1897 he wrote a memorandum, which was probably not published before the war:

Imperial aid must redress the wrongs of the Outlanders; Imperial troops must curb the insolence of the Boers. There must be no half measures. . . . Sooner or later, in a righteous cause or a picked quarrel with the approval of Europe, or in the teeth of Germany for the sake of our Empire, for the sake of our honour, for the sake of the race, we must fight the Boers.[20]

These words have the ring of some of the more bellicose language that came to be used by Sir Alfred Milner, who was sent by Chamberlain as high commissioner to South Africa in 1897. In 1898 Milner informed Chamberlain: "There is no way out of the political troubles of S[outh] Africa except reform in the Transvaal or war. And at present the chances of reform in the Transvaal are worse than ever."[21] In August 1899 Milner explained to the Liberal Sir Edward Grey that Kruger's government "want to squeeze the newcomers into the existing mould. I want them to burst it."[22]

---

[17] Winston S. Churchill, *The World Crisis*, 3d ed., 5 vols. (London: Thornton Butterworth, 1927), vol. 1, 26.

[18] Churchill, *My Early Life*, 101.

[19] Merriman Papers (South African Library, Cape Town): correspondence no. 570 of 1917, Merriman to Sir Horace Plumkett, December 12, 1917.

[20] *WSC* I 449–50.

[21] C. Headlam, ed., *The Milner Papers*, 2 vols. (London: Cassell and Company, 1931), vol. 1, 221, Milner to Chamberlain, February 23, 1898.

[22] Ibid., 478, Milner to Grey, August 7, 1899.

ORIGINS OF THE SOUTH AFRICAN WAR

During the escalation of Anglo-Transvaal tension after 1896, Churchill was fully occupied fighting in, and writing about, two other imperial wars —on the northwest frontier in India and in the Sudan.[23] Yet he does not seem to have lost sight of the South African situation. By the time he expounded his views on the causes of the South African War, which started on 11 October 1899, they had gained the further dimension of firsthand knowledge of South Africa.

In Churchill's maiden speech in the House of Commons on 18 February 1901, when the war on the African subcontinent still had more than fifteen months to run, the new Conservative member for Oldham concentrated on the South African situation. His remarks on the methods of warfare employed by British generals and the future of South Africa will be examined later. The first consideration should be his perception of the causes of the war. He stressed that it was the South African Republic that declared war: "We went to war—I mean of course we were gone to war with."[24] He saw the prime issue of difference between the Transvaal and British governments to be the extension of the franchise to "the people of the Transvaal." He added, "When I say the people of the Transvaal I mean the whole people of the Transvaal, and not necessarily those who arrived there first. At that time there were nearly two-and-a-half times as many British and non-Dutch as there were Boers."[25] He repudiated the suggestion that the war was "a war of greed" or that "certain capitalists spent money in bringing on the war in the hope that it would increase the value of their mining properties. . . . With the mass of the nation, with the whole people of the country, this war from beginning to end has only been a war of duty."[26]

In the autobiographical *My Early Life*, published thirty-one years after the outbreak of the South African War, Churchill emphasized the "personal and temperamental currents" of Kruger, Lord Salisbury, the British premier, and above all the "reinforcing and indeed overriding impulse" of Chamberlain.[27] Furthermore, he pointed to the importance of deep-level gold mining making the Witwatersrand "a factor not only in British but in world-wide financial and economic affairs"; the Transvaal became

---

[23] See Winston S. Churchill, *The Story of the Malakand Field Force* (London: Longmans, Green, 1898), and *The River War*, 2 vols. (London: Longmans, Green, 1899).
[24] *WSC* II C 3.   [25] *WSC* II C 3.
[26] *WSC* II C 7.   [27] Churchill, *My Early Life*, 102.

"the magnet of Dutch aspirations throughout South Africa ... which reached out to Holland and Germany for European support and relationships."[28] He believed the Uitlanders had the right to vote and that their watchword of "no taxation without representation" was valid. He maintained the Boers had ambitions of becoming "masters of the whole of South Africa." At the same time he recognized Kruger's fears that the Uitlanders would swamp the Transvaal Boers if they were given the vote and the Boers' perception of "British imperialism clutching for gold."[29] He pointed to Chamberlain's view that the Boers "were refusing to give civil rights to the modern productive elements who were making nine-tenths of the wealth of the country because they were afraid they would no longer be allowed to larrup their own Kaffirs."[30]

It is instructive to relate Churchill's perceptions of the Anglo-Boer conflict of 1899–1902 to the interpretations of historians who had evidence at their disposal that was not available to Churchill in 1901, or nearly thirty years later when his book *My Early Life* was published.

The first point made by Churchill in discussing the causes of the war in 1901 was that the South African Republic declared war on Britain and not vice versa, with the implication that the Boers were the aggressors. It is true that it was Kruger's government that delivered an ultimatum to the British authorities on 9 October 1899. This had been prompted by the British cabinet's decision on 8 September 1899 to send 10,000 more troops as reinforcements to South Africa. Diplomatically, the Boer cause would have been strengthened if war came as a result of a British ultimatum. A British ultimatum had in fact been agreed upon in principle by Salisbury, Chamberlain, and the cabinet at the end of September, but there were problems regarding details. Milner explained to Chamberlain: "Ultimatum has always been great difficulty, as unless we widen issue [that it is beyond the Uitlander franchise issue] there is not sufficient cause for war, and if we do so, we are abused for shifting our ground and extending our demands."[31] The British government's dilemma was resolved by the Boer ultimatum; it had been decided by the republican leadership that further delay in taking the military initiative would enable Britain to build up her military strength in South Africa to overwhelming proportions.[32] Sending the ultimatum hardly made the Boer republics the aggressors (as Britain was not the aggressor in August 1914 when the British government sent an ultimatum to Germany).

[28] Ibid.   [29] Ibid., 103.
[30] Ibid., 103–4.   [31] Marais, *Fall of Kruger's Republic*, 332.
[32] Ibid., 320.

Churchill continued his maiden speech by asserting that Britain intended extending the franchise to "the whole people of the Transvaal." Of course, this was incorrect on two counts. Britain did not intend to grant the vote to women in the Transvaal. By 1899 women had been enfranchised in only two parts of the British Empire—New Zealand and South Australia —but women in Britain and in the South African colonies and republics did not have the vote.[33] Nor was it the intention of the British government to extend the franchise to those inhabitants of the Transvaal who were not white. Granting the vote to black, colored, and Indian Transvaalers would surely not have been completely out of the question, as the Cape Colony had had a qualified, color-blind franchise since 1872.[34] Milner believed, however, that black rights should not be made an issue between Britain and the South African Republic, because of the intense resentment such a stand would raise among Transvaal Boers and "second and more important the danger that . . . British colonists elsewhere in South Africa might support the Transvaalers."[35]

Churchill further claimed that there were nearly two-and-a-half times as many British and non-Dutch in the Transvaal as there were Boers. As the first census for the whole of the Transvaal was only taken after the South African War in 1904, it is impossible to calculate the Uitlander–Boer ratio in 1899 exactly. However, the careful calculations of the historian J. S. Marais led him to state that there were probably more Boers (men, women, and children) than Uitlanders, but there may have been more Uitlander than Boer male adults owing to the fact that adult males formed a relatively large proportion of the Uitlander population.[36] More recently a modern historian has expressed agreement with Marais's calculations.[37]

In fact, historians have not found the Uitlander franchise issue nearly so simple as Churchill made it out to be (both in his maiden speech and in *My Early Life*). One view is that "the number of Uitlanders actually wanting the vote and prepared to give up their existing citizenship (an explicit condition) and accept the obligations which went with becoming a citizen of the Transvaal republic remains unknowable, but it was certainly only a minority."[38] It has also been shown that among the white

---

[33] S. B. Spies, "Women and the War," in *The South Africa War: The Anglo-Boer War 1899–1902*, ed. P. Warwick and S. B. Spies (Harlow: Longman, 1980), 161.
[34] See L. M. Thompson, *The Unification of South Africa, 1902–1910* (Oxford: Clarendon Press, 1960), 109–10.
[35] Marais, *Fall of Kruger's Republic*, 183.   [36] Ibid., 2–3.
[37] Smith, *A Reappraisal*, 44. See also the same author's *The Origins of the South African War (1899–1902)* (London: Longman, 1996).
[38] Smith, *A Reappraisal*, 47.

working class on the Witwatersrand there were those who were against Uitlanders getting the vote because "They feared the creation of a new society where the Randlords [the mining bosses] would rule."[39] That is not to deny that there were Uitlanders who intended to settle in the republic and who wanted the vote to enable them to have a voice in the government of the country.[40]

Although no actual franchise reforms were introduced by the republican government, Kruger and his advisers were not totally opposed to introducing new voting laws. Whatever offers were made were rejected by the British authorities as being inadequate.[41]

The British Liberal leader, Sir Henry Campbell-Bannerman, the day before war started, asserted that the "franchise movement was the biggest hypocrisy in the whole fraud."[42] Indeed, few modern historians would unreservedly support the interpretation that the war was fought to give the vote to Uitlanders in the Transvaal. It is today accepted by many historians that the British authorities used the Uitlander franchise issue as a pretext (or as the historian Andrew Porter put it, "a fig leaf to cover their nakedness"[43]) to veil their true motives for going to war.

Churchill, in his maiden speech, repudiated the view that the South African War was "a war of greed" or a war brought on by certain capitalists. It is often considered that J. A. Hobson, who had been a British war correspondent in South Africa in 1899, had been the first to propound a capitalist conspiracy explanation for the outbreak of the Anglo-Boer war.[44] Dr. Iain Smith has recently shown, however, that it was the pro-Kruger Johannesburg newspaper *The Standard and Diggers' News* that first argued that the capitalists were behind the agitation against the Transvaal government.[45] The connection between capitalist mining interests and the outbreak of hostilities in 1899 has featured prominently in the historical debate on the origins of the South African War.[46] Although it

---

[39] Diana Cammack, *The Rand at War, 1899–1902: The Witwatersrand and the Anglo-Boer War* (London: James Currey, 1990), 22.

[40] Ibid., 27.   [41] Smith, *A Reappraisal*, 48–9.

[42] A. N. Porter, *The Origins of the South African War: Joseph Chamberlain and the Diplomacy of Imperialism, 1895–1899* (Manchester: Manchester University Press, 1980), 261.

[43] Ibid., 257.

[44] See J. A. Hobson, *The South African War: Its Causes and Effects* (London: James Nisbet, 1900).

[45] Smith, *A Reappraisal*, 29–30.

[46] See, for instance, R. V. Kubicek, *Economic Imperialism in Theory and Practice: The Case of South African Gold Mining Finance* (Durham, North Carolina: Duke University Press, 1979); A. Jeeves, "Aftermath of Rebellion: The Randlords and Kruger's Republic after the Jameson Raid," *South African Historical Journal* 10 (1978): 102–16; Thomas Pakenham,

cannot be denied that economic factors played an important role in caus-
ing the war, the view that mine owners exercised the predominant influence has not gained general acceptance. As a recent work on British
imperialism explains, in a section entitled "Crisis and War in South Africa,"
the principal problem "is to trace the ties that bound economics, strategy
and private ambition."[47]

One may leave the notions Winston Churchill expressed on the origins
of the South African War in his maiden parliamentary speech and move
on to his later views published in *My Early Life*. In the first instance he
laid considerable emphasis on the colonial secretary, Joseph Chamberlain, championing the cause of the Uitlanders with the prime minister,
"Lord Salisbury following steadily on behind."[48] While this perception
was once quite widely accepted, a strong case has also been made against
the view that Salisbury was not in full command of the cabinet from 1895
to 1899.[49] The British official whose role has, in fact, been accorded more
weight and influence as a factor in the pre–South African War period, Sir
Alfred Milner,[50] is strangely enough not mentioned by Churchill in this
regard.

Churchill noted the importance that the discovery of gold on the Witwatersrand gave to the Transvaal from a world financial point of view.[51]
This theme, and in particular the role of the Bank of England in Britain's
dealings with the South African Republic, has continued to interest historians. J. J. Van Helten some years ago disputed that control of the gold
mines was a factor in the considerations of the Bank of England before
1899.[52] Yet Van Helten did not deny the existence of "a complex relationship between the supplies of newly mined gold, the international gold
standard and the Bank of England's financial crisis."[53] In an important
recent work on the subject, Dr. Russell Ally agrees that Britain did not

The Boer War (Johannesburg: Jonathan Ball Publishers, 1979), 88–90; and B. Porter,
"Imperialism and the Scramble," *Journal of Imperial and Commonwealth History* 9
(1980): 76–81.
[47] P. J. Cain and A. G. Hopkins, *British Imperialism: Innovation and Expansion, 1688–
1914* (London: Longman, 1993), 370.
[48] Churchill, *My Early Life*, 103.
[49] A. Porter, "Lord Salisbury, Mr. Chamberlain and South Africa 1895–99," *Journal of
Imperial and Commonwealth History* 1, no. 1 (1972): 3–26.
[50] See particularly Marais, *Fall of Kruger's Republic*, passim, and G. H. L. le May, *British
Supremacy in South Africa* (Oxford: Clarendon Press, 1965).
[51] Churchill, *My Early Life*, 102–3.
[52] J. J. Van Helten, "Empire and High Finance: South Africa and the International Gold
Standard, 1890–1914," *Journal of African History* 23 (1982): 529–48.
[53] Ibid., 548.

want to take physical control of the Transvaal simply because the Bank of England was concerned about the state of its gold reserves, but he goes on to argue that "this should not detract from the fact that there was a growing appreciation of the importance of the Witwatersrand gold for the Bank of England's safeguarding of the international gold standard."[54] There is little doubt that this involved relationship between financial interests in London and the British government relating to gold, and the Transvaal will continue to feature prominently in the ongoing historical debate on the origins of the South African War.

A further issue which has aroused considerable historical controversy—the role played by the need to ensure a satisfactory supply of black labor for the Witwatersrand—is hinted at obliquely by Churchill.[55]

This was one of the strands of J. A. Hobson's argument, namely that the British government went to war "to secure for the mines a cheap adequate supply of labour."[56] In 1974 the argument was taken further and it was argued that the demands of capital resulted in a war being fought to enable the black labor force to be driven, at its expense, into the structure required by the mining industry.[57] This interpretation has not been completely abandoned.[58] The more generally accepted view, however, is that the evidence does not support it.[59]

Churchill believed that the discovery of gold had made the South African Republic "the magnet of Dutch aspirations throughout South Africa." He maintained furthermore that "Kruger and his colleagues saw no reason why Europe should not intervene on their behalf or why they should not become masters of the whole of South Africa."[60] Historians have not found evidence to substantiate the view that Kruger and his government had intentions of bringing all of South Africa under their control. It is now, however, widely accepted that the prime factor that led to war in 1899 was the British government's intention to assert British

---

[54] Russell Ally, *Gold and Empire: The Bank of England and South Africa's Gold Producers, 1886–1926* (Johannesburg: Witwatersrand University Press, 1994), 25.

[55] Churchill, *My Early Life*, 102–3.   [56] Hobson, *Causes and Effects*, 231.

[57] D. Bransky, "The Causes of the Boer War: Towards a New Synthesis" (unpublished paper, Oxford, 1974).

[58] See S. Marks, "Southern Africa 1867–1886," in *The Cambridge History of Africa*, 8 vols., ed. R. Oliver and G. N. Sanderson (Cambridge: Cambridge University Press, 1985), vol. 6, 471.

[59] See A. Jeeves, *Migrant Labour in South Africa's Mining Economy: The Struggle for the Gold Mines' Labour Supply, 1890–1920* (Johannesburg: Witwatersrand University Press, 1985), and Patrick Harries, "Capital, State and Labour on the 19th Century Witwatersrand: A Reassessment," *South African Historical Journal* 18 (1986): 25–45.

[60] Churchill, *My Early Life*, 102–3.

supremacy in South Africa. But to say that is not enough, as it has been pointed out in recent years. In an influential essay, Shula Marks and Stan Trapido insisted on the necessity of trying "to tease out some of the embodied implications" of the concept of British supremacy.[61] More recently P. J. Cain and A. G. Hopkins have also warned against the danger of "collapsing the argument into poorly specified generalities about the defence of British supremacy."[62]

The development of the Witwatersrand gold mines made the South African Republic the most powerful state in the region—that is, more powerful economically, commercially, and politically than the self-governing British Cape Colony and Natal. It has been postulated that South Africa at the time was "a case of economic development raising the enemies of the imperial connection to political preponderance over the colonial collaborators."[63] As early as March 1896, Lord Selborne, the under secretary at the colonial office, had written a memorandum about imperial prospects in South Africa. The question, as he saw it, and as other members of the British government came to see it, was whether South Africa would become another Canada (within the British Empire) or another United States (outside the Empire). In the latter case it was assumed that Afrikaner or Boer nationalism would spread its influence over the whole subcontinent. On the other hand, if the Union Jack were raised over the Transvaal, British supremacy over the whole of South Africa would be reasserted.[64]

The reassertion of that supremacy had other strands and implications. From a political point of view it would ensure the establishment of state governments on the subcontinent that would be sympathetic (or "loyal") to imperial aspirations and prepared to cooperate (or to "collaborate") to achieve those goals. It would also ensure the acceptance of South Africa as an exclusively British sphere of influence and the elimination of European rivals (especially Germany). Administrative machinery would have to be created to meet the bureaucratic demands of a modern state. Economically, it was considered to be essential that agriculture and industry—and in particular the gold mines—be developed and organized,

---

[61] Shula Marks and Stan Trapido, "Lord Milner and the South African State," in *Working Papers in Southern African Studies*, 2 vols., ed. P. Bonner (Johannesburg: Ravan Press [Pty], Ltd, 1981), vol. 2, 58.

[62] Cain and Hopkins, *British Imperialism*, 370.

[63] R. Robinson and J. Gallagher, *Africa and the Victorians: The Official Mind of Imperialism*, 2d ed. (London: Macmillan, 1981), 468.

[64] Ibid., 434–7.

not only to bring greater prosperity to South Africa but also to bolster the trade and monetary resources of the Empire as a whole. Some officials also felt that British supremacy was necessary to ensure that the Simonstown naval base, on the Cape coast, would remain exclusively in the hands of the Royal Navy to guard the long sea route to India.[65]

These considerations must be seen in the context of Britain's position in the world at the end of the nineteenth century. Britain had lost its industrial predominance, and diplomatically, by 1894, it was the only one of the six great European powers that was not a member of one of the two blocs of alliances that had been formed. Chamberlain and others (almost certainly the young Churchill, also) regarded a strong, well-organized empire as a prerequisite for Britain to maintain its power and prestige in the world.[66] As Chamberlain put it in September 1899, "What is now at stake is the position of Great Britain in South Africa—and with it the estimate formed of our power and influence in our Colonies, and throughout the world."[67]

One will, of course, never know if Churchill was correct in asserting that if his father had been alive in 1899, it was more than likely that he would have opposed the South African War.[68] It is evident, however, that Winston Churchill himself from 1896 was in favor of Britain going to war against the South African Republic. In fact, taking into account his views at the time of the Jameson Raid, it is probably true to maintain that he wanted war before 1899, conceivably as early as 1896. Chamberlain realized the importance of having public opinion on the government's side before going to war.[69] Churchill recalled the colonial secretary saying to him, "It is no use blowing the trumpet for the charge and find nobody following."[70] It seems more than likely that Churchill shared the cabinet's perception of the importance for Britain's position as a world power of reasserting her supremacy in South Africa.

[65] S. B. Spies, "Reconstruction and Unification, 1902–1910," in *A New Illustrated History of South Africa*, ed. T. Cameron and S. B. Spies (Johannesburg: Southern Book Publishers and Human and Rousseau, 1991), 220; and Smith, *A Reappraisal*, 53. A number of historians have made the point that it was unnecessary for Britain to control the Transvaal to ensure the safety of Simonstown: see, for instance, Marais, *Fall of Kruger's Republic*, 325, and Cain and Hopkins, *British Imperialism*, 380.

[66] S. B. Spies, "British Supremacy and South African Unification," in *South Africa in the 20th Century*, ed. B. J. Liebenberg and S. B. Spies (Pretoria: J. L. Van Schaik, 1993), 6.

[67] Cabinet Memorandum, "The South African Situation," September 6, 1899, quoted in Robinson and Gallagher, *Africa and the Victorians*, 454.

[68] Churchill, *My Early Life*, 55.

[69] On Chamberlain and public opinion, see Porter, *Origins of the South African War*, passim.

[70] Churchill, *My Early Life*, 233.

THE SOUTH AFRICAN WAR

This is not the place to dwell on Winston Churchill's adventures during the South African War—his appointment as the *Morning Post*'s special correspondent at the front; his capture by the Boers near Chieveley on 15 November 1899, when they ambushed the British force in an armored train; his incarceration as a prisoner of war in Pretoria; his subsequent daring escape and journey to Delagoa Bay; his return to Natal and appointment as a lieutenant in the South African Light Horse (without abandoning his status as a war correspondent); or his experiences with the forces of Lord Roberts as they advanced to the Transvaal capital, Pretoria.[71] Nor, except in passing, will attention be given to the influence the South African War had on his personality and career.[72]

More crucial in the context of this chapter are his opinions of the enemy, the Boers, his comments on the methods of warfare employed by British forces, and his views on the settlement needed in South Africa after the war.

Before these matters are examined, one aspect of his capture by the Boers needs to be clarified. Churchill was convinced that he was captured by Louis Botha (according to Churchill, then a burgher in the ranks), who was to become commandant general of the Transvaal forces, and after the war the first premier of the self-governing British colony of the Transvaal and the first prime minister of the Union of South Africa. Churchill, furthermore, insisted that Botha himself told him in Britain after the war: "I took . . . you prisoner. I, myself."[73] It would have indeed been remarkable if the two men who played such prominent roles after 1902 as conciliators between Boers and Britons should have first met as captor and captive. The evidence does not, however, support this romantic legend. The author of the most authoritative account of the first months of the war in Natal has pointed out that Botha on 15 November 1899 was not a burgher or private soldier, but was the general in command of the Boers in the action, and it is highly unlikely that in that capacity he would have been isolated and so far ahead of the other Boers.[74] Moreover, Botha

[71] See ibid., 235–360; WSC I 438–531; Winston S. Churchill, *London to Ladysmith via Pretoria* (London: Longmans, Green, 1900); and Winston S. Churchill, *Ian Hamilton's March* (London: Longmans, Green, 1900).
[72] See WSC I 531 for a succinct summary of these matters.
[73] Churchill, *My Early Life*, 259–60.
[74] C. J. Barnard, *Generaal Louis Botha op die Natalse Front, 1899–1900* (Cape Town: A. A. Balkema, 1970), 37.

never mentioned Churchill in his official report of the action, whereas another Boer officer, Danie Theron, did mention Churchill and explicitly stated that "He [Churchill] would not stand still when Field Cornet Oosthuizen warned him to surrender. Only when he [Oosthuizen] turned his rifle on him did he surrender."[75] Another South African historian informed Winston Churchill's son, Randolph, in 1962: "It is known that Louis Botha's command of English was poor; he probably failed to make his meaning clear to Sir Winston. My guess is that Botha intended to indicate that he was in overall command of the area in which the armoured train affair took place."[76] The man who almost certainly captured Churchill was Field Cornet (later General) Sarel Oosthuizen, a brave and intrepid fighter, who was seriously wounded at Dwarsvlei in July 1900 and who died as a result of that wound in August of that year.[77]

Less than a month after the British army led by Lord Roberts had occupied Bloemfontein, the capital of the Orange Free State, Churchill stressed to Chamberlain that "the Republics must go."[78] From the time that the Boer ultimatum had been received it had in fact been the intention of the British government to annex the South African Republic, and soon afterward it was decided that the Orange Free State should also be annexed.[79] Not only was it the intention of the British government to annex both Boer republics, but contrary to international law and the opinion of the government's law advisers, the annexations were actually proclaimed before the conquest of the Boer territories was completed: the Orange Free State on 24 May (made known on 28 May) and the Transvaal on 1 September 1900.[80] The cabinet justified the premature annexations on military grounds.[81]

Churchill also argued strongly that the government should not negotiate with the Boer civil authorities or with either president except in their

[75] Ibid.; Leyds-Argief (Transvaal Archive, Pretoria), 711(c), telegram 53 of November 28, 1899, Theron to state secretary (my translation).

[76] WSC I 473, quoting Professor Arthur Davey, who was attached to the history department of the University of South Africa and of Cape Town.

[77] Gail Nattrass and S. B. Spies, eds., *Jan Smuts' Memoirs of the Boer War* (Johannesburg: Jonathan Ball Publishers, 1994), 190.

[78] WSC I 520, quoting Churchill to Chamberlain, April 7, 1900.

[79] Cabinet Papers (Public Record Office, Kew), Cab. 41/25, 26, Salisbury to Queen Victoria, December 8, 1899; Cab. 37/52, 3, Chamberlain's secret memorandum, January 10, 1900.

[80] S. B. Spies, *Methods of Barbarism? Roberts and Kitchener and Civilians in the Boer Republics, January 1900–May 1902* (Cape Town: Human and Rousseau, 1977), 59–63.

[81] Colonial Office Records (Public Record Office, Kew), CO 517/290, 14469, H. Lambert to law officers, May 19, 1900.

military capacities.[82] That was indeed the policy which was followed when negotiations were started in April 1902.[83]

But if Churchill was unrelenting in his insistence that Boer rule in the Transvaal and Orange Free State should be ended, he urged generosity, leniency, and forgiveness in the treatment of Natal rebels (that is, those Dutch-speaking British subjects in Natal who had joined Boer commandos)—for which he was abused in Natal and in Britain.[84]

When Churchill arrived back in Britain from South Africa on 20 July 1900, after the Transvaal capital had fallen to Boer forces, he, like Lord Roberts and many people in Britain, thought the war was virtually over.[85] From September he was involved in the so-called "Khaki election," in which Chamberlain's slogan, "Every seat lost by the Government is a seat gained by the Boers," set the tone. Churchill fought and won the election in Oldham on the platform that the war was just and necessary, and that it had to be fought to a definite conclusion, after which there should be a generous peace settlement.[86] In his maiden parliamentary speech on 18 February 1901, he expressed his belief "that as compared with other wars especially those in which a civil population took part this war in South Africa has on the whole been carried on with unusual humanity and generosity."[87] His views on the conduct of the war—as will become apparent later in this chapter—were not always so supportive of the British military command. Indeed, even in the maiden speech itself, hints of disapproval at actions of soldiers in South Africa surfaced: farm burning received a tantalizing brief mention and there was criticism of the way British officers, whom he regarded as the best officers in the world "in dealing with native races," treated "respectable old Boer farmers."[88]

The phrase in that maiden speech that made the most impact, however, was Churchill's statement, "If I were a Boer fighting in the field —and if I were a Boer I hope I should be fighting in the field."[89] In his autobiographical account Churchill relates that when he spoke those words, he saw Chamberlain say something to his neighbor. He later learned that the colonial secretary had said, "That's the way to throw away seats."[90] A month after he had delivered his maiden speech, Churchill reacted in the *Westminster Gazette* to a correspondent's criticism of

[82] *WSC* I 520–52.   [83] Spies, *Methods of Barbarism?*, 281–3.
[84] Churchill, *My Early Life*, 357–8.
[85] Ibid., 361; *WSC* I 529; Spies, *Methods of Barbarism?*, 70.
[86] Churchill, *My Early Life*, 364–6.   [87] *WSC* II C 2.
[88] *WSC* II C 2, 4.   [89] *WSC* II C 2.
[90] Churchill, *My Early Life*, 372.

his use of the phrase by maintaining that every man owed a duty to his country. He argued further that "While the Boer cause is certainly wrong, the Boer who fights for it is certainly right. Much more so then is the Boer who fights bravely for it."[91]

Despite his somewhat guarded defense in his maiden speech of British methods of warfare in South Africa, Churchill was to become increasingly concerned about the way matters were developing. Even before the general election he expressed astonishment at what he called "the pitiless spirit" he found prevalent in Britain. He had found that "Lord Roberts has lost a certain amount of popularity because it is thought he has not been sufficiently severe and [Roberts's chief of staff] Lord Kitchener's name has been several times mentioned to me as the kind of man for the business. I wish him joy of his reputation."[92] In fact, it was Milner (as he himself subsequently admitted) rather than Roberts who was responsible for the leniency of the first proclamation issued by the military authorities in South Africa.[93] From April 1900, however, the spirit of the earlier proclamation was reversed, and Roberts instituted far harsher measures against Boer civilians as his army advanced through the Orange Free State and the South African Republic. Farms in the vicinity of Boer attacks on British communications were burned—whether or not the owners of the farms were involved in these attacks. Subsequently farms (and villages) were destroyed for various reasons, such as that the owner of the farm was on commando, or that information had been withheld from British officers, or on grounds of clearance of supplies. There was deliberate, widespread, and ruthless devastation of Boer property in the two republics. Milner admitted after the war that as many as 30,000 houses may have been destroyed; a very high proportion of these were burnt while Roberts was in command.[94] Boer civilians were put on trains as hostages to deter commandos attacking communications.[95] Boer women and children in British-occupied towns were sent to commandos in the field. In September 1900 camps—euphemistically called refugee camps, but more commonly known as concentration camps—were established to house Boer (and black) civilians.[96] These measures were calculated to act as a lever

---

[91] *Westminster Gazette*, March 18, 1901, Churchill to editor, quoted in *WSC* II C 23–4.
[92] Milner Papers (Bodleian Library, Oxford), 28 (B), Churchill to Milner, September 8, 1900.
[93] Army Proclamation issued by Field Marshal Lord Roberts in South Africa, Cd 426, 2–3; J. E. Wrench, *Alfred Lord Milner: The Man of No Illusions, 1854–1925* (London: Eyre and Spottiswoode, 1958), 223; Spies, *Methods of Barbarism?*, 28, 34–5.
[94] Spies, *Methods of Barbarism?*, 116–27.   [95] Ibid., 115–16.
[96] Ibid., 148–50.

to induce the Boers in the field to surrender. Roberts declared: "Unless the people generally are made to suffer for misdeeds for those in arms against us the war will never end."[97]

On 29 November 1900, Kitchener succeeded Roberts as commander of British forces in South Africa. As the war dragged on, the controversial measures inaugurated by Roberts were continued by Kitchener and in some instances implemented more harshly, while further steps were taken to end Boer resistance. Increasing numbers of surrendered Boers and of black people were armed to fight against the commandos.[98] A number of Cape Afrikaners who joined invading Boer commandos were tried and publicly executed as rebels (including the Free Stater Gideon Scheepers, who was not a rebel).[99] These executions, almost certainly in conflict with international law, aroused protests in South Africa, Britain, and America. (Churchill has related that he protested against the execution of Scheepers and, moreover, that he may have played some part in averting the execution of another Boer, Commandant P. H. Kritzinger.)[100]

In January 1901 Kitchener started the "drives" or "sweeps," clearing the country of people (black and white) and supplies. The population of the concentration camps was enormously increased. Kitchener also threatened to confiscate the property of those still in the field after a certain date and to deport them to Fiji or Madagascar. "The Boers," he declared, "are uncivilized Afrikaner savages with only a thin white veneer."[101] The most important development during Kitchener's command was the rising death toll in the concentration camps. After the war it was calculated that more than 26,000 women and children died in the camps for white people, and considerably more than 13,000 people died in the black camps.[102] Some details of conditions in the camps started becoming known in Britain

[97] Telegrams and Letters sent by Field Marshal Lord Roberts (National Army Museum, London), V 12, C 4709, to Lieutenant General C. F. Clery, September 17, 1900. For a detailed account of Roberts's measures against civilians, see Spies, *Methods of Barbarism?*, 90–169.

[98] For a detailed account of Kitchener's measures against civilians, see Spies, *Methods of Barbarism?*, 170–280.

[99] See G. S. Preller, ed., *Scheepers se Dagboek en die Stryd in Kaapland, 11 Oktober 1901–18 Januarie 1902* (Cape Town: Nasionale Pers, 1938); C. J. Scheepers Strydom, *Kaapland en die Tweede Vryheidsoorlog* (Cape Town: Nasionale Pers, 1917); J. R. Snyman, "Die Afrikaner in Kaapland, 1899–1902," *Archives Year Book for South African History*, vol. 42, no. 2 (Pretoria: The Government Printer, 1979).

[100] Churchill, *My Early Life*, 374.

[101] Kitchener Papers (Public Record Office, London), PRO 30/57/22, Y62, Kitchener to St. J. Brodrick, June 22, 1901.

[102] Spies, *Methods of Barbarism?*, 265–6.

and elsewhere during the first half of 1901, particularly as a result of the revelations of the Cornish humanitarian Emily Hobhouse, who had visited the camps.[103] There is no evidence that the British authorities in South Africa were guilty of a deliberate policy of extermination in the concentration camps. They were, however, responsible for poor planning, ill-conceived control, and neglect. The concentration camps were started by Roberts and extended by Kitchener as part of the strategy to end Boer resistance. They enabled the army to clear the country of civilians whose presence on the farms was considered to be undesirable from a military point of view. It was hoped that they would induce burghers to surrender to join their families in the camps. Black women and children were housed in camps while the army utilized the labor of their menfolk.[104] The concentration camps were started by the military authorities; Milner, the head of the British civil establishment in South Africa, was adamant "that while a hundred explanations may be offered and a hundred excuses made, they do not really amount to an adequate defence."[105] Joseph Chamberlain, Milner's chief in London, believed that it was not "altogether a complete answer to say that the aggregation of people who are specially liable to infectious disease has produced a state of things which is inevitable. The natural remark is: 'Why then did you bring them together?'"[106] On 14 June 1901, the leader of the Liberal opposition in Britain answered his own question—"When is a war not a war?"—by stating, "When it is carried on by methods of barbarism in South Africa."[107] Nearly three months before Campbell-Bannerman's "methods of barbarism" speech Churchill had expressed the following views privately:

I have hated these latter stages with their barbarous features—questionable even according to the bloody precedents of 1870 [the Franco-Prussian War], certainly most horrible. I look forward to the day when we can take the Boers by the hand and say as [General U.S.] Grant said to the Confederates at Appomattox: "Go back and plough your fields." Personally I am still absolutely determined to strip them of their political independence, but I cannot face the idea of their being economically and socially ruined too.[108]

Churchill continued to plead that there should be infused "into the prosecution of the war a vigour and vitality . . . which will . . . finally lead us

---

103 Ibid., 195–8.   104 Ibid., 189 and passim.
105 Headlam, *The Milner Papers*, vol. 2, 229, Milner to Chamberlain, December 7, 1901.
106 Milner Papers, 41, Chamberlain to Milner, November 4, 1901.
107 J. A. Spender, *The Life of the Right Hon. Sir Henry Campbell-Bannerman, G.C.B.*, 2 vols. (London: Hodder & Stoughton, 1924), vol. 1, 335–6.
108 Milner Papers, 37, Churchill to Milner, March 17, 1901.

victoriously to a conclusion which shall combine the peace of Africa with the honour of Britain."[109]

As the war wound to a conclusion, Churchill thought of going to South Africa to observe and report on the final stages. His friend Lieutenant General Sir Ian Hamilton, Kitchener's chief of staff, dissuaded him on the grounds that "the Press censorship is severe and would be intolerable to you."[110] After the peace agreement had been signed, Churchill once again expressed his admiration for the Boers: "I hear it on all sides said what an extraordinary people they are." As he saw it, "They have been defeated, they recognise that they cannot beat the British Empire and they have decided to have it on their side. I am bound to say if they play their cards with their usual skill they will most certainly succeed." In contrast, Churchill confessed:

I have very little admiration for the Loyalists of Capetown [*sic*], and with a few exceptions for the Uitlanders of Johannesburg, and I am certain of this that if we can make the Boers one of the foundations of our position in South Africa, if not indeed the chief foundation, we shall be building upon the rock.[111]

POSTWAR SETTLEMENT

From 1896 until October 1900, Churchill had talked to and corresponded with influential people about South Africa; he had also written books and lectured on the topic. His election to the House of Commons in October 1900 gave him an enhanced status and provided him with a prominent new platform from which to expound his ideas. In 1904 he abandoned the Conservative Party to join the Liberals—as a result of differences regarding tariff, rather than South African, issues. Nevertheless, his stance on a South African policy had moved closer to that of the Liberals than to that adopted by members of his former party. The resignation of the Conservative Party on 4 December 1905 led to the leader of the Liberal Party, Sir Henry Campbell-Bannerman, becoming prime minister (which was confirmed by the Liberal electoral victory of January 1906). Churchill was appointed under secretary at the colonial office and was thus granted the opportunity of playing a direct role in determining policy at a crucial stage for South Africa. It would appear that Campbell-Bannerman offered

[109] *WSC* II C 90, speech at Saddworth, Yorkshire, October 4, 1901.
[110] *WSC* II C 119, Hamilton to Churchill, March 23, 1902.
[111] *WSC* II C 147, Churchill to Ian Hamilton, June 25, 1902.

the position of under secretary of the Treasury and under secretary of colonial affairs to Reginald McKenna[112] and Churchill jointly, as it were, leaving it to them to decide who would take which post. Although Churchill was not a financial expert, he did know a great deal about South Africa and held strong views about the peaceful development of the country. He must have realized too that for some years at least after the Liberal Party's ascension to power, South African policy was going to be one of the government's chief priorities. He probably also saw the advantages for him and the opportunities offered by the fact that the secretary of state for the colonies, Lord Elgin, would be in the House of Lords; the under secretary would be the government spokesman on colonial affairs in the Commons. The combination of ambition and interest made it virtually certain that Churchill would have no hesitation in opting for the under secretaryship at the colonial office.[113]

The Vereeniging peace agreement signed on 31 May 1902 had stipulated that as soon as circumstances permitted, representative government would be established in the conquered Boer territories. That would lead, it was stated, to self-government.[114] After the war the territories were governed as crown colonies, and the policy of reconstruction was instituted by Milner and a group of officials, prominent among them a group of young Oxonians, who became known as "the Kindergarten."[115] Milner modified crown colony rule in May 1903 to allow nominated civilians to serve on the legislative councils. The most influential Boers declined to serve on the legislative councils and, by January 1905, the first postwar political party, Het Volk (The People), was established in the Transvaal under the leadership of Botha and General J. C. Smuts. Before Milner left South Africa in April 1905, to be succeeded as high commissioner by Lord Selborne, Colonial Secretary Alfred Lyttelton had issued letters patent to introduce representative government to the Transvaal. Provision was made for a predominantly elective legislature, while executive power would still be wielded by British officials. Before the Conservatives

---

[112] Reginald McKenna (1863–1943) was a Liberal M.P. from 1895–1918. He was president of the Board of Education before becoming first lord of the Admiralty in 1908. When Churchill succeeded him as first lord in 1911, McKenna became home secretary, and in 1915 he became chancellor of the Exchequer.

[113] Ronald Hyam, *Elgin and Churchill at the Colonial Office, 1905–1908: The Watershed of the Empire-Commonwealth* (London: Macmillan, 1968), 41–2.

[114] J. D. Kestell and D. E. van Velden, *The Peace Negotiations . . .* (London: Richard Clay and Sons, 1912), 117.

[115] See W. Nimocks, *Milner's Young Men: The Kindergarten in Edwardian Imperial Affairs* (Durham, North Carolina: Duke University Press, 1968).

could implement the Lyttelton constitution, however, the Liberals came to power.[116]

In addition to the constitutional issue, the Liberal government was faced with another South African problem that needed urgent attention: the question of Chinese labor on the Witwatersrand gold mines. For various reasons there was a labor shortage in the gold mines after the South African War. In February 1904 the Conservative government had sanctioned the labor importation ordinance passed by the Transvaal Legislative Council. This provided for indentured laborers from the northern provinces of China, whose people had been prevented from going to work as usual in Manchuria by the Russo-Japanese War of 1904–5. In all, nearly 64,000 Chinese came to the Witwatersrand mines. Economically, the experiment was successful: the labor crisis was solved until recruitment of African workers revived in 1907 and the value of gold production soared. There were, however, many objections in the Transvaal and in Britain to the presence and treatment of the Chinese laborers, and the issue contributed to the Conservative fall from power.[117] Churchill and cabinet ministers and colonial office officials were aware of the connection between the Chinese labor problem and the constitutional issue. The foreign secretary, Sir Edward Grey, considered responsible government in the Transvaal as the way out for the British government "of the impasse on Chinese labour."[118]

Campbell-Bannerman has received much of the credit for what has been called "the magnanimous gesture" of granting responsible government to the Boer republics so soon after the South African War. While he undoubtedly believed in "the panacea of self-government among white men" in the former Boer republics, he left the details of planning and drafting a constitution to others.[119] It was in these areas that Churchill, the young under secretary for the colonies, made a considerable contribution. It would seem that some members of the cabinet, including Elgin, believed that representative government would first have to be granted to the new colonies before responsible government could be introduced. Churchill played a significant role in pointing out that this was unnecessary and that responsible government could and should be granted to the Transvaal as

---

[116] Thompson, *Unification of South Africa*, 21–3; N. G. Garson, "Het Volk: The Botha-Smuts Party in the Transvaal, 1904–1911," *Historical Journal* 9, no. 1 (1966): 101–32.

[117] See P. Richardson, *Chinese Mine Labour in the Transvaal* (London: Macmillan, 1982).

[118] Hyam, *Elgin and Churchill*, 122.   [119] Ibid., 38–9.

soon as possible.[120] He wrote numerous memoranda and minutes on the issue and corresponded with influential people in Britain and in South Africa (particularly with Selborne) on South African affairs.[121] On 26 January 1906, Churchill had an interview with Smuts, who had come to Britain to persuade the Liberals to grant the Transvaal immediate self-government. As Smuts's son subsequently wrote, "Churchill was frankly dubious"; nor did Smuts have confidence in the attitude of Elgin.[122] But, as has been explained,[123] that did not mean that they were unsympathetic to the immediate introduction of self-government; it probably meant that they were exercising the correct discretion in a controversial matter. Few modern historians still believe, as Smuts did, that it was his interview with Campbell-Bannerman that was decisive in swaying the Liberals in favor of the introduction of responsible self-government. It is virtually certain that by the time Smuts saw Campbell-Bannerman the majority of Liberal cabinet ministers had decided that self-government should be given to the Transvaal.[124] On 8 February 1906, the cabinet finally abandoned the Lyttelton constitution, and after the West Ridgeway commission had reported on the details, Churchill (and not Campbell-Bannerman) announced the terms in the Commons on 31 July 1906.[125] A general election in the Transvaal in February 1907 resulted in Het Volk, contrary to Churchill's expectations, gaining the most seats, so that the former Boer generals Louis Botha (as premier) and Jan Smuts were now the most important members of the cabinet. The first Chinese laborers on the Witwatersrand were repatriated in June 1907, the last in 1910. The Orange River Colony was granted responsible government in June 1907, and there too the Boer party Orangia Unie came to power, with Abram Fischer as prime minister and General J. B. M. Hertzog as the most influential member of his cabinet.[126]

---

[120] Ibid., 114–15, 120–1.

[121] WSC II C 496–502, 504–24; D. G. Boyce, ed., The Crisis of British Power: The Imperial and Naval Papers of the Second Earl of Selborne (London: The Historians' Press, 1990), 254–301.

[122] J. C. Smuts, Jan Christian Smuts (Cape Town: Cassell, 1952), 97; W. K. Hancock, Smuts: The Sanguine Years, 1870–1919 (Cambridge: Cambridge University Press, 1962), 213–14.

[123] Hyam, Elgin and Churchill, 126–7.

[124] Ibid., 125–7; Hancock, Sanguine Years, 214–17; Ronald Hyam, "Smuts and the Decision of the Liberal Government to Grant Responsible Government to the Transvaal, January and February 1906," Historical Journal 8 (1966): 126.

[125] Hyam, Elgin and Churchill, 148–50.

[126] G. B. Pryah, Imperial Policy and South Africa, 1902–1910 (Oxford: Clarendon Press, 1955), 177–9, 196.

It has been asserted in a recent biography of Churchill that, while he certainly played an active role in shaping the Transvaal settlement, his contribution "is easily overestimated by those looking for signs that in his political youth the lineaments of the great man of the future could be discerned."[127] Churchill himself was not modest about this period of his life. In March 1908 he informed H. H. Asquith (who was to succeed Campbell-Bannerman as premier) that during the last two years, as far as the colonial office was concerned, "Practically all the constructive action and all the parliamentary exposition has been mine."[128] Those words can be explained as an understandable exaggeration by an ambitious young politician pressing for full cabinet ranking. Yet his assiduous attention to detail, sheer hard work, and persuasive arguments undeniably had a remarkable impact on the final settlement, particularly when Churchill's subordinate position is borne in mind.

The significance of the settlement was that the loyalty of Botha and Smuts to the British Empire was ensured. Smuts marveled, "They gave us back our country in everything but name. After four years. Has such a miracle of trust and magnanimity ever happened before?"[129] On Campbell-Bannerman's death in April 1908, Botha sent the following message to Asquith:

In securing self-government for the new Colonies . . . through the policy of trust he inspired the people of South Africa with a new feeling of hopefulness and co-operation.

In making it possible for the two races [the English and the Boer] to live and work together harmoniously he has laid the foundation of a united South Africa.[130]

Hertzog, the third of the Boer generals to be premier of the Union of South Africa, believed that in granting self-government the British government was merely honoring a promise that had been made.[131] But even Hertzog, who was opposed to South African forces invading German Southwest Africa in 1914 and who proposed that South Africa should be neutral in the Second World War, was to operate within the parameters of the empire-commonwealth.

The leader of the Conservative opposition, Arthur Balfour, regarded the

---

[127] John Charmley, *Churchill: The End of Glory* (London: Hodder & Stoughton, 1993), 39.
[128] Hyam, *Elgin and Churchill*, 489.   [129] Smuts, *Smuts*, 98–9.
[130] Spender, *Life of Campbell-Bannerman*, vol. 2, 395–6 (my interpolation).
[131] C. M. van den Heever, *Generaal J. B. M. Hertzog* (Johannesburg: A. P. Boekhandel, 1946), 204.

grant of self-government to the Transvaal as "the most reckless experiment ever tried in the development of a great colonial policy."[132] Milner bluntly expressed his disgust: "We have given over the country to the Govt. of a backward race who hate us."[133]

But Churchill and other Liberal leaders had not abandoned the concept of British supremacy in South Africa. The grant of self-government was not so much a magnanimous gesture as an action grounded in the belief that it was the most effectual way to try to ensure the loyalty of South Africa's white inhabitants and to further Britain's international, economic, and strategic interests. Similarly, Botha and Smuts's attitude of cooperation within the empire-commonwealth was based more on political expediency—and indeed it was the only viable option open to them—than on a desire for reconciliation.[134]

Only white people received the vote in the newly constituted self-governing colonies, the Transvaal and the Orange River Colony. To some extent, the franchise for inhabitants of these states who were not white was governed by Article 8 of the Vereeniging peace agreement. This article had stated originally, "The Franchise will not be given to Natives until after the introduction of Self-Government." Smuts altered this to read, "The question of granting the Franchise to Natives will not be decided until after the introduction of Self-Government." That version was accepted by Milner, Kitchener, and the Conservative government.[135] And not only accepted: apparently Milner told Hertzog and Smuts: "On this question I am at one with you."[136] Article 8 of the peace agreement would seem to have precluded the British government's enfranchising black people in the former republics when they were granted self-government. But what about Indian and colored (mixed race) people in the republics? After Dr. A. Abdurahman, president of the African Political Organization in the Cape Colony, had sent a petition to London in June 1906 pleading for political rights for colored men in the Transvaal, Churchill answered a question in the Commons by stating, "I believe the precise meaning attached to the word 'native' is native of any country other than a Euro-

---

[132] Le May, *British Supremacy*, 189.

[133] Roberts Papers (National Army Museum, London), Milner to Roberts, January 4, 1908.

[134] Hyam, *Elgin and Churchill*, 184; Ronald Hyam, "The Myth of the Magnanimous Gesture: The Liberal Government, Smuts and Conciliation 1906," in Ronald Hyam and Ged Martin, *Reappraisals in British Imperial History* (London: Macmillan, 1975), 167–86.

[135] Hancock, *Sanguine Years*, 159; Kestell and van Velden, facsimile of page of the peace proposals, facing 112.

[136] André Odendaal, *Vukani Bantu: The Beginning of Black Protest Politics in South Africa to 1912* (Cape Town: David Philip, 1984), 37.

pean country."[137] Black political activity in South Africa intensified after the grant of responsible government, but pleas for imperial support for black political rights in the former republics received little sympathy from the Liberal government in Britain.[138] It has been postulated that British officials (and politicians) considered that "their task was to manipulate South African affairs, not to precipitate social change."[139]

There were two particular areas of racial tension in South Africa during Churchill's term as under secretary of the colonies. In the Transvaal the question of Indian immigration had come sharply to the fore shortly before the grant of responsible government. The Crown Colony government proposed an ordinance to prevent new Indian immigrants entering the Transvaal and to force Indian residents in the Transvaal to carry passes bearing their fingerprints. Churchill's advice to the British government regarding the ordinance was to avoid responsibility for it: "The new [Transvaal] parliament may shoulder the burden. Why should we: Dawdle or disallow—preferably the former."[140] The British government in the event chose the latter option and disallowed the ordinance, only to watch the Transvaal authorities pass an almost similar ordinance after the grant of responsible government. A campaign of passive resistance led by M. K. Gandhi was followed by mass arrests before Gandhi and Smuts reached a temporary agreement in January 1908.[141]

The most serious manifestation of black-white conflict since the Anglo-Zulu War of 1879 erupted in Zululand and Natal in 1906. Discontent, owing to land shortage and economic distress, was aggravated by the imposition of a poll tax in 1906. The Natal government imposed martial law after outbreaks of unrest, and a number of Zulu were summarily executed. The resistance by the chief, Bambatha, resulted in the rebellion assuming serious proportions. The Natal militia, with only "moral" support from a battalion of imperial forces who took no part in the fighting, and the visit of a Royal Navy battleship to Durban crushed the rebellion. Only twenty-four white soldiers and six civilians lost their lives, but over

---

[137] Le May, *British Supremacy*, 205.   [138] Odendaal, *Vukani Bantu*, 72–82.
[139] Donald Denoon, *The Grand Illusion: The Failure of Imperial Policy in the Transvaal Colony during the Period of Reconstruction, 1900–1905* (London: Longman, 1973), 5. Criticisms of the fact that African, Indian, and colored people were not enfranchised in the Transvaal and the Orange River Colony are to be found particularly in Thompson, *Unification of South Africa*, 27; and Nicholas Mansergh, *South Africa 1906–1961: The Price of Magnanimity* (London: George Allen and Unwin, 1962).
[140] Hyam, *Elgin and Churchill*, 266.
[141] Ibid., 265–72; Maureen Swan, *Gandhi: The South African Experience* (Johannesburg: Ravan Press, 1984), 93–164.

three thousand blacks were killed and seven thousand were jailed. Churchill felt strongly about the behavior of the Natal authorities. He drafted a telegram to the Natal government on 28 March 1906, urging it to exercise great caution in executing rebels and directing that executions should be suspended until further information was received in London. The telegram caused a furor in Natal—where the ministry contemplated resigning *en bloc*—and also in other self-governing colonies. The telegram was seen as an interference in the rights of colonies that had received responsible government. The British government retracted and denied any intention of interfering in the internal affairs of Natal. Churchill continued to push strongly for intervention to bring "this wretched Colony—the hooligan of the British Empire—to its sense," and accused Natal of "disgusting butchery of natives."[142]

The 1907 imperial conference in London was the first one to be attended by representatives from the Transvaal and the Orange River Colony, and Churchill played a prominent role in its organization and proceedings. Louis Botha, the former enemy, was considered by the public to be the lion of the conference, but his contribution was insignificant.[143] The secretary of state for war, R. B. Haldane, was eager for the colonial premiers to achieve uniformity in their defense organization.[144] Churchill's friend Leo Amery,[145] then a leader writer for *The Times*, considered him to be the dominant figure in the colonial office. Amery found Churchill strongly opposed to consulting the colonial leaders on foreign affairs until they had built up enough military strength to be of real value to Britain in time of war.[146] Churchill believed that Britain would never have secured the Japanese alliance of 1902 or the Entente Cordiale of 1904 if the colonies had been consulted.[147] Churchill's one idea, Amery stated, "seemed to be that the Colonial Prime Ministers should be given a good time and sent away well banqueted, but empty-handed."[148]

---

[142] Hyam, *Elgin and Churchill*, 251, and on the Bambatha rebellion in general, 239–58; see also Shula Marks, *Reluctant Rebellion: The 1906–8 Disturbances in Natal* (Oxford: Clarendon Press, 1970).

[143] L. S. Amery, *My Political Life*, 3 vols. (London: Hutchinson, 1953), vol. 1, 313.

[144] Haldane Papers (National Library of Scotland, Edinburgh), MS 5919, 118, memorandum of events between 1906 and 1915.

[145] L. S. Amery (1873–1955), compiler of *The Times History of the War in South Africa, 1899–1902*, journalist and politician, first lord of the Admiralty, 1922–24, secretary of state for the colonies and for dominion affairs, 1924–29.

[146] Amery, *Political Life*, vol. 1, 302.

[147] J. Barnes and D. Nicholson, eds., *The Leo Amery Diaries*, 2 vols. (London: Hutchinson, 1980), vol. 1, 313.

[148] Amery, *Political Life*, vol. 1, 302.

One of the last matters relating to South Africa with which Churchill was concerned before he left the colonial office in April 1908 was the advice he offered the king about the Cullinan diamond. The diamond, the largest in the world, was discovered at Premier Mine near Pretoria in January 1905. After his return from the London conference, Botha proposed in the Transvaal parliament that the stone should be presented to King Edward VII as a gesture of peace, reconciliation, and goodwill. His proposal was opposed by some English-speaking members of the Progressive Party. They opposed the proposal ostensibly on the grounds that the Transvaal could not afford the gift, but it was more likely that they believed that the publicity and prestige gained by Botha in London would receive a fillip. Churchill steadfastly urged that the diamond should be accepted by the king, as he believed that "the feeling of loyalty to the King and of gratitude for the liberties which have been restored to them in His Majesty's name, are the strongest links between this country and the Transvaal." Churchill's advice was followed and the diamond was presented to Edward VII on his birthday, 9 November 1907. The diamond was subsequently cut into a number of smaller stones, some of them set into the royal scepter and crowns.[149]

In 1908 Churchill was due for promotion to full cabinet rank under Asquith's premiership. His preference was to become secretary of state for the colonies, but in April 1908 he was appointed president of the Board of Trade.[150] Churchill was not exclusively concerned with South African affairs while he was under secretary at the colonial office, but they certainly formed the predominant feature of his work between the end of 1905 and 1908.

Neither as president of the Board of Trade, nor when he went to the home office in February 1910, was Churchill directly concerned with South Africa. In 1909, however, there were rumors that he wanted to become the first governor-general of the Union of South Africa. Apparently Asquith wanted to appoint a member of cabinet to that post: someone who would be strong enough to help the Union government stand up to Milner should he ever become colonial secretary. Charles Hobhouse, then financial secretary to the Treasury, wrote in his diary: "Winston Churchill wanted to go, but the PM wouldn't look at him."[151] The governor of the Cape Colony, Sir Walter Hely-Hutchinson, informed Merriman on 11 August 1909:

---

[149] *WSC* II 217–20.   [150] *WSC* II 240–5.
[151] Sir Charles Hobhouse Journals, 1890–1915 (British Library, London), Add MS 60505, August 3, 1909; E. David, ed., *Inside Asquith's Cabinet* (London: John Murray, 1977), 79.

A friend just out from England tells me that Winston Churchill's candidature for the governor-generalship is by no means otherwise than serious—and that it is on the cards, though not likely he may be appointed. . . . The story is that Winston wants to form a Socialist-Radical party but thinks the time is not yet, and that he had better be out of politics for two or three years.[152]

In September 1909 Asquith asked the home secretary, Herbert Gladstone, the fourth son of W. E. Gladstone, to accept the post of governor-general of the Union of South Africa, and Gladstone was created a viscount.[153] The South African Unionist politician C. P. Crewe wrote to his wife:

Haldane was talking about Herbert Gladstone . . . who is to get a peerage, [and] asked what title he was going to take. Haldane said he thought Milord Majuba would be the most suitable [a reference to his father's restoration of Transvaal independence after the British defeat at the battle of Majuba in February 1881].[154]

Elgin and Curzon were two viceroys of India who did come back to play prominent roles in British political affairs; no governor-general who returned to the mainstream of British politics comes to mind. It is futile, but tempting, to speculate whether the dynamic Churchill could have been the exception, if he had at the age of thirty-six become governor-general of the Union of South Africa. This rumor possibly had no more substance than talk at the time, in 1907, that Churchill was getting engaged to Louis Botha's daughter Helen.[155]

APPROACH OF THE GREAT WAR

After the grant of self-government to the former Boer republics, South African affairs no longer exercised the urgent priority they had earlier for British statesmen and officials. On 27 June 1908, in a confidential "Note upon British Military Needs" prepared for the cabinet, Churchill prefaced some of his recommendations with the remark: "Now that South Africa is out of the way."[156] As a senior army officer minuted in December 1908: "We have decided to trust the Boers."[157] The fact was that by the time that Churchill left the colonial office, Britain's external interests had become focused more on the possibility of a future European war;

---

[152] Thompson, *Unification of South Africa*, 448 n. 42, quoting from Merriman Papers.
[153] Ibid., 449.
[154] C. P. Crewe Papers (East London Museum), correspondence, Box B, 147, November 28, 1909 (my interpolation).
[155] WSC II 210.   [156] Cab 37/94, 89.
[157] War Office records (Public Record Office, Kew), WO, 32/7116, minute by Major General J. S. Ewart.

imperial affairs came to be considered primarily in that context, so that "defence" became the most important component of Britain's relations with the empire-commonwealth. Although not the only consideration, strategic factors had certainly helped motivate the unification of South Africa.[158]

The constitutional position of the dominions in a war in which Britain was involved had come under scrutiny when their delegates to the 1911 imperial conference had attended a meeting of the committee of imperial defense. The principle was accepted that the constitutional status of the dominions precluded any of them remaining neutral if Britain was at war; in such an eventuality they would automatically be at war. The British government did not, however, deny the assertion of the Canadian premier Sir Wilfrid Laurier that the nature and extent of the dominions' participation in such a war was a matter that could be decided only by their parliaments. Asquith, however, secured a unanimous assurance that it was unlikely that any dominion would refuse to cooperate.[159]

It has been postulated that defense considerations became of prime importance in Britain's attitude to the self-governing dominions after 1908. The cornerstone of imperial defense, it was repeatedly stressed, was the need to ensure British supremacy at sea.[160] From 1911, when he became first lord of the Admiralty, the vital matter of naval defense became Churchill's particular responsibility. The Agadir crisis had erupted in July 1911, after the imperial conference of that year; in October 1911 Asquith appointed Churchill first lord of the Admiralty. As Martin Gilbert has succinctly explained, although Churchill was not committed to war with Germany, "The principal task with which Asquith entrusted him was to ensure that the Royal Navy did not find itself in a position where Germany could gain sudden advantage over it."[161] Churchill, moreover, focused increasingly on world affairs, believing that problems could arise in Europe, Asia, or Africa.[162]

Churchill's biographers have stressed that as first lord of the Admiralty he initially pressed for a diminution of the naval arms race with Germany.

---

[158] Thompson, *Unification of South Africa*, 64, 398–9; Ronald Hyam, "British Imperial Policy in South Africa, 1908–1910," in Warwick and Spies, *The South Africa War*, 373; J. E. B. Seely, *Adventure* (London: Heinemann, 1930), 133.

[159] Cab 2/2, Committee of Imperial Defense, minutes of 11th meeting, May 26, 1911; F. S. Malan-Versameling (Cape Archives, Cape Town), Acc. 583, Aantekeningen, Mei 1910–September 1914; Indrukken van de Imperiale Konferentie, 1911; M. Hankey, *The Supreme Command*, 2 vols. (London: George Allen and Unwin, 1961), vol. 1, 131.

[160] See, for instance, *The Times*, December 17, 1910, quoting Admiral Sir George Egerton.

[161] WSC III 1.   [162] Ibid.

He did not, however, abandon his belief in the importance for the empire-commonwealth of British naval supremacy and his implementation of a policy of naval preparedness.[163] Churchill sought to involve the dominions, including the Union of South Africa, in imperial naval defense.

There was a divergence of opinion among dominion governments regarding the way in which they should contribute to the naval defense of the Empire. Some preferred to grant money or material, while Australia and Canada started laying the foundation for the establishment of navies of their own. South Africa's contribution was less than that of any of the other dominions. The total sum of £85,000 which South Africa contributed to imperial naval defense annually was the same as the Cape Colony and Natal had contributed in 1902; no further amount was contributed when the two inland colonies achieved self-government, or after the unification of South Africa. This amount, it was calculated in 1911–12, represented approximately a shilling and three pence per head of the white population and three pence per head of the total population of South Africa. Australia contributed over nine shillings per head, while the inhabitants of the United Kingdom contributed more than eighteen shillings per head.[164]

First Sea Lord Admiral Sir John Fisher once called Cape Town one of the five strategic keys that lock up the world.[165] The Admiralty and the war office had no doubt as to the strategic importance to Britain of the Cape, particularly if the Suez Canal were closed. The committee of imperial defense declared, "The importance of the Cape is paramount and the ports of the Peninsula must become the most important of our coaling stations strategically and commercially."[166] Churchill believed a "complete harmony" existed between imperial interests and South African needs: "The interruption of the trade route would arrest, its insecurity would hamper, the whole economic development of South Africa, and sensibly and immediately affect the fortunes, both as producers and consumers, of persons of every race and occupation in South Africa."[167] In a private and confidential letter sent to Louis Botha by hand, Churchill suggested that the Union government should provide a squadron of small fast cruisers

---

[163] WSC II 570–1, III 1–2.
[164] Archives of the Office of the Governor General (Central Archives, Pretoria), GG vol. 5, 1/587.
[165] Ronald Hyam, *Britain's Imperial Century: A Study of Empire and Expansion* (London: B.T. Batsford, 1976), 125.
[166] Cab 11/32, part 6, Cape of Good Hope, May 1904.
[167] WSC II C 1514, undated Admiralty memorandum by Churchill.

costing £400,000 or £500,000 apiece on the South African trade route. He explained:

It would be a very good thing from a purely S. African point of view, a considerable assistance to the Admiralty and would have the best possible effect in this country and in Europe. . . . All the other Dominions are taking action and I do not think the Union Government ought to be left out.[168]

But although Botha and Smuts were sympathetic to the pleas for a greater South African contribution in money or ships to imperial naval defense, no increase in the £85,000—which Smuts called "a paltry sum"—was made before the outbreak of the First World War.[169] One reason for this was that the newly established Union of South Africa had serious financial problems, particularly after the formation of the Union Defense Force in 1912.[170] There were also, however, internal political complications which made it difficult for the Union government to increase its naval contribution. The former Orange Free State president, M. T. Steyn, probably shrewdly assessed some segments of Afrikaner opinion when he maintained that there were some of his people who regarded the naval contribution as "the symbol of extreme jingo imperialism."[171]

The Union of South Africa was the only dominion that was contiguous to German territory. Churchill has related in his memoirs that Botha told him in 1913 that when war came he was "going to attack German South West Africa and clear them out once and for all."[172] At least two other British cabinet ministers, the secretary of state for war, Haldane, and the chancellor of the Exchequer, David Lloyd George, also received information of Botha's intentions regarding German Southwest Africa.[173]

After the outbreak of the First World War on 4 August 1914, a British war council attended by Churchill sanctioned six dominion expeditions against German colonies—including a request to the Union government

---

[168] Archives of the secretary to the department of the prime minister (Central Archives, Pretoria), PM 1/1/467, Churchill to Botha, July 30, 1912.

[169] *Union of South Africa, House of Assembly Debates*, 2d session, 1st Parliament, Col 1420, March 28, 1912; PM 1/1/467, Botha to Churchill, September 23, 1912 (copy).

[170] See, for instance, PM 1/1/467, Botha to Churchill, September 23, 1912 (copy); Merriman Papers, diary, April 25, 1911, July 1914, correspondence, Steyn to Merriman, October 8, 1913.

[171] W. K. Hancock and Jean van der Poel, *Selections from the Smuts Papers*, 7 vols. (Cambridge: Cambridge University Press, 1966), vol. 3, 23, Steyn to Smuts, January 27, 1911.

[172] Churchill, *My Early Life*, 261.

[173] Haldane Papers, MS 5909, 143, General Lord Methuen (commander in chief of British forces in South Africa) to Haldane, September 7, 1911; David Lloyd George, *War Memoirs*, 4 vols. (London: Odhams Press, 1934), vol. 4, 1789.

to invade German Southwest Africa. The official reason for these operations was to deprive the German navy of its colonial bases and radio
stations; there was also the perception that these German colonies could
be used as bargaining counters at the peace negotiations. In the case of
German Southwest Africa, the British cabinet attached importance to the
political effect of inviting the cooperation of the South African government.[174] The South African government's decision to agree to the British
request to invade German Southwest Africa precipitated an Afrikaner
rebellion. After its suppression by the Botha government, German Southwest Africa was conquered and members of the Union Defense Force
fought in East Africa, Palestine, and Flanders. The British government also
benefited financially by having a friendly government in power in South
Africa (the Bank of England obtaining the value of gold mined, though
it was retained for safety in South Africa) and by being able to purchase
war materials from the United States, despite a deteriorating balance of
trade. One of the most significant contributions made by South Africans
was the services rendered to the imperial war effort by Smuts in London
as a member of the war cabinet.[175]

While working with Churchill at the colonial office, Elgin had coined
the phrase "Churchill's latest *volte face.*" It has been maintained that
Churchill's career between 1899 and 1911 was indeed "full of contradictions and shifts of attitude."[176] If the shrewd assessment of Leo Amery
—that Churchill as "a great English patriot" was primarily motivated by
what was in England's best interests[177]—is accepted, however, the apparent contradictions and shift in attitude tend to fall away. Viewed through
this prism, Churchill's attitude, his statements, and his actions concerning
South Africa and peace and war in the period between 1896 and 1914
assume a remarkable degree of consistency.

[174] Cab 42/1, 1–3, secretary's notes of war councils, August 5–6, 1914; Asquith Papers
(Bodleian Library, Oxford), m. s. 111, proceedings of a sub-committee of the Committee
of Imperial Defense assembled on August 5, 1914 to consider the question of offensive
operations against German colonies; Hankey, *Supreme Command*, vol. 1, 167–8.

[175] S. B. Spies, "The Outbreak of the First World War and the Botha Government," *South
African Historical Journal* 1 (November 1969): 47–57; N. G. Garson, "South Africa and
World War I," *Journal of Imperial and Commonwealth History* 8, no. 1 (1979): 68–85;
S. B. Spies, "South Africa and the First World War," in Liebenberg and Spies, *South
Africa in the 20th Century*, 93–137.

[176] Hyam, *Elgin and Churchill*, 500.   [177] Amery, *Political Life*, 196.

6

The aftermath of the Great War

JAMES W. MULLER

When Winston Churchill joined the Fourth Hussars in January 1895, the British Empire had been at peace for so long that junior officers despaired of ever fighting a war on the continent of Europe.[1] Liberal statesmen like William Gladstone aimed to bind civilized nations together in a peaceful web of commercial relations, diverting energies once used for waging war to the endeavor to give citizens a richer and more comfortable life. In the first decade of the twentieth century, as storm clouds gathered on the distant horizon, British diplomatists were obliged to consort with shadowy worries about war. In the first volume of *The World Crisis*, his history of the First World War, Churchill describes the "duality" of British foreign policy in those years before the war, when British statesmen lived in "the actual visible world with its peaceful activities and cosmopolitan aims" but had to imagine "a hypothetical world, a world 'beneath the threshold,' as it were," in which polite diplomacy gave way to violence and death (I 24; cf. 48–9, 51–2).

Beginning in 1911, when he became first lord of the Admiralty, Churchill was responsible for superintending Britain's precautions against the unwonted specter of a European war. His office imposed on him the duty of finding his way in that "hypothetical world." Three years before the outbreak of war, he prepared for the Committee of Imperial Defense a memorandum that presented his idea of the likeliest scenario. He thought that the French would be driven back from the Meuse by the twentieth day

---

[1] Winston S. Churchill, *My Early Life: A Roving Commission* (London: Thornton Butterworth, 1930), 78–81, 88–9; Winston S. Churchill, *The World Crisis*, 5 vols. (London: Thornton Butterworth, 1923–31), vol. 1, 19 (parenthetical numbers in the text hereafter refer to this book by volume and page, or simply by page if the volume is the same as in the previous reference). Cf. Winston S. Churchill, *Thoughts and Adventures* (London: Thornton Butterworth, 1932), 174–7.

of the German invasion, but that by the fortieth day "Germany should be
extended at full strain" and France would have the opportunity to reverse
its fortunes. Although the memorandum "was, of course, only an attempt
to pierce the veil of the future," Churchill's predictions proved astonish-
ingly accurate (60). When the war came, the French were in full retreat on
the twentieth day, just as he had foreseen, and their prospects seemed
gloomy; but by the fortieth day the German advance was spent, and the
French army was able to make the counterattack that stabilized the western front.

While Churchill, with his fertile imagination and his excellent information, contemplated the prospects for war quite realistically, some of his
colleagues in the Liberal cabinet were hard put to imagine it, even when
it was at hand. In the deceptively still summer of 1914, with the long Victorian peace about to give way to war, they shrank from embracing their
lot, hoping that events would spare Britain from being drawn into the
fray. Even after the German declaration of war upon Russia, even after
the German invasion of Belgium, there were ministers who still hoped
that the avalanche could be recalled. Churchill recalls in *The World Crisis*
that as their hopes melted away, "The grief and horror of so many able
colleagues were painful to witness." His friend John Morley even resigned
from the government because he could not adjust to the new situation.
Those who thought like Morley were not the sort of people you would
want to take with you on a tiger hunt (199, 218–20; cf. 188, 193).[2] Fortunately for Britain, none of them, but rather a man of very different kidney
was at the helm of the Admiralty. Churchill had no inhibitions about
facing up to war. By the time the cabinet, swallowing hard, agreed to make
war against Germany, "the king's ships" had already been for several
days safely at sea (213).

At midnight on 28 July, after informing the king that the fleet had been
sent to its war station, Churchill wrote a letter to his wife. He described
the "darling cygnet" that had been born to two black swans who lived
on the lake in St. James's Park. But his observation of the swans was
only an interlude of recreation after his day of preparing for war, which
he admitted had "a hideous fascination" for him. "My darling one &
beautiful," he wrote, "Everything tends towards catastrophe & collapse.
I am interested, geared up & happy. Is it not horrible to be built like
that?" He described himself and his staff as "awake to the tips of our

[2] Cf. Winston S. Churchill, *Great Contemporaries* (London: Thornton Butterworth, 1938),
63–6. See also Asquith's letter of October 7, 1914, to Venetia Stanley, quoted in *WSC* III
120–1.

fingers."[3] Churchill's daughter Mary Soames, who wrote her mother's biography with the aid of the letters that passed between her parents, concluded that he told his wife everything;[4] this letter, written in anticipation of what Churchill must have thought would be the greatest event in his life, is one of the most revealing. He opens to her a part of his soul not fit to display in public in a regime that aims at peace and comfortable self-preservation—the part that longs for the greatest contests or challenges, ones that are more than peaceable. Why would a man be "interested, geared up & happy" at the prospect of a war that would destroy the world he had known up till then? Churchill has the kind of spirit or ambition that is not content with the comfortable, humdrum life of peacetime politics. He avows it to his wife, but others noticed it too in the waning days of summer 1914.

This is the side of Churchill that Asquith had sought out when he made him first lord of the Admiralty in 1911, foreseeing a need for such a man; this is the side of him that later caused his return to the Admiralty in 1939, when the appeasement of Neville Chamberlain had finally failed, and the nation awoke to the fact that Chamberlain himself had to be replaced in May 1940. What the Greeks might have called Churchill's *aristeia*—his finest hour, to put it into English—depended on this side of his soul. Here is the famous statesman of wartime renown, awake to the tips of his fingers, the Churchill who thrilled and affrighted both ordinary citizens and academics, though in different proportions—the intransigent foe, the bulldog, the man of war, the one who would "never give in, *never.*"[5]

When we contemplate Winston Churchill the political icon, this side of his character comes to the fore. It is only when we survey his career as a whole that we realize that, despite his remarkable success at conjuring himself onto every battlefield (it took a direct order from the king to prevent him from wading ashore with the British vanguard on D-Day), he spent the greater part of his life preparing for war or recovering from war, but not actually waging it. If battles, as he writes in his biography of Marlborough, "are the principal milestones in secular history,"[6] unseasonable though the thought may be to current academic historians, then it would be prudent

[3] Winston Churchill to Clementine Churchill, July 28, 1914, printed in *WSC* II C 1989–90, at 1989.
[4] Mary Soames, *Clementine Churchill* (London: Cassell, 1979), 92.
[5] A speech to the boys of Harrow School, October 29, 1941, printed in Winston S. Churchill, *War Speeches*, 3 vols. (London: Cassell, 1952), vol. 2, 94–96, at 95.
[6] Winston S. Churchill, *Marlborough: His Life and Times*, 2 vols. (London: George G. Harrap, 1947), vol. 2, 381.

for a statesman to learn about war, to expect war, and to prepare for war rather than trying to wish it away, as some of Churchill's colleagues did. When Churchill predicted, observing the triumph of liberal democracy at the beginning of the twentieth century, that the wars of peoples would be bloodier than the wars of kings, he was closer to the mark than those who expected the democratic revolution to put an end to war among civilized men.

But do this ability and willingness to think about war and to plan for it make a statesman too bellicose, too apt to choose violent solutions to problems that might be settled by lowering our voices and negotiating peacefully? Churchill has often been taxed by critics with having an unwonted penchant for the use of force. It has been said that some men have a martial disposition, while others are more phlegmatic. If Churchill's pacifist colleagues must be criticized for being at a loss in wartime, cannot Churchill himself be criticized for being at a loss in times of peace? The question arises in the very letter to his wife that has already been quoted, wherein Churchill asks God's forgiveness for his excitement at the prospect of war and explains:

I w[oul]d do my best for peace, & nothing w[oul]d induce me wrongfully to strike the blow. I cannot feel that we in this island are in any serious degree responsible for the wave of madness wh[ich] has swept the mind of Christendom. No one can measure the consequences. I wondered whether those stupid Kings & Emperors c[oul]d not assemble together & revivify kingship by saving the nations from hell but we all drift on in a kind of dull cataleptic trance. As if it was somebody else's operation![7]

Churchill is alive, at any rate, to the question of justice in war. He presumes that there is a difference in justice between aggression and self-defense. So far from presuming that war was inevitable, he seems to think that war was *not* inevitable, but that those who find it unthinkable, by their ostrichism, have missed their chance to try to prevent it. Certainly he drew that sort of a conclusion later about the failure of British and French appeasement in the 1930s.

Not all of Churchill's Liberal colleagues resigned from the government when war came—in fact, Morley had little company. Most of them clung to office and discharged it to the best of their varying abilities. But Morley was not alone in hesitating to join the battle. Across the Atlantic, the leader

---

[7] Winston Churchill to Clementine Churchill, July 28, 1914, printed in *WSC* II C 1989–90, at 1989.

of the great republic, President Woodrow Wilson, showed the traditional American reluctance to become involved in other people's troubles. This standoffishness on the part of the United States goes back as far as George Washington's farewell address, in which the father of his country warned compatriots to steer clear of European contests. But in the end Wilson did lead his country into the war, and Churchill's study of Wilson's conduct of war and peace in his history of the First World War illuminates his own views.

WILSON AS WAR LEADER

In the third volume of *The World Crisis*, which describes the war from 1916 until Armistice Day in November 1918, Churchill hints that the United States might better have declared war on Germany before 6 April 1917; or, alternately, that it might have persisted in indecision even after the expansion of the U-boat warfare. Englishmen expecting American support because their common "laws and language seemed to make a bridge of mutual comprehension between the two nations" were hard put to understand why the United States held back. Churchill explains that they should rather have been surprised and gratified that the American people, "grappling with the undeveloped resources of the continent which was their inheritance, absorbed in domestic life and politics, taught by long constitutional tradition to shun foreign entanglements," could finally be persuaded by some among them, "who never doubted, and who from the first discerned the inevitable path," to join hands with the Allies in a war across the Atlantic (III 227–8). He accounts for America's entry into the war by way of a digression on the United States Constitution. From its rigidity, exemplified by its provision of fixed terms for public officers, and from the superiority of the party machinery that selects them to any nationally focused public opinion, arises the great personal authority of the president. Unlike a parliamentary government in which the executive authority is vested in statesmen who belong to the legislature and are "continuously accountable to it for their tenure," the American electoral process makes it likely that the president will be an eminent citizen who has not previously held public office (228). Such a man was Woodrow Wilson, despite his brief tenure in the gubernatorial chair, and American policy depended "upon the workings of this man's mind and spirit to the exclusion of almost every other factor" (229).

Relying on the memoirs of Wilson's confidant Colonel House, Churchill

sketches a picture of the president as a partisan Democrat who hated war
and violence. Instead of recognizing in the invasion of Belgium and the
sinking of the *Lusitania* an unhesitating willingness to use force without
right, which would prove inconvenient to the United States in case of a
German victory, Wilson tried to keep America out of the war. Only as he
stood before Congress to deliver his war message did he realize where the
sympathies of his countrymen had always lain. In the end the Germans
forced his hand by declaring unlimited U-boat warfare and then, against his
hope, acting accordingly. Wilson's abhorrence of force and his unfounded
expectation that Germany would shrink from it recall the unavailing idealism of men like Morley at the beginning of the war. While Churchill
admires Wilson's war speeches, with their insistence that "the world must
be made safe for Democracy," he rues his long delay in bringing America
into the struggle, when promptitude would have saved "many million
homes . . . an empty chair" (233).

On the other hand, Churchill praises the immediate American decision
to raise an army by conscription, contrasting it with the halfhearted
measures taken in Britain. After missing the chance to require universal
service at the beginning of the war when it was not absolutely necessary,
Britain was hard put to face up to the need for it later. Compulsion did
not sit well "with the British habit of mind" (236). Even Kitchener, who
was too fond of his own popularity, liked to think "his countrymen
would give him personally whatever numbers he thought right to demand." When conscription became unavoidable, the government adopted
a bill that proved inadequate to the purpose and had to be revised several
months later. In a chapter of *The World Crisis* called "A Political Interlude" that shows his acuity as a political analyst, Churchill uses this
dispute to reflect on the different "processes of thought and methods of
management" in war and peace:

Much is gained in Peace by ignoring or putting off disagreeable or awkward questions, and avoiding clear-cut decisions which if they please some, offend others.
It is often better in Peace to persist for a time patiently in an obscure and inde-
terminate course of action rather than break up or dangerously strain a political
combination. . . . Compromise is very often not merely necessary but actually
beneficial. . . . Many an apparently insoluble political problem solves itself or
sinks to an altogether lower range if time, patience and phlegm are used. British
politicians and Parliamentarians, particularly those called upon to lead great
parties, are masters in all these arts. . . .

In War everything is different. There is no place for compromise in War. That
invaluable process only means that soldiers are shot because their leaders in

Council and camp are unable to resolve. In War the clouds never blow over, they gather unceasingly and fall in thunderbolts. Things do not get better by being let alone. . . . Clear leadership, violent action, rigid decisions one way or the other, form the only path not only of victory, but of safety and even of mercy. (238–9)

When one reads Churchill's criticism, one thinks not only of Wilson's delays in entering the war but also of Asquith's hesitations during the Dardanelles campaign. Our author must have wished that the prime minister, a devoted reader of ancient Greek texts, had hearkened to the stark contrast between peace and war drawn by Thucydides in his history of the Peloponnesian War, which Churchill restates in this passage.[8]

Churchill did not underrate the difficulty of making the adjustment from the profound peace of the Victorian era to a new kind of total war. As he wrote in *My Early Life*, reflecting on the difference in the scale of warfare in the short space of a few decades,

I wonder whether any other generation has seen such astounding revolutions of data and values as those through which we have lived. Scarcely anything material or established which I was brought up to believe was permanent and vital, has lasted. Everything I was sure or taught to be sure was impossible, has happened.[9]

In many ways, the First World War was a more astonishing event than the Second: for the Second World War marked a renewal of the first German attempt to gain control of Europe, which is why Churchill put the two struggles together and called them another Thirty Years' War.[10] But the transition from war to peace after Armistice Day in 1918 was as problematic as the transition from peace to war in 1914. In the fourth volume of *The World Crisis*, which Churchill called *The Aftermath*, he surveys the successes and failures of those who restored peace after the Great War.

MISSED OPPORTUNITIES

Taking stock of England at the end of the war, Churchill finds his country in "the highest position she has yet attained." Against a succession of Continental foes her goal had been constant. Four times in as many centuries England had championed European resistance to military tyranny and preserved the independence of the Low Countries—"a record of persistency and achievement, without parallel in the history of ancient or modern times." After the Great War, England could point to other "advantages"

[8] Thucydides 3.82.   [9] Churchill, *My Early Life*, 81.
[10] Winston S. Churchill, *The Second World War*, 6 vols. (London: Cassell, 1948–54), vol. 1, vii.

as well (IV 17). No longer did the German navy pose a threat to Britannia's rule of the waves; nor could Russia's rulers, preoccupied with their deglutition of the erstwhile empire of the czars, think any more of extending its bounds to Constantinople or to India. England was ranged with mighty allies: France, now linked to her "by ties of comradeship in suffering and in victory"; the United States, which had once more at length begun to write its history "in common" with England; and the British Empire (except for "parts of Ireland"), which had contributed loyal troops from Canada, Australia, New Zealand, India, and even South Africa (18). With all the opposing emperors and armies defeated, the English people joined their allies in rejoicing; but "too much blood had been spilt" for the celebrations to last very long (19). As soon as the soldiers realized their work was done, they were eager to return home. Far from exulting in the defeat of the Germans, the British government was bound to prevent them from starving or slipping into Bolshevism: Churchill wanted to "rush a dozen great ships crammed with provisions into Hamburg" forthwith (21).

Here was the missed opportunity of the aftermath. On Armistice Day, Lloyd George, Wilson, and Clemenceau "seemed to be the masters of the world" and might have joined hands to set its future course. Putting aside passions, party politics, and political ambition, they would have done well to hearken to the Roman motto, "Spare the conquered and war down the proud." But for the best choices "NOW was the only time": for "the hour was fleeting" (21–2). Churchill asks what they might have done, dreaming "one of the many Armistice dreams" (22).[11] He imagines that President Wilson met his British and French counterparts on an island in the channel immediately after the war, leaving partisanship and moralism behind; that Clemenceau was determined to seize the moment and make friends with Germany; that Lloyd George resolved "not to fall below the level of events," trusting the British people to do the same. The three statesmen agreed on an international but not supranational League of Nations, including "all the dominating races" (23): thus the Russians would have to be included, but not before they had freely chosen a national assembly, which meant breaking the Bolsheviks. Nor did the Allies shrink from the task in Churchill's dream, but they thought it morally necessary to enlist the aid of Germany in liberating Russia, since "Germany knows more about Russia than anyone else" does (24). Thus Germany would slip

---

[11] Lawrence of Arabia thought the "Armistice dream" the best-written part of *The Aftermath*; see T. E. Shaw to Churchill, March 18, 1929, printed in *WSC* V C (1) 1446–8, at 1448.

in "an almost unconscious transition" from enemy to ally. French security would be guaranteed by "English-speaking peoples throughout the world" (25). The victorious statesmen agreed to settle the expenses of the war by equal sacrifices all around, and they gave their League armed force to enforce its decisions, reserving to it alone both chemical and aerial warfare. Most wonderful of all, they settled everything in just three days. But when Churchill goes on to imagine the three staking their political lives on approval of these resolutions, "the spell" breaks and he awakens from his dream to find himself "in the rough, dark, sour and chilly waters in which we are swimming still" (27). Indeed, he calls the first chapter of *The Aftermath* "The Broken Spell," showing how the preternatural forgetfulness of selfish interests that sometimes obtained under pressure of war was shattered by the renewal of the ordinary lives of statesmen and peoples afterward.

The evanescence of Churchill's dream repeats the experience of millions of people whose "life had been raised to a strange intensity," who "had been appreciably exalted above death and pain and toil" by the spell of war (30). The difficulty of adjusting from peace to war was a theme of the first volume of *The World Crisis* (I 216–21, 233; cf. 24); now he claims that "the transition to peace was more violent than the entry into war, and that it involved a more complete and universal revolution of our minds" (IV 29). The British nation came gradually into the war but suddenly out of it. Until the summer of 1918, no one had thought the war would end until the next year at least. What plans had been made for peacetime were "hypothetical, contingent, remote" (28); everyone was working flat out and then abruptly brought up short by the armistice. Almost without warning, the "boundless hopes" that had sustained them through hard years gave place to "cold, grey reality" (30–1). Exertion gave place to exhaustion. Neither soldiers nor civilians were willing to make any more sacrifices, and the sudden melting of their once firm resolve left statesmen disarmed. Democracy reasserted itself, demanding a rest. Thus Churchill calls his second chapter "Demos," or the people, for the popular spirit ruled after the war. All at once, one had to consider what things cost, both in money and in strain. Economic considerations that had been banished in wartime returned, and nothing more could be expected that went beyond "the ordinary capacities of human beings" (33). As munitions minister, Churchill was responsible for ending the civilian effort that had involved millions of workers. It would have endangered "social order" to send the munitions workers home immediately (34), so he temporized.

As a general rule, workers were allowed to finish war materials that were more than 60 percent completed, which meant that armaments continued to pile up: "It was certainly waste," our author admits, "but perhaps it was a prudent waste" (35).

As things regained their ordinary proportions, party politics, in remission during the war, sprang back to life. The massive agreement on what "was deep and permanent in our island life," which those who dwelt in the British Isles "felt and cherished in common," was replaced onstage by the virulent quarrel over Irish home rule, which had engrossed the nation's energies before the outbreak of war (36). The national coalition that had sustained Lloyd George's government resolved itself into party elements. A Liberal sustained by the votes of Conservative and Labour members in Parliament, with most of his own party still loyal to his predecessor, the prime minister was naturally impatient for an election. In retrospect Churchill thinks he should have invited Asquith to join the delegation for the peace talks in Paris. At the time, however, he favored the election. His own position as a Liberal was irregular. "In the stress of war" he had "resumed intimate contact with the Conservative Party and with the friends of my youth." Now he much preferred a centrist government under Lloyd George to the partisan polarization of the prewar years; "but the Election at once raised the party issue in its crudest form" and "woefully cheapened Britain" (40–1). Liberals who had sided with Asquith were stigmatized as disloyal, and the Liberal Party never recovered from its ensuing defeat. Worse still, Lloyd George and his principal ministers pandered to the hard desire for vengeance that welled up among their constituents, "lashed by the popular press into fury" (41). Even erstwhile pacifists thirsted for punishment, and women, who were voting for the first time, were "the most bitter" (42; cf. 49).

The people made three "clangorous" demands: "to hang the Kaiser; to abolish conscription; and to make the Germans pay the uttermost farthing" (42). Against its better judgment, the government renounced conscription almost immediately. Lloyd George was eager to bring the kaiser to justice, and the Labour member of his war cabinet publicly said that the kaiser should hang. Churchill demurred, fearing lest the kaiser be elevated or even exonerated by a trial; but even he found himself unable to oppose the policy of trying him. Most urgently did the people press for the German indemnity. But they were up against the hard fact that payments could only be in goods or services, gold and securities being inadequate to the scale demanded. Yet the industrial base in the Allied countries would be ruined if the market were flooded by German goods, and no one wanted Germans in their midst serving to rebuild their shattered countries. Moreover, the robust recovery of Germany's economy required to sustain large payments to the Allies was in tension with the popular demand to cripple her industry. But the insistent demand for revenge made Churchill's factual arguments "unseasonable" (46). One minister even promised to "squeeze the German lemon till the pips squeaked" (47). Lloyd George, who might have limited himself to "words of sober restraint and of magnanimous calm," pouring "cold water upon inordinate hopes and claims," was instead addressing a public audience "night after night." In this situation he was not quite equal to "the hardest test of all," which "is to stand against the current of millions of rejoicing and admiring supporters" (49). While he won his electoral victory, Britain's "national bearing" suffered "quite a vulgar upset" in the eyes of the world (50).

ENTER CHURCHILL

Lloyd George offered Churchill either the Admiralty or the war office, giving him a day to make up his mind, and Churchill chose the Admiralty. By then, however, the prime minister had decided that his energies were needed at the war office, so Churchill became secretary of war. A demobilization scheme that paid scant regard to the spiritedness of soldiers had carried the army close to mutiny. It provided that "key men"—generally the last ones to be drafted into the army—should be the first to return to civilian jobs (53). Battle-worn veterans were loath to let the best jobs at home go to those who had suffered least, and the army had experienced "serious breaches of discipline" (54). Instead, Churchill ordered that soldiers be released according to their length of service, age, and number of wounds. He increased army pay to bring it closer to civilian wages, and he ordered young trainees who had not yet served abroad to go overseas to relieve veteran troops. These measures were taken urgently, in the face of difficulties in Parliament and in the country, in order to prevent further disturbances. Though Liberal and Labour members, "animated by a sense of detachment from responsibility," tried to defeat the conscription bill, the government's majority sustained it easily (64). The war secretary then announced the new measures to the army "in language which they would understand"—that is, he spiced up his army order with a bit of Churchillian rhetoric. For instance, his "Explanatory Note" justified the duties of occupation, which delayed the homecoming of many soldiers, on the plea that

Britain must not "be defrauded of the fruits of victory" (56); he defended the replacement of veterans with green troops so that younger men might "have a chance to see the German provinces which are now in our keeping and the battlefields where the British Army won immortal fame." He also warned that any insubordination would put a soldier's name at the bottom of the list to return home (58).

In the fortnight required before these resolutions could be taken, however, the troubles multiplied. As if to grant Montesquieu's bland prediction that the government of England would last only so long as military men respected the civil power,[12] Churchill describes the potential challenge to "the British Democracy" (61) at this moment when the Russian Revolution pointed for many to a promising alternative:

Armies of nearly four million men had been suddenly and consciously released from the iron discipline of war, from the inexorable compulsions of what they believed to be a righteous cause. All these vast numbers had been taught for years how to kill; how to punch a bayonet into the vital organs; how to smash the brains out with a mace; how to make and throw bombs as if they were no more than snowballs. . . . To all, sudden and violent death, the woeful spectacle of shattered men and dwellings was, either to see in others or expect and face for oneself, the commonest incident of daily life. If these armies formed a united resolve, if they were seduced from the standards of duty and patriotism, there was no power which could even have attempted to withstand them. (60)

In one place, "owing to the weakness of the civic authorities," the town hall was actually burned by a mob of soldiers (61). Churchill had anxious moments when a disgruntled group of armed soldiers assembled in the Horse Guards' Parade, "at the physical heart of the State," and put their demands to the army staff (63). But the change in policy, together with both firmness and self-restraint on the part of their officers, soon restored good feeling among the troops. Our author concludes by praising both the "enormous feat of British organizing capacity," which for almost half a year "disembarked, de-trained, disarmed, de-kitted, demobilized, paid off and discharged" ten thousand men a day "between sunrise and sunset," and "the noble behaviour" of nearly "four million trained and successful killers" as they peacefully "resumed their civic status" (64–5).

Churchill has less praise for the way that the Allies discharged their

---

[12] Charles-Louis de Montesquieu, *The Spirit of the Laws*, bk. XI, ch. 6, the famous chapter on the government of England, toward the end. In contrast to Montesquieu, however, who emphasizes the gap between the warlike spirit of soldiers and the peaceable temper of civilian ministers, Churchill's account in *The Aftermath* insists on persuading soldiers of the *justice* of the civil power.

responsibility to the people of Germany after the armistice, when the blockade was enforced so rigorously that only farmers and profiteers had enough to eat. With a "callous" public behind them, British and French statesmen neglected their obligation to feed Germany (66). Churchill credits a protest by British officers in the army of occupation against inaction in negotiations on the food supply, which provided him with evidence he brought before the House of Commons, with restoring the necessary provision by May 1919. By then, however, the Allies had lost the mantle of just conquerors. Similarly, the Allies—particularly the French—were reluctant to release hundreds of thousands of German prisoners of war: "It was like surrendering captured cannon" (68). But eventually the deed was done, again after prodding by Churchill, who saw no point in visiting vengeance upon the poor captives.

WILSON'S IDEALISM AND THE FOURTEEN POINTS

Three chapters of *The Aftermath* describe the peace settlement after the Great War. Here the leading role is played by Woodrow Wilson. Our author elaborates the portrait of the American president begun in the previous volume, pointing out that he "reached at the Armistice the zenith of his power and fame." On 8 January 1918, Wilson had laid before Congress his "admirably, if vaguely, phrased" statement of Fourteen Points of Allied aspiration (104). Apart from the return of Alsace and Lorraine to France and the reconstitution of Poland, which he made "definite conditions" for a settlement with Germany, his speech offered "broad principles which could be applied in varying degrees according to the fortunes of war" (105). Most famous among these was his insistence that "open covenants of peace, openly arrived at," should replace the secret treaties of old-world diplomacy (108). America's allies prized the president's speech more as a sign of his resolve than as a blueprint for making peace; but the Germans, when they sued for peace, addressed themselves to the president on the basis of his Fourteen Points. Wilson took the peace negotiations into his own hands, insisting that the Germans give themselves up entirely to the discretion of the victors; and the Allies, "though at first startled by his self-assertion," allowed him to take the initiative (106). Suddenly the meaning of the Fourteen Points became crucial to all, and the Allies began to ask themselves whether they subscribed to them. Britain, having used the sea blockade against Germany to such advantage, demurred from the idea of "absolute freedom of navigation upon the seas, outside territorial waters, alike in peace and in war" (108). France, for her part, was concerned because the return of Alsace and Lorraine was implied rather than explicitly required by the Fourteen Points, and because they did not specify that the Germans should pay reparations. Britain and France took common exception to the Fourteen Points on these grounds. They even professed themselves willing to fight on alone against Germany when Colonel House, speaking for President Wilson, threatened to make a separate peace on the basis of the Fourteen Points. But the Allied disagreement was composed by Lloyd George's agreement to discuss the principle of freedom of the seas, which of course committed Britain to nothing. The Fourteen Points, as modified by Allied reservations, thus became the basis of the peace settlement, without further specification of what they meant. Here was fertile ground for misunderstanding and recrimination.

The French premier, Georges Clemenceau, would have had the great powers (Britain, France, Italy, and the United States) draw up a preliminary peace settlement, postponing creation of a League of Nations until afterward and bringing in representatives of lesser powers only in bit parts. Although Churchill praises this plan as "logical, practical and speedy" (116), it failed to appeal to President Wilson:

> It thrust on one side all the pictures of the peace conference which his ambition and imagination had painted. He did not wish to come to speedy terms with the European Allies; he did not wish to meet their leading men around a table; he saw himself for a prolonged period at the summit of the world, chastening the Allies, chastising the Germans and generally giving laws to mankind. He believed himself capable of appealing to peoples and parliaments over the heads of their own governments. (117)

Here was Wilson's idealism, whose intellectual source was the essay on perpetual peace by the German philosopher Immanuel Kant.[13] It gave him a "mission," which he pursued with zeal. Our author admits the power of Wilson's rhetoric and faults the French for a proposal that was "injudiciously framed," or apparently even cynical—that "seemed to treat high ideals as if they were a mere garnish to agreements on sound policy" (117). The worldly French should have paid more respect to the political power of statements or professions. Churchill acknowledges Wilson's "high motives," and likewise "his remarkable abilities, his comprehensive goodwill and his readiness to arrive at practical solutions," calling him "a good friend, not only to the Allies but to Europe"; he admits that as the

---

[13] "Perpetual Peace: A Philosophical Sketch," in Immanuel Kant, *Political Writings*, ed. Hans Reiss, 2d ed. (Cambridge: Cambridge University Press, 1991), 93–130.

president "gradually got to know" the facts, he added "sympathy and common sense" to his "lofty idealism" (122). But our author clearly prefers Clemenceau's realism to Wilson's idealism, which caused the president to delay the peace settlement until the Allies lost the power to enforce it. Wilson thought that the world was at his feet and would remain so indefinitely, while in fact he lost his eminence by his insistence on being a delegate at the peace conference.[14] In mid-January, representatives of twenty-seven nations gathered in Paris to make peace. If the great powers, amongst which Churchill includes Japan, had met privily in advance of the larger gathering to draw up together the main outlines of a settlement, then the peace conference might have been a success. But because Wilson insisted on "open covenants . . . , openly arrived at," and because the European powers had their own reasons for delaying the settlement, no such conversation ever took place.

Our author contrasts the atmosphere at the ensuing conference with that at the Congress of Vienna in 1814, which restored peace after the Napoleonic Wars. It is a contrast between democracy and aristocracy, and also between the revolutionary hopes of modern idealism and an older, traditional politics; but the difference between the two centuries is not to our advantage. Those who gathered in Vienna were "aristocrats, life-trained as statesmen or diplomatists," who sought to restore "a well-understood conservative system of society." Ruling all of Europe, they had the means to accomplish their aim: they established the settled outlines of the continent in which Churchill grew up and which endured until the Great War. To Paris, on the other hand, came "orators and mass leaders" (our author frankly calls them "demagogues") who "balanced themselves precariously upon the unsure shifting platform of public opinion, and claimed to be guiding mankind to higher destinies." Churchill admits that public opinion may be "focussed and steadied" by representation, "but it was also vehemently swayed by the Press" (120). The nineteenth-century statesmen took their aims from their understanding of politics and sought self-respect and the respect of one another, but their twentieth-century counterparts took their aims from a fickle public and sought to gratify popular passions. Hence Churchill concludes that "the historian of the future" will be surprised not by the failures of the men who went to Paris but by "their substantial achievements" (121).

---

[14] Compare the judgment of Wilson by Christopher Hollis, *The American Heresy* (London: Sheed and Ward, 1927), 306, quoted by Churchill (IV 124): "The world was before him, like a class. The sight of it turned the head of the pedagogue made prince."

Among the books about the peace conference, our author singles out
Stannard Baker's *Woodrow Wilson and World Settlement*, which draws
upon the president's confidential records to fashion an apology for his
conduct in the negotiations.[15] Churchill objects to the "Hollywood" effects
of Baker's tableau, which ministers "to the more fruity forms of popular
taste," offering a "lurid contrast" between Europe's "awful depravity"
and America's "superior ideals" (122). He denies that the Americans took
for themselves all the virtues of Europe when they left their old countries
behind, or that they managed "to create an order of beings definitely
superior in morals, in culture and in humanity to their prototypes in Europe," relying on "the American sense of humour" to correct such preten-
sions. Baker's homily to the contrary, human nature is the same on both
sides of the Atlantic. Before vindicating "the old diplomacy" demonized
by Baker, Churchill recalls the president's domestic political difficulties,
which Wilson's apologist ignores (123). The president disdained to take
the occasion of his war leadership to become "a National rather than a
Party leader." The Republicans, who had given loyal support to his war
policy, turned angrily against him after he urged their defeat in the 1918
congressional election. Since that election gave them control of the House
of Representatives in addition to their already large majority in the Senate, they were in a fair way to cause trouble for Wilson's conduct of the
negotiations. Churchill therefore wonders that the president failed to
invite members of the Senate, which has the constitutional prerogative of
rejecting treaties, to join him in Paris; but Wilson's "strong Party feeling
and his sense of personal superiority led him to reject this indispensable
precaution." The president's self-righteousness also turned against his
European counterparts. En route to Paris, he told his entourage that they
would be "*the only disinterested people* at the peace conference," denying
that the other Allied statesmen actually represented "*their own people*"
(125).

How far Churchill accepted Wilson's claim to be disinterested may
be gathered from his remark that "the United States, which had lost but
125,000 lives in the whole struggle, was to settle down upon the basis
of receiving through one channel or another four-fifths of the reparations
paid by Germany to the countries she had devastated or whose manhood she had slain" (127; cf. 125–6). But he taxes the president with "an
undoubted misconception" in supposing that the Allied statesmen diverged

---

[15] Ray Stannard Baker, *Woodrow Wilson and World Settlement*, written from his unpublished and personal material, 3 vols. (Garden City, New York: Doubleday, Page, 1922).

from the popular will in seeking vengeance (126). Since the same self-righteous misconception about the people and their elected representatives is the stock-in-trade of media mavens and populist leaders today, it is well to see exactly what it is. Borrowing Kant's confidence in the simple goodness of the people and his indictment of traditional politics, Wilson held that what people really wanted was peace and security: as he explained in 1917, "The hungry expect us to feed them, the roofless look to us for shelter, the sick of heart and body depend upon us for cure" (127). Wars and political institutions contrary to the real interests of mankind were perpetrated by selfish and conniving politicians. By this account the people in the Allied countries sought only to live in peace with Germany, and it was their politicians and their old diplomacy that caused the outbreak of war and the bitterness and contention afterward.

According to Churchill, nothing could be further from the truth. In fact, the Allied statesmen were restrained by "experience, tolerance and detachment," while their electors clamored for selfish national aspirations and severity toward the Germans. Both Lloyd George and Clemenceau were criticized at home for being lukewarm or tenderhearted: they "represented their democracies best in all in which they differed from President Wilson most" (126). Nor was the president immune to this same preference of the people for "much lower and cruder views than his," for his fellow Americans fell "far short of their Chief in disinterested generosity to the world" (127). Churchill does not blame the people, who were "very resolute and persevering in war"; but he denies that they knew anything "whatever about how to make a just and durable peace." Lacking any better channel of instruction, they concentrated on their households and their business, holding only "vague, general ideas" about politics (128). Thus, while Wilson admired the moral simplicity of the people and traced their ills to the wiles of their leaders, Churchill admired the prudence of statesmen and traced its limits partly to a defect of popular discernment and support.[16] But the picture that our author paints is more complicated. Wilson's troubles were aggravated by his hypocrisy. His "spacious philanthropy" in Europe was at variance with his "calculating and brazen"

---

[16] Kant's understanding of politics borrows its premise that the people are good and their politicians devious from Machiavelli: to "Perpetual Peace," cf. Niccolò Machiavelli, *Discourses on Livy*, trans. Harvey C. Mansfield and Nathan Tarcov (Chicago: University of Chicago Press, 1996), 115–19 (bk. I, ch. 58). Churchill's doubts about the discernment of the democratic many echo the older, classical view expressed by Thucydides, Plato, and Aristotle, while his understanding of prudence is akin to that laid out in the sixth book of Aristotle's *Nicomachean Ethics*.

conduct as a party politician in America. He had "no truck" with the Republicans at home, but he wondered why the Allies were so unforgiving to Germany. "It is difficult for a man to do great things," Churchill concludes, "if he tries to combine a lambent charity embracing the whole world with the sharper forms of populist party strife" (128–9).[17]

Against Wilson's insistence on "open covenants . . . , openly arrived at," our author defends as a matter of "self-preservation" the secret treaties that tempted Italy and Romania into the war on the side of the Allies and composed the interests of Britain, France, Italy, and Russia in the postwar disposition of the old Ottoman Empire. Though some parts of those treaties could only be justified by "duress," the United States was not justified in "taking a lofty and judicial view of these transactions" (130). On the contrary, America might have made the situation less desperate by coming earlier into the war:

One has a right to stand on the bank; but if one has exercised the right for a prolonged and agonizing period without even throwing a rope to a man struggling in the rapids, some allowance should be made for the swimmer who now clutches at this rock and now at that in rough or ungainly fashion. It is not open to the cool bystander, who afterwards becomes the loyal and ardent comrade and brave rescuer, to set himself up as an impartial judge of events which never would have occurred had he outstretched a helping hand in time. (131)

Churchill likewise scoffs at Baker's claim that the Americans had never heard of the secret treaties before they arrived in Paris. He reminds us that the French proposal ignored by the Americans would have set aside those treaties before the peace negotiations, which was nothing but "masculine good sense" (133). After all, he argues, Britain and France had no more fought the Great War in order to share in the spoils of the Ottoman Empire than the United States had declared war upon Spain in 1898 in order to take the Philippines. Wars have many unintended consequences, but the Allies did not fight the war to gain territory.

OLD WORLD OBSTACLES TO "OPEN COVENANTS"

When the president arrived in Paris, his idea "of haranguing the Old World into a nobler way of life" was replaced by "silk and steel conversations with Clemenceau and Lloyd George," together with representatives of Italy

---

[17] Wilson's hypocrisy too is characteristic of Kantian idealism: Kant was pleased by the French Revolution, which in his view moved history forward, but could not countenance the deeds of the revolutionaries.

and Japan (136). Wilson objected to the idea that the five great powers should make the peace by themselves, arguing that decisions should be taken by all twenty-seven nations on equal terms. Clemenceau refused to put France on the same level as Cuba or Honduras. The other great powers agreed, and the president had to yield to the facts. So matters were to be addressed first by a council of ten, with two representatives from each of the great powers. Nor did the council adopt an open meeting rule, despite the president's insistence upon "open covenants . . . , openly arrived at." The idea that the "plain people," as Wilson called them, should have their say in the peace settlement, with the press serving as their ministers, was simply unrealistic: "The plain people were busy getting their daily bread" (138). While the press had managed to increase their power during the war, they were excluded from the peace talks, which took place behind closed doors. Our author divides the story of the peace conference into three phases. In the first, President Wilson guided the negotiators toward the drafting of the League of Nations Covenant. In the second, after the president returned to Washington, the British foreign minister, Arthur Balfour, persuaded the Allies to focus more narrowly on the peace settlement. In the third, Lloyd George, Clemenceau, and Wilson (whom Churchill calls "the Triumvirate") hammered out the peace treaties (141). Through all these discussions the former Hapsburg and Ottoman lands slipped further into chaos. "Revolutions, disorders, the vengeance of peoples upon rulers who had led them to their ruin, partisan warfare, brigandage," and even famine were rife (140), and "the greater part of Europe and Asia simply existed locally from day to day" (139).

Woodrow Wilson's objection to a peace made by the great powers did not prevent them from making peace as they wished it, but it did muddy the waters. Instead of settling the main questions in an organized way before the plenary session of the twenty-seven nations, the great powers addressed them piecemeal, and they did it concurrently with that session. The council of ten continued to meet even after the larger peace conference got under way, and because its members also had to make day-to-day decisions on Allied military dispositions, it naturally became the place where great issues arose. Wilson himself saw that twenty-seven powers could not decide the fate of great nations in public: as Churchill explains, "If platitudes and honeyed words alone were used, the proceedings would be a farce," while "If plain speaking were indulged in, they would become a bear-garden" (144). But even the council, with its suite of experts, was too large for serious negotiation. Decisions would have to be taken by "the three men on whom ultimately everything rested"—Lloyd George, Clemenceau, and Wilson—but the three never actually met for serious discussions until the end of March 1919 (143).

Wilson insisted that the negotiators devote their energies to drafting the Covenant of a League of Nations, leaving "the practical and clamant issues . . . to drum their heels outside the door" (145). Churchill attributes the origin of the League to "the fact that twenty million men had been blowing each other to pieces for more than four years, that this process had now stopped, and most people hoped it would not begin again." He deprecates the idea that the League was simply "an American inspiration," pointing out that English liberals had also mooted the idea during the war (146). Wilson himself chaired the drafting committee and presided over the composition of an organization of "Anglo-Saxon" complexion that arose "from the moral earnestness of persons of similar temperament on both sides of the Atlantic" (147). The lesser powers welcomed a renunciation of aggression in international law. Though Britain supported the League, it joined the other great powers in hesitating to cast away "the old proved safeguards while the new were a-building." But the League actually foundered upon *American* objections. Churchill explains that since "all the teachings of the Fathers of the American Union from Washington to Monroe had ingeminated non-intervention," Americans shrank from involving themselves in the broils of the Old World (148). Wilson had taken no pains to bring Congress along with him, yet without their assent he was impotent. So he led the Allies in establishing an organization that would be all but stillborn without American involvement.

Meanwhile the council debated the practical questions that could not be ignored. A dispute had erupted over the mandatory principle of the League of Nations, which required that conquered territory be held in trust by the victors rather than added to their domains. Ironically enough, the idea had come from General Jan Smuts, who had never meant to apply it to areas conquered by the British dominions, "least of all" to German Southwest Africa (now Namibia), which the South African government had taken from the Germans and planned to annex (150). Australia and New Zealand, which had made similar conquests in the Pacific, "did not mean to give them up" either (151). Canada, though without new territories of her own, nonetheless stood with the other dominions. The mother country was willing to have the mandatory principle applied to Palestine, Mesopotamia, and the Cameroons, but not against their wishes to territories acquired by her own dominions. It nonplussed President Wilson to hear from the Australian prime minister that his country "would place herself in opposition to the opinion of the whole civilized world"; but eventually the dispute was laid to rest. The dominions agreed "to veil their sovereignty under the name at any rate of Mandate," and the legalistic Wilson accepted this fig leaf (152).

Other practical questions, which our author calls "less serious" than the disposition of German territory and the foundation of the League of Nations (153; cf. 160), were assigned to commissions. One of these commissions, the supreme economic council, actually averted starvation in Vienna. But others had few practical achievements. For instance, the commission charged with setting a figure for German reparations could bring itself neither to endorse the unrealistically high figures demanded by the public in the Allied countries, nor any realistically lower figure for fear of a public outcry. Thus no limit was ever set to the reparations. Other commissions laid down rules that put the postwar German economy in a straitjacket, making it impossible for Germany to repay the Allies in any case. John Maynard Keynes, on the staff of the British negotiators, wrote a book to denounce what he called "a Carthaginian Peace."[18] Churchill endorses Keynes's economic reasoning without accepting his disapprobation for other aspects of the peace settlement. In private, Lloyd George admitted that the economic clauses of the treaties were a sop to public opinion in the Allied countries rather than a workable plan for the postwar German economy, and he relied on their provisions for periodic review.

There were similar demands for punishing war criminals, and another commission busied itself with this question. Germany was the undoubted aggressor, and her atrocities on land and sea were roundly condemned by the victors. The Turks were also taxed with the forced march that killed most of their British prisoners from Kut, and with their treatment of the Armenians. Could individual men be punished for these crimes? Particular atrocities were hard to prove, and in any case men might plead that they were only following orders. Real responsibility seemed to belong to their superiors, and accordingly the commission climbed the ladder until it blamed "all the greatest men in Germany," in particular the kaiser (158). Lloyd George insisted that he be hanged. Parliament was told that the kaiser would be tried by an international tribunal in London. Official

---

[18] John Maynard Keynes, *The Economic Consequences of the Peace* (London: Macmillan, 1919), 138, quoted by Churchill (IV 155).

Germany was alarmed, and both Hindenburg and the kaiser's sons offered themselves "as rams taken in the thicket." The kaiser almost became a martyr. But he had flown to Holland, and "the Dutch are an obstinate people." Their obstinacy protected the kaiser, whom they refused to surrender for judgment. In the prevailing climate of opinion, the Allies could not afford to thumb their noses at a small country, and the trial never took place (159).

Wilson had to leave Paris on St. Valentine's Day to return to the United States, and by an extraordinary effort the Covenant of the League of Nations was completed (though not without some inevitable "errors and imperfections") before his departure (161). At the end of his chapter on the League, Churchill asks "who can doubt" that the covenant framed by Woodrow Wilson will ultimately be the "foundation stone" of "a dwelling-place and palace to which 'all the men in all the lands' will sooner or later resort in sure trust?" (161–2). While the covenant was hammered out, the territorial settlements and all the other burning practical issues remained on the shelf; but an impatient public "temper was rising in all the countries" (160). By mid-February Europe remained without even a preliminary peace settlement. As Churchill puts the question, "How much longer were we all to go on officially bound to hate the Germans, and indeed, since the blockade was still in operation, to starve them?" (184). Our author points out that Wilson had agreed to have work on a preliminary treaty go forward even in his absence, including "territorial questions and questions of compensation," but that Baker left this key phrase out of his story of the peace conference, substituting words to suggest that the preliminary treaty was meant to address only military questions. The "discreditable" embroidery in Baker's account, which has been criticized by other historians, was necessary to sustain his fanciful charge that after Wilson's departure, the British undermined the president's intention by ignoring the League of Nations and addressing substantive issues in the preliminary treaty (187). "Lloyd George had gone home," he wrote,

but instead of leaving the liberal leaders in control in Paris, men who were imbued with the purposes laid down in the League—Cecil, Smuts, and Barnes—who were indeed Lloyd George's associates on the British Peace Commission, he sent over Winston Churchill, the most militaristic of British leaders. Churchill was not a member of the peace delegation and had had nothing before to do with the Peace Conference. Moreover, he was a rampant opponent of the League.[19]

[19] Baker, *Woodrow Wilson*, vol. 1, 296, quoted by Churchill (IV 185); cf. vol. 1, 302.

In other words, Churchill writes, Lloyd George planned to subvert the League of Nations by sending "specially to Paris the very wicked author of this book" (186). In fact, Churchill had gone to Paris only to urge the council to take action on the Russian civil war and was not involved in other questions.

In President Wilson's absence, Balfour urged the council to hasten its work on a settlement. He reined in the various commissions, directing them to focus on real rather than academic questions and setting deadlines for their reports. So far from objecting to this activity upon his return in March, Wilson was pleased that work had gone forward. Chastened by the frosty reception of his policies by Republicans at home, he was now more willing to deal with Lloyd George and Clemenceau, having perhaps finally realized that they were "not unworthy comrades" (188). But the council of ten, which in fact met as a congress of fifty people, was too big to decide the main questions. The occasion for creating "an organism more compact, more secret, more intimate" arose when one of the commissions recommended that German-speaking Upper Silesia be assigned to Poland. Lloyd George's objections in the council and French counterarguments were aired in the press, whereupon "the Prime Minister successfully broke up the Council of Ten," which briefly remained as a gathering of the foreign ministers of the great powers but then "perished painlessly of inanition" (191). Instead, he met secretly with Wilson, Clemenceau, and the Italian prime minister, Vittorio Orlando. Beginning with Lloyd George, all three great statesmen threatened to leave the conference unless it made more progress; only Orlando actually did leave, after Wilson had claimed to know the Italian people better than he (193). The remaining triumvirate then wrote the treaties that the Italian prime minister eventually returned to sign.

At this point the argument over the peace settlement began in earnest between Britain and France. Churchill quotes at length from a memorandum written by Lloyd George on 25 March urging justice for Germany: preservation of her territorial integrity, a limit of one generation to the term of her reparations, and no impediments to the restoration of its economy. In the spirit of Keynes's argument, the British prime minister pointed out that "we cannot both cripple her and expect her to pay" (195).[20] He

---

[20] Churchill's critique of Stannard Baker culminates with that writer's misattribution of this memorandum of Lloyd George, which Baker much admires, to an American general in his book: "probably the most astonishing blunder which any man claiming to write a standard history, and armed for that purpose with a mass of exclusive official and

averred that although it was "easy to patch up a peace which will last for thirty years," it was hard "to draw up a peace which will not provoke a fresh struggle when those who have had practical experience of what war means have passed away" (194). Anticipating another war if boundaries were drawn which left Germans outside their own country, Lloyd George warned his counterparts against arrogance, which would only increase the danger of Bolshevism in Germany. He recognized that France would need a guarantee from Britain and the United States against German aggression, and he recommended that Germany be invited to join the League of Nations. Clemenceau retorted that Lloyd George's magnanimity left Britain everything it wanted but only a half measure for France. In the company of the American president, the two European statesmen rehearsed their differences. Eventually they admitted to their meetings the redoubtable British civil servant Maurice Hankey, who reduced their decisions to writing. As Churchill explains,

He knew everything; he could put his hand on anything; he knew everybody; he said nothing; he gained the confidence of all; and finally he became by the natural flow of their wishes the sole recorder for the decisive six weeks of the conversations between President Wilson, M. Clemenceau and Mr. Lloyd George by which the Peace was settled. (134)

Accordingly the settlement was reached in May and signed by the Germans the next month. As Lloyd George feared, a Bolshevik Revolution did come to Germany. Our author admits that "the story requires a book to tell" (200); he can spare only two pages. The German communists used the Russian Revolution as their model. Like their Russian counterparts, they aimed "to prevent the people from choosing a Parliament" (201). The difference is that they failed, and Germany preserved her representative government.

SELF-DETERMINATION AND THE TERRITORIAL SETTLEMENTS

Dismissing "tropical colonies," reparations, and even the League of Nations, Churchill takes up "the territorial settlements in Europe," by which he holds that the peace treaties "will finally be judged" (202). In a chapter on the treaties he gives us his own judgment. Connecting the

authentic information, has ever committed" (IV 198). The American was Major General Tasker H. Bliss, a member of the peace commission. See Baker, *Woodrow Wilson*, vol. 2, 495–6; vol. 3, 449–57.

treaties ending the Great War with the long "chain of European history," he discerns "three events of the first magnitude" embodied in the settlement: "the dissolution of the Austro-Hungarian Empire; the rebirth of Poland; and the preservation of united Germany." Yet these towering events did not simply arise from the fortunes of war. Rather, they arose from "the methodical application of a principle." Our author finds the root of Wilson's insistence upon "Self-determination" in the idea of "*Selbst bestimmung*" propounded by the German philosopher Johann Gottlieb Fichte (203).[21] In Britain, Churchill remarks, the same idea would be called self-government, or government by consent. As religion was relegated to the private sphere over the course of the nineteenth century, nationalism took its place as "the most powerful moulding instrument of mankind in temporal affairs" (204). With every nation insisting that it should govern itself, even "great Empires" had to make their peace with this principle in order to survive (203). Both victors and vanquished relied upon the endorsement of self-determination in Wilson's Fourteen Points. But what constituted a nation? Generally adopting language "as the proof of nationality," with plebiscites to settle doubtful cases, the men who made the treaties could not ignore other considerations—"historical, geographical, economic or strategic"—but they put them all in the second place (205). "For the first time," Churchill argues, Europe's boundaries generally reflected "the wishes of its peoples" (206). All three main features of the European settlement arose from this principle. The polyglot empire of Austria and Hungary was dissolved into its linguistic elements. Poland was reborn by uniting Polish-speaking areas within the old boundaries of the Empire, of Germany, and of Russia. Despite her defeat, Germany was preserved as "the largest and incomparably the strongest racial mass in Europe" because her people spoke the same language (203).

Churchill applies the national principle to the frontiers of Germany fixed by the Treaty of Versailles. That principle restored Alsace and Lorraine to France but blocked the French demand for the Saar Valley, whose inhabitants considered themselves German. A bit of northern Schleswig

---

[21] *Grundlage der gesammten Wissenschaftslehre als Handschrift für seine Zuhörer* (1794–95), in Johann Gottlieb Fichte, *Gesamtausgabe der Bayerischen Akademie der Wissenschaften*, ed. Reinhard Laub and Hans Jacob, 4 vols. (Stuttgart-Ban Cannstatt: Friedrich Frommann Verlag [Günther Holzboog], 1964–), vol. 1 (2), 356, 378 ff., 389, 422, 435, 437, 450; cf. *Grundlage des Naturrechts nach Principien der Wissenschaftslehre* (1796), in *Gesamtausgabe*, vol. 1 (3), 331, 342 ff., 346, 413, 426, 434, and *Das System der Sittenlehre nach den Principien der Wissenschaftslehre* (1798), in *Gesamtausgabe*, vol. 1 (5), 27 ff., 44, 49 ff., 53, 66, 78, 80, 102, 109 ff., 121, 126, 128, 131, 139, 144, 151, 166, 194 ff., 200, 231.

was returned to Denmark on the same principle. In the east the rebirth of Poland entire—made possible only by the fall of all three empires which had partitioned her, Germany and Austria-Hungary by war and Russia by revolution—entailed a new partition of Prussia. No physical barrier in the plain between Berlin and Warsaw offered itself as a border, and populations were mixed. The settlement simply had to follow linguistic boundaries as best it could. In eastern Prussia a noncontiguous German-speaking area was separated from the rest of Germany by the Polish Corridor to the sea, with special arrangements for the port city of Danzig. The Allies divided over the assignment of Upper Silesia to Poland in the draft treaty, which outraged the Germans. Lloyd George invoked the principle of self-determination against the cession of this German-speaking area, while Wilson and Clemenceau upheld the claim of Poland. The treaty was modified to provide for a plebiscite; but later, after the vote went against Poland, the League of Nations took refuge in a compromise "bitterly resented by Germany" (214).

Yet our author points out that defeat in the Great War had brought liberalism to Germany and in many ways had left her in a favorable position. Gladstone's followers would have welcomed the replacement of royal rule with self-government and the inauguration of "a parliamentary system based on universal suffrage to which the rulers of Germany are effectively responsible" (214). They would equally have approved of the abolition of conscription and the restriction of armaments. "Absurd and monstrous" financial penalties required by the Treaty of Versailles have lapsed, Churchill writes, or have been replaced by "arrangements increasingly based on facts, on good sense and on mutual agreement." He rues the destruction of private savings by the postwar "destruction of the mark" but blames that disaster on the German government itself and predicts that Germans will recover from it. True, Germany lost her colonies, but as a land power she had acquired them only recently, and they were more in the way of a luxury to her than an integral part of national life. The advantages enjoyed by Germany appear in sharp relief if one imagines the effects of a German victory on Britain. The defeat of the Royal Navy would have meant the dissolution of the British Empire. Millions of Britons would have died of starvation and the rest would have been consigned "to universal and hopeless poverty" (215). Britain would have fared worse than Austria, and London worse than Vienna. In short, despite her defeat and attendant losses, Germany's advantages are real and her grievances slight. As for Britain, she has no choice but to fight and no future unless she prevails. Thus does Churchill offer "blunt" advice to the next generation of Germans by appealing to their "intellect" (216).

Next he considers the situation of France, whose territory he calls "the fairest portion of the globe." The size of France's population was unequal to that of Germany, and the disproportion would grow until, by 1940, Germany would "have about twice as many men of military age as France"—which "was the root problem of the Peace Conference." Churchill admits that "it is well always to talk about peace and to strive and suffer for peace; but it is better at the same time to understand the causes which lead to wars." Here is a cause that is hard to avoid: the natural inequality of strength between the two nations, which was bound to return as soon as Germany recovered from her defeat. Without Russian aid, France would be no match for Germany; but no one could count on Russia anymore. With "hundreds of miles of land frontier," France was imperiled in a way that Britain, with the channel, and America, with the ocean, need not fear (216). In half a century she had already been assailed by Germany twice. She could look to her defenses, but naturally she sought other guarantees. Assurances that the horrors of war had made men "wiser, nobler, more humane," that German democracy would be pacific, that "no one is going to fight any more" had in French ears a hollow ring (217). They wanted to be as safe as possible and "sincerely" doubted that the League of Nations would be able to protect them. Their misgivings were justified when its covenant was rewritten to exclude the use of force (218). Instead, Marshal Foch would have the left bank of the Rhine. But the people who lived on that side of the river were Germans, and wanted to remain part of Germany. Lloyd George and Wilson sympathized with the French, but they declined to expand her boundaries to the Rhine. Rather than being made to give up the Rhineland, Germany would give up her armaments. Strict limits were put on the size of the German army and navy, fortifications were forbidden in a broad strip of German territory along the French border, and the all-powerful general staff was dissolved. But the French did not trust that these changes would last. They were offered "a British and American guarantee to France against a future German invasion," which Churchill considers practically "an absolute safeguard," though he admits that France would have anxious moments before "the English-speaking world" could bring its irresistible strength to bear (221–2). Clemenceau accepted this assurance over Foch's resistance, bringing down upon himself the wrath of his country's "strongest elements"; then the United States Senate refused to ratify the president's promise, voiding the British guarantee as well since it was contingent upon the American. "Isolated and, as they claim, deceived and deserted," Frenchmen were left to prepare for their perils, consoled only by a temporary military occupation of the Rhineland "now drawing to its close" (222).

The Hapsburg Empire was "shivered into fragments" as the war ended by the principle of self-determination. Czechoslovakia and Yugoslavia declared their independence before the end of 1918 and claimed the right to sit among the victors at the peace conference (223). Likewise, Hungary seceded from the Empire as an independent monarchy. Even Austria, "with the ancient and cultured capital of Vienna," established herself as a republic and endeavored to escape punishment by this change of regime. But the "exceptional responsibility" for the war among "the ruling class in Austria and Hungary" denied these countries the same consideration that was given to Czechoslovakia and Yugoslavia, even though "the mass of the populations" of these countries were one of them no more innocent or culpable than another. They were simply "puppets of Fate," and our author concludes that "it is always unlucky to be born in the central regions of any continent" (224). Thorny problems abounded for the peacemakers. Inevitably, "many points of friction remained to cause heartburnings to the populations affected, and anxiety to Europe" (230–1). In Czechoslovakia, three million Germans lived within the limits of the old Bohemian kingdom. Despite the principle of self-determination, it was decided "to adhere to the ancient frontiers of Bohemia, well defined by mountain ranges, and consecrated by five hundred years of tradition" (225–6). On the other side, the new Czechoslovakian borders took in one million Hungarians. The Yugoslavian borders, particularly with Italy, required difficult negotiations. Romania acquired Transylvania from Hungary, leaving another million Hungarians cut off from their homeland by a Romanian "border belt." Shrunken Hungary, which lost territory to Czechoslovakia, Yugoslavia, and Romania, was in the toils of a communist revolution led by Bela Kun, "a disciple of Lenin and a paid tool of Moscow"; she could therefore command little sympathy at the peace conference (227). The "final remnant" of the Empire was Austria, which Churchill calls "pitiful indeed" (228). In fixing her border with Italy secret treaties came into play: Italy had been promised the whole southern side of the Alps, despite four hundred thousand German-speaking people who lived in South Tyrol. Self-determination gave way to the Allied promises to guarantee Italian security, and Austria lost the territory to Italy. The rump of Austria wanted to unite with Germany. But this "Anschluss," though consistent with the doctrine of self-determination, would have left "the new Germany larger in territory and population than the old Germany" (228–9)—a result unacceptable to the Allies and therefore forbidden to both countries by treaty except with the unanimous consent of the League of Nations. But when the treaty thoughtlessly tried to impose the whole financial burden of reparations from the Empire on the "two small derelict States" of Austria and Hungary, the Austrian economy collapsed (229).

Among the losers, Bulgaria fared better. Despite the Allies' grievances against her, which were so severe that no one would shake hands with her delegates when they arrived in Paris, "the Bulgarian Treaty was drafted in a far more instructed and careful mood than that which had regulated the fate of Austria and Hungary." Churchill attributes this result both to the gradual ascendance of "the best and ablest officials" and to the benevolent indifference of the great powers, whose "passions and interests" did not extend to Bulgaria (230). In judging the treaties that ended the Great War, our author concludes that the Allies applied the "fundamental principle" of self-determination as "honestly" as they could "within the limits of their waning power." Only protracted involvement by Britain, France, and the United States and "transferences of population such as were afterwards made in Turkey" might have avoided the anomalies and exceptions that remained after the new frontiers were drawn. But the Allies were exhausted, and it was by no means clear that any such tinkering would have been worth the risk it would have entailed. For the most part, Woodrow Wilson's principle was observed: in spite of his disappointments, it was he who inspired the treaties that ended the war. "According to the lights of the twentieth century," then, the settlement was practically perfect (231). But how reliable were those lights? Was it right to relegate everything but self-determination to the second place—to put the wishes of peoples before dynasties, history, strategy, economy, and geography? The settlement did make some exceptions to the imperious logic of Wilson's principle, and Churchill sympathizes with Allied statesmen who hesitated to subordinate every other consideration to the people's wishes, as very roughly represented by their native tongues. Would Europe profit by the dissolution of the Hapsburg Empire, and would the proliferation of small nations in the center of the continent contribute to the happiness of their inhabitants? Against the prevailing doctrine, our author keeps his own counsel and quietly nurses doubts—which were amply justified by the renewal of war two decades later.

THE LIMITS OF PEACEMAKING

Yet *The Aftermath* deserves to be read and pondered today not only because Churchill recognized the flaws of the peace settlement after the Great War and foresaw something of its sad sequel, but also for its realistic account of the problems of peacemaking in a democratic age. While Allied notables carved up the world on their maps in Paris, rougher characters were following other ideas and making their own dispositions on the ground. Churchill's theme is how the leisurely decisions made in Paris were eclipsed by imperious struggles on Europe's periphery. To the eastward, a war went on for the soul of Russia. Churchill describes Lenin as a "plague bacillus" unleashed upon that country, a man whose purpose was "to save the world" and whose method was "to blow it up." Attributing to him an "implacable" desire for vengeance, our author explains:

The quality of Lenin's revenge was impersonal. Confronted with the need of killing any particular person he showed reluctance—even distress. But to blot out a million, to proscribe entire classes, to light the flames of intestine war in every land with the inevitable destruction of the well-being of whole nations—these were sublime abstractions. (73–4)

As the Bolsheviks tightened their grip upon Russia, the victorious Allies gave little more than moral support to their opponents, and the country spun further into communist tyranny.

Before the war ended, of course, the collapse of the eastern front after the Bolshevik Revolution had posed grave dangers to Russia's allies. At one stroke the Germans had outflanked the Allied naval blockade. They were able to draw grain from the Ukraine and Siberia and oil from the Caspian. Eager to reanimate Russian resistance, the Allies had supported counterrevolutionaries who continued the fight against Germany. To prevent Allied munitions shipments from falling into German hands, Japan proposed to seize the Siberian railway. But President Wilson would not countenance such a move, with or without American participation. When the railway fell into the hands of enterprising Czechoslovakian soldiers, Wilson finally agreed to send aid to them. British, Japanese, and American troops, together with a detachment from the Young Men's Christian Association in the United States, landed at Vladivostok on Russia's Pacific coast, while another international force, mostly British, took control of Murmansk and Archangel on the Arctic Ocean. But the Allied help proved too little and too late, leaving the Czechs to escape from Russia as best they could.

Churchill tried to do more. At the beginning of 1919, in his new post at the war office, he urged Britain to contract her commitments but to make good on those that remained. Britain resolved to withdraw from southern Russia, where she had tried to prop up a counterrevolutionary army, but to help it by offering her surplus munitions. Churchill's aim was to establish and sustain a ring of hostile states around Soviet Russia. Lloyd George, leery of further involvement, sought a settlement. The Bolsheviks, but not the White Russians, agreed to negotiations on the island of Prinkipo in the Sea of Marmara. In February, eager for the Allies to adopt a definite policy toward Russia, Churchill secured the prime minister's permission to visit the peace conference in Paris, where he made his appeal just as President Wilson was about to return to America. Wilson refused to accept the policy Churchill was urging. Instead, he wanted "to clear out of Russia altogether" and was willing to talk to the Bolsheviks by themselves if necessary; but if negotiations were fruitless, he would help sustain the Allied military intervention (172). When the Allies decided to make negotiations at Prinkipo contingent on an end to hostilities in Russia, the Bolsheviks refused and continued to attack the White Russians. Churchill sought to establish an Allied military commission to coordinate the intervention in Russia, but no agreement could be reached at Paris. Afterward, in a letter to Lloyd George, he objected to a policy that drained British resources but lacked a definite purpose and a "will to win" (176).

Nowhere was the gap between the Allies' deliberations at the peace conference and the actual situation on the ground more glaring than in Turkey, which promptly became another trouble spot. While statesmen in Paris debated the future of Europe, the unsettled peoples of the Middle East looked on expectantly. Disinterested America, not having been party to secret treaties made during the war under the pressure of circumstances, might have helped to sweep them away. Instead of adopting this wise policy, America cleaved to the doctrine of self-determination—never less applicable than in the volatile Middle East. Again that government erred out of idealism: "It was a tragedy," writes Churchill, "that President Wilson in action did not keep a closer grip upon the realities." Insisting on the principle that rule should be by "the consent of the governed" (362), the president proposed that an international commission canvass public opinion in the region and draw up a settlement upon "the most scientific basis."[22]

---

[22] The quotation is from Baker, *Woodrow Wilson*, vol. 1, 76, quoted by Churchill (IV 363).

Such a commission, which might have been suitable for addressing a thorny domestic problem, only stirred up trouble in these inchoate nations. Churchill describes how it made "a roving progress in search of truth through all the powder magazines of the Middle East with a notebook in one hand and a lighted cigarette in the other" (363). As our author explains:

Statesmen in a crisis, like generals or admirals in war, have often to take fateful decisions without knowing a very large proportion of the essential facts. It is hard to do this, but anything is better than not taking decisions at all. To stroll around among masses of disorganized, infuriated, people, asking them what they think about it and what they would like, is the most sure and certain method of breeding strife. When one is helping in affairs which one does not understand and in which one is scarcely at all interested, a mood of elevated and airy detachment easily dominates the mind. "Let us have all the facts unfolded before we take our decision. Let us know where we are. Let us ascertain the wishes of the population." How prudent and correct it all sounds! But before the Commission, on which in the end only America was represented, had gone a third of the way through the sphere of their studies, almost all the peoples concerned were in armed revolt and almost all the Allied troops had gone home. (364)

Urgent problems were postponed by local administrators who could only await the resolutions of the commission.

Italy, determined to carve herself a joint of the Ottoman Empire, used a local disturbance as a pretext to seize Adalia (now called Antalya) on Turkey's southern coast, and then complained that Greek designs on Smyrna (the modern Izmir) would disrupt her plans to take the country's Aegean coast. To get the jump on the Italians, and because of rumors that the Turks were mistreating the Greek population, the other Allies authorized Greece to occupy Smyrna. A war promptly broke out between Greece and the Turks, who were supposed to have been beaten, but rallied themselves to defend their shrunken territory under the command of the man who had foiled the Allies at the Dardanelles, Mustafa Kemal, better known as Atatürk. Unable to sustain the Greeks whose armies they had unleashed, the Allies watched while Greece suffered a terrible defeat, leaving them to negotiate a ticklish withdrawal from Constantinople with the now-victorious Turks.

Churchill's account of President Wilson's statesmanship ends with the presidential election of 1920, which replaced him and his party with men eager to rest from "the quarrels and muddles of the benighted Old World." Lest his reader blame the three great powers for their irresolution and neglect, our author points out that

Modern forces are so ponderous and individual leaders relatively so small, so precariously balanced, so frequently changed; the collective life moves forward so irresistibly, that too much vitality or perseverance or coherent policy should not be counted on from large communities. There are moments when each is grand and noble; there are moments when all are expressionless slabs. (412)

If Wilson's hopes for universal peace were dashed in the years following the Great War, Churchill admits that at no point in his public life was the management of affairs "so difficult" as after the war, when the exhausted nations were unable to rise very high. Whether they might have done better, or whether their failings were "inevitable," is the question that he enjoins us to ponder (10). When we consider that question, *The Aftermath* affords us some timely counsel at the end of the twentieth century, reminding us that settling one conflict invariably opens the door to others; that a punitive peace sows seeds for a new war; that statesmen who aim at peace may take resolutions beyond their powers to sustain; and that even great nations must exert themselves to uphold their rights against a lesser opponent that is determined to fight.

7

The search for peace in Ireland

PAUL ADDISON

We associate Churchill with conflict. In 1908, the journalist A. G. Gardiner wrote of the thirty-four-year-old statesman, "The whole spirit of his politics is military. It is impossible to think of him except in the terms of actual warfare. The smell of powder is about his path, and wherever he appears one seems to hear the crack of musketry and the hot breath of battle."[1] It was an impression confirmed and magnified by the rest of his career, and most of all by his war leadership from 1940 to 1945. More than any other British statesman of his time, Churchill saw the world in terms of conflicts that had to be confronted and resolved; if in his view there was no alternative, he was prepared to resolve them by force or the threat of force.

This made Churchill a very controversial figure in Britain, and he was often caricatured as a kind of mad Colonel Blimp for whom the use of force was a psychological necessity or an end in itself. So much for legend: The true Churchill was a more complex character, and a statesman of extraordinary versatility. Although there were phases in which his more warlike tendencies were in the ascendant, there were others in which he displayed in abundance the qualities of the peacemaker: patience, flexibility, a capacity for negotiation and compromise, and the desire to achieve a stable and lasting settlement of the struggles between nations and classes. Much of his life was devoted to the exploration of alternatives to warfare and bloodshed.

The story of Churchill and Ireland is interesting partly as a chapter in the history of Anglo-Irish relations. More broadly, it is helpful in bringing

---

[1] A. G. Gardiner, *Prophets, Priests and Kings* (London: J. M. Dent, 1914), 229. The book reprints sketches of political personalities written six years previously.

into focus the interplay of the hawk and the dove in his politics and personality. It was no accident that at different times both North and South accused him of overaggressive behavior. The Ulster Unionists alleged that in 1914 he was one of the ringleaders in a conspiracy to compel them by military force to accept home rule. In 1920 the critics of British policy in Ireland condemned him for unleashing a campaign of terrorism against the rebellious population of the South. But in the years leading to 1914, when Ireland was poised on the brink of a civil war, no one was more active in seeking to find a solution acceptable to all parties. In the aftermath of the First World War he played a leading role in the negotiations that led to the Anglo-Irish agreement of 1921 and the creation of the Irish Free State. During the Second World War he was prepared to go even farther, holding out the promise of a reunited Ireland in return for the participation of Eire in the war. Yet Churchill's Irish policies were driven at all times by a conception of British interests.

IRISH GRIEVANCES AND IMPERIAL INTERESTS

How and why did Churchill involve himself in Irish affairs? He was never, it has to be said, an expert on the subject. Unlike his father, Lord Randolph, he never lived in Ireland, or studied its problems, or enjoyed the company of an enlightened circle of Trinity College men. His family connections with the Leslies and the Londonderrys had little bearing on his politics. But Ireland was nevertheless a country of which Churchill formed colorful and lasting impressions early in life.

He was two years old when his grandfather, the seventh duke of Marlborough, was appointed viceroy of Ireland. Under the care of his nurse, Mrs. Everest, the infant Churchill accompanied his family to Dublin, and lived with his father and mother at the Little Lodge, in the grounds of the viceroy's palace. His earliest memory was of his grandfather unveiling a statue of Lord Gough, and he remembered vividly the warnings of Mrs. Everest against the Fenians. "I gathered these were wicked people," Churchill recalled in *My Early Life*, "and there was no end to what they would do if they had their way."[2] Mrs. Everest's forebodings were amply borne out. In 1882, by which time the Churchills were safely back in London, the chief secretary for Ireland, Lord Frederick Cavendish, and the under secretary, T. F. Burke—who had once made young Winston a present

---

[2] Winston S. Churchill, *My Early Life* (London: Macmillan, 1944), 16.

of a drum—were hacked to death with surgical knives while taking a walk on the grounds of the viceregal lodge.

In later life Churchill was always aware of the hatred for Britain cherished by the more extreme Irish Nationalists. But since he did not regard them as representative of Roman Catholic Ireland as a whole, he never succumbed to a bigoted or racist view of the Irish. Both his father and grandfather were indeed strict Unionists who were strongly opposed to Irish home rule. But the seventh duke was a remarkably enlightened viceroy who sought to reconcile the Irish to Great Britain through land and educational reform and the avoidance of coercion. Lord Randolph took much the same line.[3]

By the time Churchill was a schoolboy at Brighton, the Irish question was the storm center of British politics and Lord Randolph was in the thick of the conflict. In 1886 the leader of the Liberal Party, W. E. Gladstone, announced his conversion to the cause of Irish home rule. With Lord Randolph in full cry, the Conservatives opposed him root-and-branch. The Union was in danger, Lord Randolph warned, and the Empire too. In a daring move to block home rule he traveled to Belfast and in a famous speech in the Ulster Hall (22 February 1886) urged the Protestants of Ulster to resist home rule by force if necessary. A few weeks later he summed up his policy in a phrase that was to become the battle cry of the Ulster Unionists for many years to come: "Ulster will fight, Ulster will be right."

The crisis quickly passed. Gladstone's home rule bill was defeated in the House of Commons and the Conservatives took office under Lord Salisbury, with Randolph Churchill as chancellor of the Exchequer. To the dismay of his son, however, Lord Randolph quarreled with Salisbury, overplayed his hand by resigning, and never held office again. Idolizing his father as he did, Winston Churchill turned bitterly against the leaders of the Conservative Party, whom he blamed for Lord Randolph's misfortunes. "There are no lengths to which I would not go in opposing them if I were in the House of Commons," he wrote to Lady Randolph from Bangalore in 1897. "I am a Liberal in all but name. . . . Were it not for Home Rule—to which I will never consent—I would enter Parliament as a Liberal. As it is—Tory Democracy will have to be the standard under which I will range myself."[4]

---

[3] R. F. Foster, *Paddy and Mr. Punch: Connections in Irish and English History* (London: Allen Lane, 1993), 233–41.
[4] *WSC* I C 751, Churchill to Lady Randolph, April 6, 1897.

Here then were the pieces of an Irish mosaic which Churchill inherited: a memory of Fenianism; a paternal approach to Catholic Ireland; opposition to home rule; the championship of Ulster Unionism; and a bitter resentment of the Conservative front bench. But with the death of Lord Randolph in 1895, Churchill was free to begin life on his own account. Over the next few years he roamed the world as a subaltern and war correspondent on the frontiers of the British Empire, devoured by ambition and reading voraciously with the aim of preparing himself for a political career. It was through this military and imperial apprenticeship that Churchill began to develop his own ideas, and a more coherent vision than Lord Randolph.

The romantic and warlike imperialism of the late nineteenth century affected Churchill's view of almost every question, including Ireland. As he came to appreciate, the Irish were not simply a peasant population inhabiting a poor and windswept island: they were an international people whose influence sometimes worked in favor of the British Empire, and sometimes against. It would be difficult to say with any certainty how and why this realization came to Churchill, but it may well have owed much to his experiences in the South African War of 1899–1902. Among the most notable features of the war was the performance of the Irish regiments, who served with such distinction that their deeds were celebrated in music-hall songs like "Bravo Dublin Fusiliers" and "What Do You Think of the Irish Now?"[5]

The point was not lost on Churchill the war correspondent. In his report on the relief of Ladysmith he described how the Dublin Fusiliers, in special recognition of their valor, were allowed to march at the head of the relieving army as it entered the town: "Many of the soldiers, remembering their emerald isle, had fastened sprigs of green in their helmets, and all marched with a swing that was wonderful to watch."[6] Many years later Churchill was to recall the "gallant conduct of the Irish regiments," and the readiness of "Irish manhood" to enlist in the South African War. And in old age he told his private secretary, Anthony Montague Browne, that he had always had a "soft spot" for the southern Irish "because of the many Irish soldiers who served us well."[7]

[5] Robert Kee, *The Green Flag: A History of Irish Nationalism* (London: Weidenfeld & Nicolson, 1972), 444.
[6] Frederick W. Woods, ed., *Young Winston's Wars* (London: Sphere Books, 1972), 352–3, dispatch from Durban, March 10, 1900.
[7] Winston S. Churchill, *The World Crisis: The Aftermath* (London: Thornton Butterworth, 1929), 279; Anthony Montague Browne, *Long Sunset* (London: Cassell, 1995), 203.

The Boer War also gave Churchill a taste of the anti-imperial sentiments of large numbers of Irish people who were by no means extremists.
In the House of Commons John Redmond and other Irish Nationalist
M.P.s condemned the British as warmongers. When Churchill visited the
United States to give a series of lectures on his experiences in South Africa
he found that his friend and mentor Bourke Cockran, a prominent Irish-
American and congressman from New York, was one of the foremost
critics of British policy. Lecturing in Chicago, Churchill was almost howled
down by an Irish-American crowd. He managed to win his audience
round by embroidering a tale of a battle in which for a time all seemed
lost until the Dublin Fusiliers arrived, the trumpeters sounded the charge,
and the enemy was swept from the field.[8]

With hindsight it is possible to trace, in the story of Churchill's later relations with Ireland, the effect of some of these early impressions. But at the
beginning of the twentieth century no one could possibly have anticipated
the shape of things to come. A rational prophet might have predicted that
since Churchill revered his father so much, he would remain a Tory and
uphold the Irish policies of Lord Randolph. That same prophet might also
have predicted that British politics were not likely to be much troubled
by Ireland in future. Anglo-Irish relations appeared to be more peaceful
and harmonious than ever before. The Conservative strategy of "killing
Home Rule with kindness" seemed to be working, and the Liberals were
no longer in a hurry to set up a parliament in Dublin.

Churchill, however, did not remain in the Conservative Party. Thwarted
ambition, coupled with a genuine belief in the advantages of free trade,
led him to cross the floor of the House to join the Liberals in 1904. Fortunately for Churchill, home rule was not a burning issue at this particular juncture. The Liberals had shelved it and were pledged only to the
creation of an administrative council with limited powers. Nevertheless,
it was clear that in changing parties Churchill had abandoned the clear
lines of resistance to home rule which Lord Randolph had marked out.
As it happened, he was writing the life of his father at the very same time
as he was abandoning his father's party. With typical boldness and ingenuity he sought both to justify the position his father had taken up in
1886, and at the same time to distance himself from it. Lord Randolph,
he argued, had been caught up in a crisis in which the true proportions

[8] Robert H. Pilpel, *Churchill in America, 1895–1961* (London: New English Library, 1977),
35, 54–5.

of the home rule question had been distorted out of all recognition by the passions and politics of the hour. Now that passions had cooled a new situation prevailed:

A proposal to establish by statute, subject to guarantees of Imperial supremacy, a colonial Parliament in Ireland for the transaction of Irish business may be unwise, but it is not, and ought not to be, outside the limits of calm and patient consideration. Such a proposal is not necessarily fraught with the immense and terrific consequences which were so generally associated with it. A generation may arise in England who will question the policy of creating subordinate legislatures as little as we question the propriety of Catholic emancipation and who will study the records of the fierce disputes of 1886 with the superior manner of a modern professor examining the controversies of the early church.[9]

From 1905 to 1910 the Liberal government took no action on home rule. Nor would there have been much point in doing so as long as the House of Lords retained the power to reject a home rule bill. Churchill, nevertheless, spoke out in favor of the idea. Of course it may be argued that he did so merely from expediency, to please a particular audience. But Churchill had already proved his credentials as an imperial peace-maker. Throughout the South African War he had argued in favor of a generous peace settlement—one of the issues on which he had begun to diverge from the Conservative Party.

As colonial under secretary from 1905 to 1908 he had gone on to play a part in the restoration of self-government to the defeated Boer republics, an experience that seems to have confirmed him in the belief that magnanimity was the key to imperial statesmanship. Addressing a gathering of Welsh miners in Swansea in August 1908, he declared:

If you want to make the British Empire strong . . . work for a national settlement with Ireland on the basis of some generous reconciliation which shall secure them the national rights which they most deeply deserve. Why, the problem of giving Home Rule to Ireland is nothing like so difficult or so serious or so dangerous as the problem which we have successfully solved in South Africa and which has already healed the wounds there.[10]

It seems likely, therefore, that by 1908 Churchill was already convinced on its merits of the case for home rule.

[9] Winston S. Churchill, *Lord Randolph Churchill* (London: Odhams Press, 1951), 439.
[10] Robert Rhodes James, ed., *Winston S. Churchill: His Complete Speeches, 1897–1963*, 8 vols. (New York: Chelsea House, 1974), vol. 2, 1086–7, speech of August 14, 1908 at Swansea.

When the House of Lords rejected the Lloyd George budget of 1909, the government decided to curtail the veto power of the upper house by limiting it, in effect, to a period of three years. "It was fairly clear," writes Pat Jalland, "that the Liberals would introduce a full Home Rule Bill once the veto of the Lords was overcome, and when they won a further election."[11] Asquith therefore announced, on the eve of the election of January 1910, that home rule was the only possible solution of the Irish problem. All doubts were finally dispelled when the two general elections of 1910 left the Liberals without an independent majority in the House, and dependent on the votes of Labour and the Irish Nationalists.

THE ULSTER CRISIS

Churchill's high-level involvement in Irish affairs began in January 1911, when as home secretary he was appointed by Asquith to a cabinet committee set up to prepare the appropriate legislation. After much discussion the committee decided in favor of home rule on the Gladstonian model, with a separate all-Ireland parliament for domestic affairs. In April 1912 the home rule bill was introduced into the House of Commons by Asquith himself.

Churchill gave the bill his full public support. As before, he justified it principally in terms of the advantages it would bring to the British Empire, but this time with particular reference to the effect it would have in the United States. Speaking in Belfast in February 1912, he declared:

A settlement of the long quarrel between the British government and the Irish people would be to the British Empire a boon and a blessing. . . . In their own island the Irish race have dwindled. . . . But elsewhere, all over the world, they have held their own, and in every country where the English language is spoken, the Irish are a power for good or a power for ill, a power to harm us or a power to help us. . . . The Irishmen overseas have done us much harm in the past. They have been an adverse force in our colonies. They have on more than one occasion unfavourably deflected the policy of the United States. They are now the most serious obstacle to Anglo-American friendship.[12]

It is interesting to discover that even at this early stage it was one of Churchill's aims to foster the improvement of Anglo-American relations. In the preface to a home rule pamphlet published at about the same time,

[11] Pat Jalland, *The Liberals and Ireland: The Ulster Question in British Politics to 1914* (London: Harvester Press, 1980), 26.
[12] Rhodes James, *Complete Speeches*, vol. 2, 1900, speech of February 8, 1912.

he put the point more dramatically, with a sweeping vision of the shape of things to come:

We see the four consolidations of the human family which . . . are in the ascendant—the Russian power, the Yellow races, the Teutonic alliance, and the English-speaking peoples. There is no solution of a political question which would give more unaffected pleasure than the grant of Home Rule through all the self-governing Dominions of the British Empire. We must not, as Lord Salisbury in his last great speech reminded us, expect that the vast developments which the mind foresees will take place within the compass of our own short lives. But still it must always be a guiding star of British statesmanship, not only to federate the Empire, but to draw nearer in bonds of friendship and association to the United States. . . . The road to the unity of the English-speaking races, with all that that carries with it, is, no doubt, a long one, and we cannot see the end of it. But it is an open road, and an Irish Parliament, loyal to the Crown, and free to make the best of the Emerald Isle, is assuredly the first milestone upon it.[13]

What Churchill sought was a settlement in the long-term interests of the British Empire. As Mary Bromage wrote in her perceptive study of Churchill and Ireland: "Churchill's policy was, in essence, an English policy, and not an Irish policy, either Unionist or Nationalist."[14]

This was true also in a second sense. Churchill wanted as far as possible to achieve a bipartisan settlement in which a solution was imposed on Ireland by agreement between the Liberal and Conservative Parties. The prospects were far from encouraging: Britain was entering a period of intense party warfare in which both the government and the opposition freely accused one another of activities bordering on treason. Adamantly opposed to home rule, the Conservatives followed the example of Lord Randolph, who encouraged the Ulster Unionists to defy the government by force if necessary.

Churchill replied with truculent oratory and melodramatic warnings. But behind the scenes he was busy trying to promote solutions that would be more palatable to the opposition than home rule on the Gladstonian model. Almost from the beginning there were two alternatives he preferred: a federal United Kingdom in which the Dublin parliament would be on an equal footing with other regional parliaments; or a home rule parliament from which the predominantly Protestant counties of Ulster were excluded.

---

[13] Preface by Winston S. Churchill to Jeremiah MacVeagh, M.P., *Home Rule in a Nutshell: A Pocket Book for Speakers and Electors*, 3d ed. (London: The Daily Chronicle, n.d. but the preface is dated December 1911, and the pamphlet was received by the Advocates' Library in Edinburgh on February 21, 1912).

[14] Mary C. Bromage, *Churchill and Ireland* (Notre Dame, Indiana: University of Notre Dame Press, 1964), 51.

The "home rule all round" formula envisaged separate parliaments for England, Scotland, Wales, and Ireland, with an imperial parliament to which they were all subordinate. The advantage from a Conservative point of view was that a scheme of this kind not only denied the claims of the Irish to separate treatment, but locked them into a framework from which escape would be difficult. The greatest practical objection arose from the difficulty of trying to operate an English parliament alongside a federal parliament that was also predominantly English. Recognizing this, Churchill proposed, in a cabinet paper of 1 March 1911, that England itself should be divided into seven areas, each with its own legislative and administrative body, alongside parliaments for Scotland, Ireland, and Wales. Churchill's plan found little favor with his colleagues, but he continued to pursue it and caused something of a sensation when he made it public in a speech to his constituents in Dundee in September 1912. By analogy with the seven kingdoms of Anglo-Saxon England, it became known as Churchill's scheme for a revival of the "Heptarchy."[15]

Asquith and his colleagues, meanwhile, pressed on with an all-Ireland home rule bill. The real danger of this course lay in the fact that it was likely to result in an Irish civil war. The Protestant minority, settled mainly in Ulster, regarded themselves fervently as British and attached indissolubly to the British Crown. From 1911 they were mobilizing under the leadership of Carson and pledged themselves to resist home rule by armed force if necessary. A paramilitary force, the Ulster Volunteers, was created, and began openly drilling and arming itself with the encouragement of the Tory opposition.

Churchill was very persistent in the search for a compromise. In February 1912 and again in December of the same year he urged the cabinet to offer temporary exclusion to the Protestant counties of the North. During the autumn and winter of 1913–14 he was the principal go-between in a number of secret moves to bring about a compromise between the parties. He conferred with Bonar Law at Balmoral in September 1913 and again with Austen Chamberlain in November. When Asquith and Bonar Law were unable to come to terms, Churchill continued to explore the ground through his close friendship with F. E. Smith, a leading member of the opposition front bench and ardent champion of Ulster. Both were now convinced that the exclusion of Ulster provided the basis for a solution.

---

[15] WSC II 1377–8, cabinet paper of March 1, 1911; for press cuttings illustrating the response to Churchill's speech, see Chartwell papers 2/58.

One remaining obstacle was the steady resistance of the Irish home rule party under Redmond to any solution which fell short of a united Ireland. But, as Churchill explained in his conversations with Austen Chamberlain, the Liberals were "not absolutely bound to R. [Redmond] and he was not indispensable to them."[16]

Plainly there had to be a compromise on Ulster if Churchill were to achieve his objective of a bipartisan policy. But it is tempting to speculate that Churchill was also trying to make his peace with the ghost of Lord Randolph, whose legacy he was often accused of betraying. In February 1912 Churchill actually attempted to address a Unionist audience in Belfast in the very hall where his father had spoken. His aim was to reassure the Ulster Unionists, but so great was the threat to his safety that the meeting was moved, at the last minute, to the Celtic Road football stadium.[17]

Finally, all of Churchill's attempts to come forward as the conciliator of Ulster were dashed by the so-called "Ulster plot." On 9 March 1914 Asquith announced an amendment to the home rule bill to enable any county, by a vote of the majority of its electors, to opt out of home rule for a period of six years. This was a belated move by the cabinet in the direction urged by Churchill and Lloyd George, but the proposal was immediately rejected by the Ulster Unionists and their Conservative allies. As Carson declared: "Ulster wants this problem settled now and for ever. We do not want sentence of death with a stay of execution for six years."[18] The Conservatives followed this up by threatening the rejection in the House of Lords of the annual army act, which entrusted the government with control over the armed forces.

In Churchill's view, however, the concessions made to Ulster placed the government in a new position. Now that Ulster's claims had been acknowledged, the government would have every right to ensure the passage of the home rule act and impose it on the North. Speaking at Bradford on 14 March he warned that Ulster must accept the government's offer or take the consequences: "Let us go forward together and put these grave matters to the proof!"[19] The government in fact had no plan to repress Ulster. But ministers were greatly alarmed by police reports that suggested that the Ulster Volunteers were preparing to seize control of arms

[16] *WSC* II 473–8, 480–1.
[17] Norman Rose, *Churchill: An Unruly Life* (London: Simon and Schuster, 1994), 91.
[18] Jalland, *The Liberals and Ireland*, 203.
[19] Rhodes James, *Complete Speeches*, vol. 3, 2233, speech of March 14, 1914 at Bradford; see also Rose, *Unruly Life*, 94–5.

depots, police barracks, railways, post offices, and other key points. A cabinet committee under Churchill therefore authorized precautionary troop movements, and Churchill in his other capacity as first lord of the Admiralty ordered the Fifth Battle Squadron to Lamlash, menacingly close to Belfast. Conservatives and Unionists were convinced that the government was planning a military assault on Ulster.

That impression was confirmed, shortly afterward, by the notorious episode of the Curragh Mutiny. The secretary of state for war, John Seely, summoned General Sir Arthur Paget, the officer commanding at the Curragh, to see him in London and briefed him on the possible need for preventive action in Ulster. But Seely blundered by allowing Paget to extract from him a promise that officers who objected to taking part in operations against Ulster would not be obliged to do so. Paget then compounded the blunder by summoning a meeting of all the officers under his command, warning them that operations against Ulster were impending, and advising them to "disappear" or resign their commissions if they were unable to accept orders. The mutiny followed when 57 of the 70 officers of the Third Cavalry Brigade, and their brigadier, General Hubert Gough, declared that they would rather be dismissed than move north.

The events of March 1914 convinced many Tories that Churchill had betrayed both his country and his father's memory by taking the lead in a conspiracy to coerce Ulster. This was untrue, but if a false impression was created, Churchill was partly to blame. The language he used ("there are worse things than bloodshed") was threatening and provocative. In defense of Churchill it can be argued, reasonably enough, that he often employed strident language in the service of comparatively moderate goals; extremism of style ought not therefore to be confused with extremism of policy. But apologists ought to reflect that in politics substance cannot be divorced from presentation. At many points in his career, Churchill's aggressive and insensitive manner undermined his attempts to win support for moderate programs and policies. In the case of Ireland the semi-secret maneuvers he conducted with the aim of finding common ground with the Conservatives were accompanied by slashing attacks on them, which only served to compound the mistrust with which he was regarded on the Tory side of the House. Yet Churchill had little inkling of the depth of the hostility he inspired.

The aggressive stand Churchill took against Ulster in March 1914 was even more theatrical than usual. It happened shortly after a crisis over the naval estimates in which he had almost been driven out of the cabinet, and his standing in the Liberal Party was extremely low. As Churchill admitted in his postwar account of the affair, he deliberately exploited the Irish question at this juncture to inflame party passions and win back some of the ground he had lost in his own party.[20] But it cut right across his efforts to obtain a bipartisan solution—and, unknown to him, time was running out. Within a few weeks of the Curragh Mutiny Churchill was once more engaged in secret talks with F. E. Smith in which he floated the idea of "home rule all round." In July 1914 a conference of party leaders met in a last attempt to hammer out a solution before the home rule bill became law. But they were still unable to agree on the details of a settlement when the war broke out.

THE TROUBLES AND THE TREATY

In 1914 the politics of Catholic Ireland were still dominated by the home rule party, with its apparent acceptance of the British connection and the desirability of remaining within the Empire. By the end of the war, the home rulers had been swept away by a landslide in favor of Sinn Fein, which won 73 of the 105 Irish seats.

Most historians agree that this revolution in Irish feeling was the result of a number of major blunders by the British government, including the executions which followed the Easter Rising of 1916, and the attempt to apply conscription to Ireland in the spring of 1918. Since Churchill was out of office at the time of the Easter Rising, he was free of responsibility on that score; over conscription he was thoroughly wrongheaded, but the same can be said of Lloyd George and other ministers. The truth is that few members of the government gauged the strength of Irish nationalism or understood how best to respond to it. When the Sinn Fein M.P.s set up their own parliament, the Dail, and declared Ireland a republic, there was hardly a ripple on the surface of English complacency. When the cabinet discussed Ireland on 4 February 1919, the minutes recorded that Churchill, as secretary of state for war, "did not contemplate any trouble in Ireland. In his view there was no place in the world where there was less danger at the present time, and he was satisfied that the troops there could be relied upon."[21]

Lloyd George and his colleagues were beset on all sides by problems

---

[20] Winston S. Churchill, *The World Crisis, 1911–1914* (London: Thornton Butterworth, 1923), 178.
[21] PRO CAB 23/9 WC 526, February 4, 1919.

that appeared to be more urgent. Besides, they hoped that it was only a matter of time before the Irish problem was solved. While they rejected Sinn Fein's demand for an independent republic as unthinkable for strategic and imperial reasons, they were now prepared—four years too late —to settle for the solution that had almost been reached in 1914. On 11 November 1919, the cabinet agreed to introduce legislation to set up separate home rule parliaments in Dublin and Belfast. Initially, they intended that all nine counties of the province of Ulster should be represented in the Northern Ireland parliament. But this would have produced a Roman Catholic majority in the North, a prospect which caused the Ulster Unionists to insist on the exclusion of six counties only. Home rule, it was thought, would remove the fundamental grievances behind the Irish revolt. The government of Ireland act, embodying these proposals, reached the statute book in December 1920.

For Catholic Ireland, home rule was no longer an acceptable solution. Widespread civil disobedience gradually developed into a war that was as much a psychological as a military contest. The Irish Volunteers, or IRA as they became known, consisted of no more than five thousand men scattered about the country and engaging in sporadic guerrilla warfare. They could not hope to defeat the British army, nor did they attempt to do so. Their principal target was the Royal Irish Constabulary (RIC), and they developed, during the winter of 1919–20, a strategy of assassinating policemen and attacking outlying police barracks. Owing to the support they received from the local population, it proved impossible to bring them to justice in the courts.

In theory the principal advantage of the British government was the overwhelming military force at its disposal. If the British army had been properly equipped and allowed to operate a system of martial law throughout Ireland, the opposition could probably have been crushed. But Ireland was an integral part of the United Kingdom. And although they were frequently urged to give the military authorities greater freedom of action, the politicians regarded military rule as a dangerous expedient that was likely to alienate public opinion. Time and again, therefore, they backed away from all-out military confrontation and preferred to reinforce the police. Toward the end of 1919 the viceroy of Ireland, Lord French, persuaded the RIC, a force that had previously been recruited exclusively from Ireland, to accept British ex-servicemen as recruits; the first was enrolled on 2 January 1920. Owing to the fact that they wore the khaki uniform of the British soldier together with the black and green caps and belts of the police, they were at once nicknamed, after a famous hunt in the south of Ireland, the Black and Tans. Since Churchill is often associated with them, it is worth noting that he seems to have played no part in the initial decision to recruit them.

As secretary for war, Churchill had been preoccupied throughout 1919 by his crusade against Bolshevism. It was not until January 1920, according to the diary of the chief of the imperial general staff, Sir Henry Wilson, that he realized the state of chaos in Ireland.[22] In view of the frequent caricature of Churchill as a militarist, it is interesting to observe that he was no more responsive to the pleas of the military than any other politician. Reluctant to introduce martial law, he was soon at loggerheads with Wilson on this and other issues. But Churchill was not at this stage one of the doves in the cabinet: he was spoiling for a fight by any means that avoided full-scale commitment of the army.

During the spring and summer of 1920 he gave strong support to Lloyd George's policy of converting the RIC into a paramilitary force with a license to carry out unofficial reprisals against suspected members of the IRA. The agent of this new policy was Major General Henry Hugh Tudor, one of two candidates nominated by Churchill to command the RIC. At the same time, Churchill and Lloyd George persuaded the cabinet to reinforce the RIC with an additional "gendarmerie" of ex-officers, the first of whom arrived in Ireland in August. The Auxiliary Division, or "Auxis" as they were known, had their own dark blue uniform with Glengarry caps.[23] But they were often bracketed with the other British recruits to the RIC under the general label of Black and Tans, and with good reason. Both bodies of men engaged in a campaign of counterterrorism with the full blessing of Lloyd George, Churchill, Tudor, and the secretary of state for Ireland, Hamar Greenwood.

Churchill's enthusiasm for the policy of meeting terror with terror has been scrupulously documented by Martin Gilbert.[24] On the basis of the evidence he provides it can be seen—albeit with the wisdom of hindsight—that Churchill's judgment was at fault in two main respects. First, he and Lloyd George were under the illusion that with the help of the tactics employed by the Auxis and the Black and Tans, and other measures

---

[22] *WSC* IV 1017, diary of Sir Henry Wilson for January 23, 1920.

[23] F. S. L. Lyons, *Ireland Since the Famine* (London: Fontana, 1973), 415–16. According to Lyons, the auxiliaries numbered about 770 in October 1920, increasing to 1,418 by January 1922.

[24] See especially *WSC* IV 443–71.

to escalate the war, the IRA could be decisively defeated. When Lloyd George appointed Churchill as chairman of the cabinet committee on Ireland, in June 1920, he proposed various measures to intensify the war, including the use of aircraft to bomb or machine-gun Sinn Fein. At a cabinet meeting on 23 July, he declared that it was "necessary to raise the temperature of the conflict to a real issue and a shock, and trial of strength . . . with resulting chance of settlement." This led him to propose one of the most foolish of all his ideas: the raising of a force of 30,000 Ulstermen to uphold the authority of the Crown throughout Ireland.[25]

Second, Churchill did not appreciate until it was too late the damage done to the government's cause, both at home and abroad, by the policy of unofficial reprisals. The Labour Party, the Asquithian Liberals, and such high-principled Tories as Churchill's old friend Lord Hugh Cecil were united in condemning British methods. Meanwhile, tales of British atrocities provided fertile soil for anti-British propaganda in the United States and many parts of the British Empire. In *The Aftermath*, Churchill wrote of the Black and Tans:

They acted with much the same freedom as the Chicago or New York police permit themselves in dealing with armed gangs. When any of their own men or police or military comrades were murdered they "beat up" the haunts of well-known malignants, or those whom they conceived to be malignants, and sharply challenged suspected persons at the pistol's point. Obviously there can be no defence for such conduct except the kind of attack to which it was a reply.[26]

This was one of the less candid passages in Churchill's writings. The truth was that in carrying out reprisals the Black and Tans sometimes murdered innocent people. On 21 November 1920, a party of them fired into a football crowd, killing twelve spectators. Realizing that their activities were getting out of hand, Churchill swung round to the view that it would be better to pursue a policy of official reprisals in order to avoid "excesses."[27]

Students of Churchill are familiar with his lifelong tendency to seek victory as the prelude to a magnanimous settlement with the defeated party. So it was at the height of his belligerence against the IRA. On 23 July 1920, he proposed to the cabinet a whole series of coercive measures in Ireland. But as Thomas Jones, the assistant cabinet secretary, recorded: "He was quite prepared to go much further with concessions than the

---

[25] WSC IV 453, 455, 457.
[26] Churchill, *The Aftermath*, 287.
[27] WSC IV 463–4, IV C 1229 et seq.

Government Bill, but he was not prepared to make these concessions at a time when they would be claimed as a victory for the Sinn Feiners. . . . Mr. Churchill interjected that he was not afraid of full Dominion Home Rule, except as part of a defeat."[28]

Some historians maintain that the Lloyd George government was compelled by moral and political weakness to enter into negotiations with Sinn Fein, but this was not Churchill's view at the time. When the cabinet discussed on 12 May 1921 whether or not to offer a truce, the majority of ministers were against. Speaking as one of the minority who favored a truce, Churchill argued: "I don't agree that it would be a sign of weakness. It would have been six or eight months ago. . . . Now our forces are stronger and better trained; auxiliaries are stronger; the police are extending their control over the country." But, Churchill continued, a continuation of the war would be "very unpleasant as regards the interests of this country all over the world; we are getting an odious reputation; poisoning our relations with the United States; it is in our power to go on and enlist constables and Black and Tans; but we should do everything to get away to a settlement."[29]

Churchill and the minority were overruled and preparations were made for sterner measures. The commander in chief, Nevil Macready, predicted that a hundred terrorists might have to be shot every week. The more carefully ministers examined this and other proposals for handing over the war to the army, the more apprehensive they became. On 17 June, Lloyd George announced a change of heart to the cabinet, and it was decided to send out feelers to De Valera. The fighting stopped at noon on 11 July, and nine days later the British government made a formal offer of dominion status.

This is not the place in which to retell the complex tale of the maneuvers which preceded the opening of the Anglo-Irish conference on 11 October 1921, or the history of the conference itself, which ended with the signature of the Anglo-Irish Treaty on 6 December. Churchill was a member of a British delegation led by Lloyd George, which also included three leading Tories—Austen Chamberlain, Birkenhead, and Worthington-Evans

[28] Keith Middlemas, ed., *Thomas Jones: Whitehall Diary*, 3 vols. (Oxford: Oxford University Press, 1971), vol. 3, 28–9, diary for July 23, 1920.

[29] Ibid., vol. 3, 69, diary for May 12, 1921. The line-up for and against the truce was as follows. Against: Greenwood, Winter, Macready, Anderson, Balfour, Chamberlain, Horne, Fitzalan, Shortt, Curzon, Worthington-Evans, and Denis Henry. For: Fisher, Addison, Montagu, Munro, and Churchill. Lloyd George summed up against. See also Sheila Lawlor, *Britain and Ireland, 1914–1923* (Dublin: Gill and Macmillan, 1983), 84.

—along with Hamar Greenwood and the attorney general, Gordon Hewart. On the Irish side, Eamon De Valera, the president of the Irish Republic, deliberately absented himself from the negotiations but sent a team consisting of Arthur Griffith, Michael Collins, Robert Barton, George Gavan Duffy, Eamonn Duggan, and Erskine Childers. For the Irish delegates the principal bone of contention was not the partition of Ireland, but the question of the relationship between the twenty-six counties and the United Kingdom. The negotiations were held on the basis of seeking to discover how an independent Ireland might be associated with Britain and the British Empire. The Irish delegates were fearful that too close an association with Britain would lead to the repudiation of any deal by the republican wing of Sinn Fein, and possibly by De Valera himself. The British delegates were determined to impose some formula that would keep the new Irish state within the British Empire.

The formula eventually agreed on 6 December provided for the creation of an Irish Free State whose officials were obliged to swear an oath of allegiance to the Crown. Churchill's main contribution was to negotiate with Michael Collins the sixth and seventh clauses of the treaty, which retained for the Royal Navy the right to patrol coastal waters of the Free State, and also the right to maintain naval bases at Queenstown, Berehaven, and Lough Swilly, which became known as the "treaty ports." The effect of this clause was that in time of war the Free State would be liable to attack from any power with which Britain was in a state of hostilities. Churchill rounded off his contribution to the treaty with one of the most important and successful of his great parliamentary speeches, which helped to defuse the instinctive opposition of a large section of the Tory Party. Once again he stressed that the Irish question was not a parochial affair. The removal of Irish grievances would strengthen the British Empire and improve Anglo-American relations:

Whence does this mysterious power of Ireland come? It is a small, poor, sparsely populated island, lapped about by British sea power, accessible on every side, without iron or coal. How is it that she sways our councils, shakes our parties, and infects us with her bitterness? . . . Ireland is not a daughter State. She is a parent nation. . . . "We too are," said their plenipotentiaries, "a far-flung nation." They are intermingled with the whole life of the Empire, and have interests in every part of the Empire wherever the English language is spoken, especially in those new countries with whom we have to look forward to the greatest friendship . . . and where the Irish canker has been at work.[30]

---

[30] Rhodes James, *Complete Speeches*, vol. 2, 3155, speech of December 15, 1921.

Although Churchill played some part in the making of the treaty, his main contribution to the establishment of the Free State was yet to come. In January 1922 the new Free State came nominally into existence. Since it now ranked as a British dominion, it fell within the sphere of Churchill as colonial secretary, and the primary responsibility for dealing with the new state was his. The Free State, however, was for the first six months of its existence almost paralyzed by the division of Sinn Fein into rival camps. Although the Free State was headed by the pro-treaty faction led by Griffith and Collins, it was so threatened by the activities of the anti-treaty faction, which included raids over the border into Ulster, and the occupation by irregulars under Rory O'Connor in April 1922 of the Four Courts building in Dublin, that it hesitated to implement its side of the treaty. Churchill during this period played a very difficult role with great skill. He was under constant pressure from the Tory side to enforce the treaty by taking severe measures against the Free State—measures that might well have resulted in a renewal of the war between Britain and Ireland. But realizing the extremely difficult position of Griffith and Collins, he refrained from inflammatory action and defended their conduct to the House of Commons. After much protest he even accepted the necessity of a rigged general election in which the pro-treaty faction allowed the anti-treaty faction a block of uncontested seats in the new Dail.

The election, which took place on 16 June, gave the pro-treaty party a substantial majority. At this point Churchill changed his position. Now, he argued, the Free State possessed the necessary authority to assert itself. He demanded that action should be taken against the irregulars occupying the Four Courts. Shortly after this, Collins ordered the Free State army to storm the Courts. Since this episode is often taken to mark the beginning of a civil war that was to continue until the republicans laid down their arms in May 1923, the question arises of how far Churchill himself was responsible for bringing about the civil war.

The root cause of the civil war was, of course, the Anglo-Irish Treaty, and the inability of the more extreme Nationalists to recognize that it represented, as Collins and Griffith argued, a major step toward independence and the most that could be achieved under the circumstances. The occupation of the Four Courts was itself a sign that Ireland was drifting toward civil war, as the IRA split into factions for and against the provisional government. Finally, as F. S. L. Lyons puts it, "Events in Dublin independently pushed the Provisional Government in the direction Churchill and Lloyd George wanted them to go." The Four Courts garrison forced

Collins into action by kidnapping General J. J. O'Connell, the deputy chief
of staff of the pro-treaty forces.[31] Collins himself did not blame Churchill; on the contrary he was grateful to him for the support he had given.
Hence, the famous message that Collins, a few days before his death in
an ambush, sent by word of mouth to Churchill: "Tell Winston that we
could never have done anything without him."[32] Lionel Curtis, a civil
servant in the prime minister's secretariat with special responsibility for
Ireland, wrote to Churchill in October 1922:

I feel I ought to tell you that since you took over the conduct of Irish affairs last
January an entirely new trust in British good faith has been born in the Irish mind.
De Valera has preached throughout that the pro-Treaty party would find themselves let down at the last moment. But the Provisional Gov[ernmen]t and its
supporters have really come to believe that so long as you are in charge of Irish
affairs England will not let them down.[33]

THE NORTH, THE SOUTH, AND THE SECOND WORLD WAR

How great an achievement was the Irish settlement of 1921? In politics,
it has to be said, there are no permanent and all-embracing solutions, only
temporary arrangements, some of which last much longer than others.
But in one respect the Anglo-Irish agreement was epoch making. Within
the twenty-six counties, it marked the end of centuries of conflict between
Irish rebels and English rulers. For all practical purposes the Irish were a
self-governing people, as they have remained ever since.

There remained the problem of partition. As long as Northern Ireland
remained a part of the United Kingdom, this would be unacceptable to
Irish Nationalists. And as long as Northern Ireland was a Protestant state
that discriminated against the large Catholic minority within its borders,
the territorial dispute would be fueled by grievances over civil rights. Was
Churchill in any way responsible for this outcome? Could more have been
done to anticipate and prevent the tragic long-term consequences?

Irish Nationalists sometimes claim that partition was the result of a
deliberate strategy on the part of the British government—a classic example
of the old imperial precept of divide and rule. In Britain, most historians see

---

[31] Lyons, *Ireland Since the Famine*, 461.
[32] Churchill, *The Aftermath*, 348; Chartwell papers 22/14, undated note from E [Edward
Marsh] on which Churchill has written: "Keep."
[33] Chartwell papers 22/14, Curtis to Churchill, October 13, 1922.

it as a response by the government to the demands, and indeed the threats, of the Ulster Unionists. The alternative to partition, in other words, was a civil war between Protestant and Catholic Ireland, with bloodshed on a scale much greater than has actually befallen Ireland in the twentieth century. Furthermore, British ministers in 1921 did not necessarily expect that partition would be permanent. Churchill certainly looked forward to some future date at which Northern Ireland would opt either to rejoin the rest of Ireland, or to participate with the South in the creation of an All-Ireland Council that would provide a measure of federal government for the whole of Ireland.

It does appear, however, that the Irish delegates were deceived by Lloyd George in 1921 over the critical question of the border between the North and the South. Under the government of Ireland act of 1920, the six counties of the North had been empowered to establish their own executive and legislature. But Article 12 of the agreement stated that the boundary between Northern Ireland and the Free State would be subject to revision by a boundary commission whose conclusions would be binding on all parties. Lloyd George led the Irish delegates to suppose that when the commission reported, it would award substantial areas of the six counties, including the two predominantly Catholic counties of Fermanagh and Tyrone, to the Free State. It might even remove so much territory that a separate northern Irish state ceased to be viable. According to one account, Collins gathered the same impression from his conversations with Birkenhead and Churchill, though Churchill later strenuously denied that he had ever expected or predicted such an outcome.[34]

The sequel came as a shock to the leaders of the Free State. On 7 November 1925, they were plunged into a crisis by a story in the *Morning Post* reporting that the commission would recommend only minor changes in the boundary, with some exchange of population and territory on both sides. W. T. Cosgrave and Kevin O'Higgins, the president and prime minister of the Free State, hastened to London to warn that the recommendations of the boundary commission would be generally regarded in Ireland as a breach of the treaty and would be certain to bring about the fall of the government. Churchill, who by this time was chancellor of the Exchequer, took the chair at a series of Anglo-Irish meetings that devised a compromise solution. On the grounds that they were acceptable neither to Northern Ireland nor to the Free State, the findings of the boundary commission

---

[34] Lyons, *Ireland Since the Famine*, 445.

were suppressed—and the report of the commission remained unpublished until 1969. In return, Churchill relieved the Dublin government of the heavy financial obligations it had incurred under one of the clauses in the 1921 agreement.[35]

In the early years of the Free State, Churchill believed that the Irish Treaty had succeeded in reconciling Irish nationalism and British imperialism. He failed, perhaps, to appreciate that the leaders of the Free State were not so much pro-British as realists who had been forced into compromises, like the oath of allegiance to the Crown, which they rejected in their heart of hearts. The debacle of the boundary commission demonstrated how fragile the 1921 settlement was, and also played into the hands of the irreconcilables who taught that Britain was never to be trusted.

Emerging from the wilderness, in 1927 De Valera formed a new political party, Fianna Fail, the object of which was to achieve the creation of an Irish republic through constitutional methods. In the general election of 1932 De Valera was returned to power and at once embarked on a tariff war with Britain. Churchill was dismayed and outraged by the Irishman's repudiation of the oath of allegiance. As Churchill saw it, De Valera had no right to break the treaty; if the oath were abolished, he argued, the Irish Free State would cease to exist and Ireland would become a foreign country. The Irish under De Valera's leadership, he believed, were taking a backward step that would remove them from the mainstream of history. As he wrote with more than a touch of sarcasm in 1935: "When a race so gifted with personal charm, so capable of producing in other generations poets, orators, soldiers, statesmen, and proconsuls, elects to fall out of the busy modern world and to retire into a cool, damp cloister amid green bushes, their desire should be respected."[36]

Though Churchill claimed to be tolerant of De Valera's government, he was angry when De Valera began to press for the removal of the military clauses of the treaty. He was even more angry when he discovered that Neville Chamberlain, who succeeded Baldwin as prime minister in May 1937, was prepared to negotiate away the rights of the Royal Navy to the use of the treaty ports. Churchill would have been against this under any circumstances. But at a time when Nazi Germany posed such an obvious menace, he was vehemently opposed. When Chamberlain announced this

---

[35] Keith Middlemas and John Barnes, *Baldwin* (London: Weidenfeld & Nicolson, 1969), 363–4; WSC V 137–8.
[36] *Daily Mail*, May 1, 1935, quoted in Robert Fisk, *In Time of War: Ireland, Ulster and the Price of Neutrality, 1939–1945* (London: André Deutsch, 1983), 53–4.

concession to the House of Commons in May 1938, Churchill attacked
it in no uncertain terms: "These ports," he declared,

are, in fact, the sentinel towers of the western approaches, by which the 45,000,000
people in this Island so enormously depend on foreign food for their daily bread,
and by which they carry on their trade, which is essential for their existence....
Now we are to give them up, unconditionally, to an Irish government—I do not
want to use hard words—whose rise to power has been proportionate to the
animosity with which they have acted against this country.[37]

Much of what Churchill had achieved in 1921 and 1922 unraveled during the 1930s. At the outbreak of war in 1939 De Valera declared Ireland
neutral. Churchill, who now returned to office as first lord of the Admiralty, was inclined to contest the legality of Irish neutrality, talking wildly
in the cabinet room of taking back the treaty ports by force. He continued
to distinguish between the republican extremists and the Irish people as
a whole. "Three quarters of the people of southern Ireland are with us,"
he wrote, "but the implacable malignant minority can make so much
trouble that De Valera dare not do anything to offend them." But he also
feared—understandably enough, since the IRA had recently carried out
a bombing campaign on the mainland of Britain—that hostile elements
might give aid to German U-boats sheltering in the nooks and inlets of the
Atlantic coast.[38]

Churchill's disenchantment with the Ireland of De Valera led him to
extol by comparison the virtues of the North. The southern Irish, he wrote
in February 1933, would

not be allowed to drag Ulster down into the ditch with them ... England will
defend Ulster as if it were Kent or Lancashire. We could no more allow hostile
hands to be laid on the liberties of the Protestant north than we could allow the
Isle of Wight or the castles of Edinburgh or Carnarvon to fall into the hands of
the Germans or the French.

Ulstermen should be of good cheer, for "until they wish to abandon the
British Empire, the British Empire will never abandon them."[39]

Yet in the final analysis Churchill was prepared to put the interests of
Britain above the interests of Northern Ireland. In the desperate circumstances of the summer of 1940, shortly after his appointment as prime

[37] Quoted in Fisk, *In Time of War*, 37; United Kingdom, House of Commons debates, vol.
335, cols. 1072–8.
[38] Winston S. Churchill, *The Second World War*, 6 vols. (London: Cassell, 1948–54), vol.
1, 583, minute by Churchill as first lord of the Admiralty, September 24, 1939.
[39] *Daily Mail*, February 15, 1933, quoted in Fisk, *In Time of War*, 55.

minister, he authorized Neville Chamberlain and Malcolm MacDonald
to offer the De Valera government a deal whereby the British government
issued a declaration in favor of the reunification of Ireland in return for
the immediate entry of Eire into the war. As it happened, the proposal was
of little interest to De Valera. Apart from his determination to maintain
Irish neutrality, he did not trust Churchill to fulfill his side of the bargain.
Churchill, for his part, stipulated that any agreement with Dublin was
"contingent upon Ulster agreeing."[40] In his view, it was up to De Valera
to make the running; only by repudiating neutrality, and demonstrating
his loyalty to the common cause, could De Valera hope to persuade the
North of the attractions of a united Ireland. Churchill, then, continued to
lean toward Ulster, but this was no absolute commitment. As he explained
in the first, unsent draft of a letter to Roosevelt in November 1940, he
hoped that with the help of the United States, a united Ireland might
gradually evolve:

If it were proclaimed an American interest that the resistance of Great Britain
should be prolonged and the Atlantic route kept open, this might lead Irish
elements in the United States to bring pressure upon the Government of Eire,
which would be most helpful. It is not possible for His Majesty's Government to
compel the people of Northern Ireland against their will to quit the British Commonwealth of Nations and join the Irish Republic, but I do not doubt that, as part
of a large policy of the kind outlined, a Council for Defence of all Ireland could
be set up, out of which the unity of the Island could probably in some form or
another emerge after the war.[41]

After the entry of the United States into the war, Churchill continued
to reflect on the possible consequences of American pressure on De Valera.
When Roosevelt suggested in 1943 that the Americans might ask for the
use of some bases in Ireland, Churchill was delighted. At a cabinet meeting on 22 September, he startled his colleagues by announcing that he
proposed to settle the Irish question "now, during the war." When a number of ministers spoke strongly against the idea, Churchill was forced to
retreat, and L. S. Amery noted in his diary: "Ulster will bitterly resent any
idea of trying to persuade her to come in under de Valera even if the latter
should at the last moment lend a base or two to America."[42] In his victory
broadcast at the end of the war, Churchill expressed his gratitude for the

[40] John Bowman, *De Valera and the Ulster Question, 1917–1973* (Oxford: Clarendon
Press, 1982), 224, 238.
[41] Warren F. Kimball, ed., *Churchill and Roosevelt: The Complete Correspondence*, 3 vols.
(Princeton: Princeton University Press, 1984), vol. 1, 99 (C-43x).
[42] John Barnes and David Nicholson, eds., *The Empire at Bay: The Leo Amery Diaries,
1929–1945* (London: Hutchinson, 1988), 942–3, diary entry for September 22, 1943.

loyalty and friendship of Northern Ireland, and condemned De Valera for his readiness to "frolic" with the Germans. But most Ulster Unionists would surely have been dismayed to discover how far Churchill himself had been prepared to frolic with De Valera. Nor did Churchill cease to believe that much of Catholic Ireland was still at heart pro-British. Almost in the same breath as he attacked De Valera, he paid tribute to Irish soldiers who had volunteered to fight for the British army and had been awarded the Victoria Cross.[43]

One of the most fascinating things about Churchill is that he was both a warrior and a peacemaker, with a capacity to switch rapidly from one role to the other. In both domestic and foreign affairs, his career was punctuated by attempts to prevent conflicts and negotiate settlements. In domestic politics he was by nature a coalitionist or cross-party politician. He stood for the creation or continuation of coalition governments in 1902, 1910, 1914, 1915, 1918, 1922, 1931, 1940, 1945, and 1951. In imperial affairs he was a party to the South African settlement of 1906 and the Middle Eastern settlement of 1921. Had he been in power in the 1930s he would probably have invited Hitler to discuss the terms of a lasting settlement in Europe—though no agreement would have been possible. Exhilarated though Churchill was by war and conflict, he recognized the need to seek a humane and lasting order based on the philosophy of "appeasement from strength." As he wrote in *My Early Life*: "I have always urged fighting wars and other contentions with might and main till overwhelming victory, and then offering the hand of friendship to the vanquished. Thus I have always been against the Pacifists during the quarrel, and against the Jingoes at its close."[44]

Alas for Churchill, it was no longer possible after 1918 to impose the kind of imperial and social order in which he believed. Appeasement from strength offered no foundation where strength and authority were ebbing away. In spite of a number of spirited rearguard actions, of which the Second World War was the greatest, Churchill was forced to come to terms with the long-term decline of Victorian Britain. Fortunately, he was also remarkable for his readiness to forgive and forget, and so to adjust to a changing world. In September 1953 he invited De Valera to lunch at 10 Downing Street. It was the first time the two of them had met, and afterward Churchill remarked: "A very agreeable occasion. I like the man."[45]

---

[43] Quoted in Fisk, *In Time of War*, 463–4, Churchill broadcast of May 13, 1945.
[44] Churchill, *My Early Life*, 346.
[45] Lord Moran, *Winston Churchill: The Struggle for Survival, 1940–1965* (London: Constable, 1966), 473.

8

Palestine and Zionism, 1904–1922

DOUGLAS J. FEITH

In the Great War's transformation of the Near East, Britain's pro-Zionist policy combined strategy and idealism, advancement of Britain's imperial interests, and fulfillment of a religious and romantic vision to restore a great and despised ancient people to the decayed land of their former glory. Local Arabs fought the policy, as did officials in Britain's Palestine administration, who denounced it as strategically misguided, morally indefensible, extravagantly costly, and impossible to implement. In the war's aftermath, Arab resistance to Zionism was a cause and an effect of the opposition that British officials in the Palestine administration directed against their own government's policy.

As colonial secretary in 1921 and 1922, Winston Churchill took responsibility for a series of fateful decisions on Zionism and Palestine. He created a record that defies simple categorization as pro-Zionist or anti-Zionist. On these issues, his tenure at the colonial office was marked not by the kind of pugnacity and doggedness that are commonly described as "Churchillian" traits, but rather by irresolution.

The Jews and the Zionist cause had engaged Churchill's imagination and sympathy since his early days in Parliament. He did not serve in the war cabinet that promulgated the Balfour Declaration, but he defended the document as a matter of sound policy and solemn obligation and was instrumental in defeating the postwar parliamentary effort to undo it. Yet, when his subordinates promoted measures that diluted the declaration's promise, he continually acquiesced. He banned Jewish settlement in three-quarters of mandate Palestine and approved the principle of restricting Jewish immigration into Palestine. Although he criticized the Palestine administration's efforts to mollify the local Arabs as more likely to encourage than to reduce anti-Jewish violence, he allowed policy on Palestine—

its formulation as well as its implementation—to remain largely within the administration's control. He refused to replace administration officials who were "publicly and confessedly opposed" to the Balfour Declaration.

Churchill's mixed record on Palestine in this period reflected the difficulties of his bureaucratic setting. He could not single-handedly promulgate policy, and if he did, he could not necessarily make it stick. His maneuver was constrained. The prime minister was pro-Zionist; the military leadership was ardently on the other side; the Middle East department of the colonial office was split; the Palestine administration—cagey, but distinctly anti-Zionist—had effectively captured its chief, Sir Herbert Samuel, who could use his Jewish and pro-Zionist credentials to discredit the Zionist leadership as "extremist." Churchill might have developed more options for himself if he had given deeper thought to the nature of Arab opposition to Zionism. But he assumed without skeptical analysis that economic blandishments would in time moderate the Arab stand. In any event, the amount of intellectual effort and bureaucratic exertion that would have been required to develop an alternative policy of his own and to attempt to impose it on the government and the Palestine administration was more than Churchill was willing to expend, especially as Palestine occupied but a small, relatively dim zone of his broad, bright, and busy mind.

THE JEWISH QUESTION

Victorian England—the time, place, and frame of mind that produced Winston Churchill—was fascinated with the Jewish question. Throughout the nineteenth century, what to do about the Jews was what is nowadays called an international human rights problem, and one of compelling dimensions. In the "East"—that is, mainly Romania and the Russian Empire—Jews were officially oppressed, physically abused, and periodically murdered in what were by nineteenth-century standards large numbers. In the West, limitations imposed by law and society constrained Jews in most spheres of life. Though not free of anti-Jewish laws and practices, Britain was relatively tolerant.[1]

---

[1] There even developed a tradition of outspoken sympathy for the Jews among British literary and political figures. Byron's *Hebrew Melodies* (1815) included, for example, "The Wild Gazelle," in which the Jewish persona talks of "Judah's hills":

> More blest each palm that shades those plains
> Than Israel's scattered race;
> For, taking root, it there remains

In the last quarter of the century, intensified violence against Eastern Jews impelled millions of refugees westward, aggravating the Jewish problem in the West. More than 2 million Jews moved out of Russia alone in the period between the Russian pogroms of 1881–2, which devastated the Jewish Pale of Settlement, and the beginning of the Great War. In the mid-1890s, the Dreyfus affair spawned large-scale antisemitic street demonstrations in France and French Algeria, leading to rampages against Jewish-owned property and the beating and occasional random killing of Jews.

These attacks, particularly those in Paris, inspired the Jewish journalist Theodor Herzl to write his pamphlet *The Jewish State* (1896), which advocated a guaranteed refuge for persecuted Jews. Herzl in 1897 organized the first World Zionist Congress, which declared: "The aim of Zionism is to create for the Jewish people a home in Palestine secured by public law."[2]

> In solitary grace:
> It cannot quit its place of birth,
> It will not live in other earth.
>
> But we must wander witheringly
> In other lands to die;
> And where our fathers' ashes be,
> Our own may never lie:
> Our temple hath not left a stone,
> And Mockery sits on Salem's throne.

George Eliot gave passionate expression to her Christian Zionism in the 1876 novel *Daniel Deronda*, in which one of the Jewish characters declares, "There is store of wisdom among us to found a new Jewish polity. . . . Then our race shall have an organic centre . . . ; the outraged Jew shall have a defence in the court of nations, as the outraged Englishman or American. And the world will gain as Israel gains. For there will be a community in the van of the East which carries the culture and the sympathies of every great nation in its bosom. . . .

"Let the reason of Israel disclose itself in a great outward deed, and let there be another great migration, another choosing of Israel to be a nationality whose members may still stretch to the ends of the earth, even as the sons of England and Germany, whom enterprise carries afar, but who still have a national hearth and a tribunal of national opinion. . . . Who says that the history and literature of our race are dead? Are they not as living as the history and literature of Greece and Rome, which have inspired revolutions, enkindled the thought of Europe, and made the unrighteous powers tremble? These were an inheritance dug from the tomb. Ours is an inheritance that has never ceased to quiver in millions of human frames." George Eliot, *Daniel Deronda* (Cleveland: Burrows Brothers, 1888), 492–3, 495–6 (bk. VI, ch. 42). Echoes of Eliot are distinctly detectable more than three decades later in the comments on Zionism of its most important Gentile sympathizers, including Balfour, Lloyd George, and Churchill.

2 John Norton Moore, ed., *The Arab-Israeli Conflict*, 3 vols. (Princeton: Princeton University Press, 1974), vol. 3, 4 (hereafter *Documents*). The Congress chose the term "home" rather than "state," despite the title of Herzl's historic pamphlet, hoping Ottoman officials would not view Zionist settlement as a threat to Turkish sovereignty in Palestine. See Christopher Sykes, *Two Studies in Virtue* (New York: Alfred A. Knopf, 1953), 160 n. 1.

Refugees, mainly from Russia, having nearly tripled the population of Jews in Britain since 1880, the government of Prime Minister Arthur Balfour proposed in 1904 the first legislative initiative in British history to restrict immigration. Known as the Aliens Bill, its acknowledged purpose was to stem the influx of East European Jews.[3] Most Jews opposed the legislation. Various outspoken antisemites endorsed it. A young member of Parliament at the time, Churchill assumed a leading role against the bill, stressing Britain's humanitarian tradition of welcoming refugees. For this, he received praise from Jewish political constituents. Other friends of the Jews, however, most prominently Balfour himself, supported the bill. They spoke sympathetically of Jewish suffering but contended that various economic and social factors limited Britain's capacity to absorb foreign refugees. Jews, moreover, posed special problems, for they prided themselves in maintaining their national distinctiveness—for example, by discouraging intermarriage.

In explaining—and demonstrating—that even a hospitable nation like Britain must at times limit its hospitality to aliens, Balfour vindicated Zionist warnings of the stateless Jew's vulnerability. His government grasped that this analysis meshed with that of Zionist theorists who had asked, "Where is the refugee to whom a refuge may not be refused?"[4] Accordingly, it was Balfour's colonial secretary, Joseph Chamberlain, who first engaged Herzl in negotiations to establish a haven for Jews somewhere in Britain's colonial possessions, so long as the land of Israel remained under Ottoman control.[5]

---

[3] Balfour spoke in Parliament of "the undoubted evils that had fallen upon the country from an immigration which was largely Jewish." See Leonard Stein, *The Balfour Declaration* (New York: Simon and Schuster, 1961), 79. From 1880 to 1905, the Jewish population of Britain rose approximately from 60,000 to 160,000. Contrary to predictions at the time, the Aliens Bill, as finally adopted in 1905, did not severely curtail Jewish immigration. By 1914, the Jewish population in Britain grew to approximately 300,000. Ibid., 78.

[4] Leo Pinsker, *Auto-Emancipation: An Appeal to His People by a Russian Jew* (1882), reproduced in Arthur Herzberg, *The Zionist Idea* (New York: Atheneum, 1971), 187.

[5] On October 22, 1902, in his first meeting with Chamberlain, Herzl discussed Zionist plans for settlement of El Arish in the Sinai Peninsula: "[Chamberlain] said, 'In Egypt, you know, we should have the same difficulties with the native inhabitants [as in Cyprus].'

" 'No,' said I, 'we will not go to Egypt. We have been there.'

"He laughed again, still bent deep over the [atlas]. For the first time he got the full drift of what I wanted: an assemblage center for the Jewish people in the neighborhood of Palestine. In El Arish and Sinai, there is empty land. England can give us that. In return she would gain an increase of her power and the gratitude of ten million Jews. All these factors . . . impressed him. . . . The most extraordinary thing was his ignorance of British possessions . . . under his supervision. It was like a big second-hand store whose proprietor didn't know exactly where a particular article might be." Marvin Lowenthal, ed., *The Diaries of Theodor Herzl* (New York: Dial Press, 1956), 376–7.

Even after Herzl died (1904) and Balfour resigned the premiership (1905), these negotiations continued for a time. In 1906, while serving as under secretary of state for the colonies, Churchill commented on them in a reply to an inquiring constituent:

I recognise the supreme attraction to a scattered & persecuted people of a safe & settled home under the flag of tolerance & freedom. . . . There should be room within the world-wide limits of the British Empire, & within the generous scope of Liberal institutions for the self-development & peculiar growth of many races.[6]

Chaim Weizmann, a Russian Jew active in the Zionist Organization, immigrated to Manchester in 1904 and obtained interviews with leading British political figures, including Balfour and Churchill.[7] His principal message was that Palestine alone could serve as the Jewish people's true home and refuge. He persuaded Balfour on this point at their first meeting in 1905 when he said, "Mr. Balfour, supposing I were to offer you Paris instead of London, would you take it?" Balfour answered, "But Dr. Weizmann, we have London." "That is true," Weizmann countered, "[b]ut we had Jerusalem when London was a marsh." When Weizmann then added, "I believe I speak the mind of millions of Jews whom you will never see and who cannot speak for themselves," Balfour commented: "If that is so, you will one day be a force." As Weizmann was preparing to depart, Balfour remarked: "It is curious. The Jews I meet are quite different." Weizmann answered: "Mr. Balfour, you meet the wrong Jews."[8]

In 1908, still under secretary for the colonies, Churchill prepared greetings for a conference of the English Zionist Federation. Churchill considered offering an enthusiastic endorsement not only of a Jewish refuge, but specifically of a Jewish state in Palestine. The precise language was recommended by Dr. Moses Gaster, the head of England's Sephardic community and a Zionist colleague of Weizmann:

Jerusalem must be the only ultimate goal. *When* it will be achieved it is vain to prophesy: but that it *will* some day be achieved is one of the few certainties of the

---

[6] *WSC* II C 495–6.
[7] See Oskar K. Rabinowicz, *Winston Churchill on Jewish Problems* (New York: Thomas Yoseloff, 1960), 36.
[8] Chaim Weizmann, *Illustrated Edition of Trial and Error: The Autobiography of Chaim Weizmann* (Great Britain: Harper and Brothers for East and West Library, c. 1949), 144. The prime minister confirmed to his niece and biographer Weizmann's account of the meeting and the decisive effect it had on his appreciation of Zionism. Blanche Dugdale, *Arthur James Balfour, First Earl of Balfour, K. G., O. M., F. R. S., Etc., 1848–1906*, 2 vols. (New York: G. P. Putnam's Sons, 1937), vol. 1, 324–6.

future. And the establishment of a strong, free Jewish state astride of the bridge between Europe and Africa, flanking the land roads to the East, would not be only an immense advantage to the British Empire, but a notable step towards the harmonious disposition of the world among its peoples.[9]

Churchill, however, dropped this paragraph from the final draft. His secretary apologized to Rabbi Gaster: "To his great disappointment and regret, he [Churchill] finds that he must postpone the expression of the opinions set out in [this paragraph] . . . until he returns to a position of greater freedom and less responsibility."[10]

IMPERIAL CALCULATIONS

Whatever their differences on specific questions of policy, upholders of the British Empire like Balfour and Churchill shared a general outlook on Britain's role as a liberal imperial power in world affairs. Their conviction was that a great power had responsibilities in the world, a high calling to rule less advanced peoples and to assist them to achieve progress. According to this view, a great power extended civilization, improving the government and the material well-being of lands that the natives had failed to develop. Treasuring its credibility, it made commitments cautiously and appreciated the price to be paid for not keeping them. A great power's moral confidence and self-respect—the conviction that it acted rightfully, fairly, and from virtuous motives—were chief elements of its national power. To be sure, not everyone in Britain embraced this outlook and not everyone who did applied it consistently. But this Kiplingesque sense of imperial duty, honor, and opportunity was a potent factor in British foreign policy debates in the period.

In the Victorian era, as in all previous eras, statesmen generally assumed the inevitability of future war. It was not common, as it is today, to think of diplomacy as a means to ensure perpetual peace or to create a permanently stable balance of military power. Diplomacy's purpose was to maneuver one's country into a good position for the next war. Wars were understood to have consequences; losers lost, without a right of return to the *status quo ante*, and victors gained, without apology. This reflected the immutable reality of power politics. And, when the defeated parties

---

[9] Martin Gilbert, *Exile and Return: The Struggle for a Jewish Homeland* (Philadelphia: J. B. Lippincott, 1978), 69, emphasis in original.
[10] Michael J. Cohen, *Churchill and the Jews* (London: Frank Cass, 1985), 34.

were those who provoked the war in the first place, it also served the cause of justice. Pieties along the lines of "nothing ever gets resolved by force" and "the inadmissibility of the acquisition of territory by war" had little resonance in the thinking of men of affairs in that period. (It is not that political leaders then were actually less pious or less moral in action than those in our own era. Rather, as respectable Victorians avoided blunt talk about sex, respectable persons today avoid blunt talk about war.)

WARTIME PLEDGES TO THE ARABS

Soon after the Great War got under way, the western front deteriorated into an exasperating stalemate. Britain therefore resolved to outflank Germany by opening a front against the Ottoman Empire. The Gallipoli campaign of 1915 was launched to clear a path for a head-on attack against Constantinople. Presided over by Winston Churchill, as First Lord of the Admiralty, that nine-month campaign failed at high cost. Britain then sought to outflank the flank. It resolved to hit the Ottomans not in their empire's capital but in their Asiatic provinces: the Hejaz (the western coastal region of the Arabian peninsula containing the Muslim holy cities of Mecca and Medina), Palestine, Syria, and Mesopotamia (today's Iraq).

British officials thought they could engineer an Arab uprising throughout the Near East. Britain's Egypt administration, which Field Marshal Lord Kitchener had headed immediately before moving to London to take over the war office in August 1914, reported that Arab nationalist officers in the Ottoman army were numerous and ready to rise against the Turks as soon as Britain endorsed Arab independence and provided financial and military assistance. The prime candidate to lead the revolt was Sherif Hussein ibn Ali, the head of the Hashemite clan, who as amir of Mecca was the principal figure in the Hejaz and was thought to command deference from the other Arabian notables. In the oft-dissected correspondence between Hussein and Henry McMahon, Britain's high commissioner in Egypt, the Hashemites were offered in return for their help sweeping but always vaguely formulated promises of British support for an independent Arab kingdom from Syria to the Indian Ocean.

The strategy failed to achieve its purpose, for the major premises were incorrect. There was no broad-based Arab nationalist movement in Ottoman army ranks. Regarding the popularity of the Arab nationalist cause, Britain's experts in Cairo were longer on preconceptions than actual evidence. Moreover, Arabia's tribal chiefs were not willing to subordinate themselves to Hussein. The guerrilla exploits of T. E. Lawrence ("of Arabia") and Hussein's sons, Abdullah and Feisal, represented a small return on Britain's large wartime material and political investment in the Hashemites.[11] The Hejaz forces enjoyed a few successes, but Hussein was never able to deliver more than a few thousand men at any one time. Lawrence wrote after the war: "I have never seen more than 11,000 of them together, and more often we had only a few hundreds."[12] No popular uprising of Arabs against Turks ever occurred in Palestine, Syria, or Mesopotamia; the Arabs there, with few exceptions, fought loyally for their fellow Muslim Ottomans. Not a single Arab unit defected from the Ottoman army.

Having paid for it richly—financially and politically—cabinet-level British leaders tended to speak approvingly of the Hashemites' wartime cooperation. But the Arab contribution overall was far greater on the side of the Turks than of the Allies.

THE ZIONISTS MAKE THEMSELVES USEFUL

Zionist contributions to Britain's war effort took various forms—technology, field intelligence, combat manpower, and political propaganda. Capitalizing on their own farsighted cultivation of political contacts and uncanny good fortune, the Zionists were able to win for these contributions high visibility and warm gratitude at the upper rungs of His Majesty's government. Until the war, Herbert Samuel had had no association with the Zionist movement. As the first practicing Jew to sit in a British cabinet, however, he said he felt "a special obligation" to study Zionism and

---

[11] Owing to Lawrence's gift for self-promotion, the Arab revolt had far more popular fame than military consequence. Hussein sent his first letter to McMahon in July 1915 and the latter's positive response reflected eagerness for Arab forces to relieve Turkish pressure on the British forces at Gallipoli. Hussein delayed action against the Turks, however, until June 1916, months after the British (in January 1916) were forced to abandon Gallipoli.

Though he often overstated the Arab revolt's accomplishments, Lawrence candidly related the assessment of General Edmund Allenby, commander of the Egyptian expeditionary force: "[Allenby in late 1917] asked what our railway efforts meant; or rather if they meant anything beyond the melo-dramatic advertisement they gave Feisal's cause." T. E. Lawrence, *Seven Pillars of Wisdom: A Triumph* (Garden City, N.Y.: Doubleday, Doran, 1936), 380. Writing of Allenby's views as of the final weeks of the war: "The truth was, he cared nothing for our fighting power, and did not reckon us part of his tactical strength." Ibid., 539.

[12] Jeremy Wilson, *Lawrence of Arabia: The Authorized Biography of T. E. Lawrence* (New York: Atheneum, 1990), 1061 n. 10.

Palestine.[13] In the war's early months, in conversations and by memoranda, he advocated to his cabinet colleagues British support for creation of a Jewish state in Palestine. David Lloyd George, then chancellor of the Exchequer, responded favorably. Sir Edward Grey, the foreign minister, voiced sympathy for Zionism, but, characteristically sensitive to French concerns, noted that France would want a voice in Palestine's future and, in any event, Britain should be wary of the responsibilities of establishing a new protectorate.[14] The prime minister, Henry Herbert Asquith, on the other hand, dismissed Samuel's proposal outright, invoking Lord Kitchener, the war secretary, to belittle Palestine's importance:

Kitchener, who "surveyed" Palestine when he was a young Engineer, has a very poor opinion of the place, wh.[ich] even Samuel admits to be "not larger than Wales, much of it barren mountains, & part of it waterless" &, what is more to the point, without a single decent harbour. So he (K[itchener]) is all for Alexandretta, and leaving the Jews & the Holy Places to look after themselves.[15]

Meanwhile, Zionists strove to render themselves valuable to Britain's war effort, making friends along the way whose goodwill and gratitude would in time become Zionism's most effective political asset. In 1915, both Winston Churchill, as first lord of the Admiralty, and Lloyd George, as minister of munitions, personally met with Weizmann, who was a prominent research chemist as well as a Zionist activist, to exhort him to remedy the acetone shortage that was crimping Britain's munitions production.[16] Weizmann did it. In his memoirs, Lloyd George called the Balfour Declaration the quid pro quo plain and simple for Weizmann's success in the laboratory.[17] Though extravagantly inaccurate, the remark reflects the deep impression Weizmann's breakthrough made on Lloyd George, Churchill, and others.

Personnel is policy. In 1916, Kitchener died and Lloyd George later

[13] Stein, *Balfour Declaration*, 107.
[14] See Elie Kedourie, *In the Anglo-Arab Labyrinth* (Cambridge: Cambridge University Press, 1976), 55–6.
[15] H. H. Asquith, *Letters to Venetia Stanley*, Stanley Michael and Eleanor Brock, eds. (Oxford: Oxford University Press, 1982), 477–8. This letter, dated March 13, 1915, was sarcastic about Samuel and Jews in general: "H[erbert] Samuel had written an almost dithyrambic memorandum urging that in the carving up of the Turks' Asiatic dominions, we should take Palestine, into which the scattered Jews [could] in time swarm back from all the quarters of the globe, and in due course obtain Home Rule. (What an attractive community!)"
[16] See Weizmann, *Trial and Error*, 222.
[17] David Lloyd George, *War Memoirs*, 6 vols. (London: Ivor Nicholson and Watson, 1934), vol. 2, 586.

replaced Asquith as prime minister. Balfour took Grey's place at the foreign office. Britain's war strategy and official attitude toward the Near East changed radically. The new government assigned high priority to an Eastern strategy, and, in particular, to the liberation of Palestine. The military, however, generally stuck with Kitchener's view. With little interest in Palestine and even less in the Jews, it remained reluctant to invest men and materiel in the Near East, though it hoped to cultivate the Arabs as potential allies.

The Zionist cause appealed to Lloyd George both as a device and as an end in itself. He wanted to discard the 1916 Sykes-Picot agreement by which France and Britain had fixed postwar spheres of influence for themselves in Turkey's Asiatic provinces.[18] Under Sykes-Picot, most of the Holy Land was to be internationalized. Britain could more easily assert exclusive control, however, if it conquered the land for the declared purpose of restoring it to the Jews. Moreover, that purpose—allowing downtrodden Jews to realize their millennial yearning to revive Zion—engaged Lloyd George's sense of historic justice and gratified his romantic religious and nationalist sensibilities. Lloyd George had a passion for the Holy Land and enthusiasm for Zionism. He had received intense instruction in the Bible as a child and saw parallels between his own beloved people, the Welsh, and the Jewish people, both with tiny homelands. Lord Curzon once wrote to Balfour that Lloyd George "clings to Palestine for its sentimental and traditional value, and talks about Jerusalem with almost the same enthusiasm as about his native hills."[19]

Soon after Lloyd George formed his war cabinet, Sir Mark Sykes of the cabinet secretariat engaged Britain's Zionist leaders in talks to clarify Zionism's aims and the government's attitude toward them. These talks had a lively backdrop. In March 1917, Russian revolutionaries, with Jews prominent in the front ranks, overthrew the tsar. British officials feared Russia's abandoning the Allied camp. In April, the United States entered the war, after long delay and with distinctly mixed emotions. Britain had alienated the sympathies of American Jews by allying with the antisemitic regime of the tsar. Might not a pro-Zionist declaration help Britain win favor with influential Jews in Russia and America?

---

[18] Lloyd George described the Anglo-French agreement as "a fatuous arrangement, judged from any and every point of view." Lloyd George, *War Memoirs*, vol. 4, 1825–6.

[19] Gilbert, *Exile and Return*, 131. When Herzl and Colonial Secretary Joseph Chamberlain negotiated the abortive plan for a Jewish refuge in British East Africa, Lloyd George, then a junior member of Parliament, was retained by Herzl's representative as the project's attorney. Stein, *Balfour Declaration*, 28.

Also in April, the British government approved the invasion of Palestine.[20] Lloyd George bade adieu to General Edmund Allenby, the newly appointed commander for the Palestine campaign, with the exhortation: "Jerusalem before Christmas."[21] The war plans relied heavily on information and recommendations from a Palestinian Jewish scientist named Aharon Aaronsohn and his espionage network, called NILI (a Hebrew acronym for the biblical passage "the strength of Israel will not deceive"), which Palestinian Jews on their own initiative had created to feed British intelligence. Aaronsohn maintained liaison with Captain William Ormsby-Gore and Colonel Richard Meinertzhagen, both of whom became his grateful admirers. In 1917, Ormsby-Gore was transferred to London to serve with Sykes as assistant secretary within the intimate and influential war cabinet secretariat just as the issue of an official pro-Zionist declaration was under consideration.[22] Largely under Aaronsohn's influence, Meinertzhagen became a fervent pro-Zionist who, after the war, played a unique role as a wholehearted champion of Zionism in Allenby's Cairo headquarters and then in Churchill's colonial office.[23]

In the summer of 1917, after protracted debate, the British war office consented to create a Jewish legion to fight for the liberation of Palestine. This too was a Zionist initiative, conceived and realized by Vladimir

[20] "[T]he War Cabinet . . . realised the moral and political advantages to be expected from an advance on this front, and particularly from the occupation of Jerusalem." Lloyd George, *War Memoirs*, vol. 4, 1829. Regarding the conquest of Jerusalem, the prime minister wrote, "The achievement was of immense importance, alike on military and on sentimental grounds. . . . Our 600,000 casualties in the fiascos on the Western Front had so depleted our resources in men that we could no longer exploit victory on any front, but the moral effect of the victory was tremendously important. It cheered our own people at a critical time, when defeatist elements were making their influence felt among us. It greatly encouraged our American Allies. And among that great international fraternity, the Jewish race, it was an earnest of the fulfillment of the Balfour Declaration." Ibid., vol. 4, 1838–9.

[21] Ibid., 1835.

[22] Others in the Aaronsohn family also were active in NILI. In October 1917, Aharon's sister Sarah, who led the group in his absence, was captured and committed suicide while in custody, following several days of torture. Ormsby-Gore reported to the foreign office on the Aaronsohns' contributions, noting that they "were admittedly the most valuable nucleus of our intelligence in Palestine during the war." He concluded: "In my opinion nothing we can do for the Aaronsohn family will repay the work they have done and what they have suffered for us." See Gilbert, *Exile and Return*, 102–3.

[23] "My first introduction to Zionism was in 1917 when I met the Aaronsohn family and visited the Zionist colonies of South Palestine." Colonel R. Meinertzhagen, *Middle East Diary: 1917–1956* (London: The Cresset Press, 1959), 50. Because of his name and his pro-Zionist views, Meinertzhagen was often mistakenly labeled a Jew. See also Stein, *Balfour Declaration*, 294 n. 37.

Jabotinsky, a journalist and Zionist leader from Odessa.[24] The command of the Egyptian expeditionary force responsible for the Palestine campaign did not want a "fancy" Jewish unit and affirmatively impeded recruitment.[25] But in London important officials respected Jabotinsky's intrepidity and appreciated the Zionists' desire to soldier in the Allied cause. Among Jabotinsky's key allies in bringing the Jewish legion into being was Leopold Amery, the third of the war cabinet assistant secretaries, who soon thereafter became a prime author of the Balfour Declaration.[26]

Hence, among the officials who decided whether and how the British government should publicly announce sympathy with Zionism, a remarkable number had worked hand in hand with gifted Zionists who contributed eagerly to Britain's cause. A number—such as Lloyd George, Balfour, and Sykes[27]—were also moved by what they intensely believed, for religious or humanitarian reasons, was the moral rightness of the Zionist prescription for the Jewish problem. Such men were thus primed to accept other—pragmatic—arguments for a pro-Zionist declaration. In autumn 1917, when the war cabinet finally decided the issue, the

---

[24] In 1915 in Egypt, Jabotinsky broached the Jewish legion proposal to a minor British official in Cairo named Ronald Graham. British military authorities reacted coolly, but agreed to form the volunteers into a transport unit for use outside Palestine. This became the Zion Mule Corps, which won distinction at Gallipoli but was soon after disbanded. General Ian Hamilton, commander of the Gallipoli expeditionary force, praised the courage of the Zion Mule Corps: Vladimir Jabotinsky, *The Story of the Jewish Legion* (New York: Bernard Ackerman, 1945), 44. It happened that, by 1917, Graham was transferred to London. He became a Near East department official in the foreign office, whence he enthusiastically supported the Balfour Declaration. See also Shmuel Katz, *Lone Wolf: A Biography of Vladimir (Ze'ev) Jabotinsky*, 2 vols. (New York: Barricade Books, 1996), vol. 1, 155–238.

[25] They objected, first of all, to the idea of a foreign legion within the British army. Colonel John Henry Patterson, who led both the Zion Mule Corps and the Jewish legion, has written that no precedent existed for such a unit within the British army. They also doubted the practical value of a fighting force of Jews. Certain officers opposed the legion because they disliked Jews, as Patterson states: "From the moment of debarkation it was made plain by the Army staff that our arrival was deeply resented. The anti-Jewish chief of staff, General Louis Jean Bols, did his best to destroy us." See the foreword by Colonel John Henry Patterson in Jabotinsky, *Jewish Legion*, 20; see also 16–17. Regarding impediments to recruitment, see ibid., 112.

[26] Amery was a close friend of Colonel John Henry Patterson, the Irish-born Protestant and world-famous lion hunter who had commanded the Zion Mule Corps and was later given command of the Jewish legion. Patterson introduced Amery to Jabotinsky. Ibid., 68–70.

[27] According to his son, the historian Christopher Sykes: "[Sir Mark] was a man of ardent character and he took no decision either of a public or private kind without considering his duty as a member of his [Roman Catholic] Church. This is the first point to recognise for an understanding of the part he played in the history of the Jewish people." Sykes, *Two Studies in Virtue*, 175.

immediate practical considerations that received greatest attention were, first of all, cultivating support for Britain among influential pro-Zionist Jews in Russia and the United States and, second, preempting an anticipated (but illusory) pro-Zionist declaration by Germany.[28]

THE BALFOUR DECLARATION

In July 1917, the Zionists proposed to His Majesty's government a draft declaration proclaiming acceptance of "the principle that Palestine should be reconstituted as the national home of the Jewish people."[29] The word "home" in the Zionists' draft echoed the resolution, quoted above, of Herzl's 1897 Zionist Congress. No one knew how Palestine would develop under British control. Would Jews immigrate in numbers large enough to create a Jewish majority? And how long would this take? Until that time, talk of a Jewish state was deemed premature.

Anti-Zionist Jews, who predominated in the higher reaches of Anglo-Jewish society, asserted that Zionist aims were "inconsistent with British citizenship."[30] Edwin Montagu, the prominent Jewish Liberal politician newly appointed secretary of state for India, stated the case to the government in intensely personal terms: "If you make a statement about Palestine as the National Home for Jews, every anti-Semitic organisation and newspaper will ask what right a Jewish Englishman, with the status at best of a naturalised foreigner, has to take a foremost part in the government of the British Empire."[31] Lloyd George told Weizmann: "I know that with the issue of this Declaration I shall please one group of Jews and

---

[28] Lloyd George's private secretary wrote on May 5, 1917, to a foreign office senior official that "the raising of a Jewish unit for use in Palestine, if coupled with assurances from the British Government of their sympathy with the desire of many Jews to settle in Palestine and build up a community within it, might produce a very beneficial effect in making the Jews in America and Russia much keener on helping to see the war through." Gilbert, *Exile and Return*, 96. See also war cabinet minutes from an October 31, 1917, meeting, quoted in C. J. Lowe and M. L. Dockrill, eds., *The Mirage of Power: British Foreign Policy, 1902–22*, 3 vols. (London: Routledge and Kegan Paul, 1972), vol. 3, 550: "The vast majority of Jews in Russia and America, as, indeed, all over the world, now appeared to be favourable to Zionism. If we could make a declaration favourable to such an ideal, we should be able to carry on extremely useful propaganda both in Russia and America." See also Gilbert, *Exile and Return*, 105: urging quick action on the pro-Zionist declaration, Ronald Graham of the foreign office minuted on October 24, 1917, "We might at any moment be confronted by a German move on the Zionist question."

[29] Stein, *Balfour Declaration*, 664 [appendix].   [30] Gilbert, *Exile and Return*, 99.

[31] Montagu to Lloyd George, October 4, 1917, quoted in Stein, *Balfour Declaration*, 500.

displease another. I have decided to please your group because you stand for a great idea."[32]

Lord Curzon, a member of the war cabinet, doubted whether Palestine, so long neglected and so poor in natural resources, could sustain a substantial increase in population, especially if the immigrants were to be Jews, who were not "a people inured to agriculture."[33] Aggravating these practical difficulties was the presence in Palestine already of a half-million Arabs, who "will not be content either to be expropriated for Jewish immigrants, or to act merely as hewers of wood and drawers of water to the latter."[34] Balfour disputed Curzon's analysis. Convinced that Zionist industriousness would bring prosperity to the Arabs as well as the Jews, Balfour told the cabinet that "if Palestine were scientifically developed, a very much larger population could be sustained than had existed during the period of Turkish misrule."[35]

Although Curzon called attention to local Arab discontents, neither he nor anyone else in the cabinet anticipated that Arab political opposition to Zionism would become a major problem for Britain. The rights of the Arabs in Palestine were discussed entirely in the context of protection of personal rights—civil liberties (including protection of private property) and religious freedom. The Arabs were destined eventually to be a minority in the Jewish national home, but they would retain their individual civil and religious rights. There was no thought of giving Arabs collective political rights—national rights—in Palestine to compete there with those of the Jews. This would defeat the purpose of the Jewish national

---

[32] Weizmann, *Trial and Error*, 200–1.

[33] Curzon memorandum to war cabinet, October 26, 1917, quoted in Stein, *Balfour Declaration*, 545. Regarding Curzon's doubts as to "whether the land could support any population," see Gilbert, *Exile and Return*, 105. Curzon retained the ideas he developed when he visited Palestine as a young man in 1883: "Palestine is a country to see once, not to revisit," he wrote to a friend, adding: "There is much greater need of cultivation than in Greece and much less chance of making it pay. For the surface in many places is all rocks and stones. No Jew with his eyes open (and you never saw one with them shut) would think of going back: and if the Millennium is only to arrive when they have returned, our descendants will still be expecting it in 3000 A.D." Kenneth Rose, *Superior Person: A Portrait of Curzon and His Circle in Late Victorian England* (New York: Weybright and Talley, 1969), 89.

[34] Earl of Ronaldshay, *The Life of Lord Curzon: Being the Authorized Biography of George Nathaniel, Marquess Curzon of Kedleston, K. G.*, 3 vols. (New York: Boni and Liveright, 1928), vol. 3, 157–8.

[35] October 31, 1917, war cabinet minutes, quoted in Lowe and Dockrill, *Mirage of Power*, vol. 3, 550. The land between the Jordan River and the Mediterranean Sea had a population at the time of the declaration of approximately 700,000. Today, the population is approximately ten times that figure and the country succeeds in exporting food.

home policy.[36] It was anticipated that the Arab people would receive their reward upon victory in the form of "independence" in Syria, Mesopotamia, and Arabia.

Montagu's objections played a greater role in delaying action on the pro-Zionist declaration than did Curzon's. At all events, the pro-Zionists decided to mollify their critics by diluting the declaration's language. Amery was asked to "go a reasonable distance to meeting the objections both Jewish and pro-Arab without impairing the substance of the proposed declaration."[37] He added provisos dealing with Jews remaining outside Palestine and with "non-Jewish communities in Palestine," which could apply both to the local Arabs and to non-Arab representatives of Western and Orthodox churches.[38] With minor modification, Amery's draft received the war cabinet's approval. On 2 November, the declaration was issued over the signature of the foreign secretary:

His Majesty's Government view with favour the establishment in Palestine of a national home for the Jewish people, and will use their best endeavours to facilitate the achievement of this object, it being clearly understood that nothing shall be done which may prejudice the civil and religious rights of non-Jewish communities in Palestine or the rights and political status enjoyed by Jews in any other country.[39]

The 31 October war cabinet minutes report on Balfour's interpretation:

As to the meaning of the words "national home," to which the Zionists attach so much importance, he understood it to mean some form of British, American, or other protectorate, under which full facilities would be given to the Jews to work out their own salvation and to build up, by means of education, agriculture, and industry, a real centre of national culture and focus of national life. It did not necessarily involve the early establishment of an independent Jewish State, which

---

[36] A December 19, 1917, memorandum by Arnold Toynbee and Lewis Namier of the foreign office answered the objection that the declaration was antidemocratic: "The objection raised against the Jews being given exclusive political rights in Palestine on a basis that would be undemocratic with regard to the local Christian and Mohammedan population is certainly the most important which the anti-Zionists have hitherto raised, but the difficulty is imaginary. Palestine might be held in trust by Great Britain or America until there was a sufficient population in the country fit to govern it on European lines. Then no undemocratic restrictions of the kind indicated in the memorandum would be required any longer." Gilbert, *Exile and Return*, 111–12.

[37] Stein, *Balfour Declaration*, 520.

[38] In opposing cabinet endorsement of a Jewish national home in Palestine, Curzon stressed that Christians "are vitally interested in the churches and in the country as the scene of the most sacred events in history." He cited the active engagement in Palestine activities of the Protestant, Roman Catholic, Greek Orthodox, and Russian Orthodox churches. See Ronaldshay, *Lord Curzon*, vol. 3, 158.

[39] Moore, *Documents*, 32.

was a matter for gradual development in accordance with the ordinary laws of political evolution.[40]

Lloyd George later clarified that the essence of the Jewish national home policy was a commitment to hold Palestine open to Jewish immigration. This would create the secure refuge under great power protection that Herzl had sought in his 1903 negotiations with Joseph Chamberlain. It would also give the Jews an opportunity to become a majority in Palestine. If they did, the protecting power could then transfer political authority to "representative institutions," which could evolve into the government of a Jewish state or commonwealth.[41]

In February 1918, Balfour dined in a small group with Colonel Meinertzhagen and discussed the declaration. The latter recorded the meeting in his diary:

It is an ambiguous document. . . . I cannot see how a Jewish State can ever be established which would not prejudice the civil and religious rights of the Arabs. . . . I put a straight question to Balfour. Is this a reward or bribe to the Jews for past services and given in the hope of full support during the war?

[Balfour and certain others present] were indignant. Balfour at once said, "Certainly not; both the Prime Minister and myself have been influenced by a desire to give the Jews their rightful place in the world; a great nation without a home is not right." . . . I then asked, "At the back of your mind do you regard this declaration as a charter for ultimate Jewish sovereignty in Palestine or are you trying to graft a Jewish population on to an Arab Palestine?" Balfour waited some time before he replied, choosing his words carefully, "My personal hope is that the Jews will make good in Palestine and eventually found a Jewish State. It is up to them now; we have given them their great opportunity." . . . I remarked that if this declaration did in the end found a Jewish State, it would be the only good thing which came out of this miserable war. . . . But I am not happy about the dubious wording of the document. Anti-semites, and God knows the world is full of them, will use the document against the Jews.[42]

---

[40] Lowe and Dockrill, *Mirage of Power*, vol. 3, 550–1.

[41] In testimony before a royal commission on Palestine in 1937, Lloyd George commented: "There could be no doubt as to what the cabinet then had in their minds. It was not their idea that a Jewish State should be set up immediately by the peace treaty. . . . On the other hand, it was contemplated that, when the time arrived for according representative institutions to Palestine, if the Jews had meanwhile responded to the opportunity afforded them . . . and had become a definite majority of the inhabitants, then Palestine would thus become a Jewish commonwealth.

"The notion that Jewish immigration would have to be artificially restricted in order to ensure that the Jews should be a permanent minority never entered into the head of anyone engaged in framing the policy. That would have been regarded as unjust and as a fraud on the people to whom we were appealing." Meron Medzini, *Israel's Foreign Relations: Selected Documents, 1947–1974*, 2 vols. (Jerusalem: Ministry for Foreign Affairs, 1976), vol. 1, 27.

[42] Meinertzhagen, *Middle East Diary*, 8–9 (February 7, 1918, entry).

Meinertzhagen had an impressive ability to sense how the document would be interpreted by non- or anti-Zionist British officials—such as his colleagues at British headquarters in Cairo—as opposed to how the cabinet intended it to read. He grasped that the distinction between Jewish national rights and Arab civil rights was too fine, given the lack of official support in the field for the Jewish national home. The "pro-Arab" proviso ensured that the British military authorities in Palestine and Egypt could denounce the declaration as self-contradictory and impossible to carry out.

AFTER THE WAR: CUTTING COSTS, HOLDING PALESTINE

Churchill was not in the war cabinet as the Balfour Declaration was debated. He had left the Asquith cabinet in November 1915. In 1919, he became secretary for war and air and returned to the government's inner circle. During his period as war secretary, civil war was under way in Russia. In the brutal clash of Whites and Reds, more than a hundred thousand Jews were massacred.[43] Greek and Turkish armies battled over possession of western Anatolia, while Constantinople remained under Allied occupation. And Britain and France were trying to cooperate, despite mutual suspicions, on issues of grand import ranging from German war reparations to the partition of the Ottoman Empire.

The war secretary's urgent responsibility was to demobilize millions of soldiers and cut millions of pounds sterling from daily military spending.[44] The trick was to do this while preserving Britain's bargaining position in the upcoming peace negotiations and maintaining law and order in the newly acquired territories. A victor's usual interest in preserving the fruits of war was magnified for Britain because the Great War had been a catastrophe of unprecedented proportions. Its new Middle Eastern possessions, especially the Holy Land, were among the few consolations Britain could carry away from more than four years of horrific struggle. But could the Empire afford to keep them?

In the process of netting out the imperial costs and benefits of retaining Palestine, the starting point was the Allies' agreement at Versailles not

[43] See *WSC* IV 342 n. 2.
[44] An October 17, 1919, report to the cabinet finance committee states: "The average number of discharges from the Army was 10,000 men per diem since the Armistice, while the expenditure had fallen from 4 1/8 millions sterling per day to 1 1/4 millions sterling per day. . . . The Secretary of State for War was of opinion that . . . the Army had melted away as rapidly as available shipping and political conditions had permitted." *WSC* IV C 925.

to annex outright the imperial territories captured from their enemies. Hence, Palestine could not be incorporated into the British Empire. Rather, it would have to be governed under an as-yet-unwritten mandate or trust instrument.

Holding Palestine would allow Britain to control lines of communication connecting British Mesopotamia (and the Persian Gulf) in the East with British Egypt (and the Mediterranean Sea) in the West.[45] This was roundly considered strategically valuable. Furthermore, from the British government's point of view, the list of acceptable candidates to govern Palestine was short. If the United States were unwilling to play the role, Britain would have to, for London would not countenance France's sitting next door to Egypt and the Suez Canal. Considerations of Zionism aside, it was not conceivable that Palestine would be turned over to the local Arabs, for they had no experience in self-government, no suitable governmental institutions existed and, in any event, Britain could not simply forfeit Christianity's holy places to Muslim rule after those sacred sites had been liberated through the glorious sacrifices of General Allenby and his men.

The Zionist leadership advocated a British Palestine. Weizmann made a point of disclaiming any intention to move immediately to Jewish statehood, lest Britain lack incentive to invest resources in the country.[46] When he testified before the Allies' supreme council in February 1919, the American secretary of state asked him whether "Jewish national home" meant an autonomous Jewish government.

Weizmann replied in the negative. The Zionist Organization [wanted] merely to establish in Palestine, under a Mandatory Power, an administration, not necessarily Jewish, which would render it possible to send into Palestine 70,000 to 80,000 Jews annually. The Organization would require to have permission at the same time to build Jewish schools, where Hebrew would be taught, and to develop institutions of every kind. Thus it would build up gradually a nationality, and so make Palestine as Jewish as America is American or England English.[47]

---

[45] The prevailing view among British officials at Cairo came to be that Palestine would have "considerable" value "as a bridge in peace time to Mesopotamia." Kedourie, *Anglo-Arab Labyrinth*, 85, 88.

[46] During a stroll with Weizmann at the Paris peace talks in February 1919, Meinertzhagen, then a member of the British delegation, "advised him to go all out for Jewish Sovereignty in Palestine," but "Weizmann thinks the time inopportune and might wreck the whole idea of Mandatory Zionism." Meinertzhagen, *Middle East Diary*, 15 (February 12, 1919, entry).

[47] Proceedings of the Allied supreme council (February 27, 1919), quoted in Gilbert, *Exile and Return*, 117.

This last remark was to reverberate problematically over the years.

Within the British government, not all the pro-Zionists favored Britain's accepting the mandate for Palestine. And not all the anti-Zionists favored Britain's renouncing Palestine. The military administration there, which reported to Allenby in Egypt, desired by and large to keep the territory but discard the Balfour Declaration. Some officials said it was morally wrong for Britain to create a Jewish national home contrary to the will of the Arab inhabitants. Some worried, as the Russian civil war raged, about the Jews infecting Palestine with Bolshevik ideology. Some described Zionism (à la Curzon) as unworkable. One of the pillars of anti-Zionism was the belief that the Jews could never succeed in defending themselves physically against the Arabs. In January 1919, Curzon spoke with Sir Alfred Money, chief of the Palestine administration, and reported approvingly:

His main point, and that of Allenby, is that we should go slow about the Zionist aspirations and the Zionist State. Otherwise we might jeopardise all that we have won. A Jewish Government in any form would mean an Arab rising, and the nine-tenths of the population who are not Jews would make short shrift with the Hebrews.[48]

Setting up a Jewish national home was a daunting responsibility. Even if practicable, it would be difficult and costly to implement. Discussions of this problem within the Palestine military administration, however, were not entirely a matter of unprejudiced analysis. Although some administration officials undoubtedly were loyal and open-minded, others were simply unwilling to give the government's pro-Zionist policy a fair chance of success. These latter officials resolved to oppose their government's pro-Zionist policy, building a case on their own predictions of inflexible Arab opposition to the Balfour Declaration. They then applied themselves to vindicating these predictions.

The Palestine administration did not use suasion or power to encourage the Arabs to accept the inevitability of a Jewish national home and reach a *modus vivendi* with the Jews. Allenby, in fact, barred publication of the Balfour Declaration in Palestine. In May 1919, General Gilbert

---

[48] Gilbert, *Exile and Return*, 119. Two and a half years later, on July 26, 1921, the chief of the imperial general staff, Field Marshal Sir Henry Wilson, met with Cuthbert Evans, a brigadier general then serving in Palestine. Wilson noted in his diary: "[Evans] is convinced that the Arabs will cut the throats of the Jews & that our force is quite insufficient to prevent this." Evans also said it was "preposterous that Sir Herbert Samuel, a Jew, should be High Commissioner." *WSC* IV 622.

Clayton, Allenby's chief political officer (who had been among Cairo's chief Arab revolt strategists during the war and later became chief of staff to the Palestine high commissioner), conveyed to London a report from General Money urging the government to abandon the Balfour Declaration; Clayton concurred.[49] Soon thereafter, Meinertzhagen reported that British officials in Palestine "are encouraging the Arabs to oppose Zionism" and that "the Jews regard the Administration as half-hearted regarding the National Home." Meinertzhagen concluded that Palestine's "political state . . . is unhappy . . . due to lack of a clear policy" and "failure to make it abundantly clear that the National Home is the declared policy of H. M. G." He urged that the local administration "be purged of those elements hostile to Zionism."[50]

In early August, having received counsel from Herbert Samuel and Meinertzhagen,[51] Balfour responded to Clayton and Money, cabling Cairo to instruct the Palestine administration to tell the Arab leaders that the government's pro-Zionist declaration was a "*chose jugée*" (decided policy) and that continued agitation against it would harm the country without affecting the policy.[52] Cairo did not act on the foreign office cable.

Later that month, the cabinet considered whether to accept the mandate for Palestine. Lloyd George prevailed. One participant noted: "The

---

[49] Stein *Balfour Declaration*, 645.

[50] Meinertzhagen, *Middle East Diary*, 22 (June 14, 1919, entry).

[51] At the end of July, Balfour met with Meinertzhagen: "[Balfour's] reasons for being a Zionist were complex, but were mainly based on the unsatisfactory position of the Jews in the world. There were many and powerful opponents to Zionism, headed by several rich and influential Jews. Their main argument was that a race which had for so long been parasites on other nations was not likely to succeed in an enterprise which was entirely Jewish. . . .

"Balfour went on to say that he himself was not in favour of a British Mandate over Palestine, but that he would not oppose it. The Prime Minister was very anxious to secure a British Mandate for purely sentimental reasons.

"He defined the policy of H. M. G. as follows: All development, industrial schemes of all kinds, and financial assistance must be based on the principle that Zionists are the Most-favoured Nation in Palestine. . . .

"To those who argued that the fate of Palestine should be decided by a Plebiscite, in which case the Arabs would have an overwhelming majority, he would reply that in any Palestine Plebiscite, the Jews of the world must be consulted; in which case he sincerely believed that an overwhelming majority would declare for Zionism under a British Mandate.

"I said I did not think that Arab opposition to Zionism would last for an instant in any obstructive form, if we once made it clear that Palestine was to be the National Home of the Jews and that H. M. G. was determined to see its policy through. Arab opposition would therefore be futile and would not be tolerated. He promised to dispatch a telegram in this sense to General Allenby." Meinertzhagen, *Middle East Diary*, 24–6 (July 30, 1919, entry).

[52] Stein, *Balfour Declaration*, 646–7.

PM very vehement about our keeping Palestine. The Biblical associations. Immense prestige attaching to Jerusalem. We have conquered it. The French did practically nothing."[53]

In January 1920, having recently been transferred to Cairo to replace Clayton as chief political officer, Meinertzhagen cabled to London that he was still "advocat[ing] the publication of the Declaration on Zionism." He said he was "all the more anxious" to press for publication, as it will "once and for all dispel the anti-Zionist attitude" of those "who still doubt the permanency of Zionism."[54]

BOLSHEVIKS, TURKS, JEWS, AND ARABS

With the prime minister continually complaining that demobilization was proceeding too slowly, Churchill's resentment of Lloyd George's foreign policies brimmed. To the war secretary they appeared a hash of inconsistent sympathies and notions, all of which tended to increase demands on his office for more men and money. Lloyd George was soft on the Bolsheviks and hard on the Turkish nationalists, the opposite of Churchill's preferences. Churchill pressed for more aid to the Whites in Russia. Lloyd George, condemning his colleague's "obsession" with Russia,[55] responded that the Whites were carrying out murderous pogroms and that Churchill should inquire "about this treatment of the Jews by your friends."[56] Churchill pressed for a peace settlement with Turkey. Lloyd George, whose philhellenism was worthy of Lord Byron, chose instead to support Greek designs on Anatolia that, in Churchill's view, precluded the peace settlement with Turkey required to secure Britain's position in the Middle East. Without such a settlement, Churchill feared, Turkey might move to retake its Middle Eastern provinces.

Venting frustration in a 25 October 1919 memorandum on the Turkish situation, Churchill wrote that the "French are about to over-run Syria" and will soon be fighting the Arabs, who will increasingly command British sympathies. Serious injury to Anglo-French relations will result.

---

[53] Diary of H. A. L. Fisher, quoted in Gilbert, *Exile and Return*, 123.
[54] Meinertzhagen, *Middle East Diary*, 69 (dispatch dated January 13, 1920).
[55] *WSC* IV 331.
[56] *WSC* IV 342. Churchill replied to Lloyd George by noting that there is "a very bitter feeling throughout Russia against the Jews, who are regarded as being the main instigators of the ruin of the Empire, and who, certainly have played a leading part in Bolshevik atrocities." Churchill then wrote to General Denikin of "the vital importance . . . of preventing by every possible means the ill-treatment of the innocent Jewish population." *WSC* IV 342–3.

Then "there are the Jews, whom we are pledged to introduce into Palestine and who take it for granted that the local population will be cleared out to suit their convenience." All of this, Churchill argued, will react on "our position as the greatest Mahommedan Power." India, Egypt, Mesopotamia, and Palestine "are all affected prejudicially." The cost of the Middle Eastern military establishments are gravely burdensome and "a strong force" must be maintained in and around Constantinople "for an indefinite period." Churchill "reluctantly" concluded that partitioning the Turkish Empire among the Allies "is a mistake" that will involve Britain in "abetting . . . the conquest of the Arabs by the Turks; . . . deserting and, it will be alleged, betraying those Arabs who fought so bravely with us in the war"; and spending immense sums for military forces and development work "far exceeding any possibility of return." He knew that it would be "very hard to relinquish the satisfaction of those dreams of conquest and aggrandisement which are gratified by the retention of Palestine and Mesopotamia," but the British Empire has "far more territory . . . than we shall be able to develop for many generations."[57] (As Churchill later entered more deeply into Near Eastern affairs, his comments about the Jews became, in general, less barbed and, about the Arabs, less grateful.)

Zionist leaders knew that the Arabs would not be "cleared out to suit [the Jews'] convenience." Accordingly, they were exploring possibilities for peace. Hopes for a mutual accommodation were not so fantastic as they seemed in later years. Britain had formidable leverage. It controlled vast Arab lands. The Arabs wanted much from Britain, but were owed little, given that the vast majority had fought against Britain in the war. As for Britain's Hashemite allies, they were willing to make a deal with the Zionists if this would secure British support for an independent Arab kingdom in the lands surrounding Palestine.[58]

[57] *WSC* IV C 937–9. It was a theme of Churchill's that the British colonies of long standing in Africa were a better investment than the newly acquired possessions in the Middle East. In a July 14, 1921, speech to the House of Commons, he drew the contrast amusingly: "In the Middle East you have arid countries. In East Africa you have dripping countries. There is the greatest difficulty to get anything to grow in the one place, and the greatest difficulty to prevent things smothering and choking you by their hurried growth in the other.

"In the African colonies you have a docile, tractable population, who only require to be well and wisely treated to develop great economic capacity and utility; whereas the regions of the Middle East are unduly stocked with peppery, pugnacious, proud politicians and theologians, who happen to be at the same time extremely well armed and extremely hard up." Cohen, *Churchill and the Jews*, 112.

[58] In January 1919, at the Paris peace conference, Hussein's son Feisal signed an agreement with Weizmann by which the Arab side endorsed the Balfour Declaration and "large scale"

With London holding such a strong hand, some British officials saw an opportunity to incorporate the Jewish national home into a grand bargain, a sweeping Arab-Jewish-British land-for-peace deal extending from the Persian Gulf to the Mediterranean. Balfour expounded the vision, reminding the Arabs that Britain freed them from centuries of Ottoman rule, "established the independent Arab sovereignty of the Hejaz," and desired to make Mesopotamia "a self-governing, autonomous Arab state." Balfour voiced hope that

remembering all that, they [the Arabs] will not grudge that small notch—for it is not more geographically, whatever it may be historically— . . . in what are now Arab territories being given to the people who for all these hundreds of years have been separated from it—but surely have a title to develop on their own lines in the land of their forefathers, which ought to appeal to the sympathy of the Arab people as it, I am convinced, appeals to the great mass of my own Christian fellow-countrymen.[59]

The British Palestine administration, however, evinced less interest in moving the Arabs toward compromise with the Zionists than in proving to London that the Arabs were unmovable. It offered evidence in the form of Arab violence. For two days beginning on 4 April 1920, Arab rioters attacked Jews and Jewish-owned property in Jerusalem. In the rioting 5 Jews and 4 Arabs were killed, 211 Jews and 21 Arabs were wounded, and 2 Jewish girls were raped. For some weeks before the riot, Jabotinsky had

---

Jewish immigration into Palestine in return for Zionist technical assistance for Arab economic development: Moore, *Documents*, 401. It was fundamental to the thinking of Churchill that Arab opposition to Zionism would someday soften as Jewish brains, capital, and assiduity spread prosperity to all of Palestine's inhabitants, Arab and Jewish, and to the neighboring lands. The nature of the Feisal-Weizmann deal—economic assistance in return for peace—reinforced that hope.

But one of Feisal's key constituencies, the General Syrian Congress, comprising notables from prominent Arab families in Syria, Lebanon, and Palestine, opposed his deal with Weizmann and resolved to fight both the Balfour Declaration and any French mandate for Syria. On July 2, 1919, the Congress resolved:

"1. We desire full and absolute political independence for Syria. . . .

"6. We do not recognise to the French Government any right to any part of Syria, and we reject all proposals that France should give us assistance or exercise authority in any portion of the country.

"7. We reject the claims of the Zionists for the establishment of a Jewish commonwealth in that part of southern Syria which is known as Palestine, and we are opposed to Jewish immigration. . . . We do not acknowledge that they have a title, and we regard their claims as a grave menace to our national, political and economic life. . . .

"8. We desire that there should be no dismemberment of Syria, and no separation of Palestine or the coastal regions in the west or the Lebanon from the mother country." George Antonius, *The Arab Awakening: The Story of the Arab National Movement* (London: Hamish Hamilton, 1938), 440–2 [appendix G].

[59] Israel Cohen, ed., *Speeches on Zionism by the Right Hon. The Earl of Balfour, K. G., O. M., F. R. S.* (London: Arrowsmith, 1928), 23–5.

openly been training a Jewish self-defense corps, which went into action when the riot began. Immediately thereafter, the authorities arrested defense corps personnel, including Jabotinsky. His trial was under way by 13 April and, less than a week later, this founder of Britain's Jewish legion, who fought in the Great War as a lieutenant in the Royal Fusiliers, was sentenced to fifteen years' penal servitude (for possession of a revolver; providing arms "with the evil intent of bringing about rapine, pillage, devastation"; and conspiracy).[60] Jabotinsky's treatment was protested in the House of Commons; Lord Cecil disapproved in particular that the Zionist leader's sentence was the same as that for the two Arabs who had raped the Jewish girls.[61]

On 26 April, Meinertzhagen added a stunning entry to his diary:

It gave me a shock when I found that officers of the British Administration were actively implicated and plotting against their own government. I warned both Allenby and [Major General Sir Louis] Bols [who had replaced Money as the chief of the Palestine administration] but they preferred silence to exposure; I wrote a private and secret letter to [foreign secretary] Lord Curzon just before the Jerusalem riots at Easter, setting out the following information. . . .

[Colonel] Waters-Taylor [chief of staff to Bols] saw Haj al Amin [who later became grand mufti] on the Wednesday before Easter and told him that he had a great opportunity at Easter to show the world that the Arabs of Palestine would not tolerate Jewish domination in Palestine; that Zionism was unpopular not only with the Palestine Administration but in Whitehall and if disturbances of sufficient violence occurred in Jerusalem at Easter, both General Bols and General Allenby would advocate the abandonment of the Jewish Home. Waters-Taylor explained that freedom could only be attained through violence.

On the day of the rioting the following notice was displayed all over Jerusalem: "The Government is with us, Allenby is with us, kill the Jews; there is no punishment for killing Jews." . . .

On the day of the rioting Waters-Taylor absented himself in Jericho for the day. Two days after the rioting he sent for the Mayor of Jerusalem—Moussa Kasim Pasha—and said "I gave you a fine opportunity; for five hours Jerusalem was without military protection; I had hoped you would avail yourself of the opportunity but you have failed." This conversation was confirmed from two sources.[62]

Responding to Meinertzhagen's criticism, Lieutenant General William Congreve, the Cairo-based commander of British forces in Egypt and Palestine, wrote to Allenby, by way of explanation, that "the majority of Englishmen have an inherited feeling against the Jew" and "a sympathy with the possessor of the soil." Allenby, in turn, wrote to Curzon: "A

---

[60] Joseph B. Schechtman, *Rebel and Statesman: The Early Years—The Life and Times of Vladimir Jabotinsky* (Silver Spring, Maryland: Eshel Books, 1986), 337–8.
[61] Ibid., 350.   [62] Meinertzhagen, *Middle East Diary*, 81–2.

large section of Moslem and Christian opinion in Palestine, coherent and powerful, views Zionist aspirations with deep suspicion. It is useless for Meinertzhagen or Weizmann to avoid the issue by throwing blame on the military administration."[63] Allenby then fired Meinertzhagen and sent him back to London.

The Jerusalem riots, presumably not by coincidence, occurred a few weeks before the Allies' supreme council convened at San Remo, Italy, to draft the peace treaty (including ancillary mandates) for imposition on the Ottoman Empire. It was decided there that France would become mandatory for Syria. Britain would receive two mandates, for Mesopotamia and Palestine respectively. Though the precise boundary between Syria and Palestine remained to be delineated, Britain was able to secure for itself unbroken lines of communication from the Persian Gulf to the Mediterranean, for eastern Palestine was made contiguous with Mesopotamia.

The Palestine mandate quoted the Balfour Declaration in its entirety and mandated that Britain was responsible for putting that declaration into effect. "[R]ecognition has thereby been given," the mandate stated, "to the historical connection of the Jewish people with Palestine and to the grounds for reconstituting their national home in that country."[64] The mandate acknowledged no Arab national rights in Palestine.

As war secretary, Churchill supervised the military forces running the Palestine military government. He did not in official channels challenge their opposition to the government's pro-Zionist policy, but he did at the time publish a newspaper commentary extolling Zionism as advantageous for Britain as well as the Jews. Implicitly endorsing both large-scale Jewish immigration into Palestine and the goal of a Jewish majority there, he wrote:

If, as may well happen, there should be created in our own lifetime by the banks of the Jordan a Jewish State under the protection of the British Crown which might comprise three or four millions of Jews, an event will have occurred in the history of the world which would from every point of view be beneficial, and would be especially in harmony with the truest interests of the British Empire.

In that article, entitled "Zionism versus Bolshevism," Churchill observed: "Some people like Jews and some do not, but no thoughtful man can

---

[63] Gilbert, *Exile and Return*, 129–30. Both letters were dated April 19, 1920.
[64] Moore, *Documents*, 74–83. While nowhere referring to Arabs or the Arab people, the mandate did provide, in Article 22, that Arabic, together with Hebrew and English, was to be an official language of Palestine.

doubt the fact that they are beyond all doubt the most formidable and the most remarkable race which has ever appeared in the world." He distinguished between the Jews who were assimilated into their countries of residency and those who were not. Among the latter, there was a great divide between the Jews who organize themselves in "a world-wide conspiracy for the overthrow of civilisation" and for the promotion of Bolshevism and those who labor constructively for a national Jewish center in Palestine to serve as a refuge, "a symbol of Jewish unity and the temple of Jewish glory." "The struggle which is now beginning between the Zionist and the Bolshevik Jews," Churchill wrote, "is little less than a struggle for the soul of the Jewish people."[65] Typically, Churchill insisted that Zionism be viewed from a broad perspective. The issue was not local and administrative; rather, it was an element of world politics with transcendent moral implications.

In July 1920, Britain replaced its military government in Palestine with a civil administration. Sir Herbert Samuel became Palestine's first high commissioner. Though the chief had changed, the administration's collective frame of mind—its prevailing lack of sympathy with the government's pro-Zionist policy—remained intact. Like many political appointees before and since, Samuel quickly came under the influence of his professional military and civilian subordinates. He supervised, but they led.

Within days of Samuel's arrival in Jerusalem, French forces expelled Feisal from Damascus.[66] Britain had to acquiesce in the humiliation of its Hashemite client. Meanwhile, Turkish nationalist forces threatened Allied forces in Constantinople, Ireland was in revolt, and violent Egyptian nationalists had extracted from British negotiators a pledge of independence that "bewildered"[67] Churchill, who had not been consulted. Throughout the summer, British forces in Mesopotamia strained to suppress a large-scale rebellion. In deference to the prime minister, Churchill doggedly pursued his demobilization and expenditure reduction plans, but demand for troops was rising. Mesopotamia was being reinforced with men from India, Palestine, Constantinople, Egypt, and Europe. "We

[65] *Illustrated Sunday Herald*, February 8, 1920, quoted in Gilbert, *Exile and Return*, 127–8. Meinertzhagen had earlier used the term "constructive Bolshevism" to describe Zionism in contrast to the destructive variety then gaining ground in Russia; he reported that Weizmann approved the characterization. Meinertzhagen, *Middle East Diary*, 14 (January 30, 1919, entry).

[66] The blow that ended the Hashemite kingdom of Syria also negated Feisal's agreement with Weizmann. See Antonius, *Arab Awakening*, 439 [appendix F].

[67] Cabinet memorandum dated August 24, 1920, in *WSC* IV C 1179.

are at our wits' end to find a single soldier," Churchill exclaimed to the foreign secretary.[68]

In November, General Congreve warned Churchill that, unless the garrison for eastern Palestine were increased, British forces would not be able to maintain order there. Congreve recommended as an economy measure that Britain exclude from the mandate all of Palestine east of the Jordan River.[69]

A few weeks later, Churchill wrote Lloyd George yet again to complain about the impossibility of reconciling the prime minister's demands for economy with his commitment to retain the new Middle Eastern mandates and his antagonism to Turkey:

It seems to me a most injurious thing that we, the greatest Mohammedan Empire in the world, sh[oul]d be the leading Anti-Turk power. . . . I deeply regret & *resent* being forced to ask Parl[iamen]t for these appalling sums of money for new Provinces—all the more when the pursuance of the Anti-Turk policy complicates and aggravates the situation in every one of them, & renders cheapers [sic] solutions impossible.[70]

CHURCHILL AND THE MIDDLE EAST DEPARTMENT

War secretary Churchill quarreled with the foreign secretary over Turkey, the colonial secretary over Egypt, the India secretary over Mesopotamia, and the prime minister over all of the above. Substantive and jurisdictional disputes among the offices of these ministers were depriving British Middle East policy of even the semblance of coherence. Since the grim days of the previous summer, Churchill had been recommending creation of a new Middle East department within the government. On 31 December 1920, the cabinet agreed. It located the new department within the colonial office. Lloyd George then offered his fractious friend Churchill the job of colonial secretary. The latter agreed. Among his earliest

[68] See *WSC* IV 495. In a November 23, 1920, cabinet memorandum, Churchill wrote, "The burden of carrying out the present policy at Constantinople, in Palestine, Egypt, Mesopotamia and Persia is beyond the strength of the British Army and is producing most formidable reactions upon the Indian Army, upon which we are compelled to rely. I see the very greatest difficulty in maintaining that situation through the new financial year unless our military measures are aided by a policy of reconciliation and co-operation with the Turks and the Moslem world. It is far better to do this than to give up a province like Egypt, where we have been honourable [sic] established for so many years." *WSC* IV C 1250.

[69] See *WSC* IV 502–3. The population of eastern Palestine was 250,000 in 1920: *WSC* IV C 1260 n. 1.

[70] Churchill to Lloyd George, December 4, 1920, in *WSC* IV C 1260–1 (emphasis in original).

personnel decisions was to recruit as advisers both T. E. Lawrence and Meinertzhagen.[71]

Churchill was pleased to relinquish the war office, where he had labored to cut and shift military resources to serve policies that he had neither made nor approved. In the colonial office, he could actually make policy. But though Mesopotamia and Palestine in 1921 lay before Churchill like so much unformed clay, there was limited satisfaction, indeed inherent frustration, in his new responsibilities because he did not view the Middle East as an imperial concern of the first rank. Unlike many officials, Churchill did not believe that a matter achieved paramount importance because he was put in charge of it. Churchill found it hard to concentrate—to focus narrowly—on his assigned area. His natural perspective was the strategic overview and, from that perspective, the central field was dominated by Turkey, Russia, and the Rhine. The Middle East was in the periphery. In March 1920, Churchill had written to Lloyd George: "Compared to Germany, Russia is minor; compared to Russia, Turkey is petty."[72] How then, in the grand strategic scheme of things, to evaluate the Middle East? What is less than petty?

The Middle East had some importance, at least, because it could disturb Britain's relationship with France, a point highlighted in Churchill's 11 January 1921 meeting in Paris with French president Alexandre Millerand. Churchill, according to his own report, "pointed out the absolute need . . . of appeasing Arab sentiment," lest garrison expenses force the Allies to evacuate the Middle East.

[Millerand] then instanced Zionism in Palestine as a cause of disturbing the Arab world. While in favour of it in principle, he feared that the Jews would be very high-handed when they got together there. In reply I expatiated on the virtues and experience of Sir Herbert Samuel, and pointed out how evenly he was holding the balance between Arabs and Jews and how effectively he was restraining his own people, as perhaps only a Jewish administrator could do.[73]

The foreign office had for months been contemplating a throne for Feisal in Baghdad. By transferring to him responsibility for keeping peace domestically, Britain could reduce the size of its Mesopotamian garrison. Likewise, Abdullah was deemed suitable to relieve Britain of law enforcement duties in Transjordan. Major Hubert Young, a foreign office official

---

[71] See *WSC* IV 510 (regarding Lawrence); *WSC* IV C 1296 (regarding Meinertzhagen).
[72] Lowe and Dockrill, *Mirage of Power*, vol. 3, 730.
[73] Churchill to Lloyd George, Curzon, D'Abernon, and Hardinge, January 12, 1921, in *WSC* IV C 1304.

who soon transferred into the new Middle East department, endorsed these proposals in a 25 January 1921 memorandum to Churchill that advised a deal: the Hashemites would get their kingdoms in return for renouncing revenge against the French in Syria.[74]

Immediately after taking up the colonial office seals in February 1921, Churchill decided to visit Cairo to confer with the government's leading Middle East experts on Mesopotamia and Palestine. In preparation, John Evelyn Shuckburgh, the new head of the Middle East department, coauthored a memorandum with Young and Lawrence that recommended turning eastern Palestine over to the Arabs and expediting the Jews' economic development of western Palestine. The Jewish national home would be confined to western Palestine, an Arab-led administration under the Palestine mandate would be established for Transjordan (consistent with Young's 25 January memorandum), and Britain would move immediately (rather than continue to await confirmation of the mandate by the League of Nations) to grant applications from Jews for economic development plans in western Palestine, such as the hydroelectric power project being promoted by Pinhas Rutenberg, a Russian Jewish engineer who had helped Jabotinsky launch the Jewish legion.[75] Such an approach, Shuckburgh et al. contended, would harmonize Britain's various wartime promises to the Arabs and the Jews.

In light of that memorandum, it is noteworthy that high officials responsible for Britain's wartime promises to the Hashemites had repeatedly asserted that Palestine was excluded from the area envisioned for Arab "independence."[76] They also, in any event, had conditioned those promises on a broad-based Arab uprising that had not occurred.[77] Yet

---

[74] See *WSC* IV 519.

[75] Rutenberg held high office in the Russian provisional government headed by Alexander Kerensky following the tsar's overthrow in February 1917. He was present in the Winter Palace when it fell to Bolshevik forces the following November. After a half-year of imprisonment by the Bolsheviks, he eventually (November 1919) emigrated to Palestine, where he helped Jabotinsky organize the Jewish self-defense corps that was active in the April 1920 anti-Jewish riots. See "Rutenberg, Pinhas," *Encyclopaedia Judaica*, 16 vols. (Jerusalem: Keter Publishing House Ltd., 1973), vol. 14, 516–17.

[76] Sir Henry McMahon to Shuckburgh, March 12, 1922, in *WSC* IV C 1805: "It was . . . fully my intention to exclude Palestine. . . . I did not make use of the Jordan to define the limits of the southern area, because I thought it might be considered desirable at some later stage of negotiations to . . . find some suitable frontier line east of the Jordan." See also Kedourie, *Anglo-Arab Labyrinth*, 142: "Another point which the [British and French] negotiators [in December 1915] assumed was that Palestine—however delimited—had not been committed in the negotiations with the Sharif [Hussein]." See also ibid., 161, 189–95, 222.

[77] See Kedourie, *Anglo-Arab Labyrinth*, 108–9: "McMahon's offer had been conditional not only on the separation between the Arabs and the Turks, but on the immediate active

here those promises were said to oblige the government to bar the Zionists from more than three-quarters of mandate Palestine. Shuckburgh, Young, and Lawrence recognized that some "interpretation" would be required to square this proposal with the mandate's Jewish national home provisions, so they cited the proviso (derived from the Balfour Declaration) on the "civil and religious rights" of Palestine's "non-Jewish communities" and the mandate provision (Article 3) on encouraging "local autonomy": "We consider that these two clauses, taken in conjunction, afford adequate justification for setting up in Transjordan a political system somewhat different from that in force on the other side of the river. If British promises are to stand, this system must be Arab in character."[78] This memorandum, as Meinertzhagen foresaw would happen, takes the phrase "civil and religious rights," which the Balfour Declaration used to protect the personal rights of individuals, and interprets it as a reference to collective and political rights of the Arabs of Palestine.

Alarmed at the prospect of losing all of eastern Palestine, Weizmann wrote Churchill on 1 March that "Trans-Jordania has from earliest times been an integral and vital part of Palestine." He asserted that western Palestine's economic progress depends upon Transjordan, for it forms "the natural granary of all Palestine." Weizmann acknowledged that the British government must consider its pledges to the Arabs and should satisfy their "legitimate aspirations," but, he argued, "the taking from Palestine of a few thousand square miles, scarcely inhabited and long derelict, would be scant satisfaction to Arab Nationalism, while it would go far to frustrate the entire policy of His Majesty's Government regarding the Jewish National Home."[79]

At the Cairo Conference from 12–22 March, Churchill's decisions followed the general lines of his staff's recommendations. In Mesopotamia, Feisal was to be king. Transjordan would remain within the Palestine mandate, but without the Jewish national home. Abdullah would be asked to establish an administration there. As the conference minutes relate, Lawrence urged Abdullah's appointment:

[Lawrence] trusted that in four or five years, under the influence of a just policy, the opposition to Zionism would have decreased, if it had not entirely disappeared,

---

co-operation of the Arabs against the Turks." See also ibid., 122 (quoting an India office official): "If they [the Hashemites] fail to carry out their side of the agreement, they cannot hereafter complain if we should say it was off."

[78] *WSC* IV 538.

[79] Aaron S. Klieman, *Foundations of British Policy in the Arab World: The Cairo Conference of 1921* (Baltimore: Johns Hopkins Press, 1970), 287 [Appendix G].

and it was his view that it would be preferable to use Trans-Jordania as a safety valve, by appointing a ruler on whom he could bring pressure to bear, to check anti-Zionism.[80]

Questions arose as to the legality of taking Transjordan out of the Jewish national home. Not satisfied with the Shuckburgh-Young-Lawrence analysis, Churchill cabled home on 21 March to ask if an amendment to the Palestine mandate were necessary. He signaled that he hoped not, but if it were, "it would be better to specify areas affected without referring in detail to proposed difference in treatment."[81] Colonial office and foreign office lawyers jointly recommended a new provision, which became Article 25 of the mandate and which satisfied Churchill's desire for obscure phrasing:

In the territories lying between the Jordan and the eastern boundary of Palestine as ultimately determined, the Mandatory shall be entitled, with the consent of the Council of the League of Nations, to postpone or withhold application of such provisions of this mandate as he may consider inapplicable to the existing local conditions.

The colonial office explained that this language would allow Britain, in Transjordan, "to withhold indefinitely the application of those clauses of the mandate which relate to the establishment of the National Home for the Jews."[82]

In Jerusalem, Churchill interviewed Abdullah and explained to him the plans for Transjordan, highlighting that "the Zionist clauses of the mandate would not apply" there.[83] Abdullah suggested, but did not insist, that eastern and western Palestine be combined under an Arab amir. Samuel intervened to assure Abdullah that Britain would act in good faith toward the Arabs of western Palestine. The high commissioner pressed his point with an argument that was low-key in tone but radical in its implications for British policy: "The Mandate embodied the terms of the Balfour Declaration in which two distinct promises were made—one to the Jews and the other to the Arabs." The government was "determined to fulfil both these promises."[84]

After a few hours of talk, Abdullah acceded to Churchill's proposal for Transjordan. He agreed to remain in Amman for six months to help select an Arab governor to serve under the high commissioner for

[80] WSC IV 553. [81] Klieman, *Foundations*, 123.
[82] Ibid., 123 n. 20. [83] Ibid., 130.
[84] WSC IV 562.

Palestine.[85] Meinertzhagen, who did not accompany Churchill to Cairo and Jerusalem and did not begin service as Middle East department military adviser until May, commented acidly when he learned what was done with Transjordan. He recorded in his diary that he "exploded" on hearing that Churchill had separated Transjordan from western Palestine:

> Abdullah was placated at the expense of the Jewish National Home. . . . Lawrence was of course with Churchill and influenced him. . . . This reduces the Jewish National Home to one-third of Biblical Palestine. The Colonial Office and the Palestine Administration have now declared that the articles of the mandate relating to the Jewish Home are not applicable to Transjordan. . . . This discovery was not made until it became necessary to appease an Arab Emir. . . .
>
> I told [Churchill] it was grossly unfair to the Jews, that it was yet another promise broken and that it was a most dishonest act, that the Balfour Declaration was being torn up by degrees and that the official policy of H. M. G. to establish a Home for the Jews in Biblical Palestine was being sabotaged. . . . Churchill listened and said he saw the force of my argument and would consider the question.[86]

While still in Jerusalem, Churchill met with a delegation from the Arab Palestine Congress, which presented a memorandum that condemned the "unnatural partitioning" of Syria and Palestine, which it said were a single country. It rejected the Balfour Declaration, stating that the Arabs "resent and fight" against "transforming Palestine into a home for the Jews," who lack national rights for they have "no separate political or lingual existence." Attributing to the Jews "pernicious motives . . . towards the Powers that be and towards civilisation," the memorandum says that "everyone" should read *The Protocols of the Elders of Zion*. It asks: "If Russia and Poland, with their spacious countries, were unable to tolerate [the Jews], how could Europe expect Palestine to welcome them?"[87]

Churchill replied bluntly to the call for repudiating the Balfour Declaration and ending Jewish immigration: "It is not in my power to do so, nor, if it were in my power, would it be my wish." The declaration was "made while the war was still in progress, while victory and defeat hung

---

[85] As it happened, Abdullah remained longer than planned—viz., until he was assassinated in 1951. Meanwhile, he became king of an independent Transjordan in 1946. The kingdom's name was changed from Transjordan, which means "across the Jordan," to plain Jordan after the 1948–49 war against Israel, in which Abdullah's forces conquered the region west of the Jordan River that became known as the kingdom's "West Bank."

Before that conquest, the West Bank—as attested by General Allenby's campaign maps, the 1947 United Nations partition plan, and innumerable history and geography books by Arabs, Jews, and others—had universally been called "Judea and Samaria."

[86] Meinertzhagen, *Middle East Diary*, 99–100 (June 21, 1921, entry).

[87] Klieman, *Foundations*, 259–67 [Appendix B].

in the balance" so it "must therefore be regarded as one of the facts definitely established by the triumphant conclusion of the Great War." Churchill noted cuttingly: "I thought when listening to your statements, that . . . the Arabs of Palestine had overthrown the Turkish Government. That is the reverse of the true facts. . . . You had only to look on your road here . . . to see the graveyard of 2,000 British soldiers. . . . The position of Great Britain in Palestine is one of trust, but it is also one of right." Modulating his tone, Churchill explained that creation of the Jewish national home "does not mean that [Palestine] will cease to be the National Home of other people, or that a Jewish Government will be set up to dominate the Arab people." The Arabs can see "with [their] own eyes" how the Jews have increased Palestine's prosperity, which is one of the reasons the Arabs should "take a wise and tolerant view" of Zionism. Palestine "has been very much neglected" and there is "no reason why [it] should not support a larger number of people . . . , and all of those in a higher condition of prosperity."[88]

Before a largely Jewish audience at Jerusalem's Hebrew University, Churchill invoked the Balfour Declaration and announced: "Great Britain always keeps her promises. . . . Personally, my heart is full of sympathy for Zionism. This sympathy has existed for a long time, since twelve years ago, when I was in contact with the Manchester Jews." Reflecting Samuel's influence, he offered a loose characterization of the Balfour Declaration that worried attentive Zionists: "Our promise was a double one . . . to give our help to Zionism, and . . . [to assure] the non-Jewish inhabitants that they should not suffer in consequence."[89]

Churchill cut his Palestine visit short because the Chancellor of the Exchequer resigned. Frustrated to be abroad at such a moment, Churchill hoped that with a speedy return to London he might land the post for himself. (Lloyd George soured his relations with Churchill by giving the post to someone else.) In this and many other ways, Churchill was continually demonstrating that he considered the Middle East too small and inessential an arena for his interests and ambitions.[90] Another such

---

[88] Ibid., 269–73 [Appendix C].

[89] Ibid., 283–4 [Appendix F].

[90] On July 4, 1921, after Churchill presented to the cabinet a memorandum on Anglo-Japanese relations, Curzon, the foreign secretary, voiced another in a long series of protests against the colonial secretary's meddling in foreign office affairs. Curzon passed a note to Churchill: "My dear Winston, I wonder what you would say if on a Colonial Office [question] I felt myself at liberty to make a speech . . . quite independent of the Colonial Office and critical of the attitude adopted by its chief." Churchill replied with

sign was the degree to which Churchill deferred to Samuel in the formulation of the major premises for British policy in Palestine. Even though the colonial secretary doubted Samuel's judgment and resolve, he allowed himself to be guided by Samuel, who was in turn guided by his own subordinates.

HERBERT SAMUEL AND THE DUAL PROMISE

In his nine months as high commissioner, through intercourse with his staff and the local Arab community, Samuel grew increasingly solicitous of Arab fears about Jewish immigration and an eventual Jewish majority in Palestine. As an official in London, his thinking about Palestine had focused on facilitating Zionism. As an official in Jerusalem, he concentrated on preserving domestic tranquillity, which meant, in essence, trying to pacify the Arab population. He did not view it as his purpose to press on Arab minds the harsh reality that his government's national home policy intended to encourage Jewish immigration so that the Jews could transform their homeland into a country where they could enjoy majority status. On the contrary, he sought to assuage Arab opposition to British policy by obscuring that policy's goals and by asserting that the Balfour Declaration was a dual promise to the Jewish people and the Arab people. Both peoples, he said, must be deemed prime beneficiaries of the mandate, not just with respect to mandate Palestine as a whole (in which more than three-quarters of the territory was already reserved exclusively for the Arabs), but even in western Palestine.

Samuel's reading of the Balfour Declaration was more convenient than true. As originally promulgated and incorporated in the mandate, the declaration was for and about "the Jewish people." Neither the language regarding the "civil and religious rights of existing non-Jewish communities," nor the relevant war cabinet debate, nor the San Remo decision, supports the notion that the declaration was addressing the Jewish people and the Arab people equally or about the same things. The word "Arab" appears nowhere in it (and nowhere in the mandate, for that matter). The declaration was not a promise that Palestine—much less western Palestine

a note that revealed his low estimate of the importance of his own Middle Eastern and other responsibilities: "You may say anything you like about the Colonial Office that is sincerely meant; but there is no comparison between these vital foreign matters wh[ich] affect the whole future of the world and the mere departmental topics with wh[ich] the Colonial Office is concerned." *WSC* IV C 1543.

—would be divided politically between the Jews and the Arabs. It was not a promise that Britain would ensure that political power in Palestine be balanced between the Jewish people and the Arab people. It was not a dual promise, but rather a "declaration of sympathy with Jewish Zionist aspirations,"[91] with a proviso to protect the individual "civil and religious" rights of non-Jews.[92]

The British and Allied statesmen who endorsed the Balfour Declaration envisioned eventual Jewish self-determination in Palestine and Arab self-determination in the expanses of Syria, Mesopotamia, and Arabia. This seemed not only fair to the Arabs, but generous, given that they in general fought for the enemy in the war. Samuel, from his post in Jerusalem's Government House, however, did not view the Arab-Jewish fairness issue in the broad context of all the Middle Eastern lands liberated by the Allies from the Ottomans. He now accepted the idea that fairness required the balancing of the political interests of the Arabs and the Jews within the cramped confines of western Palestine. It is evident that Samuel intended to be just and to do right. But he effectively rewrote the Balfour Declaration to create a promise—or dual promise—that was impossible to fulfill.

GIVING APPEASEMENT A CHANCE

Palestine administration officials argued that the best way to win the Arabs' consent to the Jewish national home was to assure them that it would not be imposed against their will. Immediately after the war, anti-Zionist British officials had urged the government to renounce the Balfour

---

[91] This phrase appears in the opening paragraph of the letter from Foreign Secretary Balfour to Lord Rothschild which formally transmitted the declaration: Moore, *Documents*, 32.

[92] The distinction between "political rights" and "civil rights" was drawn sharply by Churchill himself when the Palestine Arab delegation visited the colonial office in August 1921. The delegation secretary asserted that "our rights have not been safeguarded." Churchill denied this and then said: "If you mean by that political rights, I say show me in what way you can safeguard the execution of our promises to the Jews, and we will consider how the political rights should be extended." The secretary pressed his point: "You promised us self-government." Churchill answered: "No. When was that promised? Never. We promised you should not be turned off your land." *WSC* IV C 1594. (Regarding the issue of the precise date of this meeting, see Cohen, *Churchill and the Jews*, 118 n. 129.) In a subsequent meeting with this delegation, on August 22, 1921, Churchill stated: "They [the Jews] cannot take any man's lands. They cannot dispossess any man of his rights. . . . If they like to buy people's land, and people like to sell it to them, and if they like to develop and cultivate regions now barren and make them fertile, then they have the right, and we are obliged to secure their right to come into the country and to settle" (*WSC* IV C 1611).

Declaration because the local Arabs would never acquiesce in the policy. Now, having failed to get the renunciation, these intrepid officials inconsistently asserted that the Arab community could be appeased after all, if Britain would limit Zionist activity—for example, restrict immigration and withhold approvals for development projects—and institutionalize Arab political power.

Samuel and Churchill approved such measures because they believed in appeasement. They were convinced that, if Zionism progressed slowly enough to keep Arab resentments in check, Arab attitudes toward the Jews would soften. Inclined to seek economic explanations of Arab actions and attitudes toward Zionism, Samuel and Churchill both tended to depreciate the religious and cultural sources of anti-Zionism, which considered the Jewish national movement an aggression against Arab land and the Arab people and, as such, unacceptable in principle. Arabs who held that conviction would not be satisfied with slower rates of Jewish immigration or higher rates of economic growth. Such persons, furthermore, dominated the religious and political leadership of the Arab community of Palestine. And they did so, somewhat ironically and somewhat on purpose, because the British administration in Palestine gave them authority.

Following the death in March 1921 of the mufti of Jerusalem, whom the British administration treated as the head of the Muslim community, Muslim leaders convened, in line with Ottoman law and tradition, to elect the three candidates from among whom the high commissioner could appoint the new mufti. Ernest Richmond, a member of Samuel's secretariat and a "declared enemy of the Zionist policy,"[93] favored the selection of Haj Amin el-Husseini, who had led the anti-Jewish riots in Jerusalem in April 1920, for which he had received a ten-year prison sentence and then, from Samuel, a pardon. Haj Amin placed fourth in the voting, which disqualified him, but Samuel appointed him anyway.[94] Meinertzhagen promptly recorded in his diary that Haj Amin "hates both Jews and British" and his appointment "is sheer madness":

I am particularly annoyed about this as . . . I left a memorandum with Samuel warning him of appointing the man . . . and also warning him that [Ronald]

[93] Ernest T. Richmond, assistant secretary (political) in Samuel's administration, was so described by Gerard Clauson, a colonial office official. Elie Kedourie, *The Chatham House Version and Other Middle-Eastern Studies* (New York: Praeger Publishers, 1970), 65.

[94] See Norman and Helen Bentwich, *Mandate Memories: 1918–1948* (London: The Hogarth Press, 1965), 191–2. Norman Bentwich was attorney general for Palestine throughout the 1920s.

Storrs [British governor of Jerusalem] would press for his appointment purely on the grounds of hostility to Zionism.

. . . [S]ooner or later his appointment will be bitterly regretted by us. I spoke to Churchill about it today, but he did not seem to be much interested and in any case said he could do nothing about it.[95]

(Haj Amin over the coming decades instigated a series of anti-Jewish and anti-British riots and murders and terrorized his Arab opponents. During the Second World War, having engineered the pro-Nazi coup in Iraq in 1941, which Britain suppressed, he fled to Berlin and aided Hitler's efforts against the Allies and the Jews.)

In early May, soon after Churchill departed Palestine, several days of fatal attacks on Jews by Arabs began in Jaffa. Samuel promptly sought to placate the Arabs. He suspended Jewish immigration into Palestine, explaining to Churchill that the Arab rioters were distressed by the two hundred Jewish Bolshevik immigrants who had recently arrived, though he also noted that there was some Arab opposition to any Jewish immigration, "no matter what might be its character, on grounds of principle."[96] Samuel also proposed immediate establishment of "representative institutions," which Arab leaders had been demanding so that the current Arab majority could block Jewish immigration. Churchill ratified Samuel's immigration ban, though his reply cable observed: "The present agitation is doubtless engineered in the hope of frightening us out of our Zionist policy. . . . We must firmly maintain law and order and make concessions on their merits and not under duress."[97] On 23 May, General Congreve advised Churchill: "[I]f we are to continue our Zionist policy you must be prepared to pay for British troops to the full 5,000 effectives for a long time to come, or else risk a general Jew baiting and killing . . . and even with the 5,000 I think we take a risk in the event of an organised attack."[98]

Churchill understood that "representative institutions" was a slogan connoting the end of Jewish immigration.[99] He advised Samuel not to use it, but tried to mollify the high commissioner by saying he would not

---

[95] Meinertzhagen, *Middle East Diary*, 97–8 (April 27, 1921, entry).
[96] *WSC* IV 585–6.
[97] Churchill to Samuel, telegram, May 14, 1921, in *WSC* IV C 1466–7.
[98] *WSC* IV C 1473.
[99] Regarding a report by Churchill on Palestine, the May 31, 1921, cabinet minutes state that "development of representative institutions . . . was at present suspended owing to the fact that any elected body would undoubtedly prohibit further immigration of Jews." *WSC* IV C 1484.

oppose "step by step establishment of elective institutions." The "morrow of the Jaffa riots" was not, as Churchill put it, "the best moment for making such a concession."[100] A few weeks later, Churchill commented on the subject to his private secretary: There was great folly in "going out of our way to procure a hungry lion and then walking up to him with a plate of raw beef to see how much he would like to take."[101]

Samuel prepared a major policy speech for delivery on the king's birthday, 3 June. Churchill reviewed the text in advance and approved it, though he warned Samuel against "paraphrasing" the term "national home," which Samuel wanted to define as a "spiritual centre."[102] In the speech, as delivered, Samuel announced that conditions in Palestine precluded "anything in the nature of mass immigration."[103] While lifting the immigration ban he had imposed during the Jaffa riots, Samuel declared that the administration would henceforth restrict Jewish immigration to keep within the "economic capacity" of the country to absorb new arrivals.[104] Samuel stressed that Britain would "never agree to a Jewish Government being set up to rule over the Moslem and Christian majority."[105]

Zionist leaders protested. They promoted immigration so that the Jews could become a majority and then establish a democratic government in what would be a predominantly Jewish state. It was infuriating that Samuel would, on the one hand, imply that the Jews wanted to rule as a minority over the Arabs and, on the other hand, impose immigration restrictions and suggest that Britain would preserve the Arab majority.

In a speech to the House of Commons on 14 June, Churchill endorsed Samuel's absorptive capacity standard. But he stressed that "the country is greatly under-populated." He also praised the Zionist settlers for bringing about the general economic betterment of Palestine,[106] though he criticized the "ardour" of Zionist declarations, "which alarm the Arabs."

---

[100] Churchill to Samuel, telegram, June 4, 1921, in *WSC* IV C 1493.

[101] Churchill to Archibald Sinclair, message, June 18, 1921, in *WSC* IV 615–16.

[102] Klieman, *Foundations*, 182. In a June 20, 1921, memorandum, General Congreve wrote, "In Palestine we are attempting to reconcile two ideals, extreme Zionism and extreme pan-Arabism, both equally undesirable and to a great extent artificial.... The Arabs wish to find definite expression for their national sentiments—the Jews wish to found a cultural centre. It is practically impossible to find a policy which will satisfy the extremists of both parties." Note that Congreve here implies that any Jews who aspire to something more than a Jewish "cultural center" in Palestine are extremists whom Britain should not even try to satisfy: *WSC* IV C 1517.

[103] Cohen, *Churchill and the Jews*, 105.   [104] *WSC* IV 589.

[105] Cohen, *Churchill and the Jews*, 104.

[106] On his recent Palestine visit, Churchill had taken a tour, under Rutenberg's guidance, of some Jewish settlements, which had given him confidence that the new immigrants

Addressing Britain's wartime pledges to Arabs and Jews and its new mandates, Churchill said that the "paramount object" of the Middle East department was large-scale reduction of civil and military expenditures. Notwithstanding the costs, however,

we cannot repudiate light-heartedly these undertakings. We cannot . . . leave the inhabitants, for whose safety and well-being we have made ourselves responsible in the most public and solemn manner, a prey to anarchy and confusion of the worst description. We cannot . . . leave the Jews in Palestine to be maltreated by the Arabs who have been inflamed against them.

This would not accord with Britain's "duty," nor would it "be in accordance with the reputation that our country has frequently made exertions to deserve and maintain."[107]

Two days later, the *Times* editorialized that, if he had "carried his analysis of the present difficulties a little further," Churchill

might have discovered that one of the chief obstacles to peace is a fixed scepticism amongst many of the agents of the Government in Palestine about Zionism and the Jewish national home; and Sir Herbert Samuel, in prohibiting Jewish immigration after the Jaffa riots, may have been the unwilling victim of his agents. The embargo on immigration (now removed) was a profound mistake of policy.[108]

Churchill concurred with Samuel that it was undesirable to expound plainly the goals of the Jewish national home policy. Whereas Meinertzhagen believed that vagueness on this point encouraged the anti-Zionists,[109]

were not Bolsheviks and that their achievements were yielding material benefits to both themselves and their Arab neighbors. He had declared there: "I defy anybody after seeing work of this kind, achieved by so much labour, effort and skill, to say that the British Government, having taken up the position it has, could cast it all aside and leave it to be rudely and brutally overturned by the incursion of a fanatical attack by the Arab population from outside" (*WSC* IV 574).

[107] *WSC* IV 594–8. Though Churchill insisted that Britain must fulfill its obligations in the Middle East, he would have supported assigning these obligations to the United States if the latter were willing to accept them. On June 9, 1921, he enthusiastically endorsed what he thought was a suggestion to this effect from Lloyd George: *WSC* IV C 1498–9. The next day, Lloyd George disclaimed and dismissed the idea: *WSC* IV C 1500.

[108] Cohen, *Churchill and the Jews*, 111 (June 16, 1921, editorial).

[109] He wrote in his diary, "Both in Palestine and in the Colonial Office great weakness has been manifest as a result of the recent anti-Jewish riots in Jaffa. The anti-Zionists have used the occasion to demonstrate the futility and unfairness of the movement and its inevitable failure. . . . Sir Herbert Samuel has been weak. The moment the Jaffa rioting broke out, he and his staff seem to have been hypnotized by the danger and everything was done to placate the Arab . . . whereas what the Arab wanted was a good sound punishment for breaking the peace and killing Jews. The Arab is fast learning that he can intimidate a British Administration. Samuel has not been able to stand up to the solid block of anti-Zionist feeling among his military advisers and civil subordinates.

"Surely it is time we stood by our policy and told the Arab we shall not be intimidated

Churchill and Samuel thought they could avert needless provocation of the Arabs by dispensing with talk of a future Jewish majority. Churchill was continually pressed to explain what "national home" meant, and he was nearly always careful to keep the illumination dim. A rare occasion when he revealed his true expectation was the 22 June meeting of the imperial cabinet, at which he described the Balfour Declaration as an obligation incurred in wartime "to enlist the aid of Jews all over the world" and warned that Britain must be "very careful and punctilious" in discharging its obligations.[110] Churchill was asked by the Canadian prime minister whether the phrase "national home" meant giving the Jews "control of the Government." He replied, "If, in the course of many years, they become a majority in the country, they naturally would take it over."[111] No Arab or Jewish delegation ever received so direct an answer on this point from Churchill.[112]

Fearful that Samuel's 3 June speech portended the undoing of the Jewish national home policy, Weizmann traveled to London in early July. He met with Churchill and told him that the Palestine administration and the government had placed the Jews in "a vicious circle":

On the one hand, they complain about Zionism being the burden of the British tax-payer, and when we desire to lighten this burden by developing Palestine and so increasing the wealth and productiveness of the country, they refuse to let us go on with our work because they are fearing an Arab outburst.[113]

The two men met again on 22 July at Balfour's home together with Balfour, Lloyd George, and the secretary to the cabinet. According to the minutes of the meeting, Weizmann condemned Samuel's 3 June speech as the "negation of the Balfour Declaration" because the latter meant a Jewish majority but "this speech would never permit such a majority to eventuate." Churchill "demurred at this interpretation of the speech."

---

or tolerate interference. It is absurd to talk of injustice to the Arab and eviction of the original landowners. Those arguments show a complete lack of appreciation of the Zionist movement. Zionism will injure none, on the contrary it will benefit the whole community. It is not going to dispossess the Arab or interfere with his political or religious susceptibilities." Meinertzhagen, *Middle East Diary*, 101–2 (July 5, 1921, entry).

[110] Gilbert, *Exile and Return*, 135.   [111] *WSC* IV 617.

[112] At the August 1921 colonial office meeting with the Palestine Arab delegation, the delegation secretary asked Churchill: "Did you promise that you will help them [the Jews] to make Palestine a Jewish State, a Jewish Kingdom?" Churchill gave his typically evasive answer: "[Samuel] has expressed very very clearly what is his interpretation of Mr Balfour's pledge. It undoubtedly is intended [that] the Jews shall be allowed to come freely into Palestine in proportion as there is room, and there is a good livelihood, provided of course they develop the resources of the country." *WSC* IV C 1599.

[113] *WSC* IV 619.

Lloyd George and Balfour "both said that by the Declaration they always meant an eventual Jewish State." Churchill discussed the difficult situation arising from the declaration "which was opposed by the Arabs, 9/10ths of the British officials on the spot, and some of the Jews in Palestine . . . a poor country in which destitute emigrants could not be dumped." Weizmann criticized the "representative Government project." Lloyd George then spoke directly to Churchill: "You mustn't give representative Government to Palestine." Churchill replied that "questions affecting the JNH [Jewish national home] would be eliminated from the purview of the representative Government." Weizmann said this was impossible. After some additional comments, Lloyd George noted that Weizmann wanted to know "whether we are going to keep our pledges." Weizmann said, "yes," Balfour then nodded, and Lloyd George told Weizmann: "You must do a lot of propaganda. Samuel is rather weak."[114]

BALFOUR DECLARATION: REVIEWED, REDEFINED, REAFFIRMED

Thus, the prime minister, who harassed Churchill continually to cut garrison expenses, catered to Weizmann and sympathized not at all with Churchill's desire to keep Palestine quiet through cooperation with the local authorities. By supporting Samuel, a Jew who early in the Great War had established pro-Zionist credentials, Churchill antagonized the Zionist leadership. Yet, as the Balfour Declaration's chief official defender, the colonial secretary suffered imprecations from the Arabs and their camp, which comprised the bulk of the British military and the Palestine administration and important voices in Parliament and the press.[115] Under the circumstances, Churchill concluded that he needed political cover and demanded a cabinet review of Palestine policy.

In preparation for that review, Major Young, stimulated by Meinertzhagen,[116] proposed a package deal. As a concession to the Arabs, the high commissioner's advisory council would be established on an elective (i.e., "representative") rather than appointive basis. The measures to satisfy Zionist concerns were several. Most important: "Any officials, whether

---

[114] *WSC* IV C 1559–60.
[115] For example, in October 1921, General Congreve told Major Young that "he and all his officers" thought that the government was "in the hands of the Zionist Organization" and the Middle East department was "pursuing an unfair policy in favour of the Jews." *WSC* IV 636.
[116] See Meinertzhagen, *Middle East Diary*, 106–9 (August 2 and 4, 1921, entries).

civil or military, who are publicly and confessedly opposed to the declared policy of His Majesty's Government should be replaced." This would permit release of officials "who do not feel that they can conscientiously carry out what some of them regard as an unfair and unpopular measure," namely, the Balfour Declaration. It was further proposed that the military forces in Palestine report directly to the war office and not to the notoriously anti-Zionist British authorities in Egypt. Also recommended was early approval of pending public utility concessions for "Jewish enterprise," which included the Rutenberg hydroelectric proposal. In defense of the expropriation provision in these concessions, Young stated: "This cannot be regarded as conflicting in any way with the second clause of the Balfour Declaration, which was clearly not intended to protect individuals who are determined to thwart the execution of the main policy."[117]

Had His Majesty's government adopted this package, the history of Palestine and the Jews might have taken an altogether different course. Churchill distributed Young's paper to the cabinet under his own grim cover memorandum, which said that the Palestine situation "causes me perplexity and anxiety," Arabs and Jews "are ready to spring at each other's throats," and war office estimates for the Palestine garrison for 1922–3 exceed £3.3 million, an expense "almost wholly due to our Zionist policy."[118] Churchill's memorandum, however, did not discuss or even refer to Young's specific recommendations.

When the cabinet took up Palestine on 18 August, Churchill did not ask approval for Young's recommendations. Rather, the minutes report, the alternatives before the cabinet were: withdraw the Balfour Declaration, reject the mandate, establish an Arab government, and curb or halt Jewish immigration; or "carry out the present policy with greater vigour and encourage the arming of the Jews." Without attributing comments to specific ministers, the minutes highlight certain points from the discussion: the Balfour Declaration involved the government's honor and "to go back on our pledge would seriously reduce the prestige of this country in the eyes of Jews throughout the world." The inconsistency between setting up a Jewish national home and "respecting the rights of the Arab population" must result in "estrang[ing] both Arabs and Jews, while involving us in futile military expenditure." "Against this position

---

[117] August 11, 1921, memorandum, in *WSC* IV C 1588–90. See also *WSC* IV 624. As Weizmann was still in London, Young was able to obtain his consent in advance to this package deal: see Cohen, *Churchill and the Jews*, 116–17.

[118] Churchill's August 11, 1921, cabinet memorandum, in *WSC* IV C 1585–6.

it was argued that the Arabs had no prescriptive right to a country which they had failed to develop to the best advantage."[119] The cabinet took no decisions. While the coming months saw some of Young's recommendations implemented, Palestine administration officials "publicly and confessedly opposed" to the government's pro-Zionist policy remained securely in place.

The closing days of August were hard on the colonial secretary. The Palestine Arab delegation then visiting London grated on him by insisting that the Balfour Declaration be scrapped and refusing his plea that they meet informally with Weizmann. Two days after his final, prolonged, and fruitless meeting with the Arab delegates, Churchill suffered a debilitating blow: his three-and-a-half-year-old daughter Marigold, his beloved "Duckadilly," died suddenly of illness. As his mother had died just two months before, Churchill's sense of loss must have been overwhelming. Such personal trauma undoubtedly diminished his already limited patience for the bloody attacks on Jews by Arabs and the inky bickering between pro- and anti-Zionist British bureaucrats.

Samuel wrote Churchill in October to recommend a new official declaration of policy for Palestine that might facilitate Arab-Jewish "accommodation." The Zionists should agree "that their purpose is not the establishment of a State in which Jews would enjoy a position of political privilege, but a Commonwealth built upon a democratic foundation," and Britain should explicitly repudiate Weizmann's old remark that Palestine should become as Jewish as England is English.[120] Samuel thus took a personal swipe at his influential detractor while bolstering the long-standing argument that Arab hostility to British policy was largely the result of aggressive rhetoric from Zionist "extremists."[121]

This letter's main themes resurfaced in an extraordinary document distributed on 29 October as a circular "to all troops" from General Congreve. Purporting to clarify British policy for the puzzled men in uniform, Congreve declared:

Whilst the Army officially is supposed to have no politics, it is recognised there are certain problems . . . in which the sympathies of the Army are on one side

---

[119] *WSC* IV C 1606. Regarding the last point, it bears noting that in his August 22, 1921, meeting with the Palestine Arab delegation Churchill remarked: "There was a time when it [Palestine] was three or four times as numerous as at present, and it is a great pity that there are not more people dwelling there and more wealth there instead of being occupied by a few people who are not making any great use of it." *WSC* IV C 1612.
[120] See note 47 above and accompanying text.   [121] *WSC* IV C 1650–4.

or the other. . . . In the case of Palestine these sympathies are rather obviously with the Arabs, who have hitherto appeared to the disinterested observer to have been the victims of the unjust policy forced upon them by the British Government.

He assured his troops that the government "would never give any support to the more grasping policy of the Zionist Extremist, which aims at the Establishment of a Jewish Palestine in which Arabs would be merely tolerated" and "would certainly not countenance a policy which made Palestine for the Jews what England is for the Englishmen."[122]

Three days later, on the fourth anniversary of the Balfour Declaration, Arab attacks on Jews in Jerusalem resulted in the death of four Jews and one Arab. Samuel meanwhile had decided not to enforce the fines imposed on the Arabs responsible for the May riots in Jaffa. That this was likelier to encourage than prevent additional violence was clear to the Middle East department, and not just to Meinertzhagen. Department head Shuckburgh wrote on October 28 that Samuel was "afraid," but it is an "intolerable" doctrine that "offenders may defy us with impunity." On 17 November, Churchill noted: "Samuel should be held stiffly up to the enforcement of the fines on Jaffa" for "[w]e cannot allow expediency to govern the administration of justice."[123]

At this time, however, Churchill was generally disinclined to engage in Palestine affairs.[124] His official attention focused chiefly on the Irish settlement, in which he had a major hand.[125] With Churchill's mind elsewhere, Palestine policy became an arena of active domestic political combat

---

[122] *WSC* IV C 1659–60.   [123] *WSC* IV 636–7.

[124] Churchill organized a conference in London to bring Arab and Zionist delegations together in November, but then canceled it. When it was rescheduled, he decided not to attend and sent Shuckburgh in his stead. Though he received protests about the unprofessionalism, bigotry, and disloyalty exhibited in the Congreve circular, Churchill let it pass without rebuke, marking the file on the subject: "no action required." *WSC* IV C 1659 n. 1; see also *WSC* IV 641. On November 16, 1921, Meinertzhagen wrote in his diary, "Obstruction to Zionism is no longer impelled by Arab ideas and Arab pressure. [It] is now captained by British Officials, who have constituted themselves as advisers to the Arab delegation here in London, and who are working against Zionism in Palestine. It is political sabotage of the worst kind. At the present moment it is impossible for the Arab delegation to voice the views of the People of Palestine. They are instead voicing the view of the handful of ex-Palestine Officials in London. This makes negotiations between the Arab Delegation and the Zionists manifestly impossible. . . . Winston does not care two pins. . . . He is reconciled to a policy of drift. He is too wrapped up in Home Politics" (Meinertzhagen, *Middle East Diary*, 112).

[125] Diplomacy was freeing up the services of the fearsome Black and Tans—"a pretty tough lot" (Meinertzhagen, *Middle East Diary*, 114 [December 19, 1921, entry])—the force that Churchill as war secretary had originally dispatched to suppress the Irish revolt. Now, as a cost-saving measure that did not require reliance on Jewish gendarmes, Churchill arranged to use Black and Tans, including the commanding general, to keep the peace

in Britain. The anti-Zionists, led by certain prominent peers and journalists, denounced Zionism as immoral to the Arabs and costly to the British. They wanted Parliament to reject the mandate. In the meantime, the pro-Zionists—those professing to support the Balfour Declaration—were divided into opposing camps of Weizmannites and Samuelites. These skirmished continually, in particular over whether "national home" connoted a Jewish majority and a Jewish state. Samuel's 3 June 1921 "birthday" speech had hit the Weizmannites hard. Weizmann then countered impressively at Balfour's home by lining up big guns—Lloyd George and Balfour—against the high commissioner. Samuel was determined that Churchill should function as artillery for the Palestine administration. He exhorted Churchill to launch a major policy statement to vindicate the "birthday" speech and put Weizmann and the other (in Samuel's view) immoderate Zionists in their place.

Shuckburgh and Samuel worked throughout the winter of 1921–2 planning a constitution for Palestine that would incorporate measures—such as Jewish immigration limitations and an elective "Legislative Council" (albeit with restricted authority)—that Samuel believed should win the cooperation of "well-disposed" Arab leaders. When consulted about these measures, the Palestine Arab delegation in London angered Shuckburgh by reiterating its comprehensive rejection of Britain's "Zionist policy" and leaking to anti-Zionist journalists the constitutional plans it had received for comment. A delegation leader, in a 3 March speech, was reported by Shuckburgh to have spoken "about the necessity of killing Jews if the Arabs did not get their way."[126]

On 9 March Samuel wrote Churchill that it was again necessary to suspend Jewish immigration, this time because many recent immigrants were unemployed. Samuel declared that the country's economic absorptive capacity "remains at present small."[127] Zionist leaders did not object in principle to regulating immigration for economic reasons, but they feared that a suspension would shore up a bad precedent. Shuckburgh noted that the Arab delegation had demanded a halt to immigration and

in Palestine. Churchill decided to take the Palestine force out from under Congreve's Egyptian command.

Meinertzhagen observed: "Winston is inclined to pay more attention to reconstituting the Palestine Garrison than to remedying the political situation, which is, I think, an unsound policy." Meinertzhagen drafted a new policy declaration on Zionism, which Churchill rejected "flatly . . . as a stupid proposition," but Churchill "suggests no alternative beyond asking the Zionists to come to some amicable arrangement with the Arabs." Ibid., 110–11 (November 16, 1921, entry).

[126] WSC IV 645.   [127] WSC IV 645.

regretted that they "may now boast that they have bullied us into doing what they want."[128] He nevertheless recommended approving Samuel's action, and Churchill, as usual, took Shuckburgh's advice.

The best-known document from Churchill's tenure as colonial secretary was the 3 June 1922 statement on British policy in Palestine, the core of what became known as the Churchill white paper. In fact, Churchill neither wrote the statement nor proposed any changes in the draft written by Samuel and submitted to the colonial secretary by Shuckburgh on 24 May.[129] The white paper sounded all of Samuel's favorite themes, including his rebuke of Weizmann's "as Jewish as England is English" remark. Samuel calculated correctly, however, that the Zionists would accept the document. He included for their gratification a passage on Jewish rights in Palestine resting "upon ancient historic connection." With the League of Nations soon to decide whether to confirm the mandate, he knew the Zionists would not run the risk of openly breaking with Britain.

The white paper's premise was that tension in Palestine arose from Arab fears rooted in "exaggerated interpretations" of the Balfour Declaration. The government, it said, does not intend that Palestine become "as Jewish as England is English." The Balfour Declaration does not contemplate that all of Palestine "be converted into a Jewish National Home, but that such a Home should be founded *in Palestine.*"

The statement then assures the Jews that their fears that Britain may abandon the declaration "are unfounded." The term "Jewish National Home" does not mean "imposition of Jewish nationality" upon all the inhabitants but "the further development of the existing Jewish community . . . in order that it may become a centre in which the Jewish people as a whole may take . . . an interest and a pride." For the Jewish community to have the best prospect for development, "it is essential that it should know that it is in Palestine as of right and not by sufferance" and "[t]hat is the reason why it is necessary that the existence of a Jewish National Home in Palestine should be internationally guaranteed, and that it should be formally recognised to rest upon ancient historic connection." The Jewish community "should be able to increase its numbers by immigration" but cannot exceed the country's economic absorptive capacity.

[128] Shuckburgh to Masterton Smith, March 11, 1922, quoted in *WSC* IV 646.
[129] See Cohen, *Churchill and the Jews*, 142–3.

Answering claims of entitlement that the Palestine Arab delegation had asserted, the white paper notes that "Palestine west of the Jordan" was excluded from the area designated for Arab independence in McMahon's 1915 promise to Sherif Hussein. As a step toward self-government, however, a partly elected, partly appointed legislative council was to be established. The colonial secretary, it concluded, believed that a policy along these lines "cannot but commend itself to the various sections of the population" and foster "that spirit of cooperation upon which the future progress and prosperity of the Holy Land must largely depend."[130]

The statement took pains to preserve the obscurity of the term "national home." Lloyd George, Balfour, and Churchill himself had all at one point or another acknowledged that it envisioned an eventual Jewish majority and Jewish state. Having convinced himself, however, that Palestine's limited "absorptive capacity" would preclude a Jewish majority,[131] Samuel saw no point in riling the Arabs with explicit talk of unrealistic notions.

Churchill, on the other hand, was confident that the Jews could enlarge Palestine's economy many times over. In choosing to play "hide the ball" regarding the actual aims of the national home policy, Churchill appears to have reasoned that, if no one ignited the Arabs with scary rhetoric, the Jews could continue to enter and build Palestine. Anti-Zionist hostility would then eventually wane as general appreciation grew that Zionism served Arab as well as Jewish economic interests.

It was (and remains) characteristic of the liberal imperialist frame of mind to minimize the seriousness of conflicts among the colonials. In Palestine, this meant overinflated hopes of Arab-Jewish conciliation and a refusal to recognize that deep and principled convictions underlay the rejection of Zionism and the pledge to eradicate it on the part of the Arab community. Churchill was not the first statesman who thought that Arab opposition to Zionism—that is, insistence that Palestine is an Arab land to which the Jews have no valid political claim—could be bought off. He was by no means the last, either.

Less than three weeks after the white paper appeared, Lord Islington, a Liberal baron, asked the Lords in Parliament to declare that the Palestine mandate "is unacceptable to this House" on the grounds that it

---

[130] Moore, *Documents*, 64–70.
[131] On June 12, a statistician working for the Palestine administration wrote: "Sir H. Samuel told me that he thought the country could not support economically more than 6,000 immigrants per annum. If that be so then there is no conceivable chance that the Jews will ever be a majority in Palestine." *WSC* IV 648.

violated Britain's wartime pledges to Sherif Hussein and contradicted the "wishes of the great majority of the people of Palestine."[132]

Balfour, newly created earl, rose to oppose the motion. In this, his maiden speech in the House of Lords, he explained that the ground that "chiefly moves me" to support Zionism is not "materialistic" but rather a desire to help solve "the great and abiding Jewish problem."[133] As for the purported injustice to the Arabs of Palestine, he stated: "Of all the charges made against this country . . . the charge that we have been unjust to the Arab race seems to me the strangest." He noted that it was British troops, British generals, and British blood that freed the Arab people from Turkish rule, and it was Britain that established Arab kings in Mesopotamia and the Hejaz:

And that we . . . who have . . . done more than has been done for centuries past to put the Arab race in the position to which they have attained . . . should be charged with . . . having taken a mean advantage of the course of international negotiations, seems to me not only most unjust to the policy of this country, but almost fantastic in its extravagance.[134]

Balfour's heated eloquence notwithstanding, however, the Lords voted overwhelmingly—sixty to twenty-nine—that Britain should reject the mandate.

The issue of British responsibility for Palestine came to a head in the House of Commons on 4 July. As in the Lords, the anti-Zionists attacked Zionism in principle and the Rutenberg hydroelectric power concession in particular. (Churchill had approved the concession the previous September.) They protested that the Palestine administration was dominated by Jews who had "Zionised" the country.[135]

---

[132] Christopher Sykes, *Cross Roads to Israel* (London: Collins, 1965), 90.

[133] Cohen, *Speeches by Balfour*, 59, 64–5: "Surely, it is in order that we may send a message to every land where the Jewish race has been scattered . . . that Christendom is not oblivious of their faith, is not unmindful of the service they have rendered to the great religions of the world, and, most of all, to the religion that the majority of your Lordships' House profess, and that we desire . . . to give them that opportunity of developing, in peace and quietness under British rule, those great gifts which hitherto they have been compelled . . . only to bring to fruition in countries which know not their language and belong not to their race."

[134] Ibid., 57–8. In his memoirs, Lloyd George made essentially the same point: "No race has done better out of the fidelity with which the Allies redeemed their promises to the oppressed races than the Arabs. Owing to the tremendous sacrifices of the Allied Nations . . . the Arabs have already won independence in Iraq, Arabia, Syria, and Transjordania, although most of the Arab races fought [for Turkey]. . . . The Palestinian Arabs fought for Turkish rule." David Lloyd George, *Memoirs of the Peace Conference*, 2 vols. (New Haven: Yale University Press, 1939), vol. 2, 723–4.

[135] WSC IV 651.

Churchill led the defense of the government's policy. His emphasis was not so much on the wisdom and morality of the Balfour Declaration as on the solemnity of the commitment, which implicated the government's credibility and honor.

Pledges and promises were made during the War . . . not only on the merits, though I think the merits are considerable . . . because it was considered they would be of value to us in our struggle to win the War. It was considered that the support which the Jews could give us all over the world, and particularly in the United States, and also in Russia, would be a definite palpable advantage.

Churchill regaled the House by quoting passionately pro-Zionist speeches that his current critics in Parliament had made when the Balfour Declaration was first issued. He then drew "the moral" that these members "have no right to support public declarations made in the name of your country in the crisis and heat of War, and then afterwards, when all is cold and prosaic, to turn round and attack the Minister . . . faithfully and laboriously endeavouring to translate these perfervid enthusiasms into the sober, concrete facts of day-to-day administration." He appealed to the House to uphold Britain's undertakings "faithfully" and to "interpret in an honourable and earnest way the promise that Britain will do her best to fulfil her undertakings to the Zionists."

In defending the Rutenberg concession against the charge that it was unjust to the Arabs, Churchill stressed that such projects would benefit everyone in Palestine: "[W]as not this a good gift that would impress more than anything else on the Arab population that the Zionists were their friends and helpers, not their expellers and expropriators, and that . . . Palestine had before it a bright future, and that there was enough for all?" He added:

I am told that the Arabs would have done it [i.e., hydroelectric development] themselves. Who is going to believe that? Left to themselves, the Arabs of Palestine would not in a thousand years have taken effective steps towards the irrigation and electrification of Palestine. They would have been quite content to dwell—a handful of philosophic people—in the wasted sun-scorched plains, letting the waters of the Jordan continue to flow unbridled and unharnessed into the Dead Sea.[136]

Churchill's speech was as persuasive as it was entertaining. The division that followed produced 292 votes in support of the government's Palestine policy and 35 votes in opposition.

[136] WSC IV 652–6.

With this endorsement in hand, the government finally sought confirmation of the mandate from the council of the League of Nations, which it obtained on 24 July. Through a League resolution invoking Article 25, which Churchill had added to the mandate for this purpose back in 1921, Britain then formalized the exclusion of Transjordan from the Jewish national home.[137] When the Conservatives brought down the Lloyd George coalition government in October, Churchill lost his job as colonial secretary.

CONCLUSION

The term "appeasement" in international affairs acquired a disreputable ring largely through Winston Churchill's prescient excoriation in the 1930s of the Neville Chamberlain government's policy toward Nazi Germany. Before the Second World War, however, proponents of appeasement proudly embraced the term. Churchill himself often employed it favorably.

Appeasement can be a sensible and honorable method of terminating a quarrel, as any parent of small children or any government official who must resolve differences with independent-minded foreign friends will attest. Britain's appeasement policy of the 1930s failed not because of any inherent flaw in the methodology, but because the other side was not appeasable. Chamberlain is judged harshly for failing to recognize that Hitler's ambitions were neither limited nor manageable and that Nazi grievances could not be assuaged through reasonable accommodation; Churchill receives credit for apprehending that appeasement would not work with the German regime.

As colonial secretary in 1921 and 1922, however, Churchill refused to see or admit that Arab opposition to Zionism was beyond appeasement. In a historical review prepared after the Second World War by the British administration in Palestine, the failure of appeasement in the early days of the Palestine mandate was explained with impressive directness: "It had become obvious that the Arab objection was, not to the way in which the Mandate might be worked, but to the whole policy of the Mandatory and that by no concession, however liberal, were the Arabs

---

[137] Memorandum by the British representative on Article 25 of the Palestine mandate, approved by the council of the League of Nations, September 16, 1922, in Moore, *Documents*, 83–4.

prepared to be reconciled to a regime which recognised the implications of the Balfour Declaration."[138]

In 1939, just before the Second World War began, Churchill explicitly linked the Chamberlain government's efforts to appease, respectively, the Arabs in Palestine and the Germans in Europe. Both efforts, he said, were dishonorable and doomed to fail. Both undermined British influence and endangered international security because they signaled that Britain could not be counted on to fulfill its commitments. The government's white paper on Palestine of May 1939 had given the Arabs a veto over future Jewish immigration into Palestine, thereby ensuring permanent minority status for the Jews. Churchill voiced blistering indignation: "Now, there is the breach; there is the violation of the pledge; there is the abandonment of the Balfour Declaration." He asked what Britain's potential enemies will think of this "act of abjection," this "lamentable act of default": "What will those who have been stirring up these Arab agitators think? Will they not be encouraged by our confession of recoil? Will they not be tempted to say: 'They're on the run again. This is another Munich,' and be the more stimulated in their aggression?"[139]

But the white paper anticipated such criticism. It asserted that, in promising a Jewish national home, Britain had never committed itself to a Jewish majority or a Jewish state in Palestine. As evidence, it offered a lengthy quotation from the Churchill white paper of 1922, in which the then colonial secretary had played "hide the ball" regarding the aims of Britain's Zionist policy. Churchill played this game with such care that the new colonial secretary in 1939 could claim, plausibly if disingenuously, that the ball never existed in the first place.

History is not a controlled experiment. We cannot know whether a candid, forceful, and unapologetic implementation of the Jewish national home policy would have compelled the Arab world to resign itself to the inevitability of a Jewish state in western Palestine. We do know, however, that the British government's purposeful vagueness about its aims in Palestine, its severing of Transjordan from the Jewish national home, its restrictions on Jewish immigration, its courting of Arab extremists, and its other similar efforts to contain and defuse anti-Zionism did not have that effect. Rather, they persuaded anti-Zionists in the Arab community,

---

[138] Government of Palestine, *A Survey of Palestine: Prepared in December 1945 and January 1946 for the Information of the Anglo-American Committee of Inquiry*, 2 vols. (Palestine: Government Printer, 1945–6), vol. 1, 22.
[139] WSC V 1070–1.

the Palestine administration, and back home in Britain that the government lacked the resolve to maintain its pro-Zionist policy in the face of persistent, vocal, and violent opposition. Such measures in fact engendered such opposition. This is hardly amazing and did not become obvious only in hindsight, as the writings of that contemporary Cassandra, Colonel Meinertzhagen, demonstrate.

Why did Churchill consent to this policy?

Regarding Palestine and many other subjects, Churchill exhibited a liberal optimism rooted in confidence that people would act "rationally" to seek peace and material betterment for themselves and their communities. Churchill showed limited appreciation of the potency of outraged Muslim religious sentiment among the Arabs. And owing to his imperialist worldview, he was not attuned to the Arabs' increasingly intense nationalism, which both reflected and fed hostility toward the Zionists (and toward Britain and the West in general). So Churchill convinced himself that prospects for Arab-Jewish conciliation were brighter than was in fact the case. He convinced himself further that the way to realize those prospects was to dilute (though not, as he saw it, betray) the Balfour Declaration. Churchill experienced firsthand on several occasions the refusal of Palestine Arab delegations to compromise their anti-Zionist principles. This vexed him but did not cause him to repudiate appeasement as impracticable.

Such a repudiation would, in any event, have been hard to impose on the bureaucracy. Numerous civilian and military officials in Palestine and London were committed to placating Palestine's Arabs to the detriment of the Zionists. Replacing these officials with pro-Zionists would have required a Herculean clean-out. Even then, it might not have been possible. And there was no hope of actually changing the policy on the ground without changing personnel. The bureaucratic impediments to implementing an unwaveringly pro-Zionist policy surely reinforced Churchill's philosophical predisposition to seek peace in Palestine by appealing to the Arabs' moderate instincts and economic self-interest.

Churchill sympathized with Zionism, believed in the justice of the cause, and judged that a Jewish national home in Palestine would serve the interests of the British Empire. But he did not rank Palestine among the top priorities of British foreign policy. Indeed, he viewed the entire Middle East as a strategic sideshow. When he moved to the colonial office, he was given primary responsibility for an area he deemed of secondary importance. So he tended to flow with the recommendations of his principal subordinates in Middle Eastern affairs, rather than bucking the current or endeavoring to change its direction.

By any sensible measure, Churchill was a good friend of the Jews, one of their best in high government circles anywhere. But the Jews' national cause never was, and never could be, the highest priority of Churchill or his government. This rudimentary reality caused difficulties but no surprises for thoughtful Zionists. Zionism aimed to create a Jewish state, after all, precisely because otherwise there would be none in the world whose highest priority is the interest of the Jewish people.

9

Peaceful thoughts and warring adventures

PATRICK J. C. POWERS

When the young Winston Churchill said that a man's life must be nailed to the cross either of action or of thought, apparently he was not referring to himself.[1] From the start of his political career in 1898 through its climax with his last prime ministry in the 1950s, it remained unclear as to whether his life was marked more by great public action or profound political reflection. The question has never been resolved, for the simple reason that Churchill never seriously entertained separating them in his own life. On the one hand, he presumed that the healthy and elevated political deeds characteristic of England's greatest statesmen were possible only on the basis of prior reflection about the ends to be accomplished and the means to attain them. On the other hand, he presumed that political thought that is not nourished by the experience of political accomplishments and possibilities, such as that of the socialists, would soon reveal its irrelevance.

Nowhere does Churchill stress his preference for the mixed life of thought and action more than in a book of essays written in the 1920s and 1930s and fittingly entitled *Thoughts and Adventures*. Published during the long interlude between the wars when he was largely out of the political limelight and when some thought that his political career was at an end, the book bears witness to his conviction about the symbiotic character of political action and thought. His judgments in the first half of the book about the practical success or failure of the grave political events that marked the early decades of the twentieth century are based on a determination about the character of reflection that preceded specific actions. Conversely, the second half of the book details how his adventures

[1] Winston S. Churchill, *My Early Life* (London: Thornton Butterworth, 1930), 34.

263

amid these same events served as the cauldron for subsequent reflections about the political character of human nature and its future. The positioning of "thoughts" before "adventures" in the title reflects Churchill's belief in the primacy of reflection before action.

Because the essays follow the chronological order of the events discussed, his subject in the first three of the book's four parts is the succession of times of peace and war in the first decades of this century, followed by a time in the 1930s of "Exhaustion which has been described as Peace" (177, 180).[2] The fourth set of essays refers to no period in particular and extols the timeless "pleasures of life [that] are luckily still with us" (1).

The first essays recall and examine the "settled state of order" that characterized the prewar period. A greater number are devoted to "the incomparable tragedy of the War." The present time of the 1930s, which Churchill refers to as "an epoch of such pith and moment," is dissected in several essays concerned with "confusion, uncertainty and peril, the powers of light and darkness perhaps in counterpoise." He recognized that the postwar generation was threatened as much as it was challenged by "Science [which] holds the keys" to the "cities of Destruction and Enslavement." For better or worse, he realized that the actions of twentieth-century politicians and nations cannot be comprehended or judged apart from an appreciation and evaluation of the role that science's domination of nature has played in bringing the world to "the crossroads which may lead to . . . two alternative Infernos" (1). In the concluding set of essays, Churchill addresses the underlying topic of all the essays—namely his preoccupation with philosophical and religious questions about the ultimate source of vital control in human affairs.

The extent to which an examination of the modern conditions of war and peace is merely the surface topic of *Thoughts and Adventures* is reflected in Churchill's attention to the question of whether or not scientific understanding is the most suitable form of knowledge for exercising effective political leadership in the modern world. At a deeper level, he is concerned to determine the extent to which the human causality of outstanding individuals exercises any influence in modern political life. Throughout the essays, he evaluates the relative importance in human affairs of personal will, external circumstances, or an "omnipotent factor" (171). In fact, wartime events are examined more than those of

---

[2] Winston S. Churchill, *Thoughts and Adventures* (New York: W. W. Norton, 1991). Parenthetical numbers in this chapter refer to pages in this book.

peacetime because, as Churchill recognized, in the intensity of war "chance casts aside all veils and disguises and presents herself nakedly from moment to moment as the direct arbiter over all persons and events" (71). Moreover, he had concluded from his experiences that "those who can win the victory cannot make the peace," because "two opposite sides of human nature have to be simultaneously engaged" (161). This led him to seek out the profound psychological and cosmic causes in human affairs that prevent the successful exercise of a comprehensive political leadership, and to explore ways of overcoming obstacles to such a comprehensive statesmanship.

The essential connection of the last essay, "Painting as a Pastime," with the opening essay, "A Second Choice," confirms that *Thoughts and Adventures* is a more cohesive and systematic examination of the psychological and metaphysical causes of war and peace than its presentation as a collection of essays might suggest. In the last essay, Churchill returns to the themes of the opening essay about the need for an unscientific deference to nature and for a recognition of the influence of chance on the exercise of human will. Not surprisingly, the catalyst for this perspective in both essays about the political leader's need for reflection and moderation is Churchill's defining experience with the Dardanelles expedition (8, 223). More than any other event in his early life, the personal defeat he suffered in leaving the Admiralty at the end of May 1915 taught him an important political and human lesson about the need for personal moderation in a situation where one "knew everything and could do nothing" (223).

Despite Churchill's failure in the Dardanelles affair to exercise full political and military authority, which taught him that liberal democracies do not always listen to their most thoughtful leaders, the essays in *Thoughts and Adventures* are marked from start to finish by a sustained praise of the virtues of liberal democracy during times of peace and war. Not the least of modern democracy's better qualities is the opportunity it affords the private individual, which to a great extent Churchill was in the 1930s, to instruct the public in its gravest affairs. As the essays make clear, the finest compliment that Churchill pays to liberal democracy—for its intellectual and moral resiliency under modern conditions, where peace and war are barely distinguishable—is his persistence in counseling the British public with his thoughts about its adventures during his own darkest hour, when he did not know if political authority would ever again be his to exercise.

By concluding the essays with a discussion of the need in painting to learn to be a spectator when vital control passes to others, to follow nature and to be content with its order, and to turn errors to great good fortune, Churchill responds directly to the universal and autobiographical questions he posed in the opening essay about nature, fate, and fore-knowledge. From a political perspective, his understanding of the way to conduct political affairs in deference to the given natural order offers an alternative to the scientific approach to dominating nature, which char-acterized political leadership in his own and the preceding generation. On the basis of a philosophical perspective gleaned from the personal experience of painting, Churchill outlines a way in which an individual of exceptional political talent and ambition, who has been deprived of the opportunity to win the victory and make the peace, might yet survive to instruct others on the need for private reflection about public affairs.

There is only one persuasive way of confirming the foregoing observa-tions on the political and moral order and meaning of Churchill's essays about his warring adventures and peaceful thoughts in a modern liberal democracy during the first three decades of this century. One must start with the first essay, "A Second Choice," and carefully note how the suc-ceeding essays lead sensibly to the concluding essay, "Painting as a Pas-time," which in turn returns to the moral and political themes of his opening investigation into the question of whether or not he would or should wish to live his life over again.[3]

THE OPENING PERSPECTIVE: "A SECOND CHOICE"

In the opening words of the first essay, Churchill continues the auto-biographical character of his political reflections in *My Early Life*. "If I had to live my life over again in the same surroundings, no doubt I should have the same perplexities and hesitations; no doubt I should have my same sense of proportion, my same guiding lights, my same onward thrust, my same limitations" (4). The unstated justification for discussing political events from his own perspective, and for assuming that English and American readers would be interested in his personal views, is his

---

[3] *WSC* V C (2) 433, 437, 444, 462. As Churchill's correspondence with his publisher and Edward Marsh makes clear, he gave considerable thought to the ordering of the essays, as well as to the title of the work. See also James W. Muller, " 'A Kind of Dignity and Even Nobility': Winston Churchill's *Thoughts and Adventures*," *The Political Science Reviewer* 18 (1988): 85–125, from which the author has learned much.

assumption that the actions of his life are bound up with great events at both the national and world level. Thus had he kept his Mauser pistol with him in 1899 when disembarking from the armored train derailed by the Boers, he might have killed the mounted burgher named Botha who demanded his surrender. In doing so, he would have changed the course of events in South Africa and the Great War by killing the man who became commander in chief of the Boers and, later, prime minister of the South African Union. Without Botha's political ability for ending the incipient rebellion in South Africa in 1914, Australian and New Zealand troops would have been diverted to South Africa from their destination at Gallipoli, and the course of the First World War would have been decisively altered.

Churchill is saved from the charge of vanity by the modest approach he adopts in evaluating the question of whether it would be advisable to exercise a second choice and live his life over again. He surveys his past against the backdrop of general reflections about the universal causes and effects in human affairs that influence and limit the autonomy of even the greatest public leaders. His choices are always responses to varied externals that confront him. When considering the ultimate consequences of his own actions, over which he has only limited control, "Imagination bifurcates and loses itself along the ever-multiplying paths of the labyrinth" (6). On the one hand, he says that most often he acted in politics as he wanted to, and always felt ashamed whenever he refrained from doing so (7). At the same time, he acknowledges that it is not easy to assess praise and blame for beneficial and deleterious outcomes. Often, his own judgments led him imprudently into political difficulties, whereas he benefited from having been checked by others. But even then, on some occasions he saw his "mistakes and errors turn to great good fortune" (9). The seriousness of Churchill's interest in the hypothetical question of whether to live one's life over again is reflected in the fact that he devotes the rest of the essay to an elaborate examination of the factors one would have to take account of in determining whether to exercise a second choice.

By the end of the essay, the moral advantage and political purpose behind his preoccupation with the hypothetical possibility of living one's life over again comes into full view. From his reflections about the extent to which the course of events in the lives of influential political statesmen, as well as those of ordinary citizens, is beyond the individual's control, Churchill draws an essentially modest political conclusion. Despite how happy, vivid, and full of interest his previous life was, he would not choose to live it over again. Since he cannot be sure that good fortune would continue to attend him "in another chain of causation," he concludes that accepting the limits inherent in the human condition is the more prudent course to follow in one's personal and public life:

Let us be contented with what has happened to us and thankful for all we have been spared. Let us accept the natural order in which we move. Let us reconcile ourselves to the mysterious rhythm of our destinies, such as they must be in this world of space and time. (10)

Of all Churchill's writings, this is perhaps his most comprehensive statement about the character, order, and purpose of human life within the cosmos. He begins with a double moral perspective of contentment and thanksgiving for what has and has not happened to us. The moral view is set against a cosmological acceptance of the greater natural order within which human existence occurs. Finally, he reconciles the moral and natural perspectives in terms of a modest spiritual, even religious, belief that human existence within the natural whole is in some way purposeful. While our human destiny is not entirely transparent to reason, experience teaches that it is a mixture of joy and sorrow, light and shadow, good and ill.

As will become clear in the later essays, Churchill's philosophical and personal reflection on whether to live his life over again is a fitting introduction to an examination of European political life from the prewar years, through the Great War, to the uneasy peace at the beginning of the 1930s. In "A Second Choice," he points to the threefold philosophical standard of self-restraint, recognition of nature's order, and belief in human purposefulness that will guide his estimation of political events and figures in the successive eras of peace and war. Self-restraint in one's expectations about life is the essential moral quality required for successfully traversing the recurrent ebbs and flows of public affairs. Recognition of the permanent natural order establishes the boundaries that should guide and limit the exercise of political power. Finally, one should appreciate what purposefulness is possible in human affairs, though it does not satisfy our aspirations. Throughout the essays Churchill stresses the need in personal and public life for a comprehensive moderation—the fundamental human quality unifying thought and action into a whole life. He concludes "A Second Choice" with an exhortation to the practice of moderation: "Let us treasure our joys but not bewail our sorrows. The glory of light cannot exist without its shadows. Life is a whole, and good and ill must be accepted together" (10). That Churchill believes such a moderate life of balance and self-restraint to be on the whole worth living, though it does not meet all our personal or political aspirations, is confirmed by the last line of the essay: "The journey has been enjoyable and well worth making—once" (9). He believes that the great virtue of liberal democracy is its willingness to listen to arguments for moderation, and to be guided on occasion in its public affairs by leaders possessed of moderation in both their public and private lives.

PART 1: SETTLED ORDER

The five essays in the first part are marked by an unqualified and carefully defended praise of the British parliamentary democracy in which Churchill's life was played out. In the first three essays—"Cartoons and Cartoonists," "Consistency in Politics," and "Personal Contacts"—he describes the rational and open character of parliamentary politics, which has made his life worthwhile exactly as it has unfolded. He concludes with two essays, "The Battle of Sidney Street" and "The German Splendour," in which he describes the modern irrational and mechanical alternatives to civilized democratic politics in the activities of the Russian anarchists and "the spectacle of German military and Imperial splendour" (49). His argument for preferring his life in the surroundings of British parliamentary democracy to that of participating in a rapturous welcome of the German emperor by his dutiful subjects is expressed in the stark contrast between the English and German ways of life described in the opening and concluding essays. The reason an Englishman can even entertain a second choice of lives is because, as Churchill says, "so far as my own personal course has been concerned, I have mostly acted in politics as I felt I wanted to act" (7). On the contrary, he remarks that the German emperor's infantry "reminded one more of great Atlantic rollers than human formations" (49). Whereas the English habit of political and personal liberty encouraged one to "accept the natural order in which we move," the Germans became "victims of a fatal system in which they were inextricably involved" that "did not form contact with reality at any point" (10, 54, 51).

The grounds for Churchill's favoring the peaceful ways that follow from "the slow-growing continuity of British national life" over "the inexhaustible and exuberant manhood and deadly panoply" that emanate from "the bounding fortunes of martial Germany" are laid out in three essays detailing the virtues of British parliamentary democracy (50).

In "Cartoons and Cartoonists," he reviews the most famous English caricaturists, without ever questioning the political legitimacy or appropriateness of their unrelenting and unapologetic criticism of public figures. On the contrary, he assumes that cartoonists have both a right to participate in democratic politics, and a concomitant "responsibility [which] must be very great" (11). In fact, he goes so far as to argue that the burden is on the "politicians [to] get used to being caricatured," and "even [to] get to like it" (15). The political importance of cartoons and their creators is that one learns something from them, though not always about history (11). What knowledge one gains is reflected in the compliments Churchill pays to each of the six cartoonists he reviews. Tenniel's cartoons in *Punch* were the regular food that fed and nourished his views of public men and public affairs as a schoolboy (13). Poy's cartoon about Churchill's exclusion from the governmental rearrangements following Bonar Law's resignation had "quite enough truth in it for it to be more funny to others than to oneself" (17). Low had an instinct for the maliciously perceived truth about "the established order of things," and especially the "fatted soul" of the British Empire (17). Strube's Little Man captured the post-war mentality of the weak and battered Englishman. The drawings of Raemakers conveyed "a passion of protest and scorn" against the agony of the war more effectively than spoken or written words (22). Likewise, in just twelve pages of cartoons, Beerbohm portrayed one hundred years of Franco-German relations so plainly and profoundly "that even the most deeply instructed person finds his imagination and memories stirred" (22). Churchill does not worry about the damage done by the cartoonist's exaggerations, for the same liberty that allows for political caricature also permits a political figure like him to criticize the cartoonist's trade. The virtue of modern liberal democracy is its capacity for nurturing "a great tide of good nature and comprehension in civilized mankind which sweeps to and fro" between the distorting cartoonist and his distorted subjects (22).

Churchill continues his favorable evaluation of democratic political life in "Consistency in Politics." In asserting that "politics is a generous profession," which in the end judges fairly a leader's inconsistencies, he points to the great human benefit available from democratic politics (30). While representative government occasionally requires leaders "to defer to the opinions of other people," democracy recognizes equally well that a political leader must, though his heart or objective be unchanging, "give his counsel now on the one side and now on the other of many public issues" (27). Even with regard to party affiliation, the necessary vehicle of electoral and parliamentary majorities, democracy does not punish those whose sincere convictions oblige them to switch their party allegiance. Churchill's presumption that such democratic deference to political inconsistency is right and in the public interest does not derive from any impractical idealism about what democracy ought to be. Rather, he recognizes that the great promise of democratic liberty is its capacity for uncovering the truth and promoting its eventual public triumph. Far from detracting from truthfulness, the opportunity for inconsistency allows a democratic leader the flexibility to attune his policies to a change of events, his views to a change of mood or heart, and his party allegiance to a change of sincere conviction. In allowing for political inconsistency, democracy reveals its great benefit to be the opportunity afforded for exercising genuine statesmanship. For, as Churchill argues, a statesman "should always try to do what he believes is best in the long view for his country, and he should not be dissuaded from so acting by having to divorce himself from a great body of doctrine to which he formerly sincerely adhered" (29). The dependence of democratic government on the consent of the governed, who regularly call upon it to justify political changes, challenges its leaders to limit their political inconsistencies to those that, being "in harmony with the needs of the time and upon a great issue, will be found to override all other factors" (30).

Unlike the figures reviewed by Churchill in a later series of essays on *Great Contemporaries*, whose public importance he was compelled to acknowledge whether or not he agreed with their political perspectives, the five individuals described in "Personal Contacts" impress him precisely because their lives embodied the principles and strengths of modern liberal-minded democracy. The most influential people in his life turn out to be those whose virtues, if ever possessed by a single political leader such as Churchill himself, would make possible the exercise of statesmanship dedicated to fulfilling democracy's potential for widespread human excellence. Lord Randolph Churchill represented the best of modern liberalism. Winston Churchill's father transcended conventional political divisions by standing for the union of progress and tradition, and exhorting working people to become defenders of the ancient aristocratic institutions that gave birth to the acquisition of modern democratic liberties by all Englishmen. In Bourke Cockran, an American of staunch Democratic Party and specifically Tammany Hall loyalties, Churchill found a man whose unified convictions "enabled him to present a sincere and effective front in every direction according to changing circumstances" (33). Sir Francis Mowatt impressed Churchill as the epitome of a government official of "the old school" (33). Even when his perspective was destined for defeat, as in the fiscal controversy of 1903, Mowatt went "far beyond the ordinary limits of a Civil Servant" and "carried on the struggle himself" (35). Not only did he hold firm to sound principles of public finance, but also he made no secret of his views, courted dismissal, and challenged the administration in admirable state papers. Though Hugh Cecil's moral and political views were cast in an ecclesiastical form that he could not embrace, Churchill was attracted by Cecil's steadfast belief that the members of Parliament "were not playing a game" but "were discharging a solemn and indeed awful duty." If the parties did not respect the laws of Britain, "then nothing would be left standing" (37).

Lloyd George, the last of the figures who impressed Churchill, is not characterized as a statesman in this essay any more than he is elsewhere in Churchill's writings. Yet this does not prevent Churchill from admiring the magnitude of those partial political qualities that made him "the greatest master of the art of getting things done and of putting things through that I ever knew" (39). It was Lloyd George's ability to foresee the next step that set him apart from and ahead of his peers. Churchill is candid in acknowledging that "naturally such a man greatly influenced me" (39). In the postwar world, with its tangle of unresolved political conflicts, Churchill recognized that his own aspiration to political leadership would depend largely on his ability to inform the statesmanly qualities he admired in his father and the others with a capacity for foresight not unlike Lloyd George's. Fortunately, Churchill was spared knowing how closely his fate at the end of the Second World War would parallel that of Lloyd George's at the end of the First World War, when "the political forces of the Right, the moment we escaped from the war period, repulsed him so incontinently" (40).

Even at the height of parliamentary party controversy in 1910, Churchill found the "quiet, law-abiding, comfortable" functioning of ordinary British democracy to be reassuringly peaceful (45). By contrast, he experienced the foreign anarchist and militarist alternatives to domestic electoral conflict at the ballot box as political phenomena that provoked curiosity or were brilliant and deeply interesting, but that ultimately impressed him as either startling and astonishing or formidable and stupefying (41, 44, 48). It is no accident that Churchill's openly critical account in "The Battle of Sidney Street" of the "extraordinary crime" carried out by the Russian anarchists is paired with his more reserved yet equally critical account in "The German Splendour" of the "pomp and power of the German Empire," and that both immediately precede the essays detailing the Armageddon of the First World War (41, 49). At its deepest level, he conceived of the war as the greatest challenge to Britain and France's ability to demonstrate that their dedication to liberal democratic political order was both worthier and more capable of preservation than the Bolshevik liberation of Russia or the German regime of military and imperial splendor.

To be sure, Churchill recognized a significant political difference between these two foreign political orders. The former were nothing more than a "germ cell of murder, anarchy and revolution," whose fate was that of "fierce beings, living . . . just like animals" (43); the latter represented "the pomp and power of the German Empire," whose fate was that of "puppets in the world tragedy . . . held too tightly in the grip of destiny" (55). Despite the fact that the former were "thieves and murderers for personal ends," while the latter was a magnificent spectacle of "inexhaustible and exuberant manhood and deadly panoply," Churchill suggests that the distance between the two undemocratic forms of authority is not so great as the contrast between their uncivilized and civilized appearances might imply (43, 49). This is made clear in Churchill's concluding accounts of the complete demise of both groups, which left them equally "scattered, exiled, deposed, in penury, in obloquy" (54). In the case of the anarchists, these "human fiends" perished in a conflagration after being besieged amid constant gunfire (44). Similarly, in the case of the German military potentates, Churchill stresses the coming desolation of their lives ten years hence:

Upon how many of those who marched and cantered in that autumn sunlight had the dark angel set his seal! Violent untimely death, ruin and humiliation worse than death, privation, mutilation, despair to the simple soldier, the downfall of their pride and subsistence to the chiefs; such were the fates—could we but have read them—which brooded over thousands and tens of thousands of these virile figures. (54)

The source of their similarity is to be found in an exclusive reliance on overwhelming force as the means to their objectives. The anarchists resorted to ruthless ferocity, intelligence, unerring marksmanship, and modern weapons and equipment (42). The German maneuvers revealed their reliance on the grim organization of vast and terrific machines consisting of "clouds of cavalry, avalanches of field guns and . . . squadrons

of motorcars" (53, 49). In both cases, their militaristic ways led remorse-
lessly to an identical supreme catastrophe (55, 47). As to the response of
British democracy to these foreign challenges, only with regard to the
battle of Sidney Street does Churchill make clear what was the solution
to the political threat posed by the anarchists' resort to violence: "All the
resources of which a civilized community can dispose were directed to
hunting down the criminals" (43). Yet, as the second set of essays on the
Armageddon of the coming war makes clear, Churchill also understood
the meaning of the English response to the German threat, and by extension the great political difference between the English and German regimes, to be that of a defense of civilization against its enemies. While he
never describes the intentions and efforts of the German generals as crim-
inal, in his final judgment of the kaiser's actions he comes as close to such
an attribution as political respect for a magnificent, but nonetheless formidable and stupefying, enemy permits (49):

And for the Kaiser, that bright figure, the spoilt child of fortune, the envy of
Europe—for him in the long series of heart-breaking disappointments and disil-
lusions, of failure and undying self-reproach, which across the devastation of
Europe was to lead him to the wood-cutter's block at Doorn—there was surely
reserved the sternest punishment of all. (55)

PART 2: INCOMPARABLE TRAGEDY

In chronological terms, the second set of essays focuses on the military
events of the First World War. Churchill uses eight stories of wartime
matters, however, as a way of examining the proper relation of civil to
military authority. The autobiographical dimension is more significant in
these essays, because his own wartime activities embodied the tension
between the two authorities. The first five essays explain and defend
how and why British liberal democracy promotes a healthier, though
nonetheless difficult, dialogue between the political and military authorities. These essays move from an account of overly enthusiastic civilian
efforts to assist the military in "My Spy Story" to one about the successful
promotion of military reform by the political authorities in "The Dover
Barrage." Despite the ongoing tensions between the political and military
authorities, Churchill praises the success of British liberal democracy in
supporting the political restraint of the military "from outside and from
below" (96). By contrast, the sixth and central essay, "Ludendorff's 'All—
or Nothing,' " demonstrates that the failure of German political authority

to control its military high command prevented Germany from avoiding a humiliating and self-destructive defeat. The concluding two essays, "A Day with Clemenceau" and "In the Air," celebrate French and British liberal democratic leaders for meriting authority over their commanders by taking the same risks as their military subordinates.

A widespread theory held that John Bull—the average British citizen—was naïve and vulnerable to the wiles of "Continental craft and machinations." In "My Spy Story," Churchill dispels this unfounded criticism of democratic weakness in foreign affairs. He praises the voluntary vigilance of countless English citizens who, though often led on by romance and melodrama, "constituted on the whole an important additional element of security" (58). He concludes by asserting that the British secret service was probably far more effective in monitoring the enemy than were the forces of any other nation engaged in the war (57). As Churchill implies, Britain's defensive superiority was actually nurtured by its apparent democratic weakness. At the lowest and highest levels of English political life, citizens assumed that they had a right and responsibility to participate actively in the prosecution of the war by the military.

Churchill's own participation in the war reflected the twofold conviction of most Englishmen that this was a citizen's war. "With the Grenadiers" is his account of how he prepared himself for undertaking the responsibility of leading a brigade by requesting that he be allowed to "learn first hand the special conditions of trench warfare" (66). In "Plugstreet," he recounts an imagined threat to national security that almost occurred as he exercised his citizenly right to advise the commander in chief and Committee of Imperial Defense. In both situations, Churchill's insistence on doing his duty as a citizen in the trenches at the front nearly resulted in his own death. If not for a chance request by the corps commander to meet him behind the front where the Grenadiers were holed up, he would have been in his trench when it took a direct hit from German shells. He would also have died had he remained in the front room of a Belgian farmhouse working on his recommendation to the commander in chief about tank warfare. Both incidents taught him something about the character of all life, which becomes manifest under the intensities of war. The first situation, which originally irritated him when the corps commander did not rendezvous after Churchill had inconvenienced himself by leaving the trenches, made him realize that chance "is the direct arbiter over all persons and events" (71). In the second, when he realized that a secret memorandum had not been left on the table for an alert spy to snatch away, Churchill recalled the wisdom of an unknown old man's remark that "his life had been full of troubles most of which had never happened" (76). In these two essays, Churchill makes clear what is the great political benefit to be derived from the military participation of a citizen, and especially that of one such as Churchill, who would eventually return to a position of governmental leadership. War reveals the tension in political life between seemingly contradictory truths. On the one hand, during wartime chance and necessity can frustrate a citizen's efforts at exercising his political responsibilities. On the other hand, citizens must guard themselves against the worst random effects of chance by preserving their instinctual and educated habits of political self-protection.

In the next two essays, Churchill demonstrates that, despite their wartime experience of the strength of chance in human life, English citizens like him preferred to believe themselves capable of remaining in control of their military duty. He relates how the experience of the British war councils confirmed the extent to which citizens refused to take a backseat to anyone in their right and responsibility to advise the military about the conduct of the war. The preservation by English citizens of their political freedom to advise the military and, in any final showdown, to countermand military judgments, saved Britain from certain defeat at the hands of a fatalistic German army impervious to the influence of political authority. In "The U-Boat War" and "The Dover Barrage," Churchill probes the fifth and final official volume covering the naval operations of the war, in the manner of a political detective unlocking a truth that has been deliberately obscured by "important personages in the story [who] have clearly applied their pruning-knives and ink-erasers with no timid hand" (83, 100). The epic of the navy's actions during the last two years of the war and its struggle with the civilian authorities reveals how the weakness of the British military was offset by the strength of England's political authorities. In Churchill's view, "no story of the Great War is more remarkable or more full of guidance for the future than this" (89). By February 1917 and the opening of unrestricted warfare, the danger to Britain from U-boat attacks had become "mortal and near" (88). Of the three methods of defense—mechanical means, reorganization of the naval staff, and convoys—only the last would be decisive in eliminating the threat by late 1917. Yet the Admiralty was so much opposed to convoys that they would never have implemented them, had England not been a country with a political order that encouraged political authority to challenge and question military judgments:

It was a long, intense, violent struggle between the amateur politicians, thrown by democratic Parliamentary institutions to the head of affairs, on the one hand, and the competent trained, experienced experts of the Admiralty and their great sea officers on the other. . . . The politicians, representing Civil Power at bay and fighting for the life of the State, overcame and pierced the mountains of prejudice and false argument which the Admiralty raised and backed with the highest naval authority. (89)

A similar dilemma arose with regard to the effort to close the Dover Straits and prevent the easy access of German submarines to their hunting grounds in the channel. By the winter of 1917, a disagreement arose over whether the existing defense of nets, patrolling trawlers, and mines was effective in deterring U-boat activity. The Dover command would have prevailed in maintaining the status quo, which had become detrimental to the British war effort, had the civil powers not backed the freedom of "the new and somewhat irreverent junior brains of the Navy" and their new professional thought against the "august, old, honourable authority" of Admiral Bacon and his technical brilliance (100).

Churchill argues that in no other country could the civil power have successfully overridden military authority and "in both cases . . . leaned, pressed, and finally thrust in the right direction" (100). Because British military discipline always supported the conventional authority of the admiral's long-established view over the natural authority of "keen and bold minds unhampered by long routine," a nontraditional approach to "questions entirely novel in character" would never have been voluntarily forthcoming from the naval service (93). The means of salvation for the U-boat war and the Dover barrage had to be forced upon the Admiralty, "from outside and from below," by the political authorities (96). The ascendancy of political over military authority could happen in Great Britain but not in Germany, because British politicians were publicly powerful individuals who felt that they owed their positions to no one's favor (90). The war cabinet of elected members of Parliament understood themselves to be political officers of a democratic regime founded on the principle that, in discharging their ministerial obligation to act responsibly, the right to freedom of thought ought to take precedence over the tradition of obedience to conventional authority.

The essay on "Ludendorff's 'All—or Nothing'" is the centerpiece of the second part of the book, as well as the entire collection of essays, even though it does not focus on the most important lesson about the war conveyed by the book as a whole. Rather, it contains Churchill's most direct and devastating critique of the German political and military tragedy that was the root cause of the Armageddon of the First World War. Germany's failure to make peace during the winter of 1917 was not an accident, but the deliberate consequence of the German character, which sought "to procure victory at all costs" (104). Such a militaristic, and thoroughly unpolitical, view of the function of war completely dominated German political, as well as military, authorities. In fact, by late 1917 "everything in Germany had been sacrificed to the military view" to such an extent that the emperor had been reduced "to a mere function of the wartime situation" (104). In the absence of any seriously independent and authoritative political leadership whose counterweight might restrain or at least obstruct the military juggernaut, both the military and political scenes were dominated by an individual whose personality embodied an unrestrained military conviction. First Quartermaster General Ludendorff's loyalty was to the military task of unleashing "the mighty pent-up energies" of war, rather than to any political obligation to compromise and make peace with the Allies before time ran out (108). Thus, in March 1918 Ludendorff launched a massive offensive, which Churchill calls the most terrific and inhuman of all battles in the annals of war (107). Instead of destroying the Allies, the attack galvanized "the resolve of the mighty confederacy against Germany" (110). Later that year, the Germans incurred a more humiliating defeat than they would have prior to Ludendorff's reckless offensive.

For Churchill, the "fatal weakness of the German Empire" was the fact that its military leaders became the "arbiters of the whole policy of the State" (108). Who was responsible for this characteristically German blunder? Churchill does not blame Ludendorff for "thinking as a general ought to think about his own job" (104, 108). In fact, he finds a certain "dire noble quality [in] risking all for the sake of victory" (109). At the same time, given Ludendorff's strategy of exhausting every chance and consuming every vestige of strength, which reduced the art of war to the mere "slaughter of men by machinery," Churchill found little ground for holding such a narrowly professional and mechanical military man responsible for the tragic proportions of Germany's demise (104, 107). The responsibility for Germany's fatal weakness lay elsewhere: with those who acquiesced in the face of "virtually a Ludendorff Dictatorship" over the direction and destruction of all the military and political resources of the imposing German Empire (104, 108).

Churchill evaluates the political weakness of Germany in light of the political strengths of the two alternatives, democracy and monarchy. In different ways, there existed equally in France, England, and the United States a competent civil element powerful enough to confront the military and bring its "will-power and special point of view into harmony with the general salvation of the State" (109). Conversely, the unity of political and military authority in the monarchical figures of Alexander, Hannibal, Caesar, Marlborough, Frederick the Great, and Napoleon never posed a threat to the salvation of their empires, because "all understood the whole story" (109). The German Empire enjoyed the advantages of neither democratically divided nor monarchically unified executive power. At the start of the Great War, "These other qualities were either non-existent or rigorously repressed in the German nation" (109, 104). Instead, Germany experienced the worst of both alternatives when its shortsighted military authority assumed political responsibility beyond its competence, without ever being counseled about the obligation of the military to defer to the appropriate monarchical or parliamentary representatives of the consent of the governed.

The moral of the Ludendorff story is that the Great War tested the political mettle of the competing nations, with disappointing results for those with ill-defined and weak regimes. It was no accident that the survivors and victors were countries with well-founded democratic regimes in which the political and military powers were separated and balanced. For it seemed to Churchill that, in the absence of the rare possibility of government by intellectually and politically exceptional monarchs, democracy is the alternative among the worst forms of government best suited to withstanding the extreme and inhuman threats of modern warfare. This may explain why an essay on a German general ends with an account of how the French and English military leaders, during the most desperate moments of the German offensive, succeeded in avoiding mutual reproaches and resolved "to hold together at all hazards and to establish unity of command upon the whole of the front in France and Flanders" (113). Unlike the German general staff, the actions of the Allied commanders were a model of the political benefits available in a military situation from generals whose soldiering lives had been shaped, restrained, and guided by the civilian ways, goals, and leaders of a democratic people.

The final two essays on the Great War testify that modern democracies, and not the opposing monarchies, were still capable of producing modern commanders who were not "entirely divorced from the heroic aspect of war" (188). "A Day with Clemenceau" is ostensibly a recounting of Churchill's

efforts at determining the extent to which the French intended to reinforce the British troops at the height of the German offensive in March
1918. As the title suggests, however, Churchill is primarily concerned
with catching the spirit of the French premier's character. Not only was
the "Tiger's" speech both direct and disarming, but he also possessed a
daring for visiting the worst battle situations, which made the French staff
officers "increasingly concerned for the safety of their Prime Minister"
(124). Clemenceau, however, looked on such an excursion as the "reward"
of a "*moment délicieux*" or a "*grand plaisir*" for having fulfilled his oblig-
atory but less exciting political tasks. In a comment that turns out to be
personally ironic, given Churchill's penchant for serving at the front, he
chides Clemenceau. Occasionally such an excursion is acceptable; given
the gravity of his political responsibility, however, the premier "ought not
to go under fire too often" (125).

The last essay of the second part of the book, "In the Air," would seem
to confirm the extent of Churchill's thinly veiled hypocrisy in chiding
Clemenceau for his imprudence in unnecessarily endangering his life while
serving as an important government leader. Though Churchill began flying
in connection with his duties as creator and developer of the Royal Naval
Air Service, he "continued for sheer joy and pleasure" and "for another
exciting experience" (129, 138). Unlike Clemenceau, however, Churchill
came to recognize "the enormous number of hazards which beset every
moment of the airman's flight" (130). Especially during the war, when
events demanded the unending exercise of uncommon courage from pilots,
every incidence of a problem or danger while flying made one acutely
aware that "this is very likely Death" (141). Thus, as a result of feeling
responsible for injuries suffered by those who piloted him, Churchill increasingly restricted the times that he was in the air (142). In the end, his
self-imposed moderation distinguished him from both the political excesses
of Ludendorff, which trapped Germany in an untenable military position,
and the personal indulgence of Clemenceau in reckless behavior, which
compromised his official responsibility for restraining or moderating the
public behavior of others. At the same time, the tension in Churchill's own
wartime life between an attraction to serve as a commander at the battle
front and a recognition that modern commanders ought "to be found on
the day of the battle at their desks in their offices fifty or sixty miles from
the front" foreshadows the description in the third part of the book of the
eclipse in modern society of personal leadership due to "the mass effects
of modern life and science" (190).

PART 3: CONFUSION, UNCERTAINTY, PERIL

Ostensibly, the third set of essays concerns both specific and general peace-time events of the postwar period. Yet Churchill alludes to this period as one of "Exhaustion which has been described as Peace" (177). It is full of "anxious matters" that "are not less serious . . . than the years of the Great War" (173). Churchill reviews election memories, the resolution of the Irish problem, the prominence of economic problems in British political life, the destructive potential of modern science, the decline of leadership in mass society, and future challenges to the moral and spiritual concep-tions of people and nations. Common to all of these peacetime events is the threat or presence of conflict resulting from the rapidity of change in modern life. This endangers the possibilities for civilized freedom from its political expression in national elections to its most universal articulation in the form of a moral and spiritual "vision above material things" (204). More than the essays about the recent military conflict, these confirm Churchill's conviction that "the story of the human race is War. Except for brief and precarious interludes, there has never been peace in the world" (174). The interlude of peacetime provides a "blessed respite of Exhaus-tion, offering to the nations a final chance to control their destinies and avert what may well be a general doom" (180). Churchill's contribution to humanity's salvation is a philosophical examination of the enduring cause of war in the unresolved struggle of "the powers and weapons of man" against "the march of his intelligence" and "the development of his nobility" (202). His illumination of the tension between science, moral philosophy, and spiritual conceptions paves the way for his account in the fourth part of the book of the human understanding and wisdom required in order to avoid the "supreme catastrophe" and preserve human free-dom (180).

In "Election Memories," Churchill speaks of a democratic election as a "fight" or "contest" that is full of "disorder," "rowdy meetings," "vic-tory" or "grave defeat," seats being "wrested," "violent form," and "com-bative spirit." Contrary to popular impressions, however, Churchill did not generally relish political battles; in fact, he insists that he did not like elections (147). Nonetheless, after a third and most grueling defeat in the Westminster election of 1924, he confessed that he "thoroughly enjoyed the fight from start to finish" (155). More than any other, this election illu-minated the meaning of the lesson he had learned about the British cit-izenry. "They are good all through," he claimed, by which he meant that people of all ranks worked ardently "in a purely disinterested cause not unconnected with myself" (147, 155). On the whole, however, Churchill had a general dislike of elections. For, even though elections revealed the goodness of the democratic people, it was just as true that "the ups and downs of politics" disrupted the abilities of the representatives to concentrate on governing. This was especially true during the postwar period, when frequent elections became occasions for expressions of "general discontent and ill-will" by large numbers of newly enfranchised poor and working voters. Thus, after having been defeated three times in two years, he was relieved to be returned for West Essex in the general election of 1924. It was his hope that finally he had found a "resting-place amid the glades of Epping which will last me as long as I am concerned with mundane affairs" (155).

Although Churchill recognized that the give and take of electoral battles "is the way the Constitution works," he also knew how rare and fragile was the "kindliness and good sportsmanship" characteristic of all British democratic parties (144, 147). He punctuates this concern by following the account of election battles with an essay on "The Irish Treaty" that stresses the "violently conflicting emotions" aroused by the negotiations surrounding the Irish settlement (156). Despite the fact that Ireland had been intimately connected with the British Empire during its democratic development and had been tutored in the parliamentary ways of resolving political differences, it became impossible to govern Ireland "except by processes of terror and violent subjugation deeply repugnant to British institutions and to British national character" (157). Far from being an aberration in the forward march of civilized and peaceful democratic government, the Irish crisis represented the mortal threat that has been posed throughout history by the passionate struggle against the primacy of government by rational policy:

So the world moves on only very slowly and fitfully with innumerable setbacks, and the superior solutions, when from time to time as the result of great exertions they are open, are nearly always squandered. Two opposite sides of human nature have to be simultaneously engaged. Those who can win the victory cannot make the peace; those who make the peace would never have won the victory. (161)

Although the treaty of reconciliation did not follow upon a military victory by either side, Churchill believes that it resulted from another more important moral victory by England and Ireland. Peace became possible only as personal and rational relationships were gradually established between the negotiators, after they had been victorious over themselves in surmounting the "tides of distrust and hatred which had flowed between the two countries for so many centuries" (159). Despite the sadness surrounding the "curse of the centuries" which bound Ireland and England in an "odious and disastrous conflict," and the fact that the Irish settlement was reached amid "fierce Party strife," Churchill considered the Irish resolution to be an affirmation of the strength and resiliency of constitutional and parliamentary government in the face of armed rebellion that "bore no distinguishing mark and conformed in no respect to the long-established laws and customs of war" (162, 158, 157). This favorable judgment becomes even more pronounced in light of the four essays following "The Irish Treaty," which catalogue the more profound and grave threats that Churchill foresaw would confront modern civilized democracy in the near future.

His opening claim in "Parliamentary Government and the Economic Problem," delivered as the Romanes Lecture at Oxford University—that he is a "Seeker after the Truth" rather than a partisan of contemporary political controversies—is one that applies as well to the following three essays, entitled "Shall We All Commit Suicide?," "Mass Effects in Modern Life," and "Fifty Years Hence." In these essays, he is no longer concerned with specific British political and military events, which lend themselves to partisan observations, but with universal questions about the character and direction of parliamentary government, liberal democracy, and modern civilization as a whole. He argues that the only way of promoting the virtues of modern life, while preventing the victory of its vices, is to perpetuate democratic government through representative institutions.

Churchill sees four challenges confronting parliamentary government, which he acknowledges may no longer "command a consensus of world opinion" (164). The survival of parliamentary democracy is threatened by the modern preoccupation with economics over politics, the successful technology of weapons of universal destruction, the modern culture of mass effects, and the triumph of materialism over any concern for virtue and happiness. In "Parliamentary Government and the Economic Problem," Churchill examines the consequences of the fact that since the war the issues debated in Parliament are economic rather than political and social (164). In "Shall We All Commit Suicide?" he considers the possibility that democracy cannot prevent the knowledge and power of destructive modern science from exterminating the human race (177). Even if mankind avoids physical annihilation, however, Churchill asks in "Mass

Effects in Modern Life" whether democracy, with its preference for processes of mass production and collectivization, might not eventually dispense with the need for personal direction and destroy all possibilities for human greatness (188). Finally, in "Fifty Years Hence," he wonders whether parliamentary institutions and democracy can avoid being overwhelmed by the march of material progress in time to meet the real needs of the human race by bringing comfort to the soul (203). In short, parliamentary democracy is threatened by the modern preoccupation with economics, technology, mass culture, and materialism.

"Parliamentary Government and the Economic Problem" opens with a defense, as well as a critique, of government by parliamentary speech as "the best way of governing states." Its strength is that representatives of the nation, who are habituated to obeying its decisions, meet to argue out the affairs of the public at large. Better than any other form of government, parliamentary institutions provide three great political benefits for democratic peoples. They are a buffer against revolutionary violence, they are extremely adaptive, and, most important, they provide the "closest association yet achieved between the life of the people and the action of the State" (164). At the same time, parliamentary government is subject to two serious limitations, both of which came into full view only in the postwar period. The advent of universal democratic suffrage, which was initiated through Parliament itself, undermines its authority. It is subjected to the external pressures of party organizations and public opinion, and its existence is threatened by the call for direct democracy through the elimination of all processes and institutions "interposed between the elector and the assembly" (164). More serious, however, is that universal suffrage shifts the nation's interest away from political and social issues, whose resolution is effected admirably well by Parliament, toward economic questions, which are unsuitable for parliamentary debate (165, 171). After debating the differences between classes and parties, the political matter can be settled by voting and electioneering, which will ensure that the majority is satisfied.

Not so in the economic domain, where the best measures that are truly in the national interest typically prove to be vastly unpopular even to the majority of citizens. "In fact, it would probably be safe to say that nothing that is popular and likely to gather a large number of votes will do what is wanted [in economics] and win the prize which all desire" (167). Yet because of the growth in the power of public opinion, increasingly the political parties resort to proposing only those economic measures that are electorally popular. In particular, both public opinion and the parties reject tenets of the classical economic doctrine that had prevailed in England since the early nineteenth century. Yet they fail to offer any serious proposal as to the new body of economic doctrine that should supplement or replace the old laissez-faire Victorian economics. Since political leaders have their origin in the political sphere, which is a mixture of self-interest and emotion as well as national good and reason, they are largely inclined to vote on the basis of "fear, favor, or affection" to protect their local industries (172). For this reason, the greater number of political leaders are functionally incapable of exercising the "high, cold, technical, and dispassionate or disinterested decision" required for correctly resolving the nonpolitical and technical questions of economics (170). Contrary to popular opinion, the future well-being of representative parliamentary institutions is not threatened by political agitation of any kind, which it is well adapted to handle, but by economic problems, which cannot be resolved correctly by compromise and majority vote (171).

In light of this analysis of the current economic crisis, Churchill proposed a constitutional solution involving the establishment by the British Parliament of an economic sub-parliament: "Debating day after day with fearless detachment from public opinion all the most disputed questions of Finance and Trade, and reaching conclusions by voting, would be an innovation, but an innovation easily to be embraced by our flexible constitutional system" (173). This practical solution to the economic challenges facing the parliamentary political system transcended party politics and addressed the problem on the level of fundamental political principle. As in the case of his earlier constitutional plan for the establishment of an imperial parliament, however, Churchill's proposal for an economic parliament was never adopted. His failure to persuade his political colleagues certainly came as no surprise to him. He understood that the threat that representative government posed to the correct determination of economic policy applied as well to the resolution of all fundamental constitutional questions by universal suffrage. They "cannot be solved by any expression, however vehement, of the national will, but only by taking the right action. You cannot cure cancer by a majority. What is wanted is a remedy" (171).

Modern democracy is also faced with the more radical challenge of preventing the self-destruction of mankind. In "Shall We All Commit Suicide?" Churchill raises the specter that democracy is incapable of checking the unlimited destructive potential of modern science and technology.

He was not a pessimist about the survivability of the human race. History confirms, however, both that "the story of the human race is War" and that its preservation is more likely to occur through externally imposed constraints than through human self-restraint (174). Democracy's dilemma is compounded by the fact that in the modern era the forces of economics, political institutions, education, the press, religion, and especially science have cooperated to eliminate all such external checks (175). For the first time, the only barrier to self-annihilation is mankind's historically unreliable capacity for the voluntary exercise of moderation in its use of the sciences and arts. Given the world's experience with the Armageddon of the First World War and the development of new weapons of mass destruction, Churchill had serious grounds for being concerned that the human race might physically destroy itself at some point in the future. At the same time, it is clear that he is more deeply concerned with the spiritual, intellectual, and cultural corruption that fuels the practical possibility of physical annihilation. For it may happen that the last Armageddon will be averted. Should the world pull back from the brink, however, it will result from the less than noble forces of fear, ignorance, and the competition for power. Not only will contemporary society be demeaned by the effects of the spiritual blackmail, but it may lead to an irreversible decline in civilization. Not comprehending the questionably beneficent character of the forces that have been unleashed with the advent of modern science, we are ill prepared to correct the spiritual and moral corruption that follows in its wake:

Mankind has never been in this position before. Without having improved appreciably in virtue or enjoying wiser guidance, it has got into its hands for the first time the tools by which it can unfailingly accomplish its own extermination. That is the point in human destinies to which all the glories and toils of men have at last led them. They would do well to pause and ponder upon their new responsibilities. Death stands at attention, obedient, expectant, ready to serve, ready to shear away the peoples *en masse*; ready, if called on, to pulverize, without hope of repair, what is left of civilization. He awaits only the word of command. He awaits it from a frail, bewildered being, long his victim, now—for one occasion only—his Master. (177)

If the technological threat facing the human race is that for the first time it can unfailingly destroy itself, then the profoundly psychological threat is the absence of self-knowledge. Mankind "would do well to pause and ponder [its] new responsibilities" (177). Yet it stands before the threat of death as "a frail, bewildered being." While the human race has progressed technologically, it has not undergone any corresponding improvement in the virtues appropriate for using such knowledge for the benefit of humanity. In particular, it has not acquired the wisdom required for guiding this chemical power in safe and beneficial ways. In turn, the modern coincidence between an unlimited technical power and the lack of self-knowledge has triggered the deepest problem that confronts humanity. For the first time, a part of the human race possesses the technical capacity to enslave the rest, to reduce them to absolute helplessness (179). "There is no reason why a base, degenerate, immoral race should not make an enemy far above them in quality the prostrate subject of their caprice or tyranny"(179). Previously, despite the fact that those in authority were not always the most virtuous or wisest, one had every reason to believe that the cycle of nature would eventually restore authority to the virtuous and wise, even if only for a limited time. Thus, in barbarous times, physical supremacy over others depended on the exercise of superior martial virtues. In the hard evolution of mankind, the best and fittest stocks have always triumphed up till now. But in the twentieth century, the guarantees that had historically insured that physical supremacy will coincide with the presence of moral virtues have disappeared. For the first time, "the liberties of men are no longer to be guarded by their natural qualities, but by their dodges; and superior virtue and valour may fall an easy prey to the latest diabolical trick" (179).

In the aftermath of the First World War, and long before the dawn of the atomic age, Churchill grasped the roots of the intellectual and moral crisis animating the technological threat facing mankind. Modern progress has ruptured our first line of salvation. Humanity's success at self-preservation is rooted in its vigilant awareness of the need for a constant and reciprocal correspondence between the quest for knowledge and the ability to distinguish the naturally best from the worst human qualities —between reason and nature. For the first time in history, human life is menaced by the possibility of a profound and permanent disjunction between human merit and the march of science (180). In light of his understanding of the spiritual depth to the surface military crisis, Churchill's title for this essay assumes an equivocal meaning. Even if humanity avoids committing physical suicide, is it not possible that it will commit moral suicide? In present-day terms, which are nonetheless relevant to the meaning of his comments in the 1920s, we might avoid the threat of physical annihilation that modern science has triggered, but we may yet succumb to its underlying cause of moral and spiritual nihilism.

Once mankind is threatened by the dual peril of annihilation and nihilism, the only simple way of resolving the dilemma would be to eliminate war. For this is the compelling need that fuels the use of science in the service of self-destruction and without regard to human merit. But the good historian Churchill had no illusions on this score. "Shall We All Commit Suicide?" opens with the most succinct history of humanity that Churchill—or anyone else, for that matter—ever wrote: "The story of the human race is War. Except for brief and precarious interludes, there has never been peace in the world, and before history began, murderous strife was universal and unending" (174). As one reads contemporary coverage of world events, it is difficult to find any reason why Churchill would today be obliged to issue a revised second edition of his classic four-line account of the world's history. He never believed in the easy solution that, if only humanity were confronted with the consequences of its scientific efforts, then its conduct would irreversibly change for the better. In words that continue to inform the nightly news, Churchill presumed the unending presence of "the fires of hatred burning deep in the hearts of some of the greatest peoples of the world, fanned by continual provocation and unceasing fear, and fed by the deepest sense of national wrong or national danger" (180).

To be sure, at one point he seems to offer hope that mankind will come to its senses: "Surely if a sense of self-preservation still exists among men, if the will to live resides not merely in individuals or nations but in humanity as a whole, the prevention of the supreme catastrophe ought to be the paramount object of all endeavour" (180). One should notice, however, that Churchill offers no guarantee that the human race will rise to the occasion, but only asserts the moral imperative that preventing the world's annihilation *ought* to be its paramount objective. Because he believed in the reality of human liberty, he recognized that its exercise can bring harmful as well as beneficial consequences. The realist in Churchill recognized that mankind was inclined more often than not to abuse the exercise of liberty. Unlike his early modern English predecessor the philosopher Thomas Hobbes, he found no grounds for optimism that the human tendency toward baseness is governed by a principle of natural necessity that effects the perpetuation of the human species through its incessant efforts at self-destruction.

While the principles and conduct of democracy are not the ultimate causes of the threat of annihilation and nihilism, Churchill does assert that democracy provided fertile soil for the growth of such challenges to civilization. The case for democracy's vulnerability to moral and political corruption is presented most starkly in "Mass Effects in Modern Life." While he respects democracy for the benefits it brought to large numbers of people, in the debate about whether the few or the many were the cause of human progress, Churchill places himself squarely on the side of those "who view the past history of the world mainly as the tale of exceptional human beings" (182). He foresaw the coming demise of the political, social, and economic conditions conducive to the development and influence of outstanding personalities, and he wondered if their eclipse would be for "our greater good and glory" (183).

The account of modern conditions in "Mass Effects in Modern Life" is evenhanded; every instance of progress evinces both strengths and weaknesses. Though science has made enormous strides, it has been because of the efforts of a group rather than any distinctive individuals. The processes of collectivization have brought forth all the benefits of mass production. The same processes, however, are responsible for a loss in forethought, initiative, contrivance, freedom, and effective civic status (184). Likewise, the newspapers have become the world's educators through their dissemination of knowledge and formation of public opinion. Nonetheless, such easy universalization of learning dissolves the conditions of stress and effort required for genuine mental greatness (185). Nowhere is the mix of hopes and dangers to be expected from the mass effects of modernity more evident than in the experiment that was carried out by the Russian Bolsheviks. On the one hand, there is their conception, albeit tyrannical, of the beehive as the model for organizing mankind. On the other hand, there is the evidence of their results, which suggests that their methods failed to make life better for those subject to their mechanical authority (186).

The Western liberal democracies, being the most advanced nations in all respects, offer the best examples for resolving the question of the benefit or ill to be expected from the mass effects of modernity. It is taken for granted that the spread of democratic liberty, though its benefits be great, results inevitably in the decline of the influence of great guides and guardians (186). Churchill asks, "Is what we now see in the leading democracies merely a diffusion and squandering of the accumulated wisdom and treasure of the past?" Or, he wonders, "Have we for the first time reached those uplands whence all of us, even the humblest and silliest equally with the best, can discern for ourselves the beacon lights?" (186). He has no doubt that the spread of democratic equality is in many respects beneficial.

Yet he wonders if the well-ordered conduct of public affairs in war and peace, upon which depends the enjoyment of human happiness, is possible "without leaders who by their training and situation, no less than by their abilities, feel themselves to be uplifted above the general mass" (188).

Churchill senses that modern conditions have altered the character not only of peace but especially of war, where the leveling effect was seen earliest and most clearly. Despite the fact that the First World War was the worst of conflicts, it is impossible to fix responsibility for either winning or losing it on specific individuals (187). The modern military commander is a "high-souled speculator" whose faceless activity far behind the battle lines is more akin to the paper transactions of a financial manager than it is to the battlefield involvement of a Hannibal, Caesar, Turenne, Marlborough, Frederick, or Napoleon (188). Modernity has a comparable leveling effect on political leaders, from the elected parliamentary minister to the hereditary king. While their public work is useful, they have become ordinary fellows and look upon themselves as such (188).

To be sure, Churchill concedes that there are three immediate benefits to the eclipse of the individual in modern times. First, the worth of military and political leaders is reduced to their utility as efficient, but unheroic workers (188). The successful leader is no longer considered to be a genius "who by the firmness of his character, and by the mysterious harmonies and inspirations of his nature," saved the day and preserved his nation. Rather, the general perception is that the victory resulted from the concerted efforts of the greater mass of the anonymous people. Second, as a consequence, honor and glory are no longer accorded to the modern public servant, who is the faithful but unheroic successor to the great military and political captains of history. While the people at large deserve fame and recognition for their collective actions, "There are too many of them for exceptional honours" (189). In the end, the spread of modern conditions results in the practical impossibility of acquiring or awarding fame and glory. Finally, the demise of the importance of the individual and the loss of opportunities for fame and glory lead to an admirable reaction. Mankind will turn against war; the military career will lose its romantic attraction; artists will no longer immortalize the exploits of war heroes; and the Napoleons will henceforth wreak their havoc on the battlefields of business and finance. Because the demise of the hero's importance and the loss of interest in war will set "the civilization of the world . . . on a surer basis," Churchill characterizes the coming worldwide reaction against the pursuit of war as a "blessed" event (190).

While he is sincere in his claim that the demise of war is a blessing, he does not assume that the coming peace will necessarily mean the end of troubles for humanity. The last section of "Mass Effects in Modern Life," devoted to an examination of the conditions of a peace without the threat of war, opens with a series of questions that spell out the challenges facing a world dominated by modern mass democracy:

> Can modern communities do without great men? Can they dispense with hero-worship? Can they provide a larger wisdom, a nobler sentiment, a more vigorous action, by collective processes, than were ever got from the Titans? Can nations remain healthy, can all nations draw together, in a world whose brightest stars are film stars and whose gods are sitting in the gallery? Can the spirit of man emit the vital spark by machinery? Will the new problems of successive generations be solved successfully by "the common sense of most," by party caucuses, by Assemblies whose babble is no longer heeded? (191)

Churchill does not directly answer these questions. It is taken for granted that although democracy may not meet these challenges in the most perfect way, it will succeed well enough in promoting the long-term well-being and happiness of the greater part of humanity. Instead, he is concerned that, despite the improvements brought about by democracy, difficulties encountered on the path of progress will lead modern peoples to abandon their attachment to the democratic principles of equality and liberty. The preservation of modern mass democracy is threatened not by the imperfection of democratic accomplishments, but by the restlessness of democratic peoples and their inability to handle adversity (191). Churchill warns that democratic peoples lack the virtues of moderation and courage, which previously characterized the great men of less democratic societies and are always required for the ordering of public affairs. During times of adversity, and in the absence of public models of moderation and courage, democracy, in its undisciplined "mass desire," may mistakenly long once again for the unrecoverable rule of monarchs with their towering grandeur (191).

Churchill counsels us to exercise modesty in our expectations of democracy. If a sense of grandeur in public life depends on a contrast between the outstanding accomplishments of a few and the lesser deeds of the rest, then democracy is unimpressive, since it encourages relatively equal and unexceptional accomplishments from all. At the same time, because "the general levels of intelligence and of knowledge have risen" and there are now many more "eminences" who are routinely taken for granted, modern democratic life is largely healthy (191). The problem with the nostalgic quest for great leaders is that modern mass democracy runs the risk of acquiring, instead of a statesman capable of guiding a nation to genuine happiness and well-being, a petty dictator such as "El Capitan" Franco or "Il Duce" Mussolini (192). Churchill is honest in acknowledging that the victory of the modern democratic way of life entails the irrevocable loss of the aristocratic capacity for political and military greatness. On balance, however, he asserts that modern democracies "must take the loss with the gain" (191).

The material benefits secured for the human race in the modern age are unprecedented and seemingly endless. Not only are larger numbers of human beings securely maintained in existence and primary necessities, but increasingly they also enjoy life's comforts and even aspire to culture. Once the need for self-defensive warfare, which had historically constrained mankind's aspirations, is removed, however, what remains to check the dehumanizing excesses of rapidly expanding materialism? In "Fifty Years Hence," the last of the essays concerned with the postwar peace of exhaustion, Churchill offers a comprehensive evaluation of modern civilization that gives voice both to his unqualified respect for its materialist progress and to his deep concern that modernity urgently needs to nurture man's capacities for moral and religious self-restraint. Given the breadth of his review of the history of human progress and the depth of his philosophical assertion about the greater importance for human life of moral and spiritual needs over the quest for material satisfactions, "Fifty Years Hence" ranks with the most comprehensive and principled of Churchill's writings. In its articulation of the profound spiritual dangers that threaten humanity's stability and well-being in the coming age of a prosperous peace without war, this essay is an appropriate culmination to the three parts of *Thoughts and Adventures* on the alternating periods of prewar peace, the Armageddon of wartime, and the postwar peace of exhaustion. It is also a fitting prologue to the conclusion, which considers the religious and philosophical principles and practices needed in order to preserve the benefits and restrain the excesses of modern civilization.

Churchill opens his examination of modern materialism by distinguishing between two levels of existence "in every civilized country" (193). The basic form, though mentioned most often, is partial, incomplete, and merely a useful means. Civilization emerges when men learn to harness the forces of nature (195). What raises modern civilization so decisively above earlier ones in this utilitarian respect is its capacity for

science. It has overcome the main struggle of earlier civilizations to produce or procure all the food it requires, it has substituted molecular energy
for muscular energy, and it will soon replace both with nuclear energy.
In the process, it has called into question the traditional standard of measuring man's capacities by comparison with those of nature (197–200).
While the scientific and materialistic conception of civilization is necessary for survival, Churchill considers that there is another, rarer form of
civilization that is intrinsically good, true, and beautiful. His second conception of civilization concerns the "fuller life of man," which has become "larger, safer, more varied, more full of hope and choice" (193). To
be sure, this higher notion of civilization depends on the continuous
production of material things and the ongoing revolutions in scientific
application. Civilization in this fuller sense is characterized not by material progress, however, but by advances in political institutions, manners,
and customs. In genuine civilization, men lift "themselves above primary
necessities and comforts, and aspire to culture" (193). In this fuller sense
of civilization, primacy is given not to science, but to moral and political
development.

Churchill does not doubt that modern life is in principle capable of
nurturing both dimensions of civilization for greater numbers of human
beings than was the case when the world belonged to the "twice two thousand" (193). In practice, however, he is deeply concerned that mankind will become so preoccupied with the wonders of material progress
that it will fail to nurture the genuinely human ends of civilization. To be
sure, he believes in the enduring constancy of human nature throughout
the gloomiest as well as the brightest eras of history: "The present nature
of mankind is tough and resilient. It casts up its sparks of genius in the
darkest and most unexpected places" (201). At the same time, he recognizes
soberly that we have no grounds for assuming that the newly uncovered
and frightening powers of nature unleashed by modern science will always
and everywhere be restrained by the "laws of a Christian civilization"
rather than being employed for tyrannical ends by the "pitiless sub-
human wickedness" of powerful reigning governments such as the communist state (201).

Churchill's apprehensions are compounded by his awareness that the
only viable political alternative in modern times to the most horrific des-
potisms and tyrannies ever experienced is liberal democracy. On the question of how confident we should be about democracy's salvific capacities,
he comments tersely that "democracy as a guide or motive to progress

has long been known to be incompetent" (202). He then provides what seems a devastating critique of the weaknesses of democracy against the strength of communism. The latter has "a plan and a gospel," albeit one that is destructive of freedom and motivated by hate (202). By contrast, democracy's assemblies do not represent the strength and wisdom of their peoples; its governments drift without goals, policies, or fortitude; its affairs are marked by profound inconsistencies. Most important, they are not led by anyone, be it "their ablest men," "those who know most about their immediate affairs," or "those who have a coherent doctrine" (202). In short, democracy is profoundly ill prepared for the coming changes that will radically transform mankind's economic, social, and moral conceptions. Were this Churchill's last word in "Fifty Years Hence" on the moral challenge faced by democracy to order and restrain the material capacities of modern science, it would be fair for us to dismiss the remaining essays in *Thoughts and Adventures* on "the pleasures of life" as the bankrupt and escapist daydreams of a private man who has no further public counsel to offer modern liberal democracy. In fact, in the three remaining pages of "Fifty Years Hence," Churchill prepares the reader for those essays by arguing that a kind of religious and philosophic wisdom is needed in order to avoid the worst excesses of modern science. Moreover, he suggests that modern democracy is equal to the task of adhering to such wisdom and thereby advancing the higher moral ends of civilization over its necessary but less human materialist ones.

Churchill's solution to the ills of civilization suits the threats it faces. He begins with the observation that the ills of the human race are rooted in a conflict between its theoretical capacities and its moral obligations. In brief, mankind's powers and weapons have exceeded the progress of human intelligence, which has, in turn, outstripped "the development of [its] nobility" (202). He concludes from this that "above all things [it is] important that the moral philosophy and spiritual conceptions of men and nations should hold their own amid these formidable scientific evolutions" (203). Because no amount of material progress can bring comfort to the soul, the public affairs of modern democracy require the assistance of moral and spiritual forces. First, the inherent virtue of human beings must find a strong and confident expression in daily life. Second, the hope of immortality, coupled with "a disdain of earthly power and achievement," is needed "for the safety of the children of men" (203). As Churchill indicates earlier in "Mass Effects in Modern Life," only individual great men or Titans, and not the large collective majority of democratic men, can provide such a "larger wisdom, nobler sentiment, and more vigorous action." Without such spiritual and philosophic leadership, democratic peoples will be left to drift, with "comforts, activities, amenities, and pleasures crowded upon them, while their hearts ache, their lives are barren and they have not a vision above material things" (204).

One should not be alarmed that Churchill's moral medicine might undermine democracy's egalitarian and liberal foundations. He never proposes any moral or spiritual correction of democracy that requires curtailing, compromising, or contradicting the fundamental democratic principle of government of the people, by the people, and for the people. For this reason, Churchill does not leap to the conclusion that the cure for the ills of democracy is the philosophic one of rule by philosopher-kings or religious guidance by the city of God. How, then, does he propose to bring the benefits of the Titans of philosophic and religious wisdom and virtue to bear on the public life of parliamentary democracies?

PART 4: THE PLEASURES OF LIFE

At first glance, the last three essays—"Moses," "Hobbies," and "Painting as a Pastime"—seem innocent stories without political, let alone philosophic or religious significance. Innocent they are, but precisely because of that, they are intended to have political significance. In all three, Churchill focuses on the possibility that moral and political principles can guide mankind's encounter with nature, and that virtue and wisdom are capable of shaping science, rather than the reverse. For that reason, these essays reveal the extent to which Churchill the political man was capable of comprehending and explaining the necessity of a transpolitical response to the double threat of physical annihilation and moral nihilism. Do not expect, however, to find a direct application of philosophic and religious principles to the formulation of public policy on the moral consequences of modern science and military technology. Rather, Churchill responds by indirection and deflection: he broadens the horizon for examining the problem and alters the ranking of its parts. In the end, the political contribution of these essays on "the pleasures of life" is found in their articulation of the standards for measuring and improving public conduct, habituation to which by democratic nations might contribute to constraining and ameliorating the threats of annihilation and nihilism.

Churchill's subject and audience in all three essays are the character, the concerns, and the consolations of the public leader in the modern world.

The full title of the first essay is "Moses—the Leader of a People." "Hobbies" is a discussion of the remedies for overcoming the worry and mental stress felt by "persons who, over prolonged periods, have to bear exceptional responsibilities and discharge duties upon a very large scale" (216). In "Painting as a Pastime," Churchill freely acknowledges that he would never have discovered the joys of painting had he not felt like "a diver too suddenly hoisted" at his unexpected departure in 1915 from the daily routine of his intense executive activities at the Admiralty (223). Viewed from the perspective of their common concern with statesmanship, the essays are Churchill's effort at restoring, or at least compensating for, the ongoing loss of public authority in modern democracies by exceptional individuals. In this regard, the essays in the fourth part of the book address the concerns voiced in "Mass Effects in Modern Life" and "Fifty Years Hence." They reveal the extent to which Churchill refuses to resign himself to the loss of influence by the talented political leader in the public affairs of modern mass democracy. In fact, they point to Churchill's conviction that the most important task confronting modern democracy can only be carried out by such eminent leaders. With proper guidance and preparation, such as that provided in *Thoughts and Adventures*, these leaders might yet become the conveyors of the philosophic and religious wisdom that alone can preserve democracy's virtues while restraining its excesses.

The theoretical thread linking these three very different essays is Churchill's argument that the antidote to the modern obsession with the scientific perspective is learning to restrain our preoccupation with dominating nature. The increasingly dehumanizing consequences of modern technology can be ameliorated through a disciplined effort at discovering, comprehending, and appreciating the potential of the human soul for providing moral and spiritual order. In "Moses," Churchill praises the political authority of the prophet who voyaged to the "very threshold of the Promised Land" and who drew his inspiration from an inner assimilation of the most extraordinary divine revelation about the rules and virtues of civilized life (205). In "Hobbies," Churchill challenges his readers to undertake "a voyage of self-discovery" and learn to exercise moral self-control over the excesses of their worries and mental strains by diverting themselves from the rapidity of change in the modern world (217 et seq.). In "Painting as a Pastime," he recounts his successful experience of subordinating his mind to nature for the sake of discovering, rather than manipulating, nature's intrinsic and perfect original order. In short, these essays exhort Churchill's readers—and especially those who aspire to exercise political authority, but find no opportunities for it in the modern world—to make an effort at acquiring self-knowledge and psychic discipline. It is Churchill's conviction that only a combined application of the religious, psychological, and philosophic wisdom laid out in the three concluding essays can counteract and control the prevailing modern presumption that unending and complete scientific control over both nature and human nature can satisfy all of mankind's longings.

In "Moses," Churchill presents the "great leader and liberator of the Hebrew people" as a model of public authority whose ancient statesmanship can withstand the debunking scrutiny and criticism of progressive modern science and its rationalistic methods (205, 215). He is at pains to suggest that many of the forces faced by Moses have their counterparts in modern times. Ancient Egypt experienced the modern movement of anti-Semitism. Its bureaucracy and the responses of the Pharaohs would be familiar to Churchill's contemporaries (206, 208, 210). Thus, modern peoples ought to recognize that "the grand simplicity and essential accuracy of the recorded truths" of the story of Moses and his triumph over the Pharaoh are as relevant today as they were then (215). One can question the statistics on the number of Jews who marched across the Red Sea (212). One can debate the credibility of miracles on the journey out of Egypt. What is compelling, however, is the fact that the biblical story of Moses is most satisfying when it is taken literally, by identifying one of the greatest of human beings with the most decisive leap ever discerned in the human story (214). One cannot deny the miraculous character of the Jewish people's ability to grasp and proclaim "an idea of which all the genius of Greece and all the power of Rome were incapable" (213). The genius of Moses is that he allowed his leadership to be guided by the belief that "there was to be only one God, a universal God, a God of nations, a just God, a God who would punish in another world a wicked man dying rich and prosperous, a God from whose service the good of the humble and of the weak and the poor was inseparable" (213). From such a miraculous religious truth, which unaided reason failed to uncover for centuries, flows the moral and political benefit of "the tables of those fundamental laws which were henceforward to be followed, with occasional lapses, by the highest forms of human society" (213).

Eventually, this most ancient "inspiration of the Hebrew people" would inform a new revelation with further benefits for civilization. Christianity professes faith in a God of all who wish to serve him, a God of mercy as well as justice, and a God of pity, self-sacrifice, and ineffable love as well as self-preservation and survival (215). In "Fifty Years Hence," when he ponders what forces might withstand modern science's interest in "the breeding of human beings and the shaping of human nature," Churchill's only response is to hope that "the laws of a Christian civilization will prevent them" (201). The enduring vitality of the Christian teaching about the genuine human virtues, and their suitability for preserving civilized life in contemporary liberal democracies, derives fundamentally from the interior psychological strength of the prophet Moses. In encountering the burning bush, Moses communed within himself and found his heart inflamed with the word of God. Though he did not understand all that he felt, he knew that he had been endowed with superhuman power, that there was nothing that man could not do, if he willed it with sufficient resolution (209). For as Moses intuited, "Man is the epitome of the universe. All moves and exists as a result of his invincible will"—which is actually the will of God (209). While this praise of revealed religion for its exaltation of humanity is not Churchill's last word on the sources in the human soul of moral principles for modern life, it is clear that he thought that the psychological truth of Jewish and Christian belief should never be dismissed by statesmen in their efforts at redressing the moral balance in the democratic way of life.

At first glance, "Hobbies" seems to praise the most modern of scientific topics: the importance of change and our unending need for its possibility in order to escape the stresses of modern life. Gradually, it becomes clear that Churchill advocates the change characteristic of hobbies not for the sake of cooperating with the harried pace of modern life, but in order to overcome the consequences of worry and boredom through "restoring psychic equilibrium" (220). The changes of routine required to undertake hobbies are most therapeutic for the human spirit. By means of such activities, "The bitter sweets of a pious despair melt into an agreeable sense of compulsory resignation from which we turn with renewed zest to the lighter vanities of life" (219). At the essay's conclusion, change has been placed in the service of "a voyage of discovery," whose objective is the acquisition of a self-knowledge that "enlivens the mind by a different sequence and emphasis of ideas" (219). Churchill exempts no one from the need for hobbies, be they those whose work is merely work or those fortunate few whose work is also pleasure. Essential to all productive human life, which by his definition is rational, industrious, and useful, is the need "of an alternative outlook, of a change of atmosphere, of a diversion of effort" (216). To some extent, he understands that mental relief, repose, and refreshment are needed in order to remain practically industrious and useful. Yet from the beginning, it is apparent that Churchill is primarily concerned with the psychological benefit of hobbies that rest and strengthen the tired parts of the mind (216). In the final analysis, his description of hobbies as a remedy "for the avoidance of worry and mental overstrain" suggests that the genuine benefit of hobbies is ultimately less practical and more deeply connected with some intrinsically human and more theoretical preoccupation.

Churchill divides the forms of diversion into two camps: reading and handicrafts. While cataloguing the innumerable advantages of reading for mental comfort, he comes upon an apparent disadvantage. All devoted readers soon realize that they will never become acquainted with, let alone thoroughly enjoy, the accumulated knowledge and wisdom of the human race. This apparent disadvantage, however, turns out to be the source of a most important moral and spiritual benefit: "as one surveys the mighty array of sages, saints, historians, scientists, poets and philosophers ... the brief tenure of our existence here dominates mind and spirit" (218). By bringing the reader to recognize the mortality of all human works, the hobby of reading relieves the mind of its exhausting concerns about the success or failure of its projects. The refreshing moral consequence of such a humbling awareness is that "pride ... is chased from the heart by feelings of awe not untinged with sadness" (218). For the most part, Churchill does not discriminate between kinds of readers who are more or less in need of learning the humbling lesson of human mortality, for the simple reason that no human civilization is exempt from the temptation of assuming its powers to be unlimited. Nonetheless, one should recall that the essay opens by suggesting that those persons are most in need of hobbies who "have to bear exceptional responsibilities and discharge duties upon a very large scale" (216). In light of the foregoing essays, Churchill seems to suggest that modern political leaders who are most susceptible to becoming enchanted with the seemingly endless political possibilities of modern scientific knowledge and power are most in need of the intellectually liberating and morally reordering effects of hobbies.

Churchill concludes "Hobbies" by suggesting that the best diversions are those that "call into use those parts of the mind which direct both eye and hand" (220). Among the various handicrafts practiced for pleasure, he considers painting to be by far "best of all and easiest to procure" (220). It is neither unduly demanding nor excessively exhausting, it is faithful in our declining years, and it shields us from the truth about the advance of time and old age (221). Given the breadth and depth of these praises for painting, one should not be surprised when, at the end of the essay on hobbies, Churchill refers to the painter in biblical terms: "Happy are the painters, for they shall not be lonely. Light and colour, peace and hope, will keep them company to the end, or almost to the end, of the day" (221). Or when, at the end of the next essay, "Painting as a Pastime," he compares the ironically passionate tranquillity of the traveling painter in search of nature's scenes to paint to "the calm enjoyment of the philosopher, intensified by an enthralling sense of action and endeavour" (235). This analogizing of painting to religion and philosophy is not a gratuitous aesthetic metaphor. For Churchill, it has the moral and political consequence of pointing to the only way whereby modern liberal democracy might avoid death by moral and physical suicide on the horns of the conflict between nature and human nature, between science and morality.

Churchill's preoccupation with political life is the catalyst for the origin, body, and conclusion of the final essay, "Painting as a Pastime." Had he not left political life in 1915 at the height of the First World War and found that the "narrowly measured duties of a counsellor left [him] gasping," he might never have taken up painting (223). Had he never become enchanted with painting, he would never have realized that "painting a picture is like fighting a battle" (226). He might never have arrived at the insight that all the challenges of military and political action can be found in other fields of human endeavor such as the handicraft of painting. Nor would he have learned that the virtues of the man of action can be exercised successfully and with as much excitement in the nonpolitical arena of the art of painting (226–9). In turn, without the necessity of disciplining his mental powers for the sake of painting, Churchill might never have discovered that the truth about nature's order is not revealed in a scientific theory. On the contrary, as he realized, a "heightened sense of observation of Nature is one of the chief delights that have come to me through trying to paint" (277). Without the theoretical lesson learned from painting that "the soul is pleased by the conception or contemplation of harmonies," Churchill would not have had any counsel to offer future democratic leaders about the moral and political virtues required for the preservation of civilization (229).

As he makes repeatedly clear in "Painting as a Pastime," painting is about the relation of the human observer and actor to the nature of nature—its parts, processes, and purposes (222, 227, 230, 232, 234). At first glance, it seems as if the painter is a modern scientist. Painting is an experiment. One cannot explain how to paint, but only how to get enjoyment. One must be audacious with painting, even violent; in Baconian terms, it is good to squeeze the paints. Painting presents the same kind of problem as unfolding a long interlocked argument; one's aim is progress. In short, like science, painting is a battle. Yet in spite of all the comparisons with the means of modern science, the painter's intentions concerning nature go so far beyond those of the modern scientist as to transform the ends of painting for which the scientific means are enlisted from practical to theoretical ones.

Churchill's unmodern conception of the virtue of painting is reflected in his observation that, unlike utilitarian science, it affords an amusement that is delightful to oneself and at any rate not violently harmful to man or beast. The source of painting's delight is its capacity for an all-embracing view of its subject, which presents the beginning and the end, the whole and each part, as one instantaneous impression held retentively and untiringly in the mind. This is not, however, the same all-embracing view described by a man-made scientific theory, but one that derives from observation of nature's own landscape. For just this reason, Churchill preferred the paintings of Turner to those of the French school. Turner's brush followed the form of the objects he depicted. By contrast, the French often seemed to take pride in opposing nature's order. Because they were more in love with their theories, they were willing to make sacrifices of truth in order to demonstrate fidelity to those abstract ideas. The outcome of Churchill's and Turner's approach is that one comes to know rather than merely to control nature. While progress is still one's goal, it is that of a garden where one makes progress in the growth of the mind and soul. One is pleased by the conception or contemplation of harmonies, and the mind is stimulated by the aspect of a magnificent problem. One finds contentment and fun in trying to observe and depict the joyful things one observes. The whole world is open with all of its treasure, and the simplest objects are revealed to possess an intrinsic beauty. Once one has become attuned to nature through painting, one realizes that the vistas of nature's dimensions are limited only by the shortness of life.

By the conclusion of "Painting as a Pastime," Churchill is very far from the utilitarian conception of nature required for the ends of modern science. In his best formulation of nature's order with its intrinsic integrity —which requires no enhancement by scientists, but only imitation by the painter—he writes that "Nature will hardly stand a double process of beautification: one layer of idealism on top of another is too much of a good thing" (232). It is the same for the painter, who, despite the fact that the field before him is of limitless extent, is relieved entirely of the original anxiety that drove him to painting. As Churchill writes, "I know of nothing which, without exhausting the body, more entirely absorbs the mind" (234). It would seem that he derived his deepest intellectual satisfaction from the contemplative philosophical insight, learned from the non-political art of painting: "Once you begin to study it, all Nature is equally interesting and equally charged with beauty" (232).

THE CLOSING PERSPECTIVE: "A SECOND CHOICE" REVISITED

Churchill's appreciation of the theoretical benefits of painting may help us understand the deeper reason why the first and last essays of *Thoughts and Adventures* are connected through their common reference to his political troubles at the Admiralty in 1915. The Churchill who left the Admiralty was incapable of conceiving a life without the possibility of exercising political authority in war and peace. The Churchill who praises painting no longer believes that the only life worth living is one of political action. The difference is his discovery of the theoretical activity of observing and comprehending the nature of nature, which the art of painting both requires and makes possible, and his experience that that activity may be more delightful, satisfying, and fulfilling than the exercise of the greatest opportunities for political leadership.

When Churchill concludes "A Second Choice" with the assertion, "The journey has been enjoyable and well worth making—once" (10), one should not presume that he has given voice to a fundamental disappointment with human life. This conclusion follows upon a fivefold exhortation about how to live out one's life in contentment. Central to his largely moral and spiritual proposal is the theoretical obligation to "accept the natural order in which we move" and to recognize that "the glory of light cannot exist without its shadows" (10). It was the encounter with painting, Churchill tells us, that taught him to "view Nature as a mass of shimmering light . . . which gleams and glows with beautiful harmonies and contrasts of colour" (230). If his practical views about peace and war are marked by moderation, prudence, and a sense of what is possible and worthwhile in political and moral life, then it is because his political experience led him to a deeper understanding of the natural order that encompasses human life, establishes its purpose, and defines its limits. The opening essay, "A Second Choice," announces Churchill's personal preference for viewing the moral and political life of mankind examined in the rest of the essays according to a theoretical conception of the overarching natural order. By concluding the political essays with one that gives his account of the natural order, "Painting as a Pastime" fulfills the promise of "A Second Choice."

The order and succession of the essays in *Thoughts and Adventures* demonstrates why this work deserves to be remembered as a book of wisdom and counsel worth the attention of democratic leaders at the beginning of the twenty-first century. In the dark hours of the 1930s, Churchill often imagined the worst outcomes from the moral challenge posed to the human race and the democratic way of life by the powers of modern science: "There are nightmares of the future," he wrote, "from which a fortunate collision with some wandering star, reducing the earth to incandescent gas, might be a merciful deliverance" (201). Nonetheless, even as he wandered amid such bleak thoughts, he remained confident that modern liberal democracy might yet become the guardian of the higher moral, as well as the lesser material, dimensions of civilization. Democratic peoples must be presented with a persuasive public account of why observation of nature's beauty is the higher human activity that should direct, limit, and be served by the useful industry of modern science. One might be skeptical about the practical efficacy of ending a popular book about the political and moral horrors of modern science with a seemingly impractical and merely aesthetic account of the artistic standards for discovering and implementing a harmony between science and virtue, between nature and human nature. Churchill knew, however, that it remains the last best hope that a modern statesman has of preventing democracy—"the worst form of government except for all others ever tried from time to time"—from succumbing to suicide and securing infamy for having failed to make a lasting peace for all mankind.[4]

---

[4] Robert Rhodes James, ed., *Winston S. Churchill: His Complete Speeches, 1897–1963*, 8 vols. (New York: Bowker, 1974), vol. 7, 7566.

10

From Yalta to Bermuda and beyond:
In search of peace with the Soviet Union

MARTIN GILBERT

The evils of communism, both internal and external, had been clear to Churchill from the first months of the Bolshevik Revolution of November 1917. Nothing in Soviet policy or conduct after 1917 led him to change this view. In his interwar articles he had written critically of the personalities, internal policies, and external ambitions of the Soviet Union, first under Lenin and then under Stalin. He had regarded Soviet international aspirations after 1917 as dangerous to the whole Western democratic system, having seen, as secretary of state for war (1919–21) and later as chancellor of the Exchequer (1924–9), much secret information about Russia's subversive activities inside Britain.

Yet Churchill was never averse to the search for compromise, if he felt that Britain's national interest required it. In 1918, when German troops were liberated from the eastern front to join the offensive in the west, he suggested that Britain, France, and the United States should enlist the help of Lenin and Trotsky to bring Russia back into the war, under a formula that would make common action possible, such as "safeguarding the permanent fruits of the Revolution," and with an Allied representative becoming "an integral part of the Russian government."[1]

Two years later, Churchill advised the White Russian forces in southern Russia to make their peace with the Bolsheviks and obtain the best terms they could. As he wrote to Lloyd George: "I should be prepared to make peace with Soviet Russia on the best terms available to appease the general situation, while safeguarding us from being poisoned by them." He would trust "for better or for worse for peaceful influences to bring

---

[1] Memorandum of April 7, 1918: Martin Gilbert, *Churchill's Political Philosophy* (Oxford: Oxford University Press, 1981), 78–9; see also Martin Gilbert, *Churchill: A Life* (London: Heinemann, 1991), 242–3.

about the disappearance of this awful tyranny and peril."[2] Those peaceful influences would, in Churchill's view, include material prosperity.

Before the Second World War, regarding the German danger as pre-dominant, Churchill encouraged bringing the Soviet Union into a system of European collective security. During the war, at the point when Britain was facing Hitler alone, he tried to establish personal relations with Stalin, believing that it ought to be possible to use individual contacts at the highest level to enhance relations between two countries. One of his motives in sending Stalin his well-known message of April 1941, based on information derived from Enigma decrypts, about Hitler's eastward intentions, was that he hoped to open a direct channel of communication between himself and Stalin. Neither that message, however, nor several subsequent Enigma-based communications in May and early June elicited even an acknowledgment.

THE INFLUENCE OF YALTA

After June 1941, Churchill felt that the enormous military contribution Russia was making to the defeat of Hitler, and the terrible suffering of the Russian people under German occupation, some horrific details of which he knew early on from Enigma, gave Russia certain rights, and might lead after the war to a general relaxation of rigid communism. He had no illusions, but many hopes. When as a result of the October 1944 Moscow percentages agreements between him and Stalin, Britain had to acquiesce to Soviet actions in Romania, Churchill wrote to Foreign Secretary Eden: "Remember Anthony, the Bolsheviks are crocodiles."[3] Nevertheless, he was prepared to hope, especially at Yalta, that there could be an amelioration of the ideological conflict, in the aftermath of the wartime alliance, the common cause, and Soviet losses.

A month after Yalta, Stalin personally invited Clementine Churchill to make a five-week tour of Russia to visit the hospitals which had received medical aid through the British Red Cross. The amount of money her fund had collected, Churchill wrote to Stalin on 14 April 1945, "is perhaps not great, but it is a love offering not only of the rich but mainly of the pennies of the poor who have been proud to make their small weekly contributions." He ended with a statement of long-term hope: "In the

---

[2] Letter of March 24, 1920: *WSC* IV C 1053–5.
[3] Minute of May 2, 1944: *WSC* VII 754.

friendship of the masses of our peoples, in the comprehension of their governments, and in the mutual respect of their armies, the future of the world resides."[4]

When Churchill wrote this letter, the quarrel over the future of Poland, more than any other single cause, had begun to sour, and was even threatening to undo, the working relationship between Britain and the Soviet Union established after June 1941. When Molotov announced at the end of March 1945 that the Polish political leaders nominated (as agreed by Stalin at Yalta) by Britain and France would not be considered for the Polish Provisional Government, Churchill reminded Stalin of the wider relationship. "No one has pleaded the cause of Russia with more fervour and conviction than I have tried to do," he wrote. "I was the first to raise my voice on 22nd June 1941. It is more than a year since I proclaimed to a startled world the justice of the Curzon Line for Russia's western frontier, and this frontier has now been accepted both by the British Parliament and the President of the United States." Churchill went on to tell Stalin: "It is as a sincere friend of Russia that I make my personal appeal to you . . . to come to a good understanding about Poland with the Western democracies and not to smite down the hand of comradeship in the future guidance of the world which we now extend."[5]

Churchill recognized that Soviet power could be the gravest single threat to the survival of the democracies after the defeat of Hitler. He was under no illusions as to Stalin's determination to extend Soviet rule and influence as far west as possible and, after 1945, supported the Labour government's introduction of compulsory national military service, and the creation of NATO.

The influence of Yalta on Churchill's thinking was decisive. The conference had seen a sustained attempt by Britain and the United States to secure a democratic future for Poland, based upon free elections. With regard to Poland, and Eastern Europe generally, the Yalta Agreements and Declaration were models of promissory notes. Within weeks of their signature, however, Stalin had reneged on them. Churchill's public welcome for them, and his public assertion that Stalin would adhere to them, was rapidly mocked and undermined by events. The last months of the war, as communist control was imposed on Warsaw, Budapest, and Belgrade, and Soviet forces moved toward Berlin and Prague, were a time of anguish

[4] Letter of April 14, 1945: WSC VII 1267.
[5] Telegram of March 31, 1945: WSC VII 1277.

for Churchill, at the very moment when those forces were contributing so much to the defeat of Hitler.

The last days of the Second World War were a low point in Anglo-Soviet relations. The westward thrust of the Soviet Union into Austria and Yugoslavia in the final weeks of the war was an added cause for dispute and alarm. When, on 29 April 1945, Churchill wrote to Truman about "this enormous Muscovite advance into the centre of Europe,"[6] the Yalta Agreement was in tatters. The sixteen Polish emissaries had disappeared on their way to Moscow, and Signals Intelligence had shown that Soviet forces then on the Baltic coast of Germany intended to continue through Lübeck into Denmark.

AN APPEAL TO STALIN

It was at this dangerous moment for the future of Anglo-Soviet, and Western European-Soviet relations, that Churchill decided to appeal directly to Stalin, and to do so in terms of the interests of all Europe and its peoples. Here was what he believed to be his ultimate strength, one that he was to try to use again after Stalin's death: his personal standing and persuasiveness, the voice of an elder statesman and successful war leader, the appeal of one world leader to another, of a man of experience and goodwill to his opposite number. "There is not much comfort," he telegraphed Stalin, "in looking into a future where you and the countries you dominate, plus the Communist Parties in many other States, are all drawn up on one side, and those who rally to the English-speaking nations and their associates or Dominions are on the other. It is quite obvious that their quarrel would tear the world to pieces and that all of us leading men on either side who had anything to do with that would be shamed before history. Even embarking on a long period of suspicions, of abuse and counterabuse and of opposing policies would be a disaster hampering the great developments of world prosperity for the masses."[7]

This was not a mere rhetorical appeal. Churchill believed not only in the enormous dangers of a future conflict but also in the ability of individual statesmen to avert it. But Stalin made no reply, and each day that followed—each hour almost—brought new problems and new crises. It was on 3 May that Montgomery's forces, in the attempt to prevent Soviet forces entering Denmark, finally reached the Baltic, with, as Churchill

---

[6] Truman papers.   [7] Telegram no. 2255 to Moscow: *WSC* VII 1319–20.

noted to Eden, "twelve hours to spare."[8] A day later the Anglo-Soviet crisis intensified when Molotov, in San Francisco, revealed that the sixteen Polish negotiators, who six weeks earlier left Warsaw to negotiate with the Soviets, had all been arrested.

Churchill's response is instructive: not fire and brimstone, but a search for some area of compromise, some quid pro quo. The boldest action would have been to threaten delay of the withdrawal of those Allied forces who had advanced further east than the agreed line of postwar demarcation. There were also things that could be done in Russia's interest. "We may be able to please them," Churchill telegraphed Eden (who was then in San Francisco), "about the exits from the Black Sea and the Baltic as part of a general settlement." Both methods could, he thought, be tried at once, and he concluded his telegram with the sentence: "It is to this early and speedy showdown and settlement with Russia that we must now turn our hopes."[9]

The word "settlement" was in fact used twice in this message to Eden. In the path from Yalta to Bermuda, which led through the worst decade of Anglo-Soviet relations, it remained the key to Churchill's attitude to Russia, even, and perhaps especially, at this time of maximum conflict and suspicion. Such a "settlement" always required compromise, and, more important, it needed Churchill to invest in its public aspects all his abilities with regard to rhetoric, presentation, and communication. As V-E Day came to Europe, Churchill telegraphed his wife, who was still in Moscow: "It would be a good thing if you broadcast to the Russian people tomorrow, provided that were agreeable to the Kremlin." He then sent her the text of the broadcast to be made in his name. "It is my firm belief," he declared, "that on the friendship and understanding between the British and Russian peoples depends the future of mankind. Here in our island home we are thinking today very often about you all, and we send you from the bottom of our hearts our wishes for your happiness and well-being and that, after all the sacrifices and sufferings of the Dark Valley through which we have marched together, we may also in loyal comradeship and sympathy walk in the sunshine of victorious peace. I have asked my wife to speak these few words of friendship and admiration to you all."[10]

The "friendship and admiration" were real, based upon Churchill's

[8] Telegram "special unnumbered" (Top Secret): WSC VII 1327–8.
[9] Telegram no. T.754/5 to San Francisco: WSC VII 1330.
[10] Telegram no. 2504 to Moscow: WSC VII 1350.

knowledge, some of it derived in the early years of the war from Signals Intelligence reports of German behavior in Russia, of the enormous losses suffered by the Soviet Union not only on the battlefield but in all the occupied regions. But if friendship and admiration were real, so too were the vexations and fears. On that same celebratory evening, as Churchill worked through his box of telegrams from all the Allied capitals, he came to a telegram sent that day from Moscow, from the British chargé d'affaires, Frank Roberts. It contained an official Soviet complaint about the earlier British protest concerning the arrest of the sixteen Polish negotiators. Churchill's telegraphic reply, his final wartime message to Moscow, was: "We are utterly indifferent to anything that the Soviets may say by way of propaganda. No one here believes a single word. When it becomes worthwhile, devastating replies can be made in Parliament. At present however His Majesty's Government is endeavouring to shield the Soviets. It is no longer desired by us to maintain detailed arguments with the Soviet Government about their views and actions."[11]

Churchill was prepared to take up the cudgels for Poland at Potsdam, and also to continue to work for a lasting Anglo-Soviet pact, and indeed global treaty, which would serve as a basis for postwar cooperation. In a telegram to Truman on 12 May 1945, in which he had said, of the Russians, "An iron curtain is drawn down on their front," he had made a case for negotiations before confrontation, and before withdrawing the Anglo-American forces to the line agreed at Yalta. "Surely it is vital now," he wrote, "to come to an understanding with Russia, or to see where we are with her, before we weaken our armies mortally or retire to the zones of occupation. This can only be done by a personal meeting." Churchill was convinced, he told Truman, that the issue of "a settlement with Russia before our strength has gone seems to me to dwarf all others."[12]

At Potsdam, however, the Soviet policy was rigid and Stalin unwilling to accept compromise. His troops were in place in eight capitals; that was his negotiating strength. First Churchill and then his successor as prime minister, Clement Attlee, was disillusioned in particular by the hardness of the Soviet attitude to postwar Poland. Less than a year after the end of the war, however, Churchill spoke of the need to seek "the permanent prevention of war" by means of what he once more called, this time publicly, a "settlement" with Russia. The occasion of this call was his

[11] Telegram no. 2505 to Moscow: *WSC* VII 1350.
[12] Telegram no. T.895/5, cabinet papers 120/186: *WSC* VIII 7.

speech at Westminster College, in Fulton, Missouri, in which, while speaking in realistic terms of the existence of an "iron curtain" from the Baltic to the Adriatic, he also avowed that the "awful whirlpool" of the prewar years could be avoided, "by reaching now, in 1946, a good understanding on all points with Russia."[13]

THE IDEA OF A "SUMMIT"

Later that same year, in presenting his concept of a United States of Europe at the University of Zurich, Churchill first described the importance of France and Germany's coming together to take the lead in this task, and then told his listeners that, for the new Europe to flourish, its friends and sponsors would have to include Britain and the British Commonwealth, as well as "mighty America, and, I trust, Soviet Russia, for then indeed all would be well."[14] This reference to Russia was a trial balloon that met with no response across the Iron Curtain divide. Confrontation, typified by the Berlin blockade, was the policy then emanating from Moscow.

Both as a leader of the opposition until 1951, and as prime minister from 1951 to 1955, Churchill was to make this an important part of his personal and political agenda. While speaking at Edinburgh on 14 February 1950, he argued in favor of what he called a "summit." It was the first time this word had been used to describe what we now regard as a basic feature of international relations, the face-to-face meetings of heads of government to make the initial breakthrough in a change of relationship, or to give the full weight of their authority to policies that require the highest level of agreement in order to be acceptable at the grass roots of administration and public perception. "I cannot help coming back to this idea of another talk with Soviet Russia upon the highest level," Churchill told his audience at Edinburgh. "The idea appeals to me of a supreme effort to bridge the gulf between the two worlds, so that each can lead their life, if not in friendship at least without the hatreds of the cold war."[15]

The existence of the cold war, and the threats it posed to national se-

[13] Speech of March 5, 1946: Randolph S. Churchill, ed., *The Sinews of Peace: Post-War Speeches by Winston S. Churchill* (London: Cassell, 1948), 93–105.
[14] Speech of September 19, 1946: ibid., 197–202.
[15] Speech of February 14, 1950: Randolph S. Churchill, ed., *In the Balance* (London: Cassell, 1951), 208–14.

curity and even survival, as well as what he saw as the unnatural division of Europe into two implacably opposed blocs, was anathema to Churchill's whole concept of international relations and harmonies. He saw possession of the atomic bomb by the United States, and later by Britain, not only as an element of battlefield superiority, but as a factor in the future amelioration of relations between East and West. Soviet power could not be confronted "or even placated," he told the Commons on 14 December 1950, if Britain were to deprive itself of the atomic bomb "or to prevent its use by announcing gratuitously self-imposed restrictions."[16] The word "placated" was deliberately chosen.

It was as prime minister from 1951 to 1955 that Churchill made strenuous efforts to persuade the United States to join him in a summit with the Soviet Union, first while Stalin was still alive, and then after Stalin's death. But Eisenhower and Dulles were skeptical that Stalin's death betokened any real change, and reluctant to accept Churchill's conviction that his own presence, his direct involvement in any negotiations, could prove a decisive factor. Although Churchill had no illusions about the difficulties of negotiations, he believed that they should be tried, all the more so because of the advent of the atomic age.

A failure to negotiate from strength, or to be strong enough to resist aggression if it came, was in Churchill's view the basic weakness of the appeasement policy before the outbreak of war in 1939. Twelve years after the Munich Agreement, in urging the House of Commons in 1950 to seek a settlement in the Korean War, he set out his own philosophy with regard to international relations, and in particular, during the cold war, with regard to the Soviet Union: "Appeasement from weakness and fear is alike futile and fatal," he said. "Appeasement from strength is magnanimous and noble, and might be the surest, and perhaps the only path to world peace."[17] A year later, in Washington as prime minister, he told Congress: "It is my belief that by accumulating deterrents of all kinds against aggression we shall, in fact, ward off the fateful catastrophe."[18] He had no doubt what that catastrophe would be.[19]

A policy of vigilance and deterrence went hand in hand with the search for areas of agreement. The ideological gulf was not one that Churchill

---

[16] Speech of December 14, 1950: *Hansard.*   [17] Ibid.
[18] Speech of January 17, 1952: Randolph S. Churchill, ed., *Stemming the Tide* (London: Cassell, 1953), 220–7.
[19] Speech of February 25, 1954: *Hansard.*

believed could last for ever. He had given considerable thought over the years to human nature, and to the nature of tyranny. As to how Soviet tyranny would end, whether in Eastern Europe or in the Soviet heartland, he told the Massachusetts Institute of Technology in 1949, in words which, forty years later, were seen to have been prophetic: "Laws just or unjust may govern men's actions. Tyrannies may restrain and regulate their words. The machinery of propaganda may pack their minds with falsehoods and deny them truth for many generations of time. But the soul of man thus held in trance, or frozen in a long night, can be awakened by a spark coming from God knows where, and in a moment the whole structure of lies and oppression is on trial for its life. Peoples in bondage need never despair."[20]

CHURCHILL'S LAST CRUSADE

As prime minister after 1951, in his late seventies, Churchill set himself the task of Anglo-Soviet reconciliation, and gave a high priority to bringing the United States with him into this process. Other foreign policy issues also concerned him, the Arab-Israeli conflict and the war in Indochina among them, in both of which he sought to act as a mediator and conciliator. But it was the Soviet dimension that drew from him by far the greatest efforts, stimulated by his vivid imagination with regard to the nature of atomic and hydrogen warfare. In the 1920s he had predicted a weapon of such destructive power that a single bomb could destroy a whole city.[21] In the 1950s he feared the mutual annihilation that any armed conflict would bring.

Churchill was also aware, as he embarked upon what proved to be his last crusade, that he was indeed an old man. This gave his work an added urgency, which his opponents, such as Dulles (although himself a dying man) did not feel. The man who, half a decade before the First World War, had described war as "vile and utter folly, and barbarism,"[22] was not becoming afraid in his old age of maintaining what he regarded as the essential rightness of democracy, nor was he pulling back from his belief in the power of deterrence. What he was trying to do was to get back to

---

[20] Speech of March 31, 1949: Randolph S. Churchill, *In the Balance*, 40–51.
[21] Winston S. Churchill, "Shall We All Commit Suicide?" *Nash's Pall Mall*, September 1924.
[22] Letter of September 15, 1909: *WSC* II C 910–12.

what he had done so often before, the rectification of disputes and the pacification of warlike attitudes by negotiation, compromise, and a true recognition of mutual national interests.

The election of Eisenhower as president seemed to Churchill to hold out a prospect of advancing the cause of amelioration with the Soviet Union. He had known Eisenhower well in the last two years of the war, and had been, both as leader of the opposition from 1945 to 1951 and as prime minister since 1951, a staunch advocate of good relations between Britain and the United States. When they met at a private dinner party in New York in January 1953, Churchill raised with Eisenhower the possibility of renewing the wartime talks with Stalin—reopening the Potsdam conference, as it were—in an attempt to try to settle the many points of dispute that had not been resolved or had arisen since then (among them the division of Berlin and the future of Austria). Eisenhower told Churchill that he wanted to meet Stalin, and that Churchill was welcome to do so, separately, if he thought fit.[23]

It was on 11 March 1953, only six days after the death of Stalin, that Churchill raised with Eisenhower the possibility, and the desirability, of a meeting with Stalin's successors. "I have a feeling," Churchill wrote to the president, "that we might both of us together, or separately, be called to account if no attempt were made to turn over a leaf so that a new page would be started with something more coherent on it than a series of casual and dangerous incidents at many points of contact between the two divisions of the world."[24]

Churchill's call for a new initiative crossed with a message from Eisenhower that said the president had changed his mind since their meeting in New York. "I now tend to doubt the wisdom of a formal multilateral meeting," Eisenhower wrote, "since this would give our opponent the same kind of opportunity he has so often had to use such a meeting simultaneously to balk every reasonable effort of ourselves and to make of the whole occurrence another propaganda mill for the Soviet."[25]

Undeterred by Eisenhower's attitude, Churchill decided to make a direct approach to Molotov, one of the central figures of the new Politburo, whom he had met a number of times since the negotiations for the Anglo-Soviet Treaty in 1942. In a letter drafted on 28 March 1953, he asked Molotov to consider holding a "friendly and informal meeting" with

---

[23] Washington telegram no. 34 of January 8, 1953, premier papers, 11/422: *WSC* VIII 790.
[24] Telegram no. 171 to New York: *WSC* VIII 806.
[25] Telegram dated March 12, 1953, premier papers, 11/422: *WSC* VIII 806–7.

Eden, perhaps in Vienna. "Such talks," he wrote, "however they originated, might lead us all further away from madness and ruin." Churchill's
purpose, he explained to Eden, was not limited to a meeting of foreign
ministers. "At a later stage," he explained, "if all went well and everything broadened, I, and even Ike, might come in too."[26]

The senior successor to Stalin, Georgi Malenkov, had spoken publicly
of a new Soviet attitude to the West, that of "coexistence." Churchill was
encouraged by this to persevere in his search for a high-level meeting. But
a series of further exchanges between him and Eisenhower revealed the
gulf between them. Eisenhower was skeptical of any real change in Soviet
intent, wanting to issue a firm statement of Western determination not to
be weakened, and warning Churchill, with regard to opening new negotiations, that "the whole field is strewn with very difficult obstacles."[27]
Churchill, though he had no illusions about the obstacles, wanted to give
the new leaders in Moscow the chance to show a different face. Despite
the many examples of Soviet wrongdoing, he told Eisenhower, "Great
hope has arisen in the world that there is a change of heart in the vast,
mighty masses of Russia and this can carry them far and fast and perhaps into revolution. . . . I would not like it to be thought that a sudden
American declaration has prevented this natural growth of events."[28]

The correspondence between Churchill and Eisenhower that April
was dominated by Russia, and by their contrasting attitudes. Churchill
deployed his considerable powers of expression and persuasion, but to
no avail. "It would be a pity," he telegraphed Eisenhower on 12 April
1953, "if a sudden frost nipped spring in the bud, or if this could be
alleged, even if there was no real spring. I do not attempt to predict what
the Soviet change of attitude and policy, and it seems to me of mood,
means. It might mean an awful lot. Would it not be well to combine the
re-assertions of your, and our, inflexible resolves with some balancing
expressions of hope that we have entered a new era? A new hope has, I
feel, been created in the unhappy, bewildered world."[29] These were ambitious sentiments from a man who had been deceived by Stalin, less than
a decade earlier, into believing the sincerity of the Yalta assurances.

In a public speech in Glasgow, Churchill gave public expression to his
hopes with regard to the Soviet Union. "New men have obtained supreme
power in Moscow," he said, "and their words and gestures, even to some

[26] Draft dated March 28, 1953, premier papers, 11/422: *WSC* VIII 811.
[27] Letter of April 6, 1953: *WSC* VIII 813.   [28] Letter of April 11, 1953: *WSC* VIII 813.
[29] Telegram dated April 12, 1953, premier papers, 11/1074: *WSC* VIII 814.

extent their actions, seem to betoken a change of mood."[30] These interpretations were not shared by Churchill's senior colleagues. On the day
that he was speaking in Glasgow, asking his audience, "Is there a new
breeze blowing on the tormented world?" the Atlantic Committee of
the cabinet, meeting in London, came to the conclusion, as its minutes
recorded, that the conciliatory measures of the new Soviet leaders "might
well prove more dangerous to western cohesion and to the building and
maintenance of the military and economic strength of the west, than the
bludgeoning xenophobia displayed by Stalin." The committee concluded:
"We must avoid being lulled into a false sense of security."[31] This view
was supported by the British ambassador to Moscow, Sir William Hayter,
who reported to London that the new Soviet government "talks of co-
existence, but they visualise it as the co-existence of the snake and the
rabbit. The only real change is of method." In Hayter's view, speaking as
the man on the spot, "Malenkov seems to have concluded that Stalin's
methods were too rough. Other and more subtle methods of weakening
the West are henceforth to be adopted."[32]

   Churchill neglected no means of attempting to interest the Soviets in
dialogue. When Andrei Gromyko passed through London, on his way
from the embassy in Washington to his new post as first deputy minister
for foreign affairs, Churchill, who asked to see him at 10 Downing Street,
was pleased when Gromyko expressed his "broad wish that the present
situation should continue."[33] When, however, Churchill wished to respond
favorably to a proposal by Molotov for the conclusion of a "peace pact"
between the Soviet Union, the United States, France, Britain, and China,
it was pointed out in the cabinet that Molotov had not in fact come up
with a proposal of his own, but had merely endorsed an identical proposal submitted by the Congress of Peoples for Peace, "a Communist-
controlled organisation."[34]

   Amid the various competing and apparently unsatisfactory schemes,
Churchill was determined to follow through with his idea for a high-
level tripartite meeting, and on 21 April 1953, less than two months after
Stalin's death, he telegraphed Eisenhower to propose that "the three Victorious Powers, who separated at Potsdam in 1945, should come together

---

[30] Speech of April 17, 1953: Randolph S. Churchill, ed., *The Unwritten Alliance* (London:
   Cassell, 1961), 28–35.
[31] Cabinet papers, 134/766: *WSC* VIII 817.
[32] Moscow telegram of November 24, 1953, foreign office papers, 371/106527: *WSC* VIII 817.
[33] Private office letter of April 16, 1953, premier papers, 11/422: *WSC* VIII 818.
[34] Cabinet conclusions, April 28, 1953, cabinet papers, 128/26: *WSC* VIII 819–20.

again." Earlier, Eisenhower had mentioned Stockholm as a possible meeting place: "I like the idea," Churchill wrote. But Eisenhower was still hesitant, worried, he explained in reply, about giving the Soviet Union a propaganda advantage as a result of "premature action by us."[35]

As in so many similar situations over the past half century, Churchill refused to be deflected from his purpose, and used once more his considerable powers of argument and persistence to try to persuade Eisenhower to change his mind. He proposed a direct message from himself in London to Molotov in Moscow, for a meeting between them to "renew our own war-time relation and so that I could meet Monsieur Malenkov and others of your leading men."[36]

Eisenhower, strongly supported by Dulles, refused to allow Churchill to send this message. One aspect in particular had upset them. Churchill suggested that the meeting could take place in Moscow. There was no mention of Stockholm, or any other neutral city. As he had done in 1942 and 1944, Churchill would make the journey to the Soviet capital. Of course, he believed that the force of his character, his experience in negotiations with enemies or ex-enemies, going back to the Transvaal Constitution negotiations of 1906, and his record as a wartime friend of the Soviet Union, would serve him in good stead. "We have both of us lived through a good lot," he had wanted to tell Molotov, a reminder of their past working relationship (Molotov and Eden had finessed the details of the 1944 percentages agreement once Churchill and Stalin had agreed on the basic figures).

In reply to Eisenhower's letter explaining why he thought it wrong of Churchill to go to Moscow, and to do so alone, thus exhibiting, or appearing to exhibit, "weakness or overeagerness on our part," Churchill penned one of his strongest rebukes and counterarguments. "According to my experience of these people in the war," Churchill wrote, "we should gain more by goodwill on the spot by going as guests of the Soviets than we should lose by appearing to court them. This was particularly the case when Anthony and I spent a fortnight in Moscow in October 1944." As to Eisenhower's doubts about the wisdom of Churchill's going alone, without the American president, Churchill responded: "I am not afraid of the 'solitary pilgrimage' if I am sure in my heart that it may help forward the cause of peace and even at the worst can only do harm to my

[35] Telegram no. T.101/53, premier papers, 11/422: *WSC* VIII 819.
[36] Telegram dated May 4, 1953: *WSC* VIII 827.

reputation." He had a "strong belief" that Soviet self-interest would be their guide. "My hope is that it is their self-interest which will bring about an easier state of affairs."[37]

Churchill produced another argument. Of the four men ruling Russia —Malenkov, Molotov, Beria, and Bulganin—only Molotov had had any contacts outside Russia. "I am very anxious to know these men and talk to them as I think I can frankly and on the dead level. It is only by going to Moscow that I can meet them all." As to Eisenhower's general tone, Churchill expressed his disappointment in stark language, typical again of his ability to be outspoken, when he believed major issues were at stake, even where sensitivities were concerned. "I find it difficult to believe," he told Eisenhower, "that we shall gain anything by an attitude of pure negation, and your message to me certainly does not show much hope."[38]

THE BERMUDA CONFERENCE

Frustrated by Eisenhower's rebuff, Churchill took his case to the House of Commons, setting out on 11 May 1953 his belief "that a conference on the highest level should take place between the leading powers without long delay." In two sentences intended to reach the inner sanctum of the Kremlin, he declared: "We all desire that the Russian people should take the high place in world affairs which is their due, without feeling anxiety about their own security. I do not believe that the immense problem of reconciling the security of Russia with the freedom and safety of Western Europe is insoluble."

Churchill went further, reminding the House of the Locarno Agreements of 1925, whereby the former enemies, France and Germany, had signed mutual guarantees for the security of their frontiers. "It was based upon the simple provision that if Germany attacked France we should stand with the French, and if France attacked Germany we should stand with the Germans." He believed that "the master thought which animated Locarno" could play its part between Germany and Russia "in the

---

[37] It was in his first wartime broadcast, on October 1, 1939, speaking of the Soviet annexation of eastern Poland, that Churchill made his famous, and much misquoted statement: "I cannot forecast to you the action of Russia. It is a riddle wrapped in a mystery inside an enigma." He had in fact gone on to say, "But perhaps there is a key. That key is Russian national interest."

[38] Telegram dated May 5, 1953, Eisenhower papers: WSC VIII 828.

minds of those whose prime ambition is to consolidate the peace of Europe as the key to the peace of mankind." This was a reference, and a placatory one, to the Americans. There followed a reference to Russia, and also to Poland, which was once more aimed at the security fears and at the personal emotions of the bosses in the Kremlin. "Russia has a right to feel assured," he said, "that as far as human arrangements can run, the terrible events of the Hitler invasion will never be repeated, and that Poland will remain a friendly power and a buffer, though not, I trust, a puppet State."

As Churchill saw it, his reference to Poland was crucial. In 1939 he had accepted the Soviet occupation of the eastern half of Poland (under the Nazi-Soviet Pact) as an act commensurate with the national interests and security of the Soviet Union in the face of Hitler's eastward ambitions. In 1944 and 1945 he had seen how fearful the Russians were at the thought of a hostile Poland. He had endorsed the Soviet annexation of Poland's eastern regions (including the cities of Vilna and Lvov), and, in fighting before and during Yalta to establish an all-party government in Poland, had accepted that it would be one with a substantial communist component. His reference to Poland was a gesture of appeasement, albeit, as he saw it, from the basis of the strength provided by the Western alliance and NATO.

Churchill ended his public presentation of his policy of talks with Russia with a presentation of his theme at its highest level of hope. "If there is not at the summit of the nations the will to win the greatest prize and the greatest honour ever offered to mankind, doom-laden responsibility will fall upon those who now possess the power to decide. At the worst, the participants in the meeting would have established more intimate contacts. At the best we might have a generation of peace."[39]

The leaders of the West were not prepared for such an initiative, and did not like it. Eden, who was then on his sickbed and had not seen the speech in advance, later recalled that both De Gasperi in Italy and Adenauer in West Germany were hostile.[40] On the other hand, the mass of the House of Commons was enthusiastic. The main concern in France was that they would be excluded. To deflect Churchill from his purpose, and bring in a potential French opponent of any such high-level meeting, Eisenhower responded nine days later by telephoning Churchill to invite him to a

---

[39] Speech of May 11, 1953: *Hansard.*
[40] See Robert Rhodes James, *Anthony Eden* (London: Macmillan, 1987), 365 (November 27, 1954, diary entry).

meeting at which they would both be present, with the French in attendance.[41] Churchill accepted, hoping to persuade Eisenhower to move forward with a Russian summit. The French-British-American meeting was to take place in Bermuda. Meanwhile, at a meeting of Commonwealth prime ministers, Churchill again set out his reasoning for a summit with the Russians. "The Soviet Government," he told them, "must have their own anxieties about a future war. Though they had the power to overrun most of Western Europe, they must know that their central government machinery, their communications and their war potential would be shattered by atomic attack." The Russian leaders must also know that with atomic war "the mighty ocean of land in Russia and Siberia would quickly become uncontrollable and, once the peoples realised that they were free to do as they liked and could no longer be controlled by the central machinery of the Soviet Government, they might show their preference for living happily by themselves without allegiance to a unified Soviet state." If the recent Soviet pronouncements in favor of coexistence were a "trick to deceive the world," they would quickly be discovered, but there should be a sincere examination of what he hoped was a new situation. "The effort should be made, even if there was a risk that it might not succeed."

In his remarks to the Commonwealth prime ministers, Churchill addressed a foreign office and State Department criticism of his proposed summit—that there was no way that he and the Soviet leaders could, at a high-level meeting, deal with the many complex issues and details in dispute between Russia and the West. This argument has been repeated forty years after the event by some historians. Churchill answered it at the time in the following words: "This would not be a conference to settle every point of difficulty, but there might be some settlements which would lead to an easier period, and there could be further talks as time went on. Time should be allowed to play its part. The free countries had time to wait so long as they did not weaken in their resolve."

The crucial question, Churchill told the Commonwealth prime ministers, was whether the United States would allow a summit to be held without preconditions. He would have to persuade Eisenhower of this, and would try to do so at Bermuda. His aim was a meeting with the Russians, the object of which was "building bridges and not barriers."[42]

---

[41] White House staff-secretary note, May 21, 1953, Eisenhower papers: *WSC* VIII 833.
[42] Meeting of June 3, 1953, cabinet papers, 133/135: *WSC* VIII 837–8.

Churchill now prepared for the Bermuda meeting, arguably the most important meeting of his postwar career, and certainly of his postwar aspirations. But on 23 June 1953 he suffered a stroke. Bermuda was postponed, and with it the impetus of his Moscow initiative inevitably flagged. His recovery was slow, but when it came he put Bermuda, and after it Moscow, high on his agenda. During his recovery the hard-line Stalinist Lavrenti Beria was arrested. "It is very significant," Churchill told his doctor, "and supports the line I have taken."[43]

Following Churchill's stroke there were many people, his wife included, who thought he might, and even ought, to step down. But he regarded the Bermuda-Moscow route as one that he must remain in office for: a last contribution to world peace. He began to prepare once more to confront Eisenhower, and at Bermuda he put the case forcefully for seeking a summit with the Soviet leaders, and for a greater accommodation with the Soviet Union, particularly with regard to an easing of trade barriers. Eisenhower resisted him at each turn. Even Churchill's suggestion for the foreign ministers to meet alternatively in the western and eastern sectors of Berlin was not welcomed. In suggesting it, Churchill told Eisenhower: "We should always keep the 'door open' to the Russians."

Asked by Eisenhower to elaborate on his point of view, Churchill replied, in the words of the official minutes: "The hopes of a Communist utopia which had been dangled before the eyes of millions had not been borne out. At the disposal of the Soviet leaders at any moment were enormous opportunities for improving the material situation of their population. He found it reasonable to believe that these two facts, (1) opposition from the United States and (2) the need for economic hope, may well have brought about a definite change in Russian policy and outlook which may govern their actions for many years to come."

Churchill did not deny that the strength of the West was a crucial factor in preventing Soviet aggression. He had always been an advocate of a preponderance of armaments. But he did not want the relationship between East and West to be frozen at that point. "We should not repulse every move for the better," he told the conference. He wanted to see contacts improved and trade increased. And he warned Eisenhower, as the minutes recorded: "He would not be in too much of a hurry to believe that nothing but evil emanates from this mighty branch of the human

---

[43] Lord Moran, *The Struggle for Survival* (London: Constable, 1965), 428–30 (July 10, 1954, diary entry).

family, or that nothing but danger and peril could come out of this vast ocean of land in a single circle so little known and understood."

In pressing for increased trade with Russia, and greater contacts, Churchill expressed the view that there was never an occasion "where hope should be so modest and restrained," and in words recorded by the American note taker he said: "Encourage, encourage the world by stimulating prosperity and getting people in a more agreeable state of mind."

In his reply, Eisenhower shocked the British participants by launching into a short and violent diatribe against the Soviet Union, describing the country as a whore, and suggesting that "despite bath, perfume and lace, it was still the same old girl" underneath. "From their writings it was clear that there had been no change since Lenin," Eisenhower declared. To Churchill's distress, this view prevailed. Nearly three decades earlier, in 1925, he had persuaded Baldwin's cabinet to give up the idea of an Anglo-French alliance aimed at Germany, and to accept in its place, and as a better path to reconciliation as well as security, an arrangement whereby Germany would be brought in as an equal partner to an interlocking system of frontier guarantees. From this idea had come the Locarno Treaty, to which he had earlier referred in the House of Commons, specifically in the context of a possible new German-Russian Treaty. At Bermuda he urged what he called "Locarnoism or reassurances" to be the way forward with relations with Russia. But on reading the draft communiqué at the end of the conference, he wrote to Eden: "I can find nothing in this communiqué which shows the slightest desire for the success of the Conference or for easement in relation with Russia. We are to gang up against them without any reference to the 'Locarno' idea."[44]

CONTACTS AND TRADE

Churchill's Russian initiative had failed. Ironically, while he was still at Bermuda his wife was in Stockholm receiving the Nobel Prize on his behalf. It was for literature, not for peace. Denied both the peace prize and the peace initiative, Churchill did not give up. But he fully recognized the importance of the American dimension, writing to the Labour M.P. Richard Stokes, a former minister of materials: "American anxiety about Russian rearmament must be borne in mind. We cannot get through

---

[44] Bermuda conference minutes, December 4–7, 1953, Eisenhower papers: *WSC* VIII 918–35.

without them."[45] Still, he continued to take initiatives of his own. In the last week of December 1953 he saw the Soviet ambassador to Britain, Yakov Malik, who was returning briefly to Moscow. After the meeting Churchill informed Eisenhower that he had impressed on Malik "that your atomic proposal was not a mere propaganda move but a sincere attempt to break the deadlock, and though on a small scale, might also achieve valuable results and open fruitful contacts."[46]

Contacts and trade: these were the twin tracks of Churchill's search for a way to ease the East-West divide. He expanded on the trade aspect at a cabinet meeting on 18 January 1954. Britain and the United States should no longer seek, he said, to prevent the export of goods to Russia "which would help merely to strengthen their industrial economy."[47] But Eisenhower rejected this, a clear sign that he did not hold with Churchill's approach. In a message to Eden, however, Churchill made it clear nine days later that he was not to be deflected from his search for "friendly relations" with Russia, at the same time maintaining the "strongest possible combination against Soviet aggression." It might well be true, he told Eden, that the Russians "can only be friends and live decently with those who are as strong [as] or stronger than they are themselves."[48]

Eden, as foreign secretary, was carrying the brunt of negotiations with Russia. These were not succeeding, and a four-power conference on Berlin had broken up in acrimony, with Russia pressing for the inclusion of communist China in all future such meetings. At the cabinet meeting that discussed the Russian obstinacy at Berlin, it was Churchill who pressed for a continuing effort to persuade the Americans to agree to an expansion of East-West trade. "It would be evidence," he said, "that we were trying to find peaceful means of living side by side with the Soviet Union."[49]

On the wider aspect of Soviet control of Eastern Europe, Churchill maintained in 1954 the hope he had expressed in Boston in 1949, telling the House of Commons: "Time may find remedies that this generation cannot command. The forces of the human spirit and of national character alive in those countries cannot be speedily extinguished, even by large-scale movements of populations and mass education of children. Thought

---

[45] Letter dated December 21, 1953: *WSC* VIII 940.
[46] Undated telegram, Eisenhower papers: *WSC* VIII 940–1.
[47] Cabinet papers, 128/27: *WSC* VIII 944.
[48] Telegram T.9 of 1954, premier papers, 11/665: *WSC* VIII 944–5.
[49] Cabinet conclusions, February 22, 1954, cabinet papers, 128/27: *WSC* VIII 953.

is fluid and pervasive, hope is enduring and inspiring." This understanding of the hope of subject peoples was an essential element in Churchill's vision of a future Europe in which the Soviets would have an honored part, as first expressed in his Zurich speech in 1946. But he did not minimize the problem. "The vast territorial empire and multitudes of subjects, which the Soviets grasped for themselves in the hour of Allied victory," he said, "constitute the main cause of division now existing among civilised nations." But progress had been made, and at the four-power meeting in Berlin, where Eden represented Britain, the Soviet refusal to agree to an independent and neutral Austria had been offset by an apparent willingness not to shut out such a solution.

Churchill told the House of Commons that he was hopeful that agreement would soon be reached about Austria, "though I hope it will not be thought I deceive myself or try to lead the House into foolish or vain ideas." His main concern remained the wider possibility of long-term amelioration. "Patience and perseverance must never be grudged when the peace of the world is at stake," he said. "Even if we had to go through a decade of cold-war bickerings, punctuated by vain parleys, that would be preferable to the catalogue of unspeakable and also unimaginable horrors which is the alternative. We must not shrink from continuing to use every channel that is open or that we can open, any more than we should relax those defensive measures indispensable for our own strength and safety." His aim was to "create conditions under which Russia may dwell easily and peacefully side by side with us all." To those who tried to prevent an agreement with the taunt that it was trying to have it both ways, he would reply: "It is only by having it both ways at once that we shall get a chance of getting anything of it at all."[50]

Bermuda had failed. Berlin had proved indecisive. Nor had the Soviets responded directly to Churchill's appeals in a way that he could return to the charge. But he did not give up, even though the final phase of his search for an accommodation with the Soviet Union took place at a time when, aged seventy-nine, he was beginning to feel the debilitating effects of old age. His stroke had left him physically weakened and often tired. In March 1954 he told Chancellor of the Exchequer R. A. Butler: "I feel like an aeroplane at the end of its flight, in the dusk, with the petrol running out, in search of a safe landing." The only political interest he had left, he told Butler, was in "high-level conversations with the Russians."

[50] Speech of February 25, 1954: *Hansard*.

He would then be "glad" to retire.[51] It was only a month later, after a major speech by Churchill in the House of Commons, that his private secretary, Anthony Montague Browne, "realised how much his powers had waned."[52] Churchill recognized his weakness. A friend (the former prime minister Asquith's daughter Violet) who saw him in July 1954 wrote in a private letter: "He was going through a Valley of Decision, or rather of indecision, about the time when he should relinquish power and I felt that he was in great agony of mind."[53]

Failing powers did not inhibit Churchill in his continued vigilance with regard to possible amelioration in Russia's relations with the West. In 1954 Harold Wilson, a Labour backbencher and former president of the Board of Trade, was about to visit the Soviet Union on private trade business. Because Eden was again ill, Churchill was again in charge of the foreign office. He asked Wilson to see him, and told him: "What we want, you tell them, is easement." He then told Wilson to look for consumer goods while he was in Russia. "If they were allocating more materials for the production of consumer goods," Churchill said, "it was a sign that they were looking to a peaceful solution; it might mean, it did not necessarily mean, that they were having to take more notice of ordinary people."[54]

On 27 March 1954, Churchill again took up cudgels in favor of a summit, writing to Eisenhower (using the same word "easement" that had so struck Wilson): "I am anxious to promote an easement of relations with Soviet Russia and to encourage and aid any development of Russian life which leads to a wider enjoyment by the Russian masses of the consumer goods of which you speak and modern popular amenities and diversions which play so large a part in British and American life." Increased trade would have many benefits, including a better chance for Britain and the United States to compete with the growing German and Japanese successes in world trade, but the greatest benefit would be "those hopes of a broadening of Russian life and relaxation of international tension which may lead to the re-establishment of a peaceful foundation for the tormented and burdened world."[55]

---

[51] See R. A. Butler, *The Art of the Possible: The Memoirs of Lord Butler* (London: Hamish Hamilton, 1971), 173 (March 12, 1954, diary entry).
[52] Anthony Montague Browne, recollections, notes dated March 24, 1987: *WSC* VIII 970.
[53] Letter dated July 6, 1954: *WSC* VIII 974.
[54] Wilson recollection: Martin Gilbert, *In Search of Churchill* (London: Harper Collins, 1994), 252–3.
[55] Letter dated March 27, 1954, Eisenhower papers: *WSC* VIII 962–3.

The American hydrogen bomb, and Russia's growing nuclear capacity, about which Churchill was well informed from his secret sources, led him to renew his call for closer relations with Russia, and to do so with particular reference to the nuclear threat. In a speech in the House of Commons on 5 April 1954, almost a year after his last call in the Commons for a summit, he set out what he had in mind. "If Russia, the British Commonwealth, and the United States were gathered round the table talking about the commercial application of atomic energy, and the diversion of some of their uranium stockpile, it would not seem odd if the question of the hydrogen bomb, which might blow all these pretty plans sky high, cropped up, and what I have hoped for, namely a talk on supreme issues between the Heads of States and Governments concerned, might not seem so impossible as it has hitherto."[56]

The ideas were the old ones in which Churchill strongly believed. But they were intensified by Churchill's recognition of the devastating effect of nuclear war. That spring he sent his son-in-law, Christopher Soames, and his joint principal private secretary, John Colville, to the Soviet Embassy, and was encouraged when they reported back that "Malenkov would welcome a meeting with the Prime Minister." Churchill, under continuous party pressure to resign, told his doctor: "I shall not relinquish office until I meet Malenkov."[57] And to a Conservative Party gathering in London on 30 April 1954 he said by way of introducing the main speaker, Harold Macmillan, that Britain should "establish relations with Russia" in order to show them "that we long to see them play a proud and splendid part in the guidance of the human race."[58]

The pressures on Churchill to resign were mounting. Both Eden and Macmillan pressed him to name a date for his departure from office. But he had not abandoned the quest for a summit, and when he visited Eisenhower in Washington in June 1954 to discuss the bomb, the Middle East, and Indochina, he asked the president to add to their agenda the "possibility of high level talks with the Soviets." Eisenhower agreed, whereupon Churchill suggested a "reconnaissance in force," perhaps by himself, to see "if anything promising developed." He would be interested, Churchill told the president, "in finding out what sort of a man Malenkov was," and he believed that there was "a deep underlying demand on the part of the Russian people to enjoy a better life, particularly after suffering

---

[56] Speech of April 5, 1954: *Hansard*.
[57] Lord Moran, *The Struggle for Survival*, 539–41 (April 8, 1954, diary entry).
[58] Speech of April 30, 1954: Randolph S. Churchill, *The Unwritten Alliance*, 142–4.

oppression for fifty years." Eisenhower made no recorded comment. At a later session, however, he told Churchill that he would not agree to a meeting anywhere under the present Soviet rule, "but did not object to Churchill's suggestion of either Stockholm or London." Echoing his fears at Bermuda, Eisenhower was worried that any such summit would give Malenkov a chance to "hit the free world in the face."[59]

Churchill worked hard during this Washington visit to reactivate his Bermuda plan. At one point he told Eisenhower that he thought he could use such a meeting to ask the Russians to sign the Austrian Treaty. Speaking to congressional leaders, he said that high-level conferences of this kind were vitally important: "Meeting jaw to jaw is better than war."[60] Again he answered those critics who said that a summit would never be able to cope with the detailed issues involved, telling the congressmen that he "realised how complicated the problems were, and that each problem could not be thrashed out to the last inch. But it was important to have consenting minds at the summit to back up the conference table. Otherwise, the conference may go on for ever."[61] His wish was to be a catalyst and a guide, not a foreign secretary or a diplomat.

It was Dulles who stepped in to try to persuade Churchill to abandon his idea. In a note in the Eisenhower papers, the secretary of state set out his account of what he said to Churchill in private, "that it was extremely dangerous to have such a meeting unless it would have positive results. An illusion of success would be bad, and also an obvious failure would be bad, and might create the impression that the only alternative was war."[62]

The greatest barrier to Churchill's plan was that the Russians had made no response to his initiatives or speeches. On his return by sea from Washington he decided to try to rectify this. In a personal telegram to Molotov, sent on 3 July 1954, only five days after Dulles's caveat, he proposed talks with the Soviet leaders "with no agenda and no object but to find a reasonable way of living side by side in growing confidence, easement and prosperity." Although the meeting, wherever held (Churchill mentioned no venue), "would be simple and informal and last only a few days, it might be the prelude to a wider reunion where much might be settled." Churchill went on to make it clear that this was a private

[59] "Churchill-Eden Visit," June 25–26, 1954, Eisenhower papers: WSC VIII 998–1003.

[60] It was Harold Macmillan who coined (in 1958, in Canberra) the phrase usually, but wrongly, attributed to Churchill "Jaw-jaw is better than war-war." See WSC VIII 1004.

[61] "Notes . . . on remarks," June 26, 1954, Eisenhower papers: WSC VIII 1004.

[62] "Memorandum of Conversation . . . ," June 27, 1954, Eisenhower papers: WSC VIII 1006–7.

initiative on his part, telling Molotov: "I have, however, no warrant to say this beyond my own hopes."[63]

Churchill's telegram to Molotov was sent from on board ship to the British ambassador to Moscow, Sir William Hayter, to be handed personally to Molotov. It was not sent to the cabinet either for its approval or information. Eisenhower, to whom Churchill sent a copy after it had been sent to Moscow, was not amused. "You do not let any grass grow under your feet," the president replied on 7 July. "When you left here I had thought, obviously erroneously, that you were in an undecided mood about this matter, and that when you had cleared your own mind I would receive some notice if you were to put your program into action."[64]

Not only the American president, but Churchill's own senior cabinet colleagues, had received no prior notice of the telegram to Molotov. At the first cabinet meeting after his return, ministers were told, in the formal words of the official minutes, "of a proposal that the Prime Minister might meet M. Malenkov, with a view to exploring the possibility of arranging a meeting of Heads of Government of the United States, United Kingdom and Soviet Union." On hearing this, one senior Conservative, Lord Salisbury, threatened to resign. He was supported in his objections by an equally senior political figure, Lord Swinton.[65] But on the same day as the cabinet meeting (7 July 1954) a telegram arrived from Molotov, in reply to the shipboard invitation, which excited Churchill's hopes. It was the first positive Soviet reply to any of his post-Yalta feelers. "You may be sure," Molotov wrote in the course of a long and friendly missive, "that your initiative will find here favourable attitude which it fully deserves."[66]

When Churchill raised the issue of a "bilateral meeting with M. Malenkov" in cabinet on the following day, he was careful to say that he had in mind for the venue, not Moscow, but Stockholm or Vienna. But, despite Molotov's response, the mood of the meeting was not favorable, the prevailing view being that nothing must be done to alienate the Americans. One of Churchill's closest colleagues, Oliver Lyttelton, pointed out that, despite Molotov's positive reply, "It was still open to the Cabinet to decide not to proceed further with this project."[67]

[63] Undated telegram, Eisenhower papers: *WSC* VIII 1013.
[64] Letter of July 7, 1954: *WSC* VIII 1013.
[65] Cabinet conclusions, July 7, 1954, cabinet papers 128/27: *WSC* VIII 1019.
[66] Telegram of July 7, 1954, Eisenhower papers: *WSC* VIII 1020-1.
[67] Cabinet conclusions, July 8, 1954, cabinet papers, 128/27: *WSC* VIII 1023-6.

Churchill accepted defeat; it would be up to Eisenhower to approve such a course before it was proceeded with. This retreat effectively destroyed the initiative, and a bland, noncommittal reply was sent to Molotov. Churchill asked Eisenhower once more to accept the way forward, not as he had earlier hoped by means of a Churchill visit to Moscow, but by using the forthcoming foreign ministers' talks in Switzerland as a peg. "If Malenkov will come to Berne when Geneva is over," he explained to Eisenhower, "Molotov could meet him there, and Anthony and I could have a few talks on the dead level. My idea is to create conditions in which a three- or perhaps with the French a four-power conference, might be possible," perhaps in London early that September.[68]

This was a less ambitious plan than Churchill's earlier one, but when Eisenhower replied favorably, Churchill felt he might still be able to rescue something from the earlier plan. It was the British cabinet that forced him to back down altogether. At its meeting on 23 July 1954, the constitutional propriety of Churchill's shipboard telegram to Molotov was raised. Harold Macmillan was one of those who expressed dissatisfaction, claiming that the telegram was "an important act of foreign policy which engaged the collective responsibility of the Cabinet and that the Cabinet should have been consulted before it was sent." Eden also added his voice, telling the cabinet: "He did not himself believe that any good would come from a bilateral meeting with the Russians at the present time."[69] Three days later Churchill told his colleagues that he would not proceed with his plan.[70] The telegram to Molotov, despite the favorable response, was now a dead letter.

THE LAST GLIMMER AND RESIGNATION

In British domestic politics, the episode of the Molotov telegram convinced the inner circle of Conservatives that the time had come for Churchill to resign. Churchill reluctantly accepted that any future summit initiative must come from the Americans. He was not slow to point this out, and even did so with a certain admonition, writing to Eisenhower on 8 August 1954: "It will seem astonishing to future generations—such as they may be—that with all that is at stake no attempt was made by personal parley

---

[68] Letter dated July 9, 1954, Eisenhower papers: *WSC* VIII 1027–8.
[69] Cabinet conclusions, July 23, 1954, cabinet papers, 128/27: *WSC* VIII 1035–6.
[70] Cabinet conclusions, July 26, 1954, cabinet papers, 128/27: *WSC* VIII 1036.

between the Heads of Governments to create a union of consenting minds on broad and simple issues. This should surely be the foundation on which the vast elaborate departmental machinery should come into action, instead of the other way round." Churchill added, with a clear reference to a future American rather than British initiative: "Fancy that you and Malenkov should never have met, or that he should never have been outside Russia, when all the time in both countries appalling preparations are being made for measureless mutual destruction."

There then followed a last glimmer of the Churchill initiative. As with each of his appeals to Eisenhower, it was couched in powerful language, carefully worked out and worded, seeking to put forward the argument at its highest level of sophistication, and indeed of vision. "Even when the power of Britain is so much less than the United States," Churchill wrote, "I feel, old age notwithstanding, a responsibility and resolve to use any remaining influence I may have to seek, if not a solution, at any rate an easement. Even if nothing solid or decisive was gained, no harm need be done. Even if realities presented themselves more plainly, that might bring about a renewed effort for peace. After all, the interest of both sides is Survival and, as an additional attraction, measureless material prosperity of the masses."

Churchill then looked at the objections that had come from both Whitehall and the State Department. " 'No,' it is said. 'The Heads of Government must not ever meet. Human affairs are too great for human beings. Only the Departments of State can cope with them, and meanwhile let us drift and have some more experiments and see how things feel in a year or two when they are so much nearer to us in annihilating power.'" In contrast to this attitude, Churchill reiterated his own. "Now, I believe, is the moment for parley at the summit. All the world desires it. In two or three years a different mood may rule with those who have their hands upon the levers or upon the multitude whose votes they require."

In a one-sentence summary of his aim, Churchill told Eisenhower: "I am trying to explain to you my resolve to do my best to take any small practical step in my power to bring about a sensible and serious contact."[71] Eisenhower did not respond. Churchill was isolated both domestically and internationally. His one remaining task, pressed upon him by his wife and his colleagues, was to announce the date of his resignation. This he was reluctant to do. That August he was upstaged and upset when

---

[71] Letter dated August 8, 1954, Eisenhower papers: *WSC* VIII 1039–41.

Attlee and his former foreign secretary Ernest Bevin went to Moscow, where they met Malenkov, and to Peking. Although this was neither a summit nor a high-level negotiation, it was the first visit by senior British politicians to the Soviet Union since Yalta.

Churchill had not given up his search for a road to the summit, and on 1 December 1954, the day after his eightieth birthday, he told the House of Commons, amid Labour Party accusations that he was anti-Soviet, that he was not only an advocate of high-level talks with the Russians, but that "in fact, that is the only explanation of my presence here today. It is still my purpose."[72] He was supported, surprisingly, by a Labour peer, Lord Stansgate, who told the House of Lords that same day: "I believe, and I think the great bulk of the people in this country believe, that the greatest measure of defence we can have is that the Prime Minister should retain his position until his meeting with the Russians takes place."[73]

It was not to be. The pressures on Churchill to resign were strong and continuous. But in mid-January he was writing to the prime minister of France, Pierre Mendès-France, pressing the case for "direct personal contact with the new leaders of the Soviet Government."[74] He was further encouraged to reactivate this quest when early in February, Malenkov was replaced by Bulganin and Khrushchev. A resignation date had, however, now been fixed: 5 April, two days before the House of Commons rose for its Easter recess. Then, less than a month before that date, there was a sudden false dawn: a suggestion, in a telegram from Sir Roger Makins, the British ambassador in Washington, that Eisenhower might be prepared to "lay plans for a meeting with the Soviets in a sustained effort to reduce tensions and the risk of war."[75]

This was what Churchill had urged on the president, in vain, at Bermuda and since. He now proposed delaying his resignation in order to be able to participate in such a summit. "This proposal of a meeting of Heads of Government which he [Eisenhower] would attend himself," Churchill wrote to Eden, "must be regarded as creating a new situation which will affect our personal plan and timetables."[76] Eden, Churchill's designated successor, was appalled, and in cabinet the next day pointed out that it was "more likely than not that the Russians would decline an invitation"

---

[72] Speech of December 1, 1954: *Hansard.*   [73] Ibid.
[74] Letter dated January 12, 1955: *WSC* VIII 1089–90.
[75] Telegram no. 539 from Washington, March 11, 1955, Eden papers: *WSC* VIII 1102–3.
[76] Letter dated March 12, 1955: *WSC* VIII 1103–4.

at the level of heads of state and prime ministers to what was, in effect, a continuation of the existing foreign ministers' discussions.[77]

In a letter to his wife, Churchill defended his decision not to resign. "Of course, as you know, only one thing has influenced me," he wrote, "and that is the possibility of arranging with Ike for a top level meeting in the near future with the Soviets."[78] On 14 March 1955, he told the House of Commons: "I have tried very hard to set in motion the process of a conference at the top level and to bring about actual results. Although I do not pretend to measure what the recent changes in the Soviet oligarchy imply, I do not feel that they should in any way discourage us from further endeavours."

The impact of the Makins telegram had stimulated Churchill to revive thoughts of the ultimate goal of his calls for a summit. "I still believe," he told the Commons, "that, vast and fearsome as the human scene has become, personal contacts of the right people in the right place at the right time may yet have a potent and valuable part to play in the cause of peace which is in our hearts."[79] This was Churchill's last public expression of his ideal. Hardly had he returned to Downing Street than a message was brought from the foreign office "to the effect," he wrote to his wife the next day, "that Ike was not willing himself to participate in a meeting with Russia."[80] This was confirmed on the following day in a telegram from Makins, reporting that neither Eisenhower nor Dulles "was contemplating an early Four-Power meeting with the Russians."[81]

Churchill reverted to his original resignation date. The only glimmer of hope with regard to a possible revival of summit plans came on 29 March 1955, nine days before the resignation date, when he learned of a favorable comment by Bulganin about a possible four-power meeting. Churchill, still prime minister, sent a message to Eden that the timetable for resignation must be changed, and informed Buckingham Palace of a possible delay.[82] But Bulganin's remarks were not followed up, either from Moscow or London, and a day later Churchill told his principal private secretary, John Colville, that "he did not really think there was

---

[77] Cabinet conclusions, March 14, 1955: *WSC* VIII 1106.
[78] Letter dated March 15, 1955, Spencer-Churchill papers: *WSC* VIII 1107–8.
[79] Speech of March 14, 1955: *Hansard*.
[80] Letter dated March 15, 1955, Spencer-Churchill papers: *WSC* VIII 1110.
[81] Cabinet conclusions, March 16, 1955, cabinet papers, 128/28: *WSC* VIII 1111.
[82] Colville notes (written shortly after March 30, 1955): John Colville, *The Fringes of Power* (London: Hodder & Stoughton, 1985), 704–7.

much chance of a top-level conference, and that alone would be a valid reason for staying."[83]

On 6 April Churchill resigned. A decade of seeking amelioration with the Soviet Union, and a summit to set in train a wider negotiated détente, was over. It had been his last, his most sustained, and his least successful foray into international affairs.

[83] Ibid., 707–9.

Contributors

PAUL ADDISON is director of the Centre for Second World War Studies at Edinburgh University, where he has taught since 1967. In 1967–8 he served as research assistant to Randolph S. Churchill on the official biography of Winston Churchill. Author of many articles relating to Churchill, his latest book is *Churchill on the Home Front, 1900–1955*, published in 1992.

KIRK EMMERT is professor of political science at Kenyon College, where he has taught since 1978. His interest in American and British politics and government has led him to write and speak extensively on these subjects. His book *Winston S. Churchill on Empire* appeared in 1989. Professor Emmert is a member of the board of academic advisers to the Churchill Center.

DOUGLAS J. FEITH is an attorney at the Washington firm of Feith and Zell. Before establishing the firm, Feith worked in the federal government in the 1980s, where he served as deputy assistant secretary of defense for negotiations policy, as special counsel to the assistant secretary of defense, and for a term with the National Security Council as a Middle East specialist. His articles and essays on international law and foreign and defense policy have been published in *Commentary* and other journals.

MARTIN GILBERT is the official biographer of Winston Churchill and an honorary fellow of Merton College, Oxford. His current work is as editor of the Churchill war papers, the first two volumes of which have been published. He is now at work on the third volume, *The Ever-Widening War*, which covers the events of 1941. Aside from his work on Churchill, he is author of three general histories and a series of twelve historical atlases. His most recent book on Churchill is *In Search of Churchill*, published in 1994 in the United Kingdom and in 1995 in the United States. He is a winner of the Farrow Award for Excellence in Churchill Studies.

JAMES W. MULLER is professor and chairman of the Department of Political Science at the University of Alaska, Anchorage, where he has taught since 1983. He is editor of *The Revival of Constitutionalism*. Many of his articles and reviews, published in such journals as *Commentary, The Political Science Reviewer, The Review of Politics*, and *The Wilson Quarterly*, have dealt with Winston Churchill. His forthcoming book on Churchill's writings is *The Education of Winston Churchill*. Winner of the Farrow Award for Excellence in Churchill Studies, Muller is a governor of the Churchill Center and chairs its board of academic advisers.

PATRICK J. C. POWERS is associate professor of politics at Assumption College and visiting scholar at Southern New England School of Law. He has a book in preparation: *Democratic Statesmanship: Lessons of Lincoln, Churchill, and de Gaulle*. Powers has written about political philosophy from Aristotle to the present. He is a member of the board of academic advisers to the Churchill Center.

PAUL A. RAHE is Jay P. Walker Professor of History at the University of Tulsa. His areas of specialization and research include ancient history, early modern political thought, and the American Revolution. His massive work *Republics Ancient and Modern: Classical Republicanism and the American Revolution*, first published in 1992, has been reissued in a three-volume paperback edition. Rahe is a member of the board of academic advisers to the Churchill Center and a former fellow of the Woodrow Wilson Center.

ROBERT RHODES JAMES is a fellow of Wolfson College, Cambridge. He began public service in 1955 as a clerk of the House of Commons, served four years as principal officer in the office of the secretary-general of the United Nations, and represented Cambridge as member of Parliament for sixteen years. He is a fellow of the Royal Historical Society and the Royal Society of Literature, and his books include biographies of Lord Randolph Churchill, Anthony Eden, and Bob Boothby, *Churchill: A Study in Failure*, and the eight-volume work *The Complete Speeches of Sir Winston Churchill*.

S. BURRIDGE SPIES is former professor of history at the University of South Africa, where he began teaching in 1967. At present he is preparing a history of that university. His publications have focused on South African and imperial affairs in the late nineteenth and twentieth centuries. He is the author of *Methods of Barbarism? Roberts and Kitchener and*

Civilians in the Boer Republics and coeditor of, and contributor to, *The South African War, A New Illustrated History of South Africa, South Africa in the Twentieth Century*, and *Jan Smuts: Memoirs of the Boer War*.

MANFRED WEIDHORN is Abraham and Irene Guterman Professor of English at Yeshiva University, where he has taught since 1963. He has published four books on Churchill: *A Harmony of Interests, Churchill's Rhetoric and Political Discourse, Sir Winston Churchill*, and *Sword and Pen*. In addition, he is the author of two books on seventeenth-century literature, as well as nearly seventy essays in scholarly journals on theology, literature, and the humanities. Weidhorn is a member of the board of academic advisers to the Churchill Center.

Index

337